ETHICAL THEORY

ETHICAL THEORY
A CONCISE ANTHOLOGY

SECOND EDITION

EDITED BY

HEIMIR GEIRSSON
MARGARET R. HOLMGREN

broadview press

Library and Archives Canada Cataloguing in Publication

Ethical theory : a concise anthology / edited by Heimir Geirsson, Margaret R. Holmgren. — 2nd ed.

Includes bibliographical references.
ISBN 978-1-55481-015-4

1. Ethics.   I. Geirsson, Heimir   II. Holmgren, Margaret R. (Margaret Reed), 1951-

BJ1012.E87 2010   170   C2010-901338-7

Broadview Press is an independent, international publishing house, incorporated in 1985. Broadview believes in shared ownership, both with its employees and with the general public; since the year 2000 Broadview shares have traded publicly on the Toronto Venture Exchange under the symbol BDP.

We welcome comments and suggestions regarding any aspect of our publications—please feel free to contact us at the addresses below or at broadview@broadviewpress.com.

North America
Post Office Box 1243, Peterborough, Ontario, Canada K9J 7H5
2215 Kenmore Avenue, Buffalo, NY, USA 14207
Tel: (705) 743-8990; Fax: (705) 743-8353
email: customerservice@broadviewpress.com

UK, Europe, Central Asia, Middle East, Africa, India, and Southeast Asia
Eurospan Group, 3 Henrietta St., London WC2E 8LU, United Kingdom
Tel: 44 (0) 1767 604972; Fax: 44 (0) 1767 601640
email: eurospan@turpin-distribution.com

Australia and New Zealand
NewSouth Books
c/o TL Distribution, 15-23 Helles Ave., Moorebank, NSW, Australia 2170
Tel: (02) 8778 9999; Fax: (02) 8778 9944
email: orders@tldistribution.com.au

www.broadviewpress.com

This book is printed on paper containing 100% post-consumer fibre.

Typesetting and assembly: True to Type Inc., Claremont, Canada.

PRINTED IN CANADA

CONTENTS

CHAPTER ONE

ETHICAL RELATIVISM

INTRODUCTION

Some cultures approve of abortions while other cultures do not. Some cultures approve of capital punishment while other cultures do not. And some cultures approve of slavery while other cultures do not. There is a great diversity of social norms and rules, and there seem to be significant disagreements from one culture to the next about what is right and wrong. Further, ethicists often disagree among themselves about what is right and wrong, and ethical theories often give conflicting answers to the same moral problems. The evidence seems to suggest that there are no objective or universal moral values. But if there are no objective moral values, then there is no absolute right or wrong. And if there is no absolute right or wrong, we presumably have to embrace relativism of some sort.

Relativism comes in various forms and not all of them are directly relevant to ethical theory. Anthropology informs us of a wide variety of social norms, and shows us that different cultures have different moral rules. But anthropology is descriptive in nature and it only presents to us a descriptive form of relativism. It tells us how people do behave and not how they should behave.

A different kind of relativism is moral relativism. Moral relativism is the thesis that what is right or good is determined by the relevant party. If the relevant party is an individual, then we have individual moral relativism. According to individual moral relativism, what is right or good is determined by each individual. If the relevant party is a culture, then we have cultural moral relativism. According to cultural moral relativism, what is right or wrong is determined by each culture. Each of these versions of moral relativism holds that there are no objective moral values, and no basic moral demands that are binding on all moral agents. (The next section of this book addresses the latter claim more fully.)

It is important to recognize that descriptive relativism does not entail moral relativism. In order to see why this is so, assume for the sake of argument that there are objective moral values. Given this assumption, moral relativism is clearly false. In this case there is a single truth of the matter about morality, and individuals or cultures cannot stipulate for themselves what is right and wrong. If an individual or culture decides on a moral standard that conflicts with objective moral values, then their standard is mistaken. If we assume that there are objective moral values, descriptive relativism may still be correct, however. It is quite possible, and even probable, that some individuals and cultures will make mistakes in thinking about and determining moral values. Mistakes may be quite diverse, as there are many different ways of getting things wrong. Therefore, we can hold that there are objective moral values and at the same time account for the wide variation in moral standards from culture to culture and from individual to individual. It is clearly possible, then, for descriptive relativism to be true and for moral relativism to be false. By the same line of reasoning, we can see that descriptive relativism does not entail the thesis that there are no objective moral values. It is clearly possible that there are objective moral values, but that people disagree widely on the question of what these values are. Descriptive relativism provides us with many examples of how people actually behave, but by itself it tells us nothing about the truth of moral relativism or the truth of the thesis that there are no objective moral values.

Is moral relativism tenable? Many people believe that individual moral relativism is not. In order to function as a society we need to agree on some basic moral standards. We cannot simply allow each individual to make up his or her own moral code. If we were to proceed in this manner, life would be, as Hobbes put it, nasty, brutish, and short. The foregoing consideration does not show that individual moral relativism is false, but it does suggest a pragmatic reason for rejecting this position as tenable. Once we recognize that a common moral code is needed, cultural moral relativism may seem like a viable thesis even if we reject individual moral relativism.

Can we defend cultural moral relativism? Before we answer this question, let us consider more carefully what this position entails. In order to function as a society, we need to agree on some basic moral standards. But this is not to say that all societies need to agree on the same moral standards. Further, subcultures within a society do not have to agree on all moral rules. They can differ significantly from one another and for the most part coexist peacefully, although their differences may sometimes erupt in violence or even civil wars. A cultural moral relativist need only hold that the predominant moral standards accepted by a given society determine what is right and wrong for the members of that society.

At first glance, however, this position may seem to lead to inconsistencies. Suppose that Amy and Grant are talking about abortion, and that Amy is a cultural moral relativist while Grant believes there are objective moral values. Amy starts by arguing that there is nothing morally wrong with abortion. By citing a few examples, Grant gets Amy to concede that some cultures regard abortion as morally wrong. He then accuses Amy of inconsistency, claiming that her position entails both the conclusion that abortion *is not* morally wrong (because in some cultures it is not) *and* the conclusion that it *is* morally wrong. But Grant is on the wrong track here. Cultural moral relativism is not inconsistent. Suppose that culture X believes that abortion is morally wrong, and culture Y believes that abortion is not morally wrong. The cultural moral relativist will make the following two claims: (1) it is true that it is morally wrong for persons in culture X to have abortions, and (2) it is true that it is not morally wrong for persons in culture Y to have abortions. These two claims are fully compatible with one another. The cultural moral relativist holds that actions are not right or wrong per se—they are only right or wrong relative to a given moral framework. It is obviously possible for an action to be right relative to one moral framework and wrong relative to another.

If Grant is smart, he will reframe his objection to Amy's position. Although cultural moral relativism is not inconsistent, it seems to conflict with some of our most basic intuitions about morality. Suppose that you meet an individual from culture Z, a culture that practices a brutal form of slavery. This individual, Zack, informs you that the practice of slavery is considered morally legitimate in his society, and that it is morally legitimate for him to buy and sell certain individuals, to torture them at will, and to hold them as slaves. If cultural moral relativism is true, then it is true that it is morally permissible for Zack to engage in this practice, and it is also true that it would be morally wrong for you to practice slavery, given that you are a member of a culture which abhors such a practice. In the context of this position, there is really no source of disagreement between you and Zack. You might be tempted to tell Zack that slavery is morally wrong, but if you are a cultural moral relativist, the only claim you can make is that slavery is wrong relative to the moral code that your society accepts. If you look at the situation objectively, you will recognize that slavery is morally permissible relative to the moral code that Zack's society accepts. In order to respond to Zack in an appropriate and enlightened manner, you should say something like "How interesting that your society accepts such an extensive practice of slavery. My society does not accept this practice at all. Our societies are quite different, but there is no objective way to adjudicate between our competing moral codes."

Intuitively, however, most of us would not consider this to be an adequate response. We would want to argue strenuously that it is morally abhorrent to enslave and torture human beings. We would want to offer many strong reasons why one ought not to torture people and hold them as slaves, and to assert that if they constitute good reasons for people in our culture not to behave in this manner, they also constitute good reasons for people in culture Z not to behave in this manner. We would want to ask Zack what arguments he could possibly make to justify such a practice. And we would probably want to condemn culture Z in the strongest possible terms. It is not clear, then, that cultural moral relativism provides an adequate account of moral disagreement, nor is it clear that we should accept the claim that there is nothing wrong with torture and slavery in a society in which these practices are accepted as legitimate.

Similar points can be made with respect to disagreement within a society. Suppose that there is a single member of culture Z who firmly believes that their practice of slavery is morally abhorrent, and who does everything in her power to try to reform her society. If cultural relativism is true, this individual is simply mistaken about what is right and wrong. In her society, slavery actually is morally legitimate. Her disagreement with the rest of her society reflects her mistaken determination of what is right and wrong for her fellow citizens. Most of us would consider this analysis of the situation to be seriously inadequate. We tend to believe that the reformer is correct, and that she is waging a courageous battle for the moral advancement of her community and (more importantly) for the moral rights of the slaves. And we tend to believe that certain actions and practices are just wrong, regardless of whether a majority of persons within a society has yet recognized that they are wrong.

Can the cultural moral relativist provide a more adequate account of moral disagreement? It is not clear that she can. To do so, it seems that she would have to provide some method of debating about the adequacy of competing moral frameworks. But the adequacy of a moral framework can only be assessed with reference to basic moral values such as justice, fairness, utility, respect for human rights, and so forth. And the cultural moral relativist argues that there are no objective moral values. Moral values are always relative to the moral framework accepted by the culture. In the end, the cultural relativist might claim that we have to agree to disagree on the issue of whether one moral framework is better than another.

1.

SELECTIONS FROM *FOLKWAYS*

❧ ❧ ❧

WILLIAM GRAHAM SUMNER

William Graham Sumner (1840-1910) was an anthropologist and the author of Folkways *from which this selection is taken. He argues that every society has folkways, or regular ways of doing things, that evolve in the society in response to the needs, pressures, and conditions that it faces. He then argues that the folkways of any given society constitute the standards of right and wrong for that society. There are no independent standards of right and wrong in reference to which we can evaluate folkways, or in reference to which we can judge that one society's moral code is superior to another's.*

The Folkways are "Right." Rights. Morals

The folkways ... extend over the whole of life. There is a right way to catch game, to win a wife, to make one's self appear, to cure disease, to honor ghosts, to treat comrades or strangers, to behave when a child is born, on the warpath, in council, and so on in all cases which can arise. The ways are defined on the negative side, that is, by taboos. The "right" way is the way which the ancestors used and which has been handed down. The tradition is its own warrant. It is not held subject to verification by experience. The notion of right is in the folkways. It is not outside of them, of independent origin, and brought to them to test them. In the folkways, whatever is, is right. This is because they are traditional, and therefore contain in themselves the authority of the ancestral ghosts. When we come to the folkways we are at the end of our analysis. The notion of right and ought is the same in regard to all the folkways, but the degree of it varies with the importance of the interest at stake. The obligation of conformable and cooperative action is far greater under ghost fear and war than in other matters, and the social sanctions are severer, because group interests are supposed to be at stake. Some usages contain only a slight element of right and ought. It may well be believed that notions of right and duty, and of social welfare, were first developed in connection with ghost fear and other worldliness, and therefore that, in that field also, folkways were first raised to mores. "Rights" are the rules of mutual give and take in the competition of life which are imposed on comrades in the in-group, in order that the peace may prevail there which is essential to the group strength. Therefore rights can never be "natural" or "God-given," or absolute in any sense. The morality of a group at a time is the sum of the taboos and prescriptions in the folkways by which right conduct is defined. Therefore morals can never be intuitive. They are historical, institutional, and empirical.

World philosophy, life policy, right, rights, and morality are all products of the folkways. They are reflections on, and generalizations from, the experience of pleasure and pain which is won in efforts to carry on the struggle for existence under actual life conditions. The generalizations are very crude and vague in their germinal forms. They are all embodied in folklore, and all our philosophy and science have been developed out of them.

Integration of the Mores of a Group or Age

In further development of the same interpretation of the phenomena we find that changes in history are primarily due to changes in life conditions. Then the folkways change. The new philosophies and ethical rules are invented to try to justify the new ways. The whole vast body of modern mores has thus been developed out of the philosophy and ethics of the Middle Ages. So the mores which have been developed to suit the system of great secular states, world commerce, credit institutions, contract wages and rent, emigration to outlying continents, etc., have become the norm for the whole body of usages, manners, ideas, faiths, customs, and institutions which embrace the whole life of a society and characterize an historical epoch. Thus India, Chaldea, Assyria, Egypt, Greece, Rome, the Middle Ages, Modern Times, are cases in which the integration of the mores upon different life conditions produced societal states of complete and distinct individuality (ethos). Within any such societal status the great reason for any phenomenon is that it conforms to the mores of the time and place. Historians have always recognized incidentally the operation of such a determining force. What is now maintained is that it is not incidental or subordinate. It is supreme and controlling. Therefore the scientific discussion of a usage, custom, or institution consists in tracing its relation to the mores, and the discussion of societal crises and changes consists in showing their connection with changes in the life conditions, or with the readjustment of the mores to changes in those conditions.

Purpose of the Present Work

"Ethology" would be a convenient term for the study of manners, customs, usages, and mores, including the study of the way in which they are formed, how they grow or decay, and how they affect the interests which it is their purpose to serve. The Greeks applied the term "ethos" to the sum of the characteristic usages, ideas, standards, and codes by which a group was differentiated and individualized in character from other groups. "Ethics" were things which pertained to the ethos and therefore the things which were the standard of right. The Romans used "mores" for customs in the broadest and richest sense of the word, including the notion that customs served welfare, and had traditional and mystic sanction, so that they were properly authoritative and sacred. It is a very surprising fact that modern nations should have lost these words and the significant suggestions which inhere in them. The English language has no derivative noun from "mores," and no equivalent for it. The French *moeurs* is trivial compared with "mores." The German *Sitte* renders "mores" but very imperfectly. The modern peoples have made morals and morality a separate domain, by the side of religion, philosophy, and politics. In that sense, morals is an impossible and unreal category. It has no existence, and can have none. The word "moral" means what belongs or appertains to the mores. Therefore the category of morals can never be defined without reference to something outside of itself. Ethics, having lost connection with the ethos of a people, is an attempt to systematize the current notions of right and wrong upon some basic principle, generally with the purpose of establishing morals on an absolute doctrine, so that it shall be universal, absolute, and everlasting. In a general way also, whenever a thing can be called moral, or connected with some ethical generality, it is thought to be "raised," and disputants whose method is to employ ethical generalities assume especial authority for themselves and their views. These methods of discussion are most employed in treating of social topics, and they are disastrous to sound study of facts. They help to hold the social sciences under the dominion of metaphysics. The abuse has been most developed in connection with political economy, which has been almost robbed of the character of a serious discipline by converting its discussions into ethical disquisitions.

Why Use the Word Mores?

"Ethica," in the Greek sense, or "ethology," as above defined, would be good names for our present work. We aim to study the ethos of groups, in order to see how it arises, its power and influence, the modes of its operation on members of the group, and the various attributes of it (ethica). "Ethology" is a very unfamiliar word. It has been used for the mode of setting forth manners, customs, and mores in satirical comedy. The Latin word "mores" seems to be, on the whole, more practically convenient and available than any other for our purpose, as a name for the folkways with the connotations of right and truth in respect to welfare, embodied in them. The analysis and definition given above show that in the mores we must recognize a dominating force in history, constituting a condition as to what can be done, and as to the methods which can be employed.

Mores Are a Directive Force

Of course the view which has been stated is antagonistic to the view that philosophy and ethics furnish creative and determining forces in society and history. That view comes down to us from the Greek philosophy and it has now prevailed so long that all current discussion conforms to it. Philosophy and ethics are pursued as independent disciplines, and the results are brought to the science of society and to statesmanship and legislation as authoritative dicta. We also have Volkerpsychologie, Sozialpolitik, and other intermediate forms which show the struggle of metaphysics to retain control of the science of society. The "historic sense," the Zeitgeist, and other terms of similar import are partial recognitions of the mores and their importance in the science of society. We shall see below that philosophy and ethics are products of the folkways. They are taken out of the mores, but are never original and creative; they are secondary and derived. They often interfere in the second stage of the sequence—act, thought, act. Then they produce harm, but some ground is furnished for the claim that they are creative or at least regulative. In fact, the real process in great bodies of men is not one of deduction from any great principle of philosophy or ethics. It is one of minute efforts to live well under existing conditions, which efforts are repeated indefinitely by great numbers, getting strength from habit and from the fellowship of united action. The resultant folkways become coercive. All are forced to conform, and the folkways dominate the societal life. Then they seem true and right, and arise into mores as the norm of welfare. Thence are produced faiths, ideas, doctrines, religions, and philosophies, according to the stage of civilization and the fashions of reflection and generalization.

What Is Goodness or Badness of the Mores?

It is most important to notice that, for the people of a time and place, their own mores are always good, or rather that for them there can be no question of the goodness or badness of their mores. The reason is because the standards of good and right are in the mores. If the life conditions change, the traditional folkways may produce pain and loss, or fail to produce the same good as formerly. Then the loss of comfort and ease brings doubt into the judgment of welfare (causing doubt of the pleasure of the gods, or of war power, or of health), and thus disturbs the unconscious philosophy of the mores. Then a later time will pass judgment on the mores. Another society may also pass judgment on the mores. In our literary and historical study of the mores we want to get from them their educational value, which consists in the stimulus or warning as to what is, in its effects, societally good or bad. This may lead us to reject or neglect a phenomenon like infanticide, slavery, or witchcraft, as an old "abuse" and "evil," or to pass by the crusades as a folly which cannot recur. Such a course would be a great error. Everything in the mores of a time and place must be regarded as justified with regard to that time and place. "Good" mores are those which are well adapted to the situation. "Bad" mores are those which are not so adapted. The mores are not so stereotyped and changeless as might appear, because they are forever moving towards more complete adaption to conditions and interests, and also towards more complete adjustment to each other. People in mass have never made or kept up a custom in order to hurt their interests. They have made innumerable errors as to what their interests were and how to satisfy them, but they have always aimed to serve their interests as well as they could. This gives the standpoint for the student of the mores. All things in them come before him on the same plane. They all bring instruction and warning. They all have the same relation to power and welfare. The mistakes in them are component parts of them. We do not study them in order to approve some of them and condemn others. They are all equally worthy of attention from the fact that they existed and were used. The chief object of study in them is their harmonious system of life policy. For the men of the time there are no "bad" mores. What is traditional and current is the standard of what ought to be. The masses never raise any question about such things. If a few raise doubts and questions, this proves that the folkways have already begun to lose firmness and the regulative element in the mores has begun to lose authority. This indicates that the folkways are on their way to a new adjustment. The extremes of folly, wickedness, and absurdity in the mores is witch persecutions, but the best men of the seventeenth century had no doubt that witches existed, and that they ought to be burned. The religion, statecraft, jurisprudence, philosophy, and social system of that age all contributed to maintain that belief. It was rather a culmination than a contradiction of the current faiths and convictions, just as the dogma that all men are equal and that one ought to have as much political power in the state as another was the culmination of the political dogmatism and social philosophy of the nineteenth century. Hence our judgments of the good or evil consequences of folkways are to be kept separate from our study of the historical phenomena of them, and of their strength and the reasons for it. The judgments have their place in plans and doctrines for the future, not in a retrospect.

The Mores Have the Authority of Facts

The mores come down to us from the past. Each individual is born into them as he is born into the atmosphere, and he does not reflect on them, or criticize them any more than a baby analyzes the atmosphere before he begins to breathe it. Each one is subjected to the influence of the mores, and formed by them, before he is capable of reasoning about them. It may be objected that nowadays, at least, we criticize all traditions, and accept none just because they are handed down to us. If we take up cases of things which are still entirely or almost entirely in the mores, we shall see that this is not so. There are sects of free-lovers amongst us who want to discuss pair marriage. They are not simply people of evil life. They invite us to discuss rationally our inherited customs and ideas as to marriage, which, they say, are by no means so excellent and elevated as we believe. They have never won any serious attention. Some others want to argue in favor of polygamy on grounds of expediency. They fail to obtain a hearing. Others want to discuss property. In spite of some literary activity on their part, no discussion of property, bequest, and inheritance has ever been opened. Property and marriage are in the mores. Nothing can ever change them but the unconscious and imperceptible movement of the mores. Religion was originally a matter of the mores. It became a societal institution and a function of the state. It has now to a great extent been put back into the mores. Since laws with penalties to enforce religious creeds or practices have gone out of use any one may think and act as he pleases about religion. Therefore it is not now "good form" to attack religion. Infidel publications are now tabooed by the mores, and are more effectually repressed than ever before. They produce no controversy. Democracy is in our American mores. It is a product of our physical and economic conditions. It is impossible to discuss or criticize it. It is glorified for popularity, and is a subject of dithyrambic rhetoric. No one treats it with complete candor and sincerity. No one dares to analyze it as he would aristocracy or autocracy. He would get no hearing and would only incur abuse. The thing to be noticed in all these cases is that the masses oppose a deaf ear to every argument against the mores. It is only insofar as things have been transferred from the mores into laws and positive institutions that there is discussion about them or rationalizing upon them. The mores contain the norm by which if we should discuss the mores, we should have to judge the mores. We learn the mores as unconsciously as we learn to walk and eat and breathe. The masses never learn how we walk, and eat, and breathe, and they never know any reason why the mores are what they are. The justification of them is that when we wake to consciousness of life we find them facts which already hold us in the bonds of tradition, custom, and habit. The mores contain embodied in them notions, doctrines, and maxims, but they are facts. They are in the present tense. They have nothing to do with what ought to be, will be, may be, or once was, if it is not now.

Mores and Morals; Social Code

For everyone the mores give the notion of what ought to be. This includes the notion of what ought to be done, for all should cooperate to bring to pass, in the order of life, what ought to be. All notions of propriety, decency, chastity,

politeness, order, duty, right, rights, discipline, respect, reverence, cooperation, and fellowship, especially all things in regard to which good and ill
depend entirely on the point at which the line is drawn, are in the mores. The
mores can make things seem right and good to one group or one age which
to another seem antagonistic to every instinct of human nature. The thir-
teenth century bred in every heart such a sentiment in regard to heretics that
inquisitors had no more misgivings in their proceedings than men would
have now if they should attempt to exterminate rattlesnakes. The sixteenth
century gave to all such notions about witches that witch persecutors thought
they were waging war on enemies of God and man. Of course the inquisitors
and witch persecutors constantly developed the notions of heretics and witches. They exaggerated the notions and then gave them back again to the
mores in their expanded form to inflame the hearts of men with terror and
hate and to become, in the next stage, so much more fantastic and ferocious
motives. Such is the reaction between the mores and the acts of the living
generation. The world philosophy of the age is never anything but the reflection on the mental horizon, which is formed out of the mores, of the ruling
ideas which are in the mores themselves. It is from a failure to recognize the
to and fro in this reaction that the current notion arises that mores are produced by doctrines. The "morals" of an age are never anything but the con-
sonance between what is done and what the mores of the age require. The
whole revolves on itself, in the relation of the specific to the general, within
the horizon formed by the mores. Every attempt to win an outside standpoint
from which to reduce the whole to an absolute philosophy of truth and right,
based on an unalterable principle, is a delusion. New elements are brought
in only by new conquests of nature through science and art. The new conquests change the conditions of life and the interests of the members of the
society. Then the mores change by adaptation to new conditions and interests. The philosophy and ethics then follow to account for and justify the
changes in the mores; often, also, to claim that they have caused the changes.
They never do anything but draw new lines of bearing between the parts of
the mores and the horizon of thought within which they are inclosed, and
which is a deduction from the mores. The horizon is widened by more knowledge, but for one age it is just as much a generalization from the mores as for
another. It is always unreal. It is only a product of thought. The ethical
philosophers select points on this horizon from which to take their bearings,
and they think that they have won some authority for their systems when they
travel back again from the generalization to the specific custom out of which
it was deduced. The cases of the inquisitors and witch persecutors who toiled
arduously and continually for their chosen ends, for little or no reward, show
us the relation between mores on the one side and philosophy, ethics, and
religion on the other.

2.
RELATIVISM AND OBJECTIVITY IN ETHICS

❦ ❦ ❦

WILLIAM H. SHAW

William H. Shaw is a professor of philosophy at San Jose State University. His areas of specialization are ethics and political philosophy. The following article begins with an examination of ethical relativism—the theory that what is right is what a culture says is right, or that what is right is what the individual says is right. Shaw argues that neither version of this theory is tenable. He goes on to argue that meta-ethical relativism, which holds that there is no objective basis for adjudicating between conflicting moral positions, does not follow from the disagreement we find across cultures on moral standards. According to Shaw, we can find objective grounds for assessing moral standards.

1. Ethical Relativism

The peoples and societies of the world are diverse; their institutions, fashions, ideas, manners, and mores vary tremendously. This is a simple truth. Sometimes an awareness of this diversity and of the degree to which our own beliefs and habits mirror those of the culture around us stimulates self-examination. In the realm of ethics, familiarity with strikingly different cultures has led many people to suppose that morality itself is relative to particular societies, that right and wrong vary from culture to culture.

This view is generally called "ethical relativism"; it is the normative theory that what is right is what the culture says is right. What is right in one place may be wrong in another, because the only criterion for distinguishing right from wrong—the only ethical standard for judging an action—is the moral system of the society in which the act occurs. Abortion, for example, is condemned as immoral in Catholic Spain, but practiced as a morally neutral form of birth control in Japan. According to the ethical relativist, then, abortion is wrong in Spain but morally permissible in Japan. The relativist is not saying merely that the Spanish believe abortion is abominable and the Japanese do not; that is acknowledged by everyone. Rather, the ethical relativist contends that abortion is immoral in Spain because the Spanish believe it to be immoral and morally permissible in Japan because the Japanese believe it to be so. There is no absolute ethical standard, independent of cultural context, no criterion of right and wrong by which to judge other than that of particular societies. In short, morality is relative to society.

A different sort of relativist might hold that morality is relative, not to the culture, but to the individual. The theory that what is right and wrong is determined by what a person thinks is right and wrong, however, is not very plausible. The main reason is that it collapses the distinction between thinking something is right and its actually being right. We have all done things we thought were right at the time, but later decided were wrong. Our normal view is that we were mistaken in our original thinking; we believed the action to have been right, but it was not. In the relativist view under consideration, one would have to say that the action in question was originally right, but later wrong as our thinking changed—surely a confused and confusing thing to say! Furthermore, if we accept this view, there would be no point in debating ethics with anyone, for whatever he thought right would automatically be right for him and whatever we thought right would be right for us. Indeed, if right were determined solely by what we took to be right, then it would not be at all clear what we are doing when we try to decide whether something is right or wrong in the first place—since we could never be mistaken! Certainly this is a muddled doctrine. Most likely its proponents have meant to emphasize that each person must determine for himself as best he can what actually is right or to argue that we ought not to blame people for acting according to their sincere moral judgments. These points are plausible, and with some qualifications, perhaps everyone would accept them, but they are not relativistic in the least.

The theory that morality is relative to society, however, is more plausible, and those who endorse this type of ethical relativism point to the diverseness of human values and the multiformity of moral codes to support their case. From our own cultural perspective, some seemingly "immoral" moralities have been adopted: polygamy, homosexuality, stealing, slavery, infanticide, and the eating of strangers have all been tolerated or even encouraged by the moral system of one society or another. In light of this, the ethical relativist feels that there can be no nonethnocentric standard by which to judge actions. We feel the individuals in some remote tribe are wrong to practice infanticide, while other cultures are scandalized that we eat animals. Different societies have different rules; what moral authority other than society, asks the relativist, can there be? Morality is just like fashion in clothes, beauty in persons, and legality in action—all of which are relative to, and determined by, the standards of a particular culture.

In some cases this seems to make sense. Imagine that Betty is raised in a society in which one is thought to have a special obligation to look after one's maternal aunts and uncles in their old age, and Sarah lives in a society in which no such obligation is supposed. Certainly we are inclined to say that Betty really does have an obligation that Sarah does not. Sarah's culture, on the other hand, may hold that if someone keeps a certain kind of promise to you, you owe him or her a favor, or that children are not required to tell the truth to adults. Again, it seems plausible that different sorts of obligations arise in Sarah's society; in her society, promisees really do owe their promisors and children are not wrong to lie, whereas this might not be so in other cultures.

Ethical relativism explains these cases by saying that right and wrong are determined solely by the standards of the society in question, but there are other, nonrelativistic ways of accounting for these examples. In Betty's society, people live with the expectation that their sister's offspring will look after them; for Betty to behave contrary to this institution and to thwart these expectations may produce bad consequences—so there is a reason to think she has this obligation other than the fact that her society thinks she has it. In Sarah's world, on the other hand, no adult expects children to tell the truth; far from deceiving people, children only amuse them with their tall tales. Thus, we are not required to be ethical relativists in order to explain why moral obligations may differ according to the social context. And there are other cases in which ethical relativism seems implausible. Suppose Betty's society thinks that it is wicked to engage in intercourse on Sundays. We do not believe it wrong of her to do so just because her society thinks such conduct is impermissible. Or suppose her culture thinks that it is morally reprehensible to wear the fur of rare animals. Here we may be inclined to concur, but if we think it is wrong of her to do this, we do not think it so because her society says so. In this example and the previous one, we look for some reason why her conduct should be considered immoral. The fact that her society thinks it so is not enough.

Ethical relativism undermines any moral criticism of the practices of other societies as long as their actions conform to their own standards. We cannot say that slavery in a slave society like that of the American South of the last century was immoral and unjust as long as that society held it to be morally permissible. Slavery was right for them, although it is wrong for us today. To condemn slave owners as immoral, says the relativist, is to attempt to extend the standards of our society illegitimately to another culture. But this is not the way we usually think. Not only do we wish to say that a society is mistaken if it thinks that slavery (or cannibalism, cruelty, racial bigotry) is morally permissible, but we also think we have justification for so saying and are not simply projecting ethnocentrically the standards of our own culture. Indeed, far from mirroring those standards in all our moral judgments, we sometimes criticize certain principles or practices accepted by our own society. None of this makes sense from the relativist's point of view. People can be censured for not living up to their society's moral code, but that is all; the moral code itself cannot be criticized. Whatever a society takes to be morally right really is right for it. Reformers who campaign against the "injustices" of their society are only encouraging people to be immoral—that is, to depart from the moral standards of their society—unless or until the majority of society agrees with the reformers. The minority can never be right in moral matters; to be right it must become the majority.

This raises some puzzles for the theory of ethical relativism. What proportion of a society must believe, say, that abortion is permissible for it to be morally acceptable in that society—90 per cent? 75 per cent? 51 per cent? If the figure is set high (say 75 per cent) and only 60 per cent of the society condone abortion, then it would not be permissible; yet it would seem odd for the relativist to say that abortion was therefore wrong, given that a majority of the population believes otherwise. Without a sufficient majority either way, abortion would be neither morally permissible nor impermissible. On the other hand, if the figure is set lower, then there will be frequent moral flip-flops. Imagine that last year abortion was thought wrong by 51 per cent of the populace, but this year only 49 per cent are of that opinion; that means, according to the relativist, that it was wrong last year, but is now morally permissible—and things may change again. Surely, though, something is wrong with majority rule in matters of morality. In addition one might wonder what is to count, for the relativist, as a society. In a large and heterogeneous nation like the United States, are right and wrong determined by the whole country; or do smaller societies like Harlem, San Francisco, rural Iowa, or the Chicano community in Los Angeles set their own moral standards? But if these are cohesive enough to count as morality-generating societies, what about such "societies" as outlaw bikers, the drug culture, or the underworld? And what, then, does the relativist say about conflicts between these group moralities or between them and the morality of the overall society? Since an individual may be in several overlapping "societies" at the same time, he may well be receiving conflicting moral instructions—all of which, it would seem, are correct according to the relativist.

These are all questions the relativist must answer if he is to make his theory coherent. To raise them is not to refute relativism, of course, since the relativist may be able to explain satisfactorily what he means by "society," how its standards relate to those of other groups, and what is to count as moral approval by a given society. However the relativist attempts to refine his theory, he will still be maintaining that what is right is determined by what the particular society, culture, or group takes to be right and that this is the only standard by which an individual's actions can be judged. Not only does the relativist neglect to give us a reason for believing that a society's own views about morality are conclusive as to what is actually right and wrong, but also his theory does not square with our understanding of morality and the nature of ethical discourse. By contending that the moralities of different societies are all equally valid, the relativist holds that there can be no nonethnocentric ground for preferring one moral code to another, that one cannot speak of moral progress. Moralities may change, but they do not get better or worse. If words mean anything, however, it seems clear that a society that applauded the random torture of children would be immoral, even if it thought such a practice were right. It would simply be mistaken, and disastrously so. Since this is the case, ethical relativism must be false as a theory of normative ethics.

2. Meta-ethical Relativism

In fact, ethical relativism promotes conformity and supports the moral status quo. What is right is determined by society's conventions, and so if the individual wishes to be moral, to do the right thing, he should fall in step. The unheeded reformer, far from being a prophet, is a scoundrel. One suspects, however, that those who are free enough from their own cultural formation to be attracted to ethical relativism in the first place do not themselves feel compelled to follow slavishly the conventions of their society on pain of being immoral. More likely, perhaps, is that they come to take morality—as they understand it—less seriously. "Morality is solely a matter of what society thinks," we can imagine someone saying, "so who cares if they think what I'm doing is wrong!" At this point, though, our ethical relativist may be close to abandoning his own theory; insofar as he is unmoved by what society believes, he may be implicitly thinking that something is not vicious just because society says it is. Assuming that he has not eschewed moral discourse altogether— he may personally believe that Nixon's Christmas bombing of Hanoi was an enormity, that loyalty to friends is a moral virtue, and that one ought to speak the truth—then he may not be an ethical relativist at all. In the end, though, even if he does not really think that actions are right by virtue of their conforming to what society holds to be right, he may still be struck by the diversity of moral codes: is there any satisfactory way of justifying one morality over another? With so many different moral standards, how can we be sure that ours is right?

Let us pursue this further. As a normative theory, as a criterion of right and wrong, ethical relativism has not appeared at all convincing. But if it seems implausible, the worries that prompted it are real enough. People and societies do (seem to) disagree on moral matters, and one is bound to wonder how his or her own standards of morality can be justified, or why they are to be preferred (if at all) to rival standards. Consider an example from outside ethics. A Baptist in Tennessee no doubt realizes that had he been born in Tel Aviv, most likely he would be a convinced Jew, or if born in Tehran, a devout Muslim; and sometime this fact may give him pause to reflect on the justification for the tenets of his own religion. Awareness of the array of different religious faiths does not lead him to suppose that religious truth is whatever one thinks it is, but to worry about whether his own beliefs can be rationally supported. The situation is similar in ethics. Ideally one wants values and principles that can be rationally supported, since morality—if it is to mean anything—is more than a matter of personal taste, and few are happy simply to affirm any moral principle that strikes their fancy. Yet anyone can see that there is a causal influence between one's background, culture, and rearing on the one hand and one's moral ideas and principles on the other. Raised in a different environment, we no doubt would endorse a different moral code. This has led some to adopt the relativistic meta-ethical view that there is no satisfactory method for choosing among ethical codes, that conflicting ethical opinions can be equally valid.

The distinction between normative ethics and meta-ethics is a fundamental one for philosophers, and so it may be worthwhile to clarify it in this context. As a normative theory, ethical relativism offers a criterion for distinguishing right actions from wrong—namely, that right actions are those that conform to the moral principles of the society in which they occur (or from whose perspective we are judging). Utilitarianism (a more popular normative theory) says that, in John Stuart Mill's words, actions are right in proportion as they tend to promote happiness. The rival normative theory of W.D. Ross is less easy to state succinctly. It is a pluralistic theory offering, instead of a single duty to promote happiness, a list of several *prima facie* obligations; the right action is that which has the greatest balance of *prima facie* rightness over *prima facie* wrongness or, alternatively, that which coincides with our most stringent *prima facie* duty.

Distinct from principles and theories that purport to provide us with normative standards, and there are many besides those of Mill and Ross, is the realm of meta-ethics. While normative ethics tries to specify what is right and wrong, good and bad, meta-ethics involves philosophical reflection on the nature of ethics—in particular, reflection on the meaning and status of ethical terms and discourse, and on the nature and possibility of justifying ethical principles. As a meta-ethical theory, relativism does not provide a criterion for distinguishing right and wrong; rather, it states that in the case of conflicting basic ethical judgments there is no objectively valid, rational way of justifying one against the other. Two such opinions will be equally sound. The meta-ethical relativist is not, it should be noted, thereby committed to normative relativism. He may in fact subscribe to an entirely different criterion of right and wrong, for meta-ethical relativism does not entail any particular normative theory. Rather, it makes a statement about the possibility of justifying rival ethical standards; it rules out objective certification of moral principles.

Meta-ethical relativism is generally prompted by the belief that there is fundamental disagreement in ethical matters; indeed, it would have little point without that belief. Although there is wide diversity in the moral systems of different societies, on closer inspection it is not so obvious that the values and principles of these societies vary in fundamental ways. On the one hand, the same moral principle (for example, promote the greatest happiness of the greatest number) may enjoin different conduct in different situations: perhaps monogamy will produce the most happiness in a society where the sexes are numerically balanced, polygamy in one where they are not. Moral principles frequently permit us to do something (like break a promise) in some circumstances, while forbidding it in others. So, the fact that actions condemned by one society are approved in a different cultural context by another society does not imply that antagonistic moral principles must be at work. On the other hand, many ethical disagreements are due to different factual beliefs (especially about the consequences of actions) and not to conflicting values. Some primitive tribes, for example, are reported by anthropologists to authorize the killing of one's parents before they get too old. Such a practice strikes us in Western cultures as monstrously wicked. Yet these people are not evil; they believe, rather, that one spends the afterlife in the physical state in which one dies. One does one's parents a great service by not letting them grow old and feeble before they die. If we shared this belief, we would probably do the same. To take a less exotic example, people in our society may disagree about how we ought to raise children, and yet this disagreement might stem, not from a divergence of values, but from differing estimates of the likely consequences and relative effectiveness of rival child-rearing programs. Ethical disagreements are fundamental only if they remain after there is full agreement about the factual characteristics of whatever is being evaluated.

Is there, then, fundamental ethical disagreement between cultures? The answer is hard to know, largely because it is difficult to determine whether two cultures are referring to the same action when both their factual beliefs about that action and its social context differ. For example, are South Sea islanders really approving what is to us "stealing" if they have no institution of private property in the first place? Because of intersocietal differences in conceptual understanding and factual assessment, many people remain convinced that there is no fundamental ethical disagreement, and this view has not yet been demonstrated to be wrong. On the other hand, there do seem to be areas of moral variance—for example, concerning the treatment of animals—which do not result from differing factual beliefs or conceptual schemas.

Suppose that fundamental ethical disagreement exists, that different cultures really do have conflicting, basic moral principles. This fact, if it were a fact, would not establish meta-ethical relativism. In ethical matters as in factual matters, a divergence of opinion does not mean that there is no one, right answer, that all opinions are equally sound. The existence of disagreement fails to undermine the claim that there is an objective truth to the matter. Philosophers have generally recognized this point, but they have not always acknowledged the reverse point that agreement on fundamental ethical principles—if it existed—would not ipso facto justify them nor refute meta-ethical relativism. After all, this concurrence might be a happy accident, or it might simply reflect some fact of human psychology. While it would mean that we would be able to resolve our ethical disputes—since once we were clear about the facts there would be shared principles to which we could appeal—this moral agreement would not show that these principles were really justified; and it is this that bothers the meta-ethical relativist.

3. Naturalism, Intuitionism, and Emotivism

Whether in fact people and cultures agree or disagree on their moral principles, then, is not as crucial as one might have supposed. What matters is whether there is some procedure or reasoning by which ultimate ethical standards can be justified to rational and clear-headed people. If there is, then there is objectivity in ethics, even if people as they now are disagree. If there is not, then ethics will not be objectively validated even if people as they are happen to agree. We can look then at three main positions that philosophers have staked out on this crucial issue of justifying ethical standards.

One traditional way (called "naturalism") in which philosophers have attempted to demonstrate the correctness of certain normative principles is by contending that the key concepts of ethics can be analyzed or defined in empirical, descriptive, or natural terms. To say that "right" means "brings about a good result" is to define the word in terms of another ethical concept, namely "good." But to say that it means "conducive to the survival of the species," "would be approved by an ideal observer," or "promotes the greatest happiness of the greatest number," would be to define it in terms of certain natural, non-ethical properties. If "right" or "good" can be analyzed in this way, then it will be a straight-forward factual matter to decide what sorts of actions and things have the property in question. If we disagree about the rightness of some course of action, and "right" means simply "promotes the greatest possible happiness," then it would seem that our disagreement could be resolved by investigating further the action in question to see to what extent it will promote happiness.

The attractiveness of this approach is that once we get our ethical definitions straight, then agreement on normative matters can be reached. Detailed objections, however, have been raised to every attempt to define "good" or "right" in nonmoral terms or to specify the natural property to which goodness (or rightness) refers. It seems that these moral words do not have a uniform, descriptive meaning for all people in our culture, let alone all cultures. Different people may simply mean different (even if related) things by the word "right"; if this is so, this whole meta-ethical approach will fail to produce satisfactory results. Agreeing with this, a philosopher might recommend that we assign some clear, non-ethical meanings to our ethical words, so that we could then agree on how to apply them; by choosing useful factual definitions for our terms, we could then resolve our normative disputes. But this does not solve the underlying problem, since people must still be persuaded to use their ethical words in the proposed way—and what sort of reasoning will persuade them to do so? Defending the stipulated definition will amount to arguing for a moral principle, so the crucial issue of justifying basic ethical standards still remains.

Philosophers have in fact overestimated what would be accomplished if the project of discovering nonmoral definitions or analyses of how we use our ethical terms were successful. Once naturalistic translations were found, it would be an easy matter to decide if an action were a case of rightness or wrongness; moral disputes could be resolved objectively. Or so it seems. Yet one could still wonder whether things would not have been better if our moral concepts had been different. Let us take an analogy from law. As a legal concept, murder has a fairly precise definition that does not rely on other legal terms. Murder is not defined simply as an illegal homicide, but as a certain kind of action, performed in a certain frame of mind. Thus, if all the facts were known, there should be little disagreement about whether the term applies or not. Yet one could still ask if this was the best way to use the word, if it would be better to adopt a different meaning, if there is some justification for using the word "murder" as it is now used, rather than in some other way.

Now the same sorts of questions can be asked about a moral term like "right," even if it were to be discovered that it does have some clear, stable definition in factual terms. Granted that "right" means thus-and-so, and that thus-and-so can be empirically determined, would it be better, wiser, more helpful, socially useful, or psychologically tenable to use "right" in a different way? It would be a dodge to rule out such a question on linguistic grounds (by saying, for example, that it makes no sense to ask if it would be good if "good" meant something different). There is a real worry here that cannot be dismissed in an offhand fashion. We said before that uniformity of opinion, although it makes possible ethical agreement, does not itself justify a moral principle, and something similar can be said about uniformity of definition. Definitional unanimity does not show that our moral system could not be improved with different concepts (or different meanings to our concepts), that our present definitions are as illuminating or helpful as others might be, or that those definitions assist us in answering the questions that we really want answered about how to live our lives.

Troubled by the difficulties of supplying empirical translations of ethical concepts, or by what if anything such translations would show, some philosophers (known as "intuitionists" or "nonnaturalists")[1] have argued instead that ethical terms cannot, in principle, be defined or analyzed in nonmoral, empirical terms. We have knowledge of right and wrong, good and bad, but our ethical concepts refer to distinctively moral properties. It has been held, for example, that "good" does not denote some empirical property (like "would be approved by an impartial person") but rather a peculiarly moral characteristic; like the word "yellow," "good" designates some simple, unanalyzable property. Ethical discourse is *sui generis;* it cannot be translated into empirical language. If "good" and "right" do not refer to factual properties, how do we know what is good or right? Philosophers taking this view of the meaning of moral terms have held that we know these moral properties through intuition. That is, we witness (or think about) some act, such as Tom's breaking a promise, and we simply "see" or intuit that it is wrong, that it has a certain moral characteristic, even though this is not a scientifically discernible property. Of course, to see that Tom is behaving badly is not the same as seeing that his banana is yellow, but they are alike in being the direct apprehension of some simple property.

Philosophers have been troubled by the nature of the properties to which moral terms are supposed, on this view, to refer and have puzzled over the exact character of the intuition by which they are known. But it must be acknowledged that this position has a certain plausibility; it is true to much of our moral experience, and it aligns well with our commonsense thinking. We see a couple of young boys knocking down an old social security pensioner and taking her purse. We know that it is wrong, immediately and without doubt. Assuming the act is what we take it to be, our moral evaluation is as certain as it can be.

Nonetheless, there is an alternative way of accounting for our reaction. Rather than supposing that we intuit some objective, but nonempirical, moral characteristic about the boys' action, it may be that we have been raised to be averse to hurting, or seeing hurt, people who are old, helpless, or innocent; and we react sharply and with moral outrage to those who hurt them. No doubt this is a good way to have been raised, and we may wish that everyone had moral reflexes like ours, but the problems that troubled our relativist are just around the corner. After all, some people have the same sort of adverse, moral reaction to homosexuality, interracial marriage, or oral sex that we do to the teen-age muggers. We certainly do not think they are intuiting some objective moral feature about homosexuality that we have overlooked. Rather, we are likely to believe that their attitudes can be explained by certain psychological facts about them: how they were raised, their early experiences, and perhaps their innate dispositions. In comparing cultures, as the relativist will remind us, we seem to find people who take as clearly right (or obviously wrong) actions we evaluate spontaneously and naturally in the reverse fashion. "Intuitions" conflict—so how can they ever provide us with ethical knowledge?

As a result, philosophers have taken a third meta-ethical position (known as "emotivism")[2] and contend that we do not have ethical knowledge at all, that our moral concepts do not denote either natural or nonnatural properties. Rather, ethical language expresses our emotions or is used to evoke an emotional response in our listeners. Thus, when we say it was wicked of the boys to mug old Mrs. Higgens, we are simply venting our feelings or trying to elicit similar feelings in others. Now there is something to be said for this view. It emphasizes a cardinal feature of our moral experience, namely, that morality involves personal commitment and that people are characteristically attached to their values—to their conception of right and wrong— in a way in which the earlier mentioned, more intellectualized pictures of morality seem to overlook. Disagreements about, say, the moral permissibility of abortion tend to get heated in a way a controversy about the existence of quarks does not. Moreover, moral discourse is frequently, perhaps usually, used to persuade, guide, and influence others; to stir them, move them, and influence their attitudes. This is a position the meta-ethical relativist will find comfortable. Ethical judgments cannot be objectively justified because they cannot be justified at all, because they are not really judgments. They are emotional ejaculations, neither true nor false. It could turn out that people everywhere have the same basic emotional reactions to certain situations, so the emotivist theory does not imply that ethical standards vary from culture to culture. But if they did, the emotive theory could explain why.

Although emotivism seems to capture important aspects of our moral experience, it neglects others. If we say "Tom was wrong to break his date with Betty in order to see Jane" or "Tom would have been wrong to stand her up," we seem—at least sometimes—to be asserting an opinion, not expressing an emotion. The fact that moral language may express feeling or be used to arouse others does not imply it is itself no more than this. The meaning of "euthanasia is immoral" should not be confused with the use to which it is put in a certain situation, which may well be to alter someone's proposed course of action, or be confused with whatever it happens to reveal about the speaker's own preferences, feelings, or attitudes. Indeed, if "euthanasia is immoral" did not make a claim about how things are, if it expressed only a feeling, then it is not clear how it could be used to influence others. At least some moral judgments seem to be just that—judgments that something is or is not the case—rather than an exclamation. Further, the speaker, if asked, will most likely say that his attitude of reprobation, disgust, anger, or whatever, is based on (what he takes to be) the fact that euthanasia is immoral; he feels the way he does because he thinks it is wrong. Emotivists equate our believing that something is wrong with our feeling a certain way, but in fact we feel indignation or moral disapproval *because* we think, say, that preferential hiring is unfair. Our thinking it unfair is not identical with our feeling indignant about it, although the two may be related. Emotivists owe us an explanation of how we are all mistaken in believing that we are ascribing moral predicates to subjects, that is, making moral judgments, when according to their theory, we are doing nothing of the kind.

4. The Nature of Morality

All three of these traditional meta-ethical positions have problems. Philosophers have been ingenious in trying to make variations on them work, and I have not attempted to do justice to these efforts. Certainly, the last word has yet to be written, but enough has perhaps been said for one to wonder if there could be a route across this tricky terrain that would satisfy everyone. One may well doubt that an analysis of ethical language itself, even if successful, would solve the issue of justification that faces us. By changing tack, however, and pursuing some points raised by our criticisms of the emotivist theory, we should be able to throw some light on the nature of morality and illuminate—if not resolve—the problem of justification.

We said that the emotivist account of morality correctly emphasizes certain important features about the practice of morality but ignores others. In particular, it overlooks the fact that basic to morality is the giving of reasons and argument for one's moral position. Morality can be taught; principles defended; children instructed. When people make moral judgments, they suppose that there is justification for what they say—even if they are uncertain what form that justification would take. The logic of "is wrong" is not that of "I don't like." An emotivist believes that in moral disputes reasoning is only relevant to determining the empirical properties of an action; one's moral evaluation itself—being an expression of emotion rather than an intellectual judgment—is not subject to dispute. But in moral discussions we generally go beyond merely drawing certain factual characteristics of the subject under debate to the attention of our interlocutor and hoping he will respond to them as we do. We seek the moral principles underlying his judgment, examine their plausibility, measure them for consistency with other principles, and test them against hypothetical cases. We reason with our principles just as a judge works with various legal principles in seeking a solution to a case: he does not simply listen to the facts and respond one way or another.

Reason-giving is essential to the nature of morality, at least as we understand it. Suppose that Smith and Jones both think that incest is immoral. Smith, when challenged, argues that it is unnatural, harmful to the family unit, and psychologically destructive to the individuals involved. Each of these reasons can be pursued in greater detail: For example, what is "unnatural," and is the unnatural always immoral? And we can raise other relevant issues with Smith about, say, consent, age, or individual rights. Jones, on the other hand, offers no reasons and does not assent to those Smith gives. When pressed, Jones merely says, "I don't need to give a reason; incest is simply wrong." At this point, one may doubt that Jones is making a moral judgment. He may well be troubled by the thought of incest; it may agitate him; he may be adamant in condemning it. But if he resists offering a justification for his opinion, we shall very likely refuse to recognize it as a moral position at all.[3] Instead, we would suspect that he is only expressing a personal quirk or emotional reaction. The point I am making about our practice of morality— namely, that reason-giving and argumentation are essential to it—is attested to by the fact that prejudice frequently dresses itself in the language of reason. We recognize that the racist is only rationalizing his visceral bias when he attempts to justify segregation with spurious theories of racial differences, but his effort to so justify his prejudice at least acknowledges the fact that one must have reasons to back one's views if they are to count as a moral position in the first place—let alone be taken seriously.

Two related points are relevant here. The first is that not only are reasoning and argumentation basic to our practice of morality, but only certain sorts of reasons are countenanced by it. If Jones were to offer, as a justification of his judgment that incest is immoral, the reason that the idea is too gross for him to contemplate, or if a racist were to try to justify segregation by pointing to the skin color of the group he disdains, their "arguments" would simply be ruled out of bounds. By contrast, appeals to other sorts of considerations— for example, the rights of the persons involved, fairness, or the happiness produced—are perfectly appropriate and often suffice to establish at least the *prima facie* rightness or wrongness of the action. In other words, within moral discourse there are certain standard moves and relevant considerations— acknowledged by the vast majority of those who engage in it—just as there is an accepted framework of legal principles, policies, rules, and precedents on which a lawyer can and must draw in making his case.

The second point is that the relevant standards are fairly clear and can be applied with a reasonable claim to objectivity. Within the complex institution of morality it is not the case that it is all subjective, that all judgments are equal. There are criteria, and they can be interpreted and applied with a substantial degree of objectivity—just as judges can decide cases, teachers grade essays, or referees call penalties with a legitimate claim to be doing so correctly and objectively. And mistakes can be made: the fact that a judge's decision can be appealed implies that there are accepted standards against which it can be measured. Within our society we do not see eye to eye on everything, but our considered and reflective moral judgments do enjoy extensive agreement. Moral life is, to a large extent, a common life. We have a feel for morality; we understand what constitutes a legitimate moral position and what counts as a moral argument; we share certain institutional practices as well as paradigms of moral and immoral, just and unjust, conduct. There are agreed-upon standards in our moral practice, and within limits most moral determinations can be said to be correct or incorrect, justified or unjustified.

The emotivist overlooks all this in reducing moral judgments to attitudes and feelings. He disregards the extent to which morality is a rule-governed activity, the extent to which moral judgments can claim to be objective. Within the framework of a particular moral system—and, more specifically, internal to the practice of morality as we know it—judgments about right and wrong can, at least within limits, be said correctly to be true or false. They can be either more or less justified, and they can be rationally defended or liable to objective criticism. But what about the moral system itself—can its rules be justified? Can the practice as a whole be defended?

The last question may appear, at least to nonphilosophers, a little silly, if one understands it to be asking why morality itself is necessary or how having a moral code at all can be justified. After all, it would seem that every human society must have some form of social control, some rules regulating the conduct of its members. No society, to take an extreme example, has ever tolerated—or could tolerate—random killing by anyone who felt so inclined. And these restraints, if they are to be successful, must be internalized by the bulk of the populace. Armchair anthropology is generally risky, but looking at the human predicament as a whole—which, as Warnock puts it, is "inherently such that things are liable to go badly" because of our limited resources, limited information, limited intelligence, limited rationality, and limited sympathy for others[4]—it does seem fortunate that human beings do have a moral capacity. As a result our common lot is made better, and society is rendered more secure and predictable. As Hobbes argued long ago, even an egoist recognizes that the absence of any moral code at all would be the worst possible state of affairs. Certain constraints on conduct are prerequisites of communal existence, let alone civilization.

According to one traditional view of morality, it would make no sense—though for a different reason—to ask why morality is necessary. Morality is simply there (or "out there"), waiting to be apprehended by us; rightness and wrongness, duties and obligations, are built into the very fabric of the universe. This view holds there are values or some objective "oughtness" that is presumed to exist apart from human minds, attitudes, or societies. Moral principles are as independent of us and as autonomously true as the theorems of mathematics or the laws of nature. Contemporary philosophers, however, have generally abandoned this conception of morality. Instead of seeing ethical conduct as objectively prescribed, independent of society and history, and values as simply part of the furniture of the world, they locate normative entities within human thinking and practice. Moral values, standards, principles, and ideals are not things to be discovered. Whether explicitly or implicitly, they are laid down, posited, or adopted.

An analogy can be drawn with legal theory. In the old-fashioned natural law tradition, legal philosophers held that there were certain natural, eternal principles of conduct, which only await discovery by human reason, and that an earthly legal system was legitimate only to the extent that it succeeded in reflecting these eternal verities. Modern legal theorists, however, perceive law as a purely human institution, in which legal validity is determined by mundane conditions (like the existence of sanctions) rather than transcendental ones. Similarly, morality must be viewed as a human construction, a complex social practice with necessary functions to perform. This does not imply that individuals do not have their own moral codes nor that these might not conflict with parts of the socially dominant moral system. What it does imply is that morality is essentially a cooperative, social enterprise in which we all participate.

This way of looking at morality accommodates the insights made by each of the three main meta-ethical positions sketched in the preceding section. On the one hand, we do have moral knowledge and our ethical judgments can be correct or incorrect because our common moral practice provides standards by which we can certify ethical claims. These standards are intimately intertwined with—indeed, the whole complex institution of morality is designed to further—human needs, goals, and desires, and so there is some truth in the naturalist's claim that ethical terms have an empirical, descriptive content. The point, brought home to us by the intuitionist, that we simply "see" that such-and-such is wrong, immediately and with full confidence, is accounted for by the fact that these standards become second nature to those raised within a particular moral system. On the other hand, the view of morality endorsed here respects the emotivist's strong points: moral codes involve commitment; people internalize and identify with their moral principles; and among the functions of morality is that of influencing the behavior of others.

Since a moral code cannot be proved by showing that it accords with transcendentally certified values or principles, the question of how the particular rules of a moral code can be justified, of whether one moral system can be rationally preferred to another, remains. The relativist, it will be recalled, argues that there are no grounds for recommending one set of principles over another. This is the challenge that needs to be met.

5. Justifying a Moral System

Some philosophers have tried to answer the relativist by arguing that there are certain features or principles of a moral system which are required by the concept of morality itself. By definition, morality involves guidelines or rules for conduct—principles by which one not only regulates one's life but judges others. That is, morality implies regulations which are thought to apply to everyone. This distinguishes morality from personal preference, taste, and goals. Some moral theorists have pursued this point by arguing not only that moral judgments are universalizable (in the sense that when one judges an action right or wrong, one is committed to judging all relevantly similar actions the same way) but that because of this one can only subscribe to a moral principle if one would be willing to accept it from the vantage points of all the other persons who would be affected by one's acting on that principle.[5] If this point, which is supposed to follow from the logic of our moral terms, is correct, then it has important implications for the validation of particular moral principles and ways of reasoning.

Other philosophers have argued that the nature of ethical discourse is such that it involves a commitment to impartiality, rational benevolence, and liberty as ultimate principles—that is, that moral discussion itself presupposes these fundamental values.[6] (Thus, for example, it is maintained that because moral discourse is intended to guide action rationally, and interfering with a person's chosen course determines his actions by force, not reason, moral discourse presupposes the principle that special justification is required to infringe on another's liberty.) A third, although related, approach has been for philosophers to argue that our earlier definition of morality is too lean, since certain guidelines to which a person might be committed are too bizarre to constitute a morality. Rather, they argue, morality is distinguished from other value systems by giving certain kinds of reasons for its rules and by giving weight to distinct sorts of considerations; in particular, morality involves consideration of others for their own sakes. Morality, in other words, implies taking the moral point of view, respecting persons as ends, and making judgments accordingly.[7] Because of this, certain ultimate moral principles are underwritten by the nature of morality itself.

If successful, these three strategies, which take off from the definition or concept of morality, would take us a fair distance toward justifying a determinate set of moral rules. It is open to the relativist, however, to claim that they do not highlight some inescapable features of morality, but underline only our particular institutional practices. We recognize certain sorts of considerations (the moral point of view) as being virtually definitive of moral practice, and in using our moral terms, logic may require us to universalize our judgments and even to approve them from the point of view of all those concerned. Perhaps, also, our very conception of moral discourse and reasoning commits us to certain ultimate values and principles, but can we be confident that these facts (if that is what they are) derive from some unavoidable moral necessity, rather than from our own moral customs, definitions, and practices? Could not someone simply opt for a radically different moral code, one without these features? We could, of course, deny the title "morality" to his code, but then he may not care about words.

These remarks are not intended as a full rebuttal to the above concept-of-morality strategies, but they should raise doubt that these approaches could provide conclusive justification of certain basic moral principles. Something like this justification, however, can be attained by focusing on the social nature and purpose of morality. By examining the function of a moral code and how it can best be fulfilled, we can give reasonable and objective grounds for preferring some moral systems over others—though not a logical demonstration of their superiority based on the concept of morality. Given that a moral code is supposed to regulate social conduct, that it is a human institution with a necessary role to play—a human creation open to modification—certain criteria for evaluating moral systems spring to mind. It would be self-defeating for a society to endorse a moral code that was not conducive to what we might call human flourishing, that failed to further—in some broad sense—human ends, purposes, desires, and needs. To adopt a moral code which thwarted the very things it is, as a morality, supposed to promote would be irrational. A given morality, like a given legal code, can fulfill its functions in a better or worse fashion, can satisfy or fail to satisfy our aims in having moral (or legal) ties in the first place. Not all moral codes will perform equally well, and because of this we can evaluate rival normative systems and alternative ethical principles with a reasonable claim to objectivity.

For one thing, a moral system must work, and if it is to work it must be acceptable to all the various segments of the population. As literacy and education spread, and superstition and slavish adherence to custom decline, no social group will accept a morality that ignores or slights its interests. No moral code, for example, could neglect to affirm racial and sexual equality and hope to be workable, given modern social conditions. A moral code cannot afford to fall into disrespect or to lose the allegiance of a significant number of people. A tenable morality must be one whose public affirmation can win and retain the support of the vast majority of the population. In addition to questions of social feasibility, there are related considerations of psychological viability. A moral code must be teachable; it must be consistent in its instructions and coherent in its basic objectives. What will be the psychological strain of adhering to it and the psychological costs of inculcating it? Will people be able to comply with it successfully? Will they wish to do so?

Already one can see that any feasible moral code will have a fundamental commitment to general principles of impartiality, equality, and equity—not as a result of the definition of morality nor the logic of moral terms—but as a consequence of the practical function and social nature of morality. In addition, excellent reasons in terms of the human predicament and the object of morality can be given for the basic moral prohibitions of our present system, and it would seem that any social morality would have to endorse institutions like truth-telling and promise-keeping. While some possible moral codes are obvious non-starters and others can be confidently ruled out, one may wonder how far we can go in selecting among the rival codes that remain. Three related points are worth mentioning here. The first is that inevitably there will be some arbitrariness in the system, for the simple reason that the exact nature of certain conventions will not matter as long as there is some such convention. To take a legal parallel as an example: it is necessary that people adhere to the practice of driving on one side of the road, though whether it is the right or left side makes no difference, as long as they all stick to the same side. Secondly, a moral code must function in a particular cultural and historical context; thus, variations will be inevitable between societies, since different situations, customs, needs, and individual aspirations must be accommodated. The third point is the rather practical one that although morality is a human construction, it does not need to be reconstructed from the ground up. Indeed, it would be impossible to do so. We must work incrementally with what we have—modifying, elaborating, and reweaving as necessary our existing morality.

One might be skeptical that the considerations of the preceding paragraphs will delimit our choice of moral systems sufficiently. In particular, one might argue that selecting a suitable social morality differs in an important way from the weighing of alternative legal systems, to which we have been comparing it. In choosing a legal system we have moral criteria by which to judge, but no such criteria are available to us in elaborating those standards in the first place. Two moral systems may be equally feasible and their realization in a particular society equally possible, yet they may differ drastically in their principles. How, then, could we justify one code over another? One might maintain that we could not: perhaps up to a point there are objective grounds for preferring some possible moral systems, but beyond that we must simply choose. The objections of the meta-ethical relativist would be largely met, though not entirely since certain features of our moral code could not be objectively justified. Of course, the range of arbitrary choice might not be large and by understanding our position as one of fashioning a moral system, we would at least be sure that our thinking about the alternatives was clear-headed.

There are, however, two ways in which it might be possible to eliminate even this residue of relativism. The first[8] is to justify certain foundational moral principles by showing that they would be chosen by people convening (hypothetically) for the purpose of laying the moral groundwork of society. In order that agreement be reached, it is assumed that these people are ignorant of their own position in society, as well as of their particular talents and interests. This ignorance makes the conditions of choice fair and impartial, since no one is able to bias the decision in his favor, and guarantees unanimity. A moral code chosen under such conditions, it is argued, would be rationally justified. Critics can object, however, that the particular limitations placed on the conditions of decision presuppose a moral position: why these restrictions on knowledge and not others? If we allow our intuitive notions of fairness to govern the construction of the hypothetical contract situation are we not taking for granted what needs to be demonstrated? In addition, an individual might remain unmoved by what he would choose under such fictitious and literally impossible conditions.

The second approach[9] gets around this last point by seeking those moral principles which a rational person would choose for his society, where a rational person is one who has all the available relevant information vividly before his mind and whose desires have survived cognitive psychotherapy. Since cognitive psychotherapy (the confronting of one's desires with certain kinds of information) is not supposed to involve any value judgments, the ideal of rationality used here does not employ any question-begging assumptions. And it is a fact that people are motivated to do what would be rational, in this sense, for them to do; so the criticism of a moral principle as irrational has bite to it. Still, even if this strategy can be worked out, there is no guarantee that one moral code will emerge which it would be rational for all persons to choose (given that people have different native inclinations, desires, and social positions). Since on this view people are permitted knowledge denied to them by the hypothetical contract approach, consensus seems unlikely— though perhaps there will be a small set of moral codes, with an overlapping core, that would be chosen by any rational person.

Much more could be said about these two approaches and how they could help us in the identification of an ideal moral code. This paper, however, must be content to sketch the problem facing us and to outline the various considerations that enter into the working out of a satisfactory normative system. By viewing morality in the way I have proposed and by searching for moral principles that, given the object of morality and the nature of our present moral system, can be defended as coherent, reasonable, psychologically attractive, and socially feasible, we can go a long way toward answering the relativist and showing the legitimacy of our ethical standards. How far we can go toward objectively justifying one particular moral system over all its rivals remains to be seen, but it should be clear that we need not worry further about the claims of the relativist.

Notes

1. Ross is one of these philosophers; see *The Right and the Good,* especially chaps. 1 and 2.
2. A.J. Ayer provides the classic statement of this view in *Language, Truth, and Logic.*
3. Reasons are construed broadly here, so that one who claimed such a judgment was self-evident, axiomatic, or an intuitive moral insight would be offering a kind of justification for it. How plausible the justification is, is another matter.
4. G.J. Warnock, *The Object of Morality* (London: Methuen, 1971), p. 17.

5. The view sketched here has been given its fullest statement by R.M. Hare; see in particular his *Freedom and Reason* (Oxford: Oxford UP, 1965).

6. A. Phillips Griffiths, "Ultimate Moral Principles: Their Justification" in Paul Edwards, ed., *The Encyclopedia of Philosophy* (New York: Macmillan, 1967).

7. For an example of this position, see William K. Frankena, *Ethics* 2nd ed. (Englewood Cliffs, NJ: Prentice-Hall, 1973), p. 113, and "The Concept of Morality" in G. Wallace and A.D.M. Walker, eds., *The Definition of Morality* (London: Methuen, 1970), esp. p. 156.

8. John Rawls, *A Theory of Justice* (Cambridge, MA: Harvard UP, 1971).

9. Richard B. Brandt, A *Theory of the Good and the Right* (Oxford: Oxford UP, 1979).

3.
ENCOUNTERING DIVERSITY
MEDICAL ETHICS AND PLURALISM

✸ ✸ ✸

JOSEPH J. FINS

Joseph J. Fins, MD is an Assistant Professor of Medicine at Cornell University Medical College and Associate for Medicine at the Hastings Center. In this selection, Dr. Fins addresses the question of how physicians and other health care professionals ought to respond to the increasing religious and ethnic diversity found in American hospitals. He argues that we must attempt to ascertain the patient's wishes as nearly as possible, and that respect for pluralism and cultural and religious differences is required.

One Friday night several years ago, a Hassid met an unaffiliated young Jewish physician in the corridors of the hospital. Dressed in hospital whites, the resident was a study in contrast with his co-religionist dressed in black. To the surprise of the Hassid, the young physician said, "Good Shabbos." Thus began a relationship which would have implications for the doctor and the Hassid, whose 82-year old father lay in a room down the hall dying of inoperable lung cancer, suffering from end stage chronic obstructive lung disease.

"You're Jewish?" asked the Hassid glancing at the doctor's name tag. "Yes," said the resident. "My name is Sephardic." "Oh." "Are you Mr. Friedman's son?" "Yes." "Good. I'm just coming on the case. I'll be his resident for the next five weeks." The young doctor introduced himself and they shook hands. "How is your father doing? When I saw him an hour ago he was having some difficulty breathing. I ordered a change in his inhalers and asked the nurse to give him a treatment. I was just coming back around to check on him." "Thank you. He's doing a little better, but he still is not able to talk."

The resident and the Hassid walked back to Mr. Friedman's room and the resident listened to his lungs. They were still obstructed, but the recent treatment had made things a little better. Though gratified that the patient was more comfortable, the resident knew that the situation was extremely grave. A decision would soon have to be made about Mr. Friedman, as to whether he would go down to the Intensive Care Unit and be placed on a respirator or if they would try to keep him comfortable and let nature take its course. As the resident placed his stethoscope in his pocket, he asked the patient's son if they could go outside and talk.

The resident felt in his own heart as a doctor and a Jew that placing Mr. Friedman on a ventilator at such a late stage in his illness would place a terrible burden upon him and do little more than prolong the dying process. The ventilator would also cause the patient some discomfort. In addition, being in an ICU bed would limit the time that the patient could be with his family. He asked the son to consider these choices because his father did not have the capacity to participate in these decisions.

The doctor shared these views with Mr. Friedman's son and waited for the inevitable response.

"You know, doctor, we value life. Its worth is infinite. Each breath is of infinite worth because it is a piece of infinity. Besides, I cannot make such a decision." "But, you're his only child and closest relative. Who else can make this decision?" "My Rabbi." "Yes, of course. Will you speak with him and tell him what we spoke about? I am sure he is a learned man and that he will help you."

To the resident's surprise, the patient's son agreed to raise these issues with the Rabbi. Again they went over his father's prognosis, what might be accomplished by a transfer to the Intensive Care Unit, and at what cost.

They agreed to meet Saturday evening and discuss things further. For the young doctor, the time before that meeting was a reflection on the different worlds that he and the Hassid inhabited. They were both Jews, yet lived very different lives. Still, there was a bond and a closeness that Shabbos evening when they greeted each other and spoke as Jews about the dying patient who was also the stricken father. He was glad they could communicate across the cultural divide that has fractionalized modern American Judaism. He was pleased that their common history had bound them closely enough to allow them to work together on the patient's behalf.

Later, as he checked the computer for his patient's labs, the resident was glad he had had this discussion with the patient's son. He had seen too many times when end-of-life issues were not brought to the attention of families and patients. He knew how these omissions often led to treatment decisions which proved futile and burdensome. He had learned from reading the work of the medical ethicist Lawrence Schneiderman to distinguish the effect of these treatment decisions from their hoped for benefits to patients.[1] ICU care may produce a physiologic effect like raising the blood pressure or increasing the amount of oxygen in the blood stream. But the resident had seen how these physiological effects do not always result in benefit to the patient as a whole.

Thinking about the son's response the resident decided that whatever the Rabbi counselled, at least he had given the patient's family the medical information it would need to make decisions about care rendered at the end of life. The decision was now out of the hands of doctors who did not know the patient; it rested comfortably in the hands of his son. With the counsel of his Rabbi and the father's doctors, he had all the information he would need to make these value-laden decisions for himself.

Although it struck the doctor as ironic that the son would take this new-found authority and give it to the Rabbi, he was pleased that the decision would be reflective of the patient's values and beliefs and not imposed from without.

Only in America, the resident thought as he continued his rounds. Next to the old Hassidic Jew was a Chinese woman with liver cancer. A midwestern college kid was down the hall recovering from a bone marrow transplant. The patients each had their own religious and secular beliefs and personal and cultural views on issues at the end of life. A prevailing state, religious, or insti-tutional ideology circumscribing the choices they could make could not sat-isfy them all and would be burdensome to most.

The young resident thought about this some more. If he had not been respectful of pluralism, a decision would have been imposed upon the patient which had little resemblance to the one they might have chosen. Curi-ously, he was most respectful of the patient's traditional beliefs by telling him of the rights which secular bioethics had secured for him. In our pluralist society one theological view, though prized by an individual group, can never be embraced as the exclusive religion. In America, Jewish doctors take care of Christian patients, Christian physicians attend to Jewish patients, to men-tion but some of the diverse possibilities. Here, where the enterprise of med-ical care and medical illness is equally shared by all religions and nationali-ties, we must respect pluralism. Indeed if one chooses to live in a theocratic community, it is a shared respect for pluralism that allows one to be different without being called deviant.

Difference counts and individuals have a right to make decisions about the care they receive. No one has a greater stake in these decisions than the patients themselves. This sentiment is articulated in the opinions of the great jurist Benjamin Cardozo. He wrote in 1914 that

> Every human being of adult years and sound mind has a right to deter-mine what shall be done with his own body; and a surgeon who performs an operation without his patient's consent commits an assault for which he is liable in damages. This is true except in cases of emergency where the patient is unconscious and where it is necessary to operate before consent can be obtained.[2]

More recently, the Supreme Court decided in the Cruzan case that a com-petent adult patient has the constitutional right to refuse treatment and that refusals to accept artificial nutrition and hydration are no different from other interventions.[3]

These legal decisions follow from a decision-making hierarchy that instructs us to respect the choices individuals make for themselves and not to impose our own values upon others.[4]

This hierarchy starts with what the patient tells the physician or once told his or her doctor. This is called "expressed wishes." If we do not know just what the patient said, we try to reconstruct his or her beliefs through a process we call substituted judgment. Here we try to be true to the patient's philosophy and views. If we do not know what the patient said and cannot imagine what he or she might say, we are left with a "best interests standard." That is, what would a reasonable person do in the given situation.

A quick consideration will demonstrate that the best-interests standard is the most problematic. For example, if a patient were unconscious and we neither had knowledge of what was said nor knowledge of their beliefs, then the decision would have to reflect community standards.

Because community standards can vary, what is perceived as being in the patient's best interest may depend upon who is making the determination. For example, an unconscious pregnant woman who is transferred to a Catholic hospital in an emergency will likely receive obstetrical care that reflects Catholic teaching. In that hospital, the best-interests standard might favor the life of a fetus over the mother's. In a Jewish hospital it would be the life of the woman which is protected before the potential life of the fetus.

Resorting to a best-interests standard when considering this contentious point makes most decisions no more than an approximate fit. Unlike decisions which stem from articulated preferences, the best-interests standard does not accommodate individuals or individuality. In a liberal society, our individual personal and religious beliefs are protected when we value what patients articulate for themselves and do not try to impose a religious ideology upon them based on venue. Parochial institutions in a secular society, if they receive federal funds, have to respect a divergence of views under federal law if not American decency.

But even if we share the same religious beliefs, we may look at choices at the end of life differently. The work of Pearlman, Uhlmann, and Cain illustrates this point.[5] They asked doctors, patients over 65 with chronic medical conditions, and their spouses about decisions to receive cardiac resuscitation under several scenarios.

First, would they want to receive resuscitation in their current health status? In this scenario, patients wanted to be resuscitated more than their doctors predicted but less than their spouses did. Suppose, however, the patients had a serious lung condition or suffered a stroke, what then? In this case the patients would want resuscitation more than their doctors predicted and not less. The spouses again were more likely to desire resuscitation for their husband and wife.

What does this tell us? Basically, that we view things differently and that we might make choices that do not represent the wishes of the patient if we fail to discuss these issues with them in the first place. Even well-intentioned doctors and spouses tend to misrepresent the wishes of patients because they fail to invoke the decision-making hierarchy just advanced. Instead they bring their own personal views to these decisions.

As the young resident was thinking about these issues, he planned for his upcoming meeting with Mr. Friedman's son. He decided that in the absence of clearly expressed wishes by the patient, he would encourage the son to make a decision that his father might have made. When they met later, they sat together in the quiet afforded by the solarium.

Without prompting, the son told the doctor, "My father never talked with me about his death and so I did not know what to do. I talked with the Rabbi. They were very close. At first we spoke about the value of my father's life, but I also told him what you said about the pain and the little time we'd have with father once he got into the Intensive Care Unit." The doctor waited, and to his surprise, the son continued. "The Rebbi agreed with you. He said it would prolong the dying process and *halakically*—that is our law—it would be permissible for him not to go to the Intensive Care Unit." The son wiped a tear from his eye, and said, "Thank you, doctor."

The Friedman family asked to take their father home so he could die with his family. With oxygen, inhalers, and high-dose steroids which would temporarily help his breathing, the old man was readied for discharge. Amidst his family and in familiar surroundings, his condition initially improved. He survived several days and then died with his son and grandchildren by his side.

The following year, Mr. Friedman's son moved to Israel and sent the young doctor *shmura matzoh* for his Passover seder.[6] He also included a note that he had just had a son whom he had named Jacob after his father.

Notes

1. Schneiderman, L.J., Jecker, N.S., Jonsen, A.: "Medical Futility: Its Meanings and Ethical Implications," *Annals of Internal Medicine* (1990); 112:949-54.
2. *Schloendorff v. Society of The New York Hospital.* 211 NY, 127, 129, 105 N.E. 92, 93 (1914).
3. *Cruzan v. Director, Missouri Department of Health.* 497 US, 111L ed 2 224, 110 S. Ct. 2841 (1990).
4. Fins, J.J.: "The Patient Self-Determination Act and Patient-Physician Collaboration," in *New York State Journal of Medicine* (1992); 92:489-93.
5. Uhlmann, R.F., Pearlman, R.A., Cain, K.C.: "Physicians' and Spouses' Predictions of Elderly Patients' Resuscitation Preferences," *J Geront* (1988); 43:M115-21.
6. *Shmura matzoh* is handmade matzoh that is prepared under strict Rabbinical supervision.

CHAPTER TWO

DIVINE COMMAND THEORY

INTRODUCTION

A divine command theory incorporates two basic claims:

1. A god or gods approve of or command certain actions.
2. The actions that the god or gods approve of or command are morally right because of this approval or command.

Someone who accepts a divine command theory then has the task of finding out what the god or gods approve of.

Some version of the divine command theory is accepted by many religious people. Typically these people not only accept the two basic claims of a divine command theory, they also claim to know something about what their god or gods approve of. Divine command theory is sometimes associated in people's minds with extremists, because followers of the theory have at times done outrageous things in the name of their gods and their religions. For example, in the United States some physicians who have performed abortions have been killed by anti-abortionists who supposed they were "following the word of God." Similarly radical acts have been performed in countless other nations in many ages by the proponents of a wide variety of religions. But while the idea of a divine command theory may call to many people's minds such images of dangerous extremism, it is much more common for the followers of a divine command theory to be people who are law-abiding and who are, like most of us, considered good citizens and good people. From an ethical point of view, however, there are at least two questions that should be raised about divine command theory. First, is such a theory defensible, and second, even if we grant that it is defensible, can its followers be described as responsible moral agents?

As an abstract philosophical proposition, divine command theory encounters some problems. The first claim on which it depends is that a god or gods approve of or command certain actions. However, the theory itself does not stipulate *which* god, and here we have the first problem for the theory. It is true that Western people often assume that there is only one god—namely Jehovah, or Yahweh, the Judeo-Christian/Islamic God—and that people of various religions only have different ways of worshipping the same god. But this is an overly simple assumption, for throughout history and still today people have worshipped many different gods and goddesses, and some of them are quite incompatible with others. Christians and Muslims, for example, believe in one god, while the ancient Greek and Nordic people had a multitude of gods. The god of today's Christians and Muslims is a benevolent and forgiving god, while the gods of the ancient Greek and Nordic people had magnified versions of human characteristics—including human weaknesses and vices—and were, accordingly, far from being consistently benevolent and forgiving. The first problem that faces a divine command theorist is therefore to determine which god she should seek out and listen to.

Assuming that the divine command theorist is able to choose a god or gods, she will probably find herself confronted with further philosophical dilemma. Suppose for the sake of argument that it is the Judeo-Christian God to whom she should listen. If she looks to a holy book to find out what God approves of, should she look to the Old Testament or the New Testament? Christians might argue that it does not make much difference because, as they see it, the Old Testament and the New Testament are talking about the same god. But it does not take a very close reading of the two books to see that the god described in the Old Testament has some characteristics that are not found in the god of the New Testament, and vice versa. For example, the god of the Old Testament is often jealous and vengeful while the god of the New Testament is generally benevolent and forgiving. The moral lessons of the Old and New Testaments are also different. The Old Testament teaches us "an eye for an eye and a tooth for a tooth" while the New Testament teaches us to turn the other cheek.

Suppose, again for the sake of argument, that our divine command theorist decides to put the Old Testament aside and settle on the New Testament as a source of information about God's approval and commands. Further philosophical issues lie in wait for her. One problem turns on how accurate the New Testament is. If we view the Bible as an historical document describing the life and teachings of Jesus, then it fails to meet some widely accepted criteria for historical accuracy. Historians are likely to view the New Testament as having been written by highly biased writers, people who were devout followers of Jesus first, and chroniclers of history second. This fact alone is enough to raise serious questions about its historical accuracy. Furthermore, a long time lapsed between the time when the events described took place and the time when they were written down—anywhere from about thirty to a hundred years. This time lapse further increases the likelihood of historical inaccuracy—the apostles, for example, are not writing their gospels with the events fresh in their memories but many, many years after the fact.

Suppose then that we do not view the New Testament as a historical account of Jesus' life. Suppose instead that we assume that God wrote the Bible using humans as His instrument. If we regard the New Testament in this way, then we sidestep the question of historical accuracy. But we still may wonder how it is that we have so many different Christian sects that disagree strongly about the meaning of God's words and messages. Even if God wrote the New Testament, somewhere along the way humans started translating it, selecting the stories that should be included in it (the basic selection of books and letters that now makes up the New Testament with which most Christians are familiar was only decided upon in the fourth century) and then interpreting these stories. Given the diversity of translations and interpretations, it seems unlikely that God participated in all of them. It seems clear that, at least in some instances, we humans have distorted God's word with our translations and interpretations. Thus, someone whose ethics are based on a divine command theory may have difficulty deciding on a divinity to follow and assuring herself that it is, indeed, that divinity and not human intermediaries whose command she is following.

We have used Christianity as an example here, but the problems raised above are not limited to Christianity. Other religions have religious books and documents that need to be translated and interpreted, and other religions are strongly divided into sects that often feud bitterly among themselves.

Four centuries before Christ, the Greek philosopher Plato raised a problem that applies to all religious commands as well as to all commands issued by authority figures. He asked us to consider the difference between the following two statements:

    a. God loves/commands/approves of an action because it is good.
    b. An action is good because God loves/commands/approves of it.

Plato thought, appropriately, that statement (a) is true and statement (b) is false. There is a reason why God commands something, and the reason is that what he commands is good. But if this is so, then what should be our basic reason for acting on one of God's commands? Should we act on a command simply because God commands it? Or should we look for the reasons that lie behind the command and act on them, if they are good reasons? During the Nuremberg trials following the Second World War, one war criminal after another tried to excuse his behaviour by claiming that he was just following orders. The judges were not sympathetic. Because the war criminals had followed morally reprehensible orders, they were found guilty. They had blindly acted on commands instead of evaluating the reasons behind these commands.

The following analogy may shed some light on the judges' reasoning. Everyone agrees that a robot that acts out a program is not responsible for what it does. If it does something destructive when acting out its program—for example, if it kills an innocent person—then we do not look for a fault in the robot. Instead, we look for a fault in the program. We would also look at the programmer, and at her reasons for programming the robot in such a way that it would kill an innocent person. If she deliberately created the program with this result in mind, then we would hold her morally responsible for the wrongful death. Clearly, though, the robot is not to blame for killing the person and cannot be held morally responsible for this act. The robot is simply not a moral agent.

Now consider a person who blindly follows a divine command theory, and let us draw an analogy with the robot described above. This person acts on (divine) commands, just as the robot acts out a program. If this person does something bad when acting on a divine command, such as killing an innocent human being, then just as with the robot, one might argue, it is not her fault. Instead, we should look for a fault in the religious document that the person looks to (namely the person's "program"). We should also look for a fault in the "programmer," this argument would continue, namely the god that issued the command. The conclusion that this analogy would force one towards is that we should not blame the person who follows the commands. Just as the robot is not a moral agent, the person who follows the commands is not a moral agent.

But this is a conclusion that we should not accept. Something is wrong with the analogy. While it is true that the robot is not a moral agent, the person *is* a moral agent. While the robot does not have a choice in the matter and has to follow the algorithm the program lays out, the person who blindly follows commands has a choice about how she proceeds. The choice is this: she can evaluate the reasons that lie behind the command, or she can act blindly on the commands. The choice is a moral choice. She is no less a moral agent if she chooses to act blindly on the commands. In this case, she has simply chosen to be an *irresponsible* moral agent. Thus, a person who blindly follows divine commands, or a person who blindly follows her god, is an irresponsible moral agent.

She can try to become a responsible moral agent by figuring out the reasons that lie behind the commands, and then by acting on the basis of those reasons. But if she proceeds in this manner, she will be taking a crucial step towards creating ethics without a god. Now she will be acting on the reasons rather than commands, and the relevant god has become a middleman who is not needed in order for her to act morally.

Are we being too hard on the divine command theory? Some people will think so. They will argue that we need the support of and the trust in a god to act morally. Some will also say that we need the threat of a god to ensure moral behaviour. Gods give us a powerful incentive to behave morally, for if we disobey them we end up in a less than desirable place when we die, for example.

Can we do the right thing without heeding a divine command? Most philosophers after Plato seem to think so. The normative ethical theories that follow this chapter are all examples of moral systems that do not rely on divine commands. Although some of the proponents of these theories claim that they are compatible with the Judeo-Christian God's will, they all seem to agree to some extent that we can only be good or moral when we act for the right reasons. A divine command theorist might suggest that it does not hurt to accept divine command theory. After all, we regard most of the people who accept this theory as good people and good citizens. But, goes the rejoinder, it is not enough simply to behave as a good citizen or good person would behave. To truly be good, we need to do the right thing for the right reasons.

4.
EUTHYPHRO

❀ ❀ ❀

PLATO

The great Athenian philosopher, Plato (427-347 BC), wrote a number of dialogues that feature Socrates, his teacher, as a protagonist. In his dialogues, Plato raises many of the fundamental problems in philosophy. In Euthyphro *he challenges any command that is carried out blindly, without reflection on the reasons that lie behind the command. Since the divine command theory asks one to act blindly on divine commands, Plato's arguments apply to this theory. He puts his point in the following way: do the gods love what is holy (good, right) because it is holy (good, right), or is it holy (good, right) because the gods love it? Plato, who was a moral realist, thought it was the former. But if so, then the gods love what is holy for a reason. The general question we are left with, then, is whether we should blindly follow a command, or find out the reasons that lie behind the command and, then, if they are good, act on those reasons.*

EUTHYPHRO. What trouble has arisen, Socrates, to make you leave your haunts in the Lyceum, and spend your time here today at the Porch of the King Archon? Surely you of all people don't have some sort of lawsuit before him, as I do?

SOCRATES. Well no; Athenians, at any rate, don't call it a lawsuit, Euthyphro—they call it an indictment.

EUTHYPHRO. What's that you say? Somebody must have indicted you, since I can't imagine your doing that to anyone else.

SOCRATES. No, I haven't.

EUTHYPHRO. But someone else has indicted you?

SOCRATES. Exactly.

EUTHYPHRO. Who is he?

SOCRATES. I hardly even know the man myself, Euthyphro; I gather he's young and unknown—but I believe he's named Meletus. He belongs to the Pitthean deme—can you picture a Meletus from that deme, with straight hair, not much of a beard, and a rather aquiline nose?

EUTHYPHRO. No, I can't picture him, Socrates. But tell me, what is this indictment he's brought against you?

SOCRATES. The indictment? I think it does him credit. To have made such a major discovery is no mean achievement for one so young: he claims to know how the young people are being corrupted, and who are corrupting them. He's probably a smart fellow; and noticing that in my ignorance I'm corrupting his contemporaries, he is going to denounce me to the city, as if to his mother.

Actually, he seems to me to be the only one who's making the right start in politics: it *is* right to make it one's first concern that the young should be as good as possible, just as a good farmer is likely to care first for the young plants, and only later for the others. And so Meletus is no doubt first weeding out those of us who are "ruining the shoots of youth," as he puts it. Next after this, he'll take care of the older people, and will obviously bring many great blessings to the city: at least that would be the natural outcome after such a start.

EUTHYPHRO. So I could wish, Socrates, but I'm afraid the opposite may happen: in trying to injure you, I really think he's making a good start at damaging the city. Tell me, what does he claim you are actually doing to corrupt the young?

SOCRATES. Absurd things, by the sound of them, my admirable friend: he says that I'm an inventor of gods; and for inventing strange gods, while failing to recognize the gods of old, he's indicted me on their behalf, so he says.

EUTHYPHRO. I see, Socrates; it's because you say that your spiritual sign visits you now and then. So he's brought this indictment against you as a religious innovator, and he's going to court to misrepresent you, knowing that such things are easily misrepresented before the public. Why, it's just the same with me: whenever I speak in the Assembly on religious matters and predict the future for them, they laugh at me as if I were crazy; and yet not one of my predictions has failed to come true. Even so, they always envy people like ourselves. We mustn't worry about them, though—we must face up to them.

SOCRATES. Yes, my dear Euthyphro, being laughed at is probably not important. You know, Athenians don't much care, it seems to me, if they think someone clever, so long as he's not imparting his wisdom to others; but once they think he's making other people clever, then they get angry—whether from envy, as you say, or for some other reason.

EUTHYPHRO. In that case I don't much want to test their feelings towards me.

SOCRATES. Well, they probably think you give sparingly of yourself, and aren't willing to impart your wisdom. But in my case, I fear my benevolence makes them think I give all that I have, by speaking without reserve to every comer; not only do I speak without charge, but I'd gladly be out of pocket if anyone cares to listen to me. So, as I was just saying, if they were only going to laugh at me, as you say they laugh at you, it wouldn't be bad sport if they passed the time joking and laughing in the courtroom. But if they're going to be serious, then there's no knowing how things will turn out—except for you prophets.

EUTHYPHRO. Well, I dare say it will come to nothing, Socrates. No doubt you'll handle your case with intelligence, as I think I shall handle mine.

SOCRATES. And what is this case of yours, Euthyphro? Are you defending or prosecuting?

EUTHYPHRO. Prosecuting.

SOCRATES. Whom?

EUTHYPHRO. Once again, someone whom I'm thought crazy to be prosecuting.

SOCRATES. How's that? Are you chasing a bird on the wing?

EUTHYPHRO. The bird is long past flying: in fact, he's now quite elderly.

SOCRATES. And who is he?

EUTHYPHRO. My father.

SOCRATES. *What?* Your own *father!*

EUTHYPHRO. Precisely.

SOCRATES. But what is the charge? What is the case about?

EUTHYPHRO. It's a case of murder, Socrates.

SOCRATES. Good heavens above! Well, Euthyphro, most people are obviously ignorant of where the right lies in such a case, since I can't imagine any ordinary person taking that action! It must need someone pretty far advanced in wisdom.

EUTHYPHRO. Goodness yes, Socrates. Far advanced indeed!

SOCRATES. And is your father's victim one of your relatives? Obviously, he must be—you'd hardly be prosecuting him for murder on behalf of a stranger.

EUTHYPHRO. It's ridiculous, Socrates, that you should think it makes any difference whether the victim was a stranger or a relative, and not see that the sole consideration is whether or not the slaying was lawful. If it was, one should leave the slayer alone; but if it wasn't, one should prosecute, even if the slayer shares one's own hearth and board—because the pollution is just the same, if you knowingly associate with such a person, and fail to cleanse yourself and him by taking legal action.

In point of fact, the victim was a day-labourer of mine: when we were farming in Naxos, he was working there on our estate. He had got drunk, flown into a rage with one of our servants, and butchered him. So my father had him bound hand and foot, and flung into a ditch; he then sent a messenger here to find out from the religious authority what should be done. In the mean time, he disregarded his captive, and neglected him as a murderer, thinking it wouldn't much matter even if he died. And that was just what happened: the man died of hunger and cold, and from his bonds, before the messenger got back from the authority.

That's why my father and other relatives are now upset with me, because I'm prosecuting him for murder on a murderer's behalf. According to them, he didn't even kill him. And even if he was definitely a killer, they say that, since the victim was a murderer, I shouldn't be troubled on such a fellow's behalf—because it is unholy for a son to prosecute his father for murder. Little do they know, Socrates, of religious law about what is holy and unholy.

SOCRATES. But heavens above, Euthyphro, do you think you have such exact knowledge of religion, of things holy and unholy? Is it so exact that in the circumstances you describe, you aren't afraid that, by bringing your father to trial, you might prove guilty of unholy conduct yourself?

EUTHYPHRO. Yes it is, Socrates; in fact I'd be good for nothing, and Euthyphro wouldn't differ at all from the common run of men, unless I had exact knowledge of all such matters.

SOCRATES. Why then, my admirable Euthyphro, my best course is to become your student, and to challenge Meletus on this very point before his indictment is heard. I could say that even in the past I always used to set a high value upon religious knowledge; and that now, because he says I've gone astray by free-thinking and religious innovation, I have become your student. "Meletus," I could say: "if you agree that Euthyphro is an expert on such matters, then you should regard me as orthodox too, and drop the case. But if you don't admit that, then proceed against that teacher of mine, not me, for corrupting the elderly—namely, myself and his own father—myself by his teaching, and his father by admonition and punishment."

Then, if he didn't comply and drop the charge, or indict you in my place, couldn't I repeat in court the very points on which I'd already challenged him?

EUTHYPHRO. By God, Socrates, if he tried indicting me, I fancy I'd soon find his weak spots; and we'd have *him* being discussed in the courtroom long before I was.

SOCRATES. Why yes, dear friend, I realize that, and that's why I'm eager to become your student. I know that this Meletus, amongst others no doubt, doesn't even seem to notice you; it's me he's detected so keenly and so readily that he can charge me with impiety.

So now, for goodness' sake, tell me what you were just maintaining you knew for sure. What sort of thing would you say that the pious and the impious are, whether in murder or in other matters? Isn't the holy itself the same as itself in every action? And conversely, isn't the unholy the exact opposite of the holy, in itself similar to itself, or possessed of a single character, in anything at all that is going to be unholy?

EUTHYPHRO. Indeed it is, Socrates.

SOCRATES. Tell me, then, what do you say that the holy is? And the unholy?

EUTHYPHRO. All right, I'd say that the holy is just what I'm doing now: prosecuting wrongdoers, whether in cases of murder or temple-robbery, or those guilty of any other such offence, be they one's father or mother or anyone else whatever; and failing to prosecute is unholy.

See how strong my evidence is, Socrates, that this is the law—evidence I've already given others that my conduct was correct: one must not tolerate an impious man, no matter who he may happen to be. The very people who recognize Zeus as best and most righteous of the gods admit that he put his father in bonds for wrongfully gobbling up his children; and that that father in turn castrated *his* father for similar misdeeds. And yet they are angry with me, because I'm prosecuting *my* father as a wrongdoer. Thus, they contradict themselves in what they say about the gods and about me.

SOCRATES. Could this be the reason why I'm facing indictment, Euthyphro? Is it because when people tell such stories of the gods, I somehow find them hard to accept? That, I suppose, is why some will say that I've gone astray. But now, if these stories convince you—with your great knowledge of such matters—then it seems that the rest of us must accept them as well. What can we possibly say, when by our own admission we know nothing of these matters? But tell me, in the name of friendship, do you really believe that those things happened as described?

EUTHYPHRO. Yes, and even more remarkable things, Socrates, of which most people are ignorant.

SOCRATES. And do you believe that the gods actually make war upon one another? That they have terrible feuds and fights, and much more of the sort related by our poets, and depicted by our able painters, to adorn our temples—especially the robe which is covered with such adornments, and gets carried up to the Acropolis at the great Panathenaean festival? Are we to say that those stories are true, Euthyphro?

EUTHYPHRO. Not only those, Socrates, but as I was just saying, I'll explain to you many further points about religion, if you'd like, which I'm sure you'll be astonished to hear.

SOCRATES. I shouldn't be surprised. But explain them to me at leisure some other time. For now, please try to tell me more clearly what I was just asking. You see, my friend, you didn't instruct me properly when I asked my earlier question: I asked what the holy might be, but you told me that the holy was what you are now doing, prosecuting your father for murder.

EUTHYPHRO. Yes, and there I was right, Socrates.

SOCRATES. Maybe. Yet surely, Euthyphro, there are many other things you call holy as well.

EUTHYPHRO. So there are.

SOCRATES. And do you recall that I wasn't urging you to teach me about one or two of those many things that are holy, but rather about the form itself whereby all holy things are holy? Because you said, I think, that it was by virtue of a single character that unholy things are unholy, and holy things are holy. Don't you remember?

EUTHYPHRO. Yes, I do.

SOCRATES. Then teach me about that character, about what it might be, so that by fixing my eye upon it and using it as a model, I may call holy any action of yours or another's,—which conforms to it, and may deny to be holy whatever does not.

EUTHYPHRO. All right, if that's what you want, Socrates, that's what I'll tell you.

SOCRATES. Yes, that *is* what I want.

EUTHYPHRO. In that case, what is agreeable to the gods is holy, and what is not agreeable to them is unholy.

SOCRATES. Splendid, Euthyphro!—You've given just the sort of answer I was looking for. Mind you, I don't yet know whether it's correct, but obviously you will go on to show that what you say is true.

EUTHYPHRO. I certainly will.

SOCRATES. All right then, let's consider what it is we're saying. A thing or a person loved-by-the-gods is holy, whereas something or someone hated-by-the-gods is unholy; and the holy isn't the same as the unholy, but is the direct opposite of it. Isn't that what we're saying?

EUTHYPHRO. Exactly.

SOCRATES. And does it seem well put?

EUTHYPHRO. I think so, Socrates.

SOCRATES. And again, Euthyphro, the gods quarrel and have their differences, and there is mutual hostility amongst them. Hasn't that been said as well?

EUTHYPHRO. Yes, it has.

SOCRATES. Well, on what matters do their differences produce hostility and anger, my good friend? Let's look at it this way. If we differed, you and I, about which of two things was more numerous, would our difference on these questions make us angry and hostile towards one another? Or would we resort to counting in such disputes, and soon be rid of them?

EUTHYPHRO. We certainly would.

SOCRATES. Again, if we differed about which was larger and smaller, we'd soon put an end to our difference by resorting to measurement, wouldn't we?

EUTHYPHRO. That's right.

SOCRATES. And we would decide a dispute about which was heavier and lighter, presumably, by resorting to weighing.

EUTHYPHRO. Of course.

SOCRATES. Then what sorts of questions would make us angry and hostile towards one another, if we differed about them and were unable to reach a decision? Perhaps you can't say offhand. But consider my suggestion, that they are questions of what is just and unjust, honourable and dishonourable, good and bad. Aren't those the matters on which our disagreement and our inability to reach a satisfactory decision occasionally make enemies of us, of you and me, and of people in general?

EUTHYPHRO. Those are the differences, Socrates, and that's what they're about.

SOCRATES. And what about the gods, Euthyphro? If they really do differ, mustn't they differ about those same things?

EUTHYPHRO. They certainly must.

SOCRATES. Then, by your account, noble Euthyphro, different gods also regard different things as just, or as honourable and dishonourable, good and bad; because unless they differed on those matters, they wouldn't quarrel, would they?

EUTHYPHRO. Correct.

SOCRATES. And again, the things each of them regards as honourable, good, or just, are also the things they love, while it's the opposites of those things that they hate.

EUTHYPHRO. Indeed.

SOCRATES. And yet it's the same things, according to you, that some gods consider just, and others unjust, about which their disputes lead them to quarrel and make war upon one another. Isn't that right?

EUTHYPHRO. It is.

SOCRATES. Then the same things, it appears, are both hated and loved by the gods, and thus the same things would be both hated-by-the-gods and loved-by-the-gods.

EUTHYPHRO. It does appear so.

SOCRATES. So by this argument, Euthyphro, the same things would be both holy and unholy.

EUTHYPHRO. It looks that way.

SOCRATES. So then you haven't answered my question, my admirable friend. You see, I wasn't asking what self-same thing proves to be at once holy and unholy. And yet something which is .loved-by-the-gods is apparently also hated-by-the-gods. Hence, as regards your present action in punishing your father, Euthyphro, it wouldn't be at all surprising if you were thereby doing something agreeable to Zeus but odious to Cronus and Uranus, or pleasing to Hephaestus but odious to Hera; and likewise for any other gods who may differ from one another on the matter.

EUTHYPHRO. Yes Socrates, but I don't think any of the gods do differ from one another on this point, at least: whoever has unjustly killed another should be punished.

SOCRATES. Really? Well, what about human beings, Euthyphro? Have you never heard any of them arguing that someone who has killed unjustly, or acted unjustly in some other way, should not be punished?

EUTHYPHRO. Why yes, they are constantly arguing that way, in the lawcourts as well as elsewhere: people who act unjustly in all sorts of ways will do or say anything to escape punishment.

SOCRATES. But do they admit acting unjustly, Euthyphro, yet still say, despite that admission, that they shouldn't be punished?

EUTHYPHRO. No, they don't say that at all.

SOCRATES. So it isn't just anything that they will say or do. This much, I imagine, they don't dare to say or argue: if they act unjustly, they should not be punished. Rather, I imagine, they deny acting unjustly, don't they?

EUTHYPHRO. True.

SOCRATES. Then they don't argue that one who acts unjustly should not be punished; but they do argue, maybe, about who it was that acted unjustly, and what he did, and when.

EUTHYPHRO. True.

SOCRATES. Then doesn't the very same thing also apply to the gods—if they really do quarrel about just and unjust actions, as your account suggests, and if each party says that the other acts unjustly, while the other denies it? Because surely, my admirable friend, no one among gods or men dares to claim that anyone should go unpunished who *has* acted unjustly.

EUTHYPHRO. Yes, what you say is true, Socrates, at least on the whole.

SOCRATES. Rather, Euthyphro, I think it is the individual act that causes arguments among gods as well as human beings—if gods really do argue: it is with regard to some particular action that they differ, some saying it was done justly, while others say it was unjust. Isn't that so?

EUTHYPHRO. Indeed.

SOCRATES. Then please, my dear Euthyphro, instruct me too, that I may grow wiser. When a hired man has committed murder, has been put in bonds by the master of his victim, and has died from those bonds before his captor can find out from the authorities what to do about him, what proof have you that all gods regard that man as having met an unjust death? Or that it is right for a son to prosecute his father and press a charge of murder on behalf of such a man? Please try to show me plainly that all gods undoubtedly regard that action in those circumstances as right. If you can show that to my satisfaction, I'll never stop singing the praises of your wisdom.

EUTHYPHRO. Well, that may be no small task, Socrates, though I *could* of course prove it to you quite plainly.

SOCRATES. I see. You must think me a slower learner than the jury, because obviously you will show them that the acts in question were unjust, and that all the gods hate such things.

EUTHYPHRO. I will show that very clearly, Socrates, provided they listen while I'm talking.

SOCRATES. They'll listen all right, so long as they approve of what you're saying.

But while you were talking, I reflected and put to myself this question: "Even suppose Euthyphro were to instruct me beyond any doubt that the gods all do regard such a death as unjust, what more have I learnt from him about what the holy and the unholy might be? This particular deed would be hated-by-the-gods, apparently; yet it became evident just now that the holy and unholy were not defined in that way, since what is hated-by-the-gods proved to be loved-by-the-gods as well."

So I'll let you off on that point, Euthyphro; let *all* the gods consider it unjust, if you like, and let *all* of them hate it. Is this the correction we are now making in our account: whatever *all* the gods hate is unholy, and whatever they *all* love is holy; and whatever some gods love but others hate is neither or both? Is that how you would now have us define the holy and the unholy?

EUTHYPHRO. What objection could there be, Socrates?

SOCRATES. None on my part, Euthyphro. But consider your own view, and see whether, by making that suggestion, you will most easily teach me what you promised.

EUTHYPHRO. Very well, I would say that the holy is whatever all the gods love; and its opposite, whatever all the gods hate, is unholy.

SOCRATES. Then shall we examine that in turn, Euthyphro, and see whether it is well put? Or shall we let it pass, and accept it from ourselves and others? Are we to agree with a position merely on the strength of someone's say-so, or should we examine what the speaker is saying?

EUTHYPHRO. We should examine it. Even so, for my part I believe that this time our account is well put.

SOCRATES. We shall soon be better able to tell, sir. Just consider the following question: is the holy loved by the gods because it is holy? Or is it holy because it is loved?

EUTHYPHRO. I don't know what you mean, Socrates.

SOCRATES. All right, I'll try to put it more clearly. We speak of a thing's "being carried" or "carrying," of its "being led" or "leading," of its "being seen" or "seeing." And you understand, don't you, that all such things are different from each other, and how they differ?

EUTHYPHRO. Yes, I think I understand.

SOCRATES. And again, isn't there something that is "being loved," while that which loves is different from it?

EUTHYPHRO. Of course.

SOCRATES. Then tell me whether something in a state of "being carried" is in that state because someone is carrying it, or for some other reason.

EUTHYPHRO. No, that is the reason.

SOCRATES. And something in a state of "being led" is so because someone is leading it, and something in a state of "being seen" is so because someone is seeing it?

EUTHYPHRO. Certainly.

SOCRATES. Then someone does not see a thing because it is in a state of "being seen," but on the contrary, it is in that state because someone is seeing it; nor does someone lead a thing because it is in a state of "being led," but rather it is in that state because someone is leading it; nor does someone carry a thing because it is in a state of "being carried," but it is in that state because someone is carrying it. Is my meaning quite clear, Euthyphro? What I mean is this: if something gets into a certain state or is affected in a certain way, it does not get into that state because it possesses it; rather, it possesses that state because it gets into it; nor is it thus affected because it is in that condition; rather, it is in that condition because it is thus affected. Don't you agree with that?

EUTHYPHRO. Yes, I do.

SOCRATES. Again, "being loved" is a case of either being in a certain state or being in a certain condition because of some agent?

EUTHYPHRO. Certainly.

SOCRATES. Then this case is similar to our previous examples: it is not because it is in a state of "being loved" that an object is loved by those who love it; rather, it is in that state because it is loved by them. Isn't that right?

EUTHYPHRO. It must be.

SOCRATES. Now what are we saying about the holy, Euthyphro? On your account, doesn't it consist in being loved by all the gods?

EUTHYPHRO. Yes.

SOCRATES. Is that because it is holy, or for some other reason?

EUTHYPHRO. No, that is the reason.

SOCRATES. So it is loved because it is holy, not holy because it is loved.

EUTHYPHRO. So it seems.

SOCRATES. By contrast, what is loved-by-the-gods is in that state—namely, being loved-by-the-gods—because the gods love it.

EUTHYPHRO. Of course.

SOCRATES. Then what is loved-by-the-gods is not the holy, Euthyphro, nor is the holy what is loved-by-the-gods, as you say, but they differ from each other.

EUTHYPHRO. How so, Socrates?

SOCRATES. Because we are agreed, aren't we, that the holy is loved because it is holy, not holy because it is loved?

EUTHYPHRO. Yes.

SOCRATES. Whereas what is loved-by-the-gods is so because the gods love it. It is loved-by-the-gods by virtue of their loving it; it is not because it is in that state that they love it.

EUTHYPHRO. That's true.

SOCRATES. But if what is loved-by-the-gods and the holy were the same thing, Euthyphro, then if the holy were loved because it is holy, what is loved-by-the-gods would be loved because it is loved-by-the-gods; and again, if what is loved-by-the-gods were loved-by-the-gods because they love it, then the holy would be holy because they love it. In actual fact, however, you can see that the two of them are related in just the opposite way, as two entirely different things: one of them is lovable because they love it, whereas the other they love for the reason that it is lovable.

And so, Euthyphro, when you are asked what the holy might be, it looks as if you'd prefer not to explain its essence to me, but would rather tell me one of its properties—namely, that the holy has the property of being loved by all the gods; but you still haven't told me what it is.

So please don't hide it from me, but start again and tell me what the holy might be—whether it is loved by the gods or possesses any other property, since we won't disagree about that. Out with it now, and tell me what the holy and the unholy are.

EUTHYPHRO. The trouble is, Socrates, that I can't tell you what I have in mind, because whatever we suggest keeps moving around somehow, and refuses to stay put where we established it.

SOCRATES. My ancestor Daedalus seems to be the author of your words, Euthyphro. Indeed, if they were my own words and suggestions, you might make fun of me, and say that it's because of my kinship with him that my works of art in conversation run away from me too, and won't stay where they're placed. But in fact those suggestions are your own; and so you need a different joke, because you're the one for whom they won't stay put—as you realize yourself.

EUTHYPHRO. No, I think it's much the same joke that is called for by what we said, Socrates: I'm not the one who makes them move around and not stay put. I think you're the Daedalus because, as far as I'm concerned, they would have kept still.

SOCRATES. It looks then, my friend, as if I've grown this much more accomplished at my craft than Daedalus himself: he made only his own works move around, whereas I do it, apparently, to those of others besides my own. And indeed the really remarkable feature of my craft is that I'm an expert at it without even wanting to be. You see, I'd prefer to have words stay put for me, immovably established, than to acquire the wealth of Tantalus and the skill of Daedalus combined.

But enough of this. Since I think you are being feeble, I'll join you myself in an effort to help you instruct me about the holy. Don't give up too soon, now. Just consider whether you think that everything that is holy must be just.

EUTHYPHRO. Yes, I do.

SOCRATES. Well then, is everything that is just holy? Or is everything that is holy just, but not everything that is just holy? Is part of it holy, and part of it something else?

EUTHYPHRO. I can't follow what you're saying, Socrates.

SOCRATES. And yet you are as much my superior in youth as you are in wisdom. But as I say, your wealth of wisdom has enfeebled you. So pull yourself together, my dear sir—it really isn't hard to see what I mean: it's just the opposite of what the poet meant who composed these verses:

With Zeus, who wrought it and who generated all these things,
You cannot quarrel;— for where there is fear, there is also shame.

I disagree with that poet. Shall I tell you where?

EUTHYPHRO. By all means.

SOCRATES. I don't think that "where there is fear, there is also shame"; because many people, I take it, dread illnesses, poverty, and many other such things. Yet although they dread them, they are not ashamed of what they fear. Don't you agree?

EUTHYPHRO. Certainly.

SOCRATES. On the other hand, where there is shame, there is also fear: doesn't anyone who is ashamed and embarrassed by a certain action both fear and dread a reputation for wickedness?

EUTHYPHRO. Indeed he does.

SOCRATES. Then it isn't right to say that "where there is fear, there is also shame"; nevertheless, where there is shame there is also fear, even though shame is not found everywhere there is fear. Fear is broader than shame, I think, since shame is one kind of fear, just as odd is one kind of number. Thus, it is not true that wherever there is number there is also odd, although it is true that where there is odd, there is also number. You follow me now, presumably?

EUTHYPHRO. Perfectly.

SOCRATES. Well, that's the sort of thing I meant just now: I was asking, "Is it true that wherever a thing is just, it is also holy? Or is a thing just wherever it is holy, but not holy wherever it is just?" In other words, isn't the holy part of what is just? Is that what we're to say, or do you disagree?

EUTHYPHRO. No, let's say that: your point strikes me as correct.

SOCRATES. Then consider the next point: if the holy is one part of what is just, it would seem that we need to find out which part it might be. Now, if you asked me about one of the things just mentioned, for example, which kind of number is even, and what sort of number it might be, I'd say that it's any number which is not scalene but isosceles. Would you agree?

EUTHYPHRO. I would.

SOCRATES. Now you try to instruct me, likewise, which part of what is just is holy. Then we'll be able to tell Meletus not to treat us unjustly any longer, or indict us for impiety, because I've now had proper tuition from you about what things are pious or holy, and what are not.

EUTHYPHRO. Well then, in my view, the part of what is just that is pious or holy has to do with ministering to the gods, while the rest of it has to do with ministering to human beings.

SOCRATES. Yes, I think you put that very well, Euthyphro. I am still missing one small detail, however. You see, I don't yet understand this "ministering" of which you speak. You surely don't mean "ministering" to the gods in the same sense as "ministering" to other things. That's how we talk, isn't it? We say, for example, that not everyone understands how to minister to horses, but only the horse-trainer. Isn't that right?

EUTHYPHRO. Certainly.

SOCRATES. Because, surely, horse-training is ministering to horses.

EUTHYPHRO. Yes.

SOCRATES. Nor, again, does everyone know how to minister to dogs, but only the dog-trainer.

EUTHYPHRO. Just so.

SOCRATES. Because, of course, dog-training is ministering to dogs.

EUTHYPHRO. Yes.

SOCRATES. And again, cattle-farming is ministering to cattle.

EUTHYPHRO. Certainly.

SOCRATES. And holiness or piety is ministering to the gods, Euthyphro? Is that what you're saying?

EUTHYPHRO. It is.

SOCRATES. Well, doesn't all ministering achieve the same thing? I mean something like this: it aims at some good or benefit for its object. Thus, you may see that horses, when they are being ministered to by horse-training, are benefited and improved. Or don't you think they are?

EUTHYPHRO. Yes, I do.

SOCRATES. And dogs, of course, are benefited by dog-training, and cattle by cattle-farming, and the rest likewise. Or do you suppose that ministering is for harming its objects?

EUTHYPHRO. Goodness, no!

SOCRATES. So it's for their benefit?

EUTHYPHRO. Of course.

SOCRATES. Then, if holiness is ministering to the gods, does it benefit the gods and make them better? And would you grant that whenever you do something holy, you're making some god better?

EUTHYPHRO. Heavens, no!

SOCRATES. No, I didn't think you meant that, Euthyphro—far from it—but that was the reason why I asked what sort of ministering to the gods you did mean. I didn't think you meant that sort.

EUTHYPHRO. Quite right, Socrates: that's not the sort of thing I mean.

SOCRATES. Very well, but then what sort of ministering to the gods would holiness be?

EUTHYPHRO. The sort which slaves give to their masters, Socrates.

SOCRATES. I see. Then it would appear to be some sort of service to the gods.

EUTHYPHRO. Exactly.

SOCRATES. Now could you tell me what result is achieved by service to doctors? It would be health, wouldn't it?

EUTHYPHRO. It would.

SOCRATES. And what about service to shipwrights? What result is achieved in their service?

EUTHYPHRO. Obviously, Socrates, the construction of ships.

SOCRATES. And service to builders, of course, achieves the construction of houses.

EUTHYPHRO. Yes.

SOCRATES. Then tell me, good fellow, what product would be achieved by service to the gods? You obviously know, since you claim religious knowledge superior to any man's.

EUTHYPHRO. Yes, and there I'm right, Socrates.

SOCRATES. Then tell me, for goodness' sake, just what that splendid task is which the gods accomplish by using our services?

EUTHYPHRO. They achieve many fine things, Socrates.

SOCRATES. Yes, and so do generals, my friend. Yet you could easily sum up their achievement as the winning of victory in war, couldn't you?

EUTHYPHRO. Of course.

SOCRATES. And farmers too. They achieve many fine things, I believe. Yet they can be summed up as the production of food from the earth.

EUTHYPHRO. Certainly.

SOCRATES. And now how about the many fine achievements of the gods? How can their work be summed up?

EUTHYPHRO. I've already told you a little while ago, Socrates, that it's a pretty big job to learn the exact truth on all these matters. But I will simply tell you this much: if one has expert knowledge of the words and deeds that gratify the gods through prayer and sacrifice, those are the ones that are holy: such practices are the salvation of individual families, along with the common good of cities; whereas practices that are the opposite of gratifying are impious ones, which of course upset and ruin everything.

SOCRATES. I'm sure you could have given a summary answer to my question far more briefly, Euthyphro, if you'd wanted to. But you're not eager to teach me—that's clear because you've turned aside just when you were on the very brink of the answer. If you'd given it, I would have learnt properly from you about holiness by now. But as it is, the questioner must follow wherever the person questioned may lead him. So, once again, what are you saying that the holy or holiness is? Didn't you say it was some sort of expertise in sacrifice and prayer?

EUTHYPHRO. Yes, I did.

SOCRATES. And sacrifice is giving things to the gods, while prayer is asking things of them?

EUTHYPHRO. Exactly, Socrates.

SOCRATES. So, by that account, holiness will be expertise in asking from the gods and giving to them.

EUTHYPHRO. You've gathered my meaning beautifully, Socrates.

SOCRATES. Yes, my friend, that's because I'm greedy for your wisdom, and apply my intelligence to it, so that what you say won't fall wasted to the ground. But tell me, what is this service to the gods? You say it is asking from them, and giving to them?

EUTHYPHRO. I do.

SOCRATES. Well, would asking rightly be asking for things we need from them?

EUTHYPHRO. Why, what else could it be?

SOCRATES. And conversely, giving rightly would be giving them in return things that they do, in fact, need from us. Surely it would be inept to give anybody things he didn't need, wouldn't it?

EUTHYPHRO. True, Socrates.

SOCRATES. So then holiness would be a sort of skill in mutual trading between gods and mankind?

EUTHYPHRO. Trading, yes, if that's what you prefer to call it.

SOCRATES. I don't prefer anything unless it is actually true. But tell me, what benefit do the gods derive from the gifts they receive from us? What they give, of course, is obvious to anyone—since we possess nothing good which they don't give us. But how are they benefited by what they receive from us? Do we get so much the better bargain in our trade with them that we receive all the good things from them, while they receive none from us?

EUTHYPHRO. Come, Socrates, do you really suppose that the gods are benefited by what they receive from us?

SOCRATES. Well if not, Euthyphro, what ever would they be, these gifts of ours to the gods?

EUTHYPHRO. What else do you suppose but honour and reverence, and—as I said just now—what is gratifying to them?

SOCRATES. So the holy is gratifying, but not beneficial or loved by the gods?

EUTHYPHRO. I imagine it is the most loved of all things.

SOCRATES. Then, once again, it seems that this is what the holy is: what is loved by the gods.

EUTHYPHRO. Absolutely.

SOCRATES. Well now, if you say that, can you wonder if you find that words won't keep still for you, but walk about? And will you blame me as the Daedalus who makes them walk, when you're far more skilled than Daedalus yourself at making them go round in a circle? Don't you notice that our account has come full circle back to the same point? You recall, no doubt, how we found earlier that what is holy and what is loved-by-the-gods were not the same; but different from each other? Don't you remember?

EUTHYPHRO. Yes, I do.

SOCRATES. Then don't you realize that now you're equating holy with what the gods love? But that makes it identical with loved-by-the-gods, doesn't it?

EUTHYPHRO. Indeed.

SOCRATES. So either our recent agreement wasn't sound; or else, if it was, our present suggestion is wrong.

EUTHYPHRO. So it appears.

SOCRATES. Then we must start over again, and consider what the holy is, since I shan't be willing to give up the search till I learn the answer. Please don't scorn me, but give the matter your very closest attention and tell me the truth—because you must know it, if any man does; and like Proteus you mustn't be let go until you tell it.

You see, if you didn't know for sure what is holy and what unholy, there's no way you'd ever have ventured to prosecute your elderly father for murder on behalf of a labourer. Instead, fear of the gods would have saved you from the risk of acting wrongly, and you'd have been embarrassed in front of human beings. But in fact I'm quite sure that you think you have certain knowledge of what is holy and what is not; so tell me what you believe it to be, excellent Euthyphro, and don't conceal it.

EUTHYPHRO. Some other time, Socrates: I'm hurrying somewhere just now, and it's time for me to be off.

SOCRATES. What a way to behave, my friend, going off like this, and dashing the high hopes I held! I was hoping I'd learn from you what acts are holy and what are not, and so escape Meletus' indictment, by showing him that Euthyphro had made me an expert in religion, and that my ignorance no longer made me a free-thinker or innovator on that subject: and also, of course, that I would live better for what remains of my life.

5.
THE STORY OF ABRAHAM

❀ ❀ ❀

THE BIBLE

According to divine command theory an act is right if, and only if, a god com-
mands, or approves of it. In Christianity the relevant god is, of course, Jehovah.
Upon hearing or finding out about God's command, should we ever take a step
back and wonder whether or not to follow that command? The story of Abraham
from the Bible gives one answer to that question.

Genesis, Chapter 22

1. And it came to Pass after these things, that God did tempt Abraham, and
said unto him, Abraham: and he said, Behold, here I am.
2. And he said, Take now thy son, thine only son Isaac, whom thou lovest,
and get thee into the land of Moriah; and offer him there for a burnt offering upon one of the mountains which I will tell thee of.
3. And Abraham rose up early in the morning, and saddled his ass, and took
two of his young men with him, and Isaac his son, and clave the wood for the
burnt offering, and rose up, and went unto the place of which God had told
him.
4. Then on the third day Abraham lifted up his eyes, and saw the place afar
off.
5. And Abraham said unto his young men, Abide ye here with the ass; and I
and the lad will go yonder and worship, and come again to you.
6. And Abraham took the wood of the burnt offering, and laid it upon Isaac
his son; and he took the fire in his hand, and a knife; and they went both of
them together.
7. And Isaac spake unto Abraham his father, and said, My father: and he said,
Here am I my son. And he said, Behold the fire and the wood: but where is
the lamb for a burnt offering?
8. And Abraham said, My son, God will Provide himself a lamb for a burnt
offering: so they went both of them together.
9. And they came to the place which God had told him of; and Abraham
built an altar there, and laid the wood in order, and bound Isaac his son, and
laid him on the altar upon the wood.
10. And Abraham stretched forth his hand, and took the knife to slay his son.

11. And the angel of the Lord called unto him out of heaven, and said, Abraham, Abraham: and he said, Here am I.

12. And he said, Lay not thine hand upon the lad, neither do thou any thing unto him: for now I know that thou fearest God, seeing thou hast not withheld thy son, thine only son from me.

13. And Abraham lifted up his eyes, and looked, and behold behind him a ram caught in a thicket by his horns: and Abraham went and took the ram, and offered him up for a burnt offering in the stead of his son.

14. And Abraham called the name of that place Jehovahjireh: as it is said to this day, In the mount of the Lord it shall be seen.

15. And the angel of the Lord called unto Abraham out of heaven the second time,

16. And said, By myself have I sworn, saith the Lord, for because thou hast done this thing, and hast not withheld thy son, thine only son:

17. That in blessing I will bless thee, and in multiplying I will multiply thy seed as the stars of the heaven and as the sand which is upon the sea shore; and thy seed shall possess the gate of his enemies;

18. And in thy seed shall all the nations of the earth be blessed; because thou hast obeyed my voice.

19. So Abraham returned unto his young men, and they rose up and went together to Beersheba; and Abraham dwelt at Beersheba.

20. And it came to pass after these things, that it was told Abraham, saying, Behold, Milcah, she hath also born children unto thy brother Nahor;

21. Huz his firstborn, and Buz his brother, and Kemuel the father of Aram,

22. And Chesed, and Hazo, and Pildash, and Jidlaph, and Bethuel.

23. And Bethuel begat Rebekah: these eight Milcah did bear to Nahor, Abraham's brother.

24. And his concubine, whose name was Reumah, she bare also Tebah, and Gaham, and Thahash, and Maachah.

CHAPTER THREE

EGOISM

INTRODUCTION

For years you have wanted a good stereo system and a nice motorcycle but you have not been able to afford them. You do not waste your money. Your income is simply so low that you cannot afford any luxuries. All your money goes towards your college tuition, and you can only afford a few night classes each year. After struggling for years it finally seems that you might be getting a break. It turns out that by an unusual series of coincidences, you can get everything you want without suffering any negative consequences. You have a chance to drive the motorcycle out of the store without paying for it, and no one will see you or try to hunt you down. You can also take home the stereo system of your dreams without paying for it. No one will realize that you took it, and no one will attempt to collect any payments from you or to punish you for the theft. In short, you can steal without ever suffering any bad consequences for having done so. Of course, those you steal from will suffer. The question is, should you take advantage of your newly discovered opportunities?

There are people who would hold that as long as they will benefit from these acts, they would and should take advantage of the situation. The main reason they do not take things without permission is that they fear the ramifications of getting caught. Once that fear is removed there is nothing to stop them. If they can get the money, the toys, the women or men they want without the fear of being caught, they will take them. In terms of ethical philosophy, these people are egoists.

There are two basic technical uses of the term egoism: psychological egoism and ethical egoism. Psychological egoism is a theoretical description about how persons are motivated, while ethical egoism is a normative thesis about how persons ought to behave.

Psychological egoism is the thesis that we are so constituted by nature that we always seek what is to our own advantage. At first glance, it might seem that chaos would result if each person were focused exclusively on pursuing his or her own good. However, Thomas Hobbes, a psychological egoist, argued that it is in fact in each person's best interest to enter into a contract with others stipulating that everyone will comply with certain rules of conduct, and then to appoint a ruler to ensure that everyone complies with the contract. According to this view, then, psychological egoism is compatible with social cooperation, as long as we all benefit from the cooperation. Each of us can pursue his or her own advantage and at the same time cooperate with others.

Psychological egoism is sometimes used to support arguments for ethical egoism, which is the thesis that each person always *ought* to seek his or her own advantage. Some contend that if psychological egoism is true and we always seek our own good, our moral principles must also be based on the pursuit of our own good. Any other normative position would fly in the face of the facts. Not everyone, though, thinks that psychological egoism supports such a strong case for ethical egoism. Some people favour the weaker claim that because psychological egoism is true, it is unreasonable to construct a moral theory that does not acknowledge it and take it into account. If our nature is such that we seek our own advantage, our moral theories will be more plausible if they accommodate this fact.

Is psychological egoism correct? Psychological egoism is a thesis about our psychological makeup, and it is therefore an empirical thesis. Accordingly, any evidence against this thesis, as well as any support for it, must be empirical in nature. In individual experience, the evidence must come from looking at the motivations for our actions and asking, when I did so-and-so, did I do it because I thought it would be to my own advantage, or for some other reason? If in the last analysis the answer is that I sometimes act for reasons other than pursuing my own advantage, then psychological egoism is false. So, can we find a case in which we are not motivated to seek our own advantage? If we cannot, then psychological egoism is most likely true.

One might think that it is easy to provide an example of an act that is done to promote the welfare of someone other than the person doing it. Suppose, for example, that without thinking of your own well-being you give a homeless person food. Isn't this an example of such an act? If so, then psychological egoism is false. But the psychological egoist will respond to this example by casting your motivation in a different light. She will argue that you gave the homeless person food not out of concern for her well-being, but out of concern for your own. Giving the person food made you feel good about yourself, and not giving her food would have made you feel guilty and ashamed. Therefore it was clearly to your advantage to give her the food. This reinterpretation of your act seems to save psychological egoism.

It is important to examine this exchange with the psychological egoist more closely, however. You told the psychological egoist that you were not motivated to seek your own advantage. Instead, your motive was altruistic: you simply acted out of concern for the person you helped. Or perhaps you acted out of duty, thinking that you have a moral obligation to help others. At this point, the psychological egoist tried to redescribe your motive. She claimed that although you thought your motive was altruistic, you were actually helping the homeless person because it made you feel good. But here it is important to notice that a redescription of your motive does not irrefutably change your motive. Even though the psychological egoist is able to redescribe your motives in such a way that she gives them an egoistic interpretation, you alone know the true motivation for your act. The psychological egoist's redescription is not verifiable. It shows some ingenuity on her part, but it may not correctly describe your motivation.

Suppose that the psychological egoist meets a psychological altruist, a person who believes we are constituted by nature in such a way that we always act purely out of concern for others. Whenever the psychological altruist does anything, the psychological egoist redescribes her motive and gives it an egoistic spin, trying to show the altruist that she is in fact always acting in her own best interest. But at the same time whenever the psychological egoist does anything, the psychological altruist redescribes *her* motive and gives it an altruistic spin, trying to show the egoist that she in fact always acts out of concern for others. Both might be ingenious and create convincing stories, but neither one is necessarily describing the other person's true motives. Furthermore, both leave out the possibility that we act on mixed motives, namely that although we may have concern for ourselves, we can also have concern for others, and that both concerns may motivate our actions.

While psychological egoism is intended as an empirical description, ethical egoism is a moral position that could be correct even if psychological egoism were not. An ethical egoist holds that we always *ought* to pursue our own best interest even if we are sometimes motivated to help others. Ethical egoists can hold various positions on what constitutes "our own best interest." Some may claim that it is in our best interest to seek pleasure, for example, while others may claim that it is in our best interest to seek power. And regardless of what an ethical egoist thinks is in her own best interest, she need not constantly pursue it in her daily activities. She has to think about the future, and if it is in her long term best interest to behave in an altruistic manner for awhile, then that is what she ought to do. But it is important to notice that if she does so, she only acts in an altruistic manner while she is motivated by the final payoff of securing her own advantage.

It is sometimes argued that the ethical egoist contradicts herself. On the one hand she advocates an ethical theory that claims that everyone always ought to act in his or her own best interest, but on the other hand it cannot be to her personal advantage for everyone else to behave in this manner. Instead, it would probably be to the ethical egoist's advantage if she were the only egoist in the world while everyone else was an altruist. But this objection against ethical egoism (that it is not in the egoist's best interest to recommend egoism to everyone else) is not well founded, for it is possible that in the long run ethical egoism will benefit everyone. Nevertheless, while the objection does not prove that the ethical egoist is self-contradictory, it does show that she may not serve her own interest well by openly advocating ethical egoism.

A more compelling objection to ethical egoism is that it conflicts with our intuitions about justice, fairness, advice, and friendship. True friendship requires that we take a genuine interest in our friends' well-being. A good friend is there for the other person when times are hard, and she does not take advantage of her friend whenever it is in her own best interest to do so. Instead, a good friend might even pass up opportunities of her own in order to help her friend without ever telling anyone, even the friend, that she had done so. It might be in our own best interest to be more calculating and drop our friends when times are hard in favour of new friends that serve us better. But most people do not do that, and do not think that we should.

Further, if you go to someone you trust for advice, then you expect that person to try to help you, or to promote the best interests of all the parties involved in the situation at issue. Most of us believe that it would be seriously inappropriate for the person you confide in to manipulate you or others in order to promote her own advantage. And our most common conceptions of justice and fairness seem to require that one take a disinterested, not a self-interested, attitude. A judge ruling on a case or a minister giving advice will generally not think about what she can get out of the situation, or at least we feel that she *should not* do so. Instead, she should try to be just to everyone involved and to find the solution that is best for everyone.

It seems, therefore, that although ethical egoism may be an internally consistent theory, it fosters in people qualities that we do not appreciate and that fall far short of most people's moral ideals. The ethical egoist can, of course, reply that while we might not appreciate her moral position, nothing we have said shows that her position is actually wrong.

6.
THE MYTH OF GYGES

✳ ✳ ✳

PLATO

The following selection is taken from one of Plato's masterpieces, The Republic. *Thrasymachus, with the help of Glaucon, is setting up the challenge that Plato deals with in the dialogue—namely, that it is better to be unjust rather than just. Although the issue is framed in terms of justice, the selection applies to egoism as well. If we can get away with anything we want to do, then why should we be concerned with the welfare of others at all when doing so does not serve our own interests?*

I thought that, with these words, I was quit of the discussion; but it seems this was only a prelude. Glaucon, undaunted as ever, was not content to let Thrasymachus abandon the field.

Socrates, he broke out, you have made a show of proving that justice is better than injustice in every way. Is that enough, or do you want us to be really convinced?

Certainly I do, if it rests with me.

Then you are not going the right way about it. I want to know how you classify the things we call good. Are there not some which we should wish to have, not for their consequences, but just for their own sake, such as harmless pleasures and enjoyments that have no further result beyond the satisfaction of the moment?

Yes, I think there are good things of that description.

And also some that we value both for their own sake and for their consequences—things like knowledge and health and the use of our eyes?

Yes.

And a third class which would include physical training, medical treatment, earning one's bread as a doctor or otherwise—useful, but burdensome things, which we want only for the sake of the profit or other benefit they bring.

Yes, there is that third class. What then?

In which class do you place justice?

I should say, in the highest, as a thing which anyone who is to gain happiness must value both for itself and for its results.

Well, that is not the common opinion. Most people would say it was one of those things, tiresome and disagreeable in themselves, which we cannot avoid practising for the sake of reward or a good reputation.

I know, said I: that is why Thrasymachus has been finding fault with it all this time and praising injustice. But I seem to be slow in seeing his point.

Listen to me, then, and see if you agree with mine. There was no need, I think, for Thrasymachus to yield so readily, like a snake you had charmed into submission; and nothing so far said about justice and injustice has been established to my satisfaction. I want to be told what each of them really is, and what effect each has, in itself, on the soul that harbours it, when all rewards and consequences are left out of account. So here is my plan, if you approve. I shall revive Thrasymachus' theory. First, I will state what is commonly held about the nature of justice and its origin; secondly, I shall maintain that it is always practised with reluctance, not as good in itself, but as a thing one cannot do without; and thirdly, that this reluctance is reasonable, because the life of injustice is much the better life of the two—so people say. That is not what I think myself, Socrates; only I am bewildered by all that Thrasymachus and ever so many others have dinned into my ears; and I have never yet heard the case for justice stated as I wish to hear it. You, I believe, if anyone, can tell me what is to be said in praise of justice in and for itself; that is what I want. Accordingly, I shall set you an example by glorifying the life of injustice with all the energy that I hope you will show later in denouncing it and exalting justice in its stead. Will that plan suit you?

Nothing could be better, I replied. Of all subjects this is one on which a sensible man must always be glad to exchange ideas.

Good, said Glaucon. Listen then, and I will begin with my first point: the nature and origin of justice.

What people say is that to do wrong is, in itself, a desirable thing; on the other hand, it is not at all desirable to suffer wrong, and the harm to the sufferer outweighs the advantage to the doer. Consequently, when men have had a taste of both, those who have not the power to seize the advantage and escape the harm decide that they would be better off if they made a compact neither to do wrong nor to suffer it. Hence they began to make laws and covenants with one another; and whatever the law prescribed they called lawful and right. That is what right or justice is and how it came into existence; it stands half-way between the best thing of all—to do wrong with impunity— and the worst, which is to suffer wrong without the power to retaliate. So justice is accepted as a compromise, and valued, not as good in itself, but for lack of power to do wrong; no man worthy of the name, who had that power, would ever enter into such a compact with anyone; he would be mad if he did. That, Socrates, is the nature of justice according to this account, and such the circumstances in which it arose.

The next point is that men practise it against the grain, for lack of power to do wrong. How true that is, we shall best see if we imagine two men, one just, the other unjust, given full licence to do whatever they like, and then follow them to observe where each will be led by his desires. We shall catch the just man taking the same road as the unjust; he will be moved by self-interest, the end which it is natural to every creature to pursue as good, until forcibly turned aside by law and custom to respect the principle of equality.

Now, the easiest way to give them that complete liberty of action would be to imagine them possessed of the talisman found by Gyges, the ancestor of the famous Lydian. The story tells how he was a shepherd in the King's service. One day there was a great storm, and the ground where his flock was feeding was rent by an earthquake. Astonished at the sight, he went down into the chasm and saw, among other wonders of which the story tells, a brazen horse, hollow, with windows in its sides. Peering in, he saw a dead body, which seemed to be of more than human size. It was naked save for a gold ring, which he took from the finger and made his way out. When the shepherds met, as they did every month, to send an account to the King of the state of his flocks, Gyges came wearing the ring. As he was sitting with the others, he happened to turn the bezel of the ring inside his hand. At once he became invisible, and his companions, to his surprise, began to speak of him as if he had left them. Then, as he was fingering the ring, he turned the bezel outwards and became visible again. With that, he set about testing the ring to see if it really had this power, and always with the same result: according as he turned the bezel inside or out he vanished and reappeared. After this discovery he contrived to be one of the messengers sent to the court. There he seduced the Queen, and with her help murdered the King and seized the throne.

Now suppose there were two such magic rings, and one were given to the just man, the other to the unjust. No one, it is commonly believed, would have such iron strength of mind as to stand fast in doing right or keep his hands off other men's goods, when he could go to the market-place and fearlessly help himself to anything he wanted, enter houses and sleep with any woman he chose, set prisoners free and kill men at his pleasure, and in a word go about among men with the powers of a god. He would behave no better than the other; both would take the same course. Surely this would be strong proof that men do right only under compulsion; no individual thinks of it as good for him personally, since he does wrong whenever he finds he has the power. Every man believes that wrongdoing pays him personally much better, and, according to this theory, that is the truth. Granted full licence to do as liked, people would think him a miserable fool if they found him refusing to wrong his neighbours or to touch their belongings, though in public they would keep up a pretence of praising his conduct, for fear of being wronged themselves. So much for that.

Finally, if we are really to judge between the two lives, the only way is to contrast the extremes of justice and injustice. We can best do that by imagining our two men to be perfect types, and crediting both to the full with the qualities they need for their respective ways of life. To begin with the unjust man: he must be like any consummate master of a craft, a physician or a captain, who, knowing just what his art can do, never tries to do more, and can always retrieve a false step. The unjust man, if he is to reach perfection, must be equally discreet in his criminal attempts, and he must not be found out, or we shall think him a bungler; for the highest pitch of injustice is to seem just when you are not. So we must endow our man with the full complement of injustice; we must allow him to have secured a spotless reputation for virtue while committing the blackest crimes; he must be able to retrieve any mistake, to defend himself with convincing eloquence if his misdeeds are denounced, and, when force is required, to bear down all opposition by his courage and strength and by his command of friends and money.

Now set beside this paragon the just man in his simplicity and nobleness, one who, in Aeschylus' words, "would be, not seem, the best." There must, indeed, be no such seeming; for if his character were apparent, his reputation would bring him honours and rewards, and then we should not know whether it was for their sake that he was just or for justice's sake alone. He must be stripped of everything but justice, and denied every advantage the other enjoyed. Doing no wrong, he must have the worst reputation for wrongdoing, to test whether his virtue is proof against all that comes of having a bad name; and under this lifelong imputation of wickedness, let him hold on his course of justice unwavering to the point of death. And so, when the two men have carried their justice and injustice to the last extreme, we may judge which is the happier.

My dear Glaucon, I exclaimed, how vigorously you scour these two characters clean for inspection, as if you were burnishing a couple of statues![1]

I am doing my best, he answered. Well, given two such characters, it is not hard, I fancy, to describe the sort of life that each of them may expect; and if the description sounds rather coarse, take it as coming from those who cry up the merits of injustice rather than from me. They will tell you that our just man will be thrown into prison, scourged and racked, will have his eyes burnt out, and, after every kind of torment, be impaled. That will teach him how much better it is to seem virtuous than to be so. In fact those lines of Aeschylus I quoted are more fitly applied to the unjust man, who, they say, is a realist and does not live for appearances: "he would be, not seem" unjust,

> reaping the harvest sown
In those deep furrows of the thoughtful heart
Whence wisdom springs.

With his reputation for virtue, he will hold offices of state, ally himself by marriage to any family he may choose, become a partner in any business, and,

having no scruples about being dishonest, turn all these advantages to profit.
If he is involved in a lawsuit, public or private, he will get the better of his
opponents, grow rich on the proceeds, and be able to help his friends and
harm his enemies.[2] Finally, he can make sacrifices to the gods and dedicate
offerings with due magnificence, and, being in a much better position than
the just man to serve the gods as well as his chosen friends, he may reasonably hope to stand higher in the favour of heaven. So much better, they say,
Socrates, is the life prepared for the unjust by gods and men.

Here Glaucon ended, and I was meditating a reply, when his brother
Adeimantus exclaimed:

Surely, Socrates, you cannot suppose that that is all there is to be said.

Why, isn't it? said I.

The most essential part of the case has not been mentioned, he replied.

Well, I answered, there is a proverb about a brother's aid. If Glaucon has
failed, it is for you to make good his shortcomings; though, so far as I am concerned, he has said quite enough to put me out of the running and leave me
powerless to rescue the cause of justice.

Nonsense, said Adeimantus; there is more to be said, and you must listen
to me. If we want a clear view of what I take to be Glaucon's meaning, we must
study the opposite side of the case, the arguments used when justice is praised
and injustice condemned. When children are told by their fathers and all
their pastors and masters that it is a good thing to be just, what is commend-
ed is not justice in itself but the respectability it brings. They are to let men
see how just they are, in order to gain high positions and marry well and win
all the other advantages which Glaucon mentioned, since the just man owes
all these to his good reputation.

In this matter of having a good name, they go farther still: they throw in
the favourable opinion of heaven, and can tell us of no end of good things
with which they say the gods reward piety. There is the good old Hesiod,[3] who
says the gods make the just man's oak-trees "bear acorns at the top and bees
in the middle; and their sheep's fleeces are heavy with wool," and a great
many other blessings of that sort. And Homer[4] speaks in the same strain:

> As when a blameless king fears the gods and upholds right judgment; then
> the dark earth yields wheat and barley, and the trees are laden with fruit;
> the young of his flocks are strong, and the sea gives abundance of fish.

Musaeus and his son Eumolpus[5] enlarge in still more spirited terms upon
the rewards from heaven they promise to the righteous. They take them to
the other world and provide them with a banquet of the Blest, where they sit
for all time carousing with garlands on their heads, as if virtue could not be
more nobly recompensed than by an eternity of intoxication. Others, again,
carry the rewards of heaven yet a stage farther: the pious man who keeps his

oaths is to have children's children and to leave a posterity after him. When they have sung the praises of justice in that strain, with more to the same effect, they proceed to plunge the sinners and unrighteous men into a pool of mud in the world below, and set them to fetch water in a sieve. Even in this life, too, they give them a bad name, and make out that the unjust suffer all those penalties which Glaucon described as falling upon the good man who has a bad reputation: they can think of no others. That is how justice is recommended and injustice denounced.

Besides all this, think of the way in which justice and injustice are spoken of, not only in ordinary life, but by the poets. All with one voice reiterate that self-control and justice, admirable as they may be, are difficult and irksome, whereas vice and injustice are pleasant and very easily to be had; it is mere convention to regard them as discreditable. They tell us that dishonesty generally pays better than honesty. They will cheerfully speak of a bad man as happy and load him with honours and social esteem, provided he be rich and otherwise powerful; while they despise and disregard one who has neither power nor wealth, though all the while they acknowledge that he is the better man of the two.

Most surprising of all is what they say about the gods and virtue: that heaven itself often allots misfortunes and a hard life to the good man, and gives prosperity to the wicked. Mendicant priests and soothsayers come to the rich man's door with a story of a power they possess by the gift of heaven to atone for any offence that he or his ancestors have committed with incantations and sacrifice, agreeably accompanied by feasting. If he wishes to injure an enemy, he can, at a trifling expense, do him a hurt with equal ease, whether he be an honest man or not, by means of certain invocations and spells which, as they profess, prevail upon the gods to do their bidding. In support of all these claims they call the poets to witness. Some, by way of advertising the easiness of vice, quote the words: "Unto wickedness men attain easily and in multitudes; smooth is the way and her dwelling is very near at hand. But the gods have ordained much sweat upon the path to virtue"[6] and a long road that is rough and steep.

Others, to show that men can turn the gods from their purpose, cite Homer: "Even the gods themselves listen to entreaty. Their hearts are turned by the entreaties of men with sacrifice and humble prayers and libation and burnt offering, whensoever anyone transgresses and does amiss."[7] They produce a whole farrago of books in which Musaeus and Orpheus, described as descendants of the Muses and the Moon, prescribe their ritual; and they persuade entire communities, as well as individuals, that, both in this life and after death, wrongdoing may be absolved and purged away by means of sacrifices and agreeable performances which they are pleased to call rites of initiation. These deliver us from punishment in the other world, where awful things are in store for all who neglect to sacrifice.

Now, my dear Socrates, when all this stuff is talked about the estimation in which virtue and vice are held by heaven and by mankind, what effect can we suppose it has upon the mind of a young man quick-witted enough to gather honey from all these flowers of popular wisdom and to draw his own conclusions as to the sort of person he should be and the way he should go in order to lead the best possible life? In all likelihood he would ask himself, in Pindar's words: "Will the way of right or the by-paths of deceit lead me to the higher fortress," where I may entrench myself for the rest of my life? For, according to what they tell me, I have nothing to gain but trouble and manifest loss from being honest, unless I also get a name for being so; whereas, if I am dishonest and provide myself with a reputation for honesty, they promise me a marvellous career. Very well, then; since "outward seeming," as wise men inform me, "overpowers the truth" and decides the question of happiness, I had better go in for appearances wholeheartedly. I must ensconce myself behind an imposing facade designed to look like virtue, and trail the fox behind me, "the cunning shifty fox"[8]—Archilochus knew the world as well as any man. You may say it is not so easy to be wicked without ever being found out. Perhaps not; but great things are never easy. Anyhow, if we are to reach happiness, everything we have been told points to this as the road to be followed. We will form secret societies to save us from exposure; besides, there are men who teach the art of winning over popular assemblies and courts of law; so that, one way or another, by persuasion or violence, we shall get the better of our neighbours, without being punished. You might object that the gods are not to be deceived and are beyond the reach of violence. But suppose that there are no gods, or that they do not concern themselves with the doings of men; why should we concern ourselves to deceive them? Or, if the gods do exist and care for mankind, all we know or have ever heard about them comes from current tradition and from the poets who recount their family history, and these same authorities also assure us that they can be won over and turned from their purpose "by sacrifice and humble prayers" and votive offerings. We must either accept both these statements or neither. If we are to accept both, we had better do wrong and use part of the proceeds to offer sacrifice. By being just we may escape the punishment of heaven, but we shall be renouncing the profits of injustice; whereas by doing wrong we shall make our profit and escape punishment into the bargain, by means of those entreaties which win over the gods when we transgress and do amiss. But then, you will say, in the other world the penalty for our misdeeds on earth will fall either upon us or upon our children's children. We can counter that objection by reckoning on the great efficacy of mystic rites and the divinities of absolution, vouched for by the most advanced societies and by the descendants of the gods who have appeared as poets and spokesmen of heavenly inspiration.

What reason, then, remains for preferring justice to the extreme of injustice, when common belief and the best authorities promise us the fulfilment of our desires in this life and the next, if only we conceal our ill-doing under a veneer of decent behaviour? The upshot is, Socrates, that no man possessed of superior powers of mind or person or rank or wealth will set any value on justice; he is more likely to laugh when he hears it praised. So, even one who could prove my case false and were quite sure that justice is best, far from being indignant with the unjust, will be very ready to excuse them. He will know that, here and there, a man may refrain from wrong because it revolts some instinct he is graced with or because he has come to know the truth; no one else is virtuous of his own will; it is only lack of spirit or the infirmity of age or some other weakness that makes men condemn the inequities they have not the strength to practise. This is easily seen: give such a man the power, and he will be the first to use it to the utmost.

What lies at the bottom of all this is nothing but the fact from which Glaucon, as well as I, started upon this long discourse. We put it to you, Socrates, with all respect, in this way. All you who profess to sing the praises of right conduct, from the ancient heroes whose legends have survived down to the men of the present day, have never denounced injustice or praised justice apart from the reputation, honours, and rewards they bring; but what effect either of them in itself has upon its possessor when it dwells in his soul unseen of gods or men, no poet or ordinary man has ever yet explained. No one has proved that a soul can harbour no worse evil than injustice, no greater good than justice. Had all of you said that from the first and tried to convince us from our youth up, we should not be keeping watch upon our neighbours to prevent them from doing wrong to us, but everyone would keep a far more effectual watch over himself, for fear lest by wronging others he should open his doors to the worst of all evils.

That, Socrates, is the view of justice and injustice which Thrasymachus and, no doubt, others would state, perhaps in even stronger words. For myself, I believe it to be a gross perversion of their true worth and effect; but, as I must frankly confess, I have put the case with all the force I could muster because I want to hear the other side from you. You must not be content with proving that justice is superior to injustice; you must make clear what good or what harm each of them does to its possessor, taking it simply in itself and, as Glaucon required, leaving out of account the reputation it bears. For unless you deprive each of its true reputation and attach to it the false one, we shall say that you are praising or denouncing nothing more than the appearances in either case, and recommending us to do wrong without being found out; and that you hold with Thrasymachus that right means what is good for someone else, being the interest of the stronger, and wrong is what really pays, serving one's own interest at the expense of the weaker. You have agreed that justice belongs to that highest class of good things which are worth having not only for their consequences, but much more for their own sakes—things like sight and hearing, knowledge, and health, whose value is genuine and intrinsic, not dependent on opinion. So I want you, in commending justice, to consider only how justice, in itself, benefits a man who has it in him, and how injustice harms him, leaving rewards and reputation out of account. I might put up with others dwelling on those outward effects as a reason for praising the one and condemning the other; but from you, who have spent your life in the study of this question, I must beg leave to demand something better. You must not be content merely to prove that justice is superior to injustice, but explain how one is good, the other evil, in virtue of the intrinsic effect each has on its possessor, whether gods or men see it or not.

Notes

1. At Elis and Athens officials called *phaidryntai*, "burnishers," had the duty of cleaning cult statues (A.B. Cook, Zeus, iii. 967). At 612 c, where this passage is recalled, it is admitted to be an extravagant supposition, that the just and unjust should exchange reputations.
2. To help friends and harm enemies, offered as a definition of justice by Polemarchus, now appears as the privilege of the unjust.
3. Hesiod, *Works and Days*, 232.
4. *Odyssey*, xix. 109.
5. Legendary figures, to whom were attributed poems setting forth the doctrines of the mystery religion known as Orphism.
6. Hesiod, *Works and Days*, 287.
7. *Iliad*, ix. 497.
8. An allusion to a fable by Archilochus.

7.
EGOISM AND MORAL SCEPTICISM

🌸 🌸 🌸

JAMES RACHELS

James Rachels (1941-2003) was a professor of philosophy at the University of Alabama at Birmingham, and wrote extensively on theoretical and applied ethics. In the following selection Rachels discusses the assumptions on which Glaucon's claims (in Plato's Republic*) rest, namely ethical egoism and psychological egoism.*

1. Our ordinary thinking about morality is full of assumptions that we almost never question. We assume, for example, that we have an obligation to consider the welfare of other people when we decide what actions to perform or what rules to obey; we think that we must refrain from acting in ways harmful to others, and that we must respect their rights and interests as well as our own. We also assume that people are in fact capable of being motivated by such considerations, that is, that people are not wholly selfish and that they do sometimes act in the interests of others.

Both of these assumptions have come under attack by moral sceptics, as long ago as by Glaucon in Book II of Plato's *Republic*. Glaucon recalls the legend of Gyges, a shepherd who was said to have found a magic ring in a fissure opened by an earthquake. The ring would make its wearer invisible and thus would enable him to go anywhere and do anything undetected. Gyges used the power of the ring to gain entry to the Royal Palace where he seduced the Queen, murdered the King, and subsequently seized the throne. Now Glaucon asks us to determine that there are two such rings, one given to a man of virtue and one given to a rogue. The rogue, of course, will use his ring unscrupulously and do anything necessary to increase his own wealth and power. He will recognize no moral constraints on his conduct, and, since the cloak of invisibility will protect him from discovery, he can do anything he pleases without fear of reprisal. So, there will be no end to the mischief he will do. But how will the so-called virtuous man behave? Glaucon suggests that he will behave no better than the rogue: "No one, it is commonly believed, would have such iron strength of mind as to stand fast in doing right or keep his hands off other men's goods, when he could go to the market-place and fearlessly help himself to anything he wanted, enter houses and sleep with any woman he chose, set prisoners free and kill men at his pleasure, and in a word go about among men with the powers of a god. He would behave no better than the other; both would take the same course."[1] Moreover, why shouldn't he? Once he is freed from the fear of reprisal, why shouldn't a man simply do what he pleases, or what he thinks is best for himself? What reason is there for him to continue being "moral" when it is clearly not to his own advantage to do so?

These sceptical views suggested by Glaucon have come to be known as *psychological egoism* and *ethical egoism* respectively. Psychological egoism is the view that all men are selfish in everything that they do, that is, that the only motive from which anyone ever acts is self-interest. On this view, even when men are acting in ways apparently calculated to benefit others, they are actually motivated by the belief that acting in this way is to their own advantage, and if they did not believe this, they would not be doing that action. Ethical egoism is, by contrast, a normative view about how men *ought* to act. It is the view that, regardless of how men do in fact behave, they have no obligation to do anything except what is in their own interests. According to the ethical egoist, a person is always justified in doing whatever is in his own interests, regardless of the effect on others.

Clearly, if either of these views is correct, then "the moral institution of life" (to use Butler's well-turned phrase) is very different than what we normally think. The majority of mankind is grossly deceived about what is, or ought to be, the case, where morals are concerned.

2. Psychological egoism seems to fly in the face of the facts. We are tempted to say: "Of course people act unselfishly all the time. For example, Smith gives up a trip to the country, which he would have enjoyed very much, in order to stay behind and help a friend with his studies, which is a miserable way to pass the time. This is a perfectly clear case of unselfish behavior, and if the psychological egoist thinks that such cases do not occur, then he is just mistaken." Given such obvious instances of "unselfish behavior," what reply can the egoist make? There are two general arguments by which he might try to show that all actions, including those such as the one just outlined, are in fact motivated by self-interest. Let us examine these in turn:

A. The first argument goes as follows. If we describe one person's action as selfish, and another person's action as unselfish, we are overlooking the crucial fact that in both cases, assuming that the action is done voluntarily, *the agent is merely doing what he most wants to do*. If Smith stays behind to help his friend, that only shows that he wanted to help his friend more than he wanted to go to the country. And why should he be praised for his "unselfishness" when he is only doing what he most wants to do? So, since Smith is only doing what he wants to do, he cannot be said to be acting unselfishly.

This argument is so bad that it would not deserve to be taken seriously except for the fact that so many otherwise intelligent people have been taken in by it. First, the argument rests on the premise that people never voluntarily do anything except what they want to do. But this is patently false; there are at least two classes of actions that are exceptions to this generalization. One is the set of actions which we may not want to do, but which we do anyway as a means to an end which we want to achieve; for example, going to the dentist in order to stop a toothache, or going to work every day in order to be able to draw our pay at the end of the month. These cases may be regarded as consistent with the spirit of the egoist argument, however, since the ends mentioned are wanted by the agent. But the other set of actions are those which we do, not because we want to, nor even because there is an end which we want to achieve, but because we feel ourselves *under an obligation* to do them. For example, someone may do something because he has promised to do it, and thus feels obligated, even though he does not want to do it. It is sometimes suggested that in such cases we do the action because, after all, we want to keep our promises; so, even here, we are doing what we want. However, this dodge will not work: if I have promised to do something, and if I do not want to do it, then it is simply false to say that I want to keep my promise. In such cases we feel a conflict precisely because we do *not* want to do what we feel obligated to do. It is reasonable to think that Smith's action falls roughly into this second category: he might stay behind, not because he wants to, but because he feels that his friend needs help.

But suppose we were to concede, for the sake of the argument, that all voluntary action is motivated by the agent's wants, or at least that Smith is so motivated. Even if this were granted, it would not follow that Smith is acting selfishly or from self-interest. For if Smith wants to do something that will help his friend, even when it means forgoing his own enjoyments, that is precisely what makes him *un*selfish. What else could unselfishness be, if not wanting to help others? Another way to put the same point is to say that it is the *object* of a want that determines whether it is selfish or not. The mere fact that I am acting on *my* wants does not mean that I am acting selfishly; that depends on *what it is* that I want. If I want only my own good, and care nothing for others, then I am selfish; but if I also want other people to be well-off and happy, and if I act on *that* desire, then my action is not selfish. So much for this argument.

B. The second argument for psychological egoism is this. Since so-called unselfish actions always produce a sense of self-satisfaction in the agent,[2] and since this sense of satisfaction is a pleasant state of consciousness, it follows that the point of the action is really to achieve a pleasant state of consciousness, rather than to bring about any good for others. Therefore, the action is "unselfish" only at a superficial level of analysis. Smith will feel much better with himself for having stayed to help his friend—if he had gone to the country, he would have felt terrible about it—and that is the real point of the action. According to a well-known story, this argument was once expressed by Abraham Lincoln:

Mr. Lincoln once remarked to a fellow-passenger on an old-time mud-coach that all men were prompted by selfishness in doing good. His fellow-passenger was antagonizing this position when they were passing over a corduroy bridge that spanned a slough. As they crossed this bridge they espied an old razor-backed sow on the bank making a terrible noise because her pigs had got into the slough and were in danger of drowning. As the old coach began to climb the hill, Mr. Lincoln called out, "Driver, can't you stop just a moment?" Then Mr. Lincoln jumped out, ran back, and lifted the little pigs out of the mud and water and placed them on the bank. When he returned, his companion remarked: "Now, Abe, where does selfishness come in on this little episode?" "Why, bless your soul, Ed, that was the very essence of selfishness. I should have had no peace of mind all day had I gone on and left that suffering old sow worrying over those pigs. I did it to get peace of mind, don't you see?"[3]

This argument suffers from defects similar to the previous one. Why should we think that merely because someone derives satisfaction from helping others this makes him selfish? Isn't the unselfish man precisely the one who *does* derive satisfaction from helping others, while the selfish man does not? If Lincoln "got peace of mind" from rescuing the piglets, does this show him to be selfish, or, on the contrary, doesn't it show him to be compassionate and good-hearted? (If a man were truly selfish, why should it bother his conscience that *others* suffer—much less pigs?) Similarly, it is nothing more than shabby sophistry to say, because Smith takes satisfaction in helping his friend, that he is behaving selfishly. If we say this rapidly, while thinking about something else, perhaps it will sound all right; but if we speak slowly, and pay attention to what we are saying, it sounds plain silly.

Moreover, suppose we ask *why* Smith derives satisfaction from helping his friend. The answer will be, it is because Smith cares for him and wants him to succeed. If Smith did not have these concerns, then he would take no pleasure in assisting him: and these concerns, as we have already seen, are the marks of unselfishness, not selfishness. To put the point more generally: if we have a positive attitude toward the attainment of some goal, then we may derive satisfaction from attaining that goal. But the *object* of our attitude is *the attainment of that goal;* and we must want to attain the goal *before* we can find any satisfaction in it. We do not, in other words, desire some sort of "pleasurable consciousness" and then try to figure out how to achieve it; rather, we desire all sorts of different things—money, a new fishing-boat, to be a better chess-player, to get a promotion in our work, etc—and because we desire these things, we derive satisfaction from attaining them. And so, if someone desires the welfare and happiness of another person, he will derive satisfaction from that; but this does not mean that this satisfaction is the object of his desire, or that he is in any way selfish on account of it.

It is a measure of the weakness of psychological egoism that these insupportable arguments are the ones most often advanced in its favor. Why, then, should anyone ever have thought it a true view? Perhaps because of a desire for theoretical simplicity: In thinking about human conduct, it would be nice if there were some simple formula that would unite the diverse phenomena of human behavior under a single explanatory principle, just as simple formulae in physics bring together a great many apparently different phenomena. And since it is obvious that self-regard is an overwhelmingly important factor in motivation, it is only natural to wonder whether all motivation might not be explained in these terms. But the answer is clearly No; while a great many human actions are motivated entirely or in part by self-interest, only by a deliberate distortion of the facts can we say that all conduct is so motivated. This will be clear, I think, if we correct three confusions which are commonplace. The exposure of these confusions will remove the last traces of plausibility from the psychological egoist thesis.

The first is the confusion of selfishness with self-interest. The two are clearly not the same. If I see a physician when I am feeling poorly, I am acting in my own interest but no one would think of calling me "selfish" on account of it. Similarly, brushing my teeth, working hard at my job, and obeying the law are all in my self-interest but none of these are examples of selfish conduct. This is because selfish behavior is behavior that ignores the interests of others, in circumstances in which their interests ought not to be ignored. This concept has a definite evaluative flavor; to call someone "selfish" is not just to describe his action but to condemn it. Thus, you would not call me selfish for eating a normal meal in normal circumstances (although it may surely be in my self-interest); but you would call me selfish for hoarding food while others about are starving.

The second confusion is the assumption that every action is done *either* from self-interest or from other-regarding motives. Thus, the egoist concludes that if there is no such thing as genuine altruism then all actions must be done from self-interest. But this is certainly a false dichotomy. The man who continues to smoke cigarettes, even after learning about the connection between smoking and cancer, is surely not acting from self-interest, not even by his own standards—self-interest would dictate that he quit smoking at once—and he is not acting altruistically either. He is, no doubt, smoking for the pleasure of it, but all that this shows is that undisciplined pleasure-seeking and acting from self-interest are very different. This is what led Butler to remark that "The thing to be lamented is, not that men have so great regard to their own good or interest in the present world, for they have not enough."[4]

The last two paragraphs show (*a*) that it is false that all actions are selfish, and (*b*) that it is false that all actions are done out of self-interest. And it should be noted that these two points can be made, and were, without any appeal to putative examples of altruism.

The third confusion is the common but false assumption that a concern for one's own welfare is incompatible with any genuine concern for the welfare of others. Thus, since it is obvious that everyone (or very nearly everyone) does desire his own well-being, it might be thought that no one can really be concerned with others. But again, this is false. There is no inconsistency in desiring that everyone, including oneself *and* others, be well-off and happy. To be sure, it may happen on occasion that our own interests conflict with the interests of others, and in these cases we will have to make hard choices. But even in these cases we might sometimes opt for the interests of others, especially when the others involved are our family or friends. But more importantly, not all cases are like this: sometimes we are able to promote the welfare of others when our own interests are not involved at all. In these cases not even the strongest self-regard need prevent us from acting considerately toward others.

Once these confusions are cleared away, it seems to me obvious enough that there is no reason whatever to accept psychological egoism. On the contrary, if we simply observe people's behavior with an open mind, we may find that a great deal of it is motivated by self-regard, but by no means all of it; and that there is no reason to deny that "the moral institution of life" can include a place for the virtue of beneficence.[5]

3. The ethical egoist would say at this point, "Of course it is possible for people to act altruistically, and perhaps many people do act that way—but there is no reason why they *should* do so. A person is under no obligation to do anything except what is in his own interests."[6] This is really quite a radical doctrine. Suppose I have an urge to set fire to some public building (say, a department store) just for the fascination of watching the spectacular blaze: according to this view, the fact that several people might be burned to death provides no reason whatever why I should not do it. After all, this only concerns *their* welfare, not my own, and according to the ethical egoist the only person I need think of is myself.

Some might deny that ethical egoism has any such monstrous consequences. They would point out that it is really to my own advantage not to set the fire—for, if I do that I may be caught and put into prison (unlike Gyges, I have no magic ring for protection). Moreover, even if I could avoid being caught it is still to my advantage to respect the rights and interests of others, for it is to my advantage to live in a society in which people's rights and interests are respected. Only in such a society can I live a happy and secure life; so, in acting kindly toward others, I would merely be doing my part to create and maintain the sort of society which it is to my advantage to have.[7] Therefore, it is said, the egoist would not be such a bad man; he would be as kindly and considerate as anyone else, because he would see that it is to his own advantage to be kindly and considerate.

This is a seductive line of thought, but it seems to me mistaken. Certainly it is to everyone's advantage (including the egoist's) to preserve a stable society where people's interests are generally protected. But there is no reason for the egoist to think that merely because *he* will not honor the rules of the social game, decent society will collapse. For the vast majority of people are not egoists, and there is no reason to think that they will be converted by his example—especially if he is discreet and does not unduly flaunt his style of life. What this line of reasoning shows is not that the egoist himself must act benevolently, but that he must encourage *others* to do so. He must take care to conceal from public view his own self-centered method of decision-making, and urge others to act on precepts very different from those on which he is willing to act.

The rational egoist, then, cannot advocate that egoism be universally adopted by everyone. For he wants a world in which his own interests are maximized; and if other people adopted the egoistic policy of pursuing their own interests to the exclusion of his interests, as he pursues his interests to the exclusion of theirs, then such a world would be impossible. So he himself will be an egoist, but he will want others to be altruists.

This brings us to what is perhaps the most popular "refutation" of ethical egoism current among philosophical writers—the argument that ethical egoism is at bottom inconsistent because it cannot be universalized.[8] The argument goes like this:

To, say that any action or policy of action is *right* (or that it *ought* to be adopted) entails that it is right for *anyone* in the same sort of circumstances. I cannot, for example, say that it is right for me to lie to you, and yet object when you lie to me (provided, of course, that the circumstances are the same). I cannot hold that it is all right for me to drink your beer and then complain when you drink mine. This is just the requirement that we be consistent in our evaluations; it is a requirement of logic. Now it is said that ethical egoism cannot meet this requirement because, as we have already seen, the egoist would not want others to act in the same way that he acts. Moreover, suppose he *did* advocate the universal adoption of egoistic policies: he would be saying to Peter, "You ought to pursue your own interests even if it means destroying Paul"; and he would be saying to Paul, "You ought to pursue your own interests even if it means destroying Peter." The attitudes expressed in these two recommendations seem clearly inconsistent—he is urging the advancement of Peter's interest at one moment, and countenancing their defeat at the next. Therefore, the argument goes, there is no way to maintain the doctrine of ethical egoism as a consistent view about how we ought to act. We will fall into inconsistency whenever we try.

What are we to make of this argument? Are we to conclude that ethical egoism has been refuted? Such a conclusion, I think, would be unwarranted; for I think that we can show, contrary to this argument, how ethical egoism can be maintained consistently. We need only to interpret the egoist's position in a sympathetic way: we should say that he has in mind a certain kind of world which he would prefer over all others; it would be a world in which his own interests were maximized, regardless of the effects on other people. The egoist's primary policy of action, then, would be to act in such a way as to bring about, as nearly as possible, this sort of world. Regardless of however morally reprehensible we might find it, there is nothing *inconsistent* in someone's adopting this as his ideal and acting in a way calculated to bring it about. And if someone did adopt this as his ideal, then he would not advocate universal egoism; as we have already seen, he would want other people to be altruists. So, if he advocates any principles of conduct for the general public, they will be altruistic principles. This would not be inconsistent; on the contrary, it would be perfectly consistent with his goal of creating a world in which his own interests are maximized. To be sure, he would have to be deceitful; in order to secure the good will of others, and a favorable hearing for his exhortations to altruism, he would have to pretend that he was himself prepared to accept altruistic principles. But again, that would be all right; from the egoist's point of view, this would merely be a matter of adopting the necessary means to the achievement of his goal—and while we might not approve of this, there is nothing inconsistent about it. Again, it might be said: "He advocates one thing, but does another. Surely *that's* inconsistent." But it is not; for what he advocates and what he does are both calculated as means to an end (the *same* end, we might note); and as such, he is doing what is rationally required in each case. Therefore, contrary to the previous argument, there is nothing inconsistent in the ethical egoist's view. He cannot be refuted by the claim that he contradicts himself.

Is there, then, no way to refute the ethical egoist? If by "refute" we mean to show that he has made some *logical* error, the answer is that there is not. However, there is something more that can be said. The egoist challenge to our ordinary moral convictions amounts to a demand for an explanation of why we should adopt certain policies of action, namely policies in which the good of others is given importance. We can give an answer to this demand, albeit an indirect one. The reason one ought not to do actions that would hurt other people is: other people would be hurt. The reason one ought to do actions that would benefit other people is: other people would be benefited. This may at first seem like a piece of philosophical sleight-of-hand, but it is not. The point is that the welfare of human beings is something that most of us value for *its own sake,* and not merely for the sake of something else. Therefore, when *further* reasons are demanded for valuing the welfare of human beings, we cannot point to anything further to satisfy this demand. It is not that we have no reason for pursuing these policies, but that our reason *is* that these policies are for the good of human beings.

So: if we are asked "Why shouldn't I set fire to this department store?" one answer would be "Because if you do, people may be burned to death." This is a complete, sufficient reason which does not require qualification or supplementation of any sort. If someone seriously wants to know why this action shouldn't be done, that's the reason. If we are pressed further and asked the sceptical question "But why shouldn't I do actions that will harm others?" we may not know what to say—but this is because the questioner has included in his question the very answer we would like to give: "Why shouldn't you do actions that will harm others? Because, doing those actions would harm others."

The egoist, no doubt, will not be happy with this. He will protest that *we* may accept this as a reason, but *he* does not. And here the argument stops: there are limits to what can be accomplished by argument, and if the egoist really doesn't care about other people—if he honestly doesn't care whether they are helped or hurt by his actions—then we have reached those limits. If we want to persuade him to act decently toward his fellow humans, we will have to make our appeal to such other attitudes as he does possess, by threats, bribes, or other cajolery. That is all that we can do.

Though some may find this situation distressing (we would like to be able to show that the egoist is just *wrong*), it holds no embarrassment for common morality. What we have come up against is simply a fundamental requirement of rational action, namely, that the existence of reasons for action always depends on the prior existence of certain attitudes in the agent. For example, the fact that a certain course of action would make the agent a lot of money is a reason for doing it only if the agent wants to make money; the fact that practicing at chess makes one a better player is a reason for practicing only if one wants to be a better player; and so on. Similarly, the fact that a certain action would help the agent is a reason for doing the action only if the agent cares about his own welfare, and the fact that an action would help others is a reason for doing it only if the agent cares about others. In this respect ethical egoism and what we might call ethical altruism are in exactly the same fix: both require that the agent *care* about himself, or about other people, before they can get started.

So a nonegoist will accept "It would harm another person" as a reason not to do an action simply because he cares about what happens to that other person. When the egoist says that he does *not* accept that as a reason, he is saying something quite extraordinary. He is saying that he has no affection for friends or family, that he never feels pity or compassion, that he is the sort of person who can look on scenes of human misery with complete indifference, so long as he is not the one suffering. Genuine egoists, people who really don't care at all about anyone other than themselves, are rare. It is important to keep this in mind when thinking about ethical egoism; it is easy to forget just how fundamental to human psychological makeup the feeling of sympathy is. Indeed, a man without any sympathy at all would scarcely be recognizable as a man; and that is what makes ethical egoism such a disturbing doctrine in the first place.

4. There are, of course, many different ways in which the sceptic might challenge the assumptions underlying our moral practice. In this essay I have discussed only two of them, the two put forward by Glaucon in the passage that I cited from Plato's *Republic*. It is important that the assumptions underlying our moral practice should not be confused with particular judgments made within that practice. To defend one is not to defend the other. We may assume—quite properly, if my analysis has been correct—that the virtue of beneficence does, and indeed should, occupy an important place in "the moral institution of life"; and yet we may make constant and miserable errors when it comes to judging when and in what ways this virtue is to be exercised. Even worse, we may often be able to make accurate moral judgments, and know what we ought to do, but not do it. For these ills, philosophy alone is not the cure.

Notes

1. *The Republic of Plato*, translated by F.M. Cornford (Oxford, 1941), p. 45.
2. Or, as it is sometimes said, "It gives him a clear conscience," or "He couldn't sleep at night if he had done otherwise," or "He would have been ashamed of himself for not doing it," and so on.
3. Frank C. Sharp, *Ethics* (New York, 1928), pp. 74-75. Quoted from the Springfield (Ill.) *Monitor* in the *Outlook*, vol. 56, p. 1059.
4. *The Works of Joseph Butler*, edited by W.E. Gladstone (Oxford, 1896), vol. 11, p. 26. It should be noted that most of the points I am making against psychological egoism were first made by Butler. Butler made all the important points; all that is left for us is to remember them.
5. The capacity for altruistic behavior is not unique to human beings. Some interesting experiments with rhesus monkeys have shown that these animals will refrain from operating a device for securing food if this causes other animals to suffer pain. See Masserman, Wechkin, and Terris, "'Altruistic' Behavior in Rhesus Monkeys," *The American Journal of Psychiatry*, vol. 121 (1964), 584-85.
6. I take this to be the view of Ayn Rand, in so far as I understand her confusing doctrine.
7. Cf. Thomas Hobbes, *Leviathan* (London, 1651), chap. 17.
8. See, for example, Brian Medlin, "Ultimate Principles and Ethical Egoism," *Australasian Journal of Philosophy*, vol. 35 (1957), 111-18; and D.H. Monro, *Empiricism and Ethics* (Cambridge, 1967), chap. 16.

CHAPTER FOUR

CONSEQUENTIALISM

INTRODUCTION

In standard modern approaches to ethical theory, the right and the good are taken to be the two central moral concepts. Consequentialist theories and deontological theories define these concepts differently and connect them in different ways. Consequentialist theories hold that the good is the more fundamental of these two moral concepts. Whether or not an act is right is determined by whether the consequences of that act are good. Consequentialist theories first identify the characteristic or set of characteristics by virtue of which a state of affairs can be ranked from best to worst, as judged from an impartial perspective. They then hold that acts are right if they promote the best overall state of affairs and wrong if they do otherwise.

Consider the following scenario constructed by Gilbert Harman.[1] You are the physician in charge of an emergency room. An accident occurs and six people are brought to your ER in critical condition. You have the resources and personnel to save five of the patients if you act immediately. The remaining patient can be saved, but only if the entire staff ignores the first five patients to work on him. If they do so, the first five patients will die. In this case, unless there is something truly exceptional about the one patient, most of us would opt to save the first five, and it seems that we would do so for consequentialist reasons. We believe that a state of affairs in which five people are saved and one dies is better than a state of affairs in which one person is saved and five die, and we want to create the best possible state of affairs.

A central question that must be answered by the consequentialist is what constitutes the best overall state of affairs as judged from an impartial perspective. Consequentialists take different positions on this issue. The most familiar consequentialist position is classical utilitarianism. Bentham advocated a hedonistic version of utilitarianism in which pleasure is the only good and pain the only evil. The best overall state of affairs according to Bentham is the state of affairs in which there is the greatest possible net amount of pleasure (or absence of pain) among all sentient beings. Mill argued that this position was too simplistic. He held that pleasures and pains vary not only in quantity but also in quality. Even if a pig gets intense waves of pleasure all day every day from eating and wallowing in the mud, these pleasures do not compare to the pleasures that we humans get from developing close personal relationships with one another or from pursuing a path of spiritual growth, even if these later activities are not always free from pain. For Mill, then, the best overall state of affairs is defined in terms of both the quantity and the quality of the pleasures that can be produced.

Some authors have gone further and questioned whether the best overall state of affairs should be defined so narrowly in terms of a state of mind like pleasure or happiness. Suppose that we all experienced large quantities of high quality pleasure by artificially stimulating our brains for hours on end, in isolation from our friends and relatives who were doing the same thing. Would this be the best possible state of affairs? Some consequentialists think not. They define the best overall state of affairs as the state of affairs in which there is the greatest total amount of satisfaction of individual preferences, or the greatest possible realization of some other particular value or set of values.

Consequentialists also disagree on whether the best overall state of affairs would be the state of affairs in which the greatest total accumulated amount of happiness, pleasure, preference satisfaction, etc. was achieved, or whether it would be the state of affairs in which the greatest average amount of happiness *per person* was achieved. Although the results of following these two approaches may often be essentially the same, they would presumably diverge on the important issue of population growth. If our goal is to produce the greatest possible total amount of happiness, then we should keep adding to the population as long as each person added can be sustained in a state that is slightly happier than it is unhappy. On the other hand, if our goal is to produce the greatest possible average happiness per person, then we should probably aim for a much smaller population in which each person is treated to a much happier existence.

Consequentialists disagree further on the question of whether we should pursue the best overall state of affairs through acts or rules. Act-consequentialists hold that each of us is always required to act in such a way that we produce the best overall state of affairs as judged from an impartial perspective. Rule-consequentialists hold that we are required to adopt and comply with the set of rules which, if consistently followed, will produce the best overall state of affairs as judged from an impartial perspective. Act-consequentialists argue that rule-consequentialists have an irrational obsession with rules. Suppose that you are in a situation in which you could produce the best results overall by surreptitiously breaking a rule. No one would ever find out that you had broken it, and no bad consequences would result from your doing so. If your goal is really to produce the best possible state of affairs, shouldn't you violate the rule in this case?

In any case, consequentialist theories have certain advantages to offer. First, they offer the benefit of theoretical simplicity. They give us a single principle in reference to which we can resolve any moral dilemma—from the smallest questions that arise in our personal lives to the largest global issues. Second, it seems that most of us do in fact use consequentialist reasoning much of the time, even if we have never been introduced to these theories. As we saw at the outset, most of us would save five patients in the ER as opposed to one, assuming that all of the patients had roughly the same value to us and to humanity. Finally, the claim that we ought to produce the best possible results overall, as judged from an impartial perspective, has a strong intuitive plausibility. It sounds almost absurd to suggest that we should not perform the act that would produce the best overall results. Some philosophers have argued that it would simply be irrational to depart from consequentialism.

However, the problem with consequentialist theories in general and utilitarian theories in particular is that they also seem to generate implications that conflict with some of our most basic moral convictions. Consider a second example offered by Harman.[2] Suppose that you are a prominent surgeon and you have five patients who are about to die. One needs a heart transplant, one a liver transplant, one a kidney transplant, and so on. No suitable organs have become available for these patients, nor can they be expected to become available in time to save these patients' lives. A sixth patient, Smith, enters the hospital complaining of severe chest pain and shortness of breath. The tests you run on Smith reveal that his organs are healthy and would be a perfect match for the other five patients who are about to die, and his chart reveals that he is an organ donor. Now suppose that you could take Smith into surgery, arrange for him to die, and harvest his organs for the other patients, all without arousing any suspicion that you had done so. Many would argue that consequentialist reasoning leads inextricably to the conclusion that you should kill Smith in order to save the five other patients. The important thing is to produce the best results overall, as judged from an impartial perspective, and this end justifies whatever means you need to use to achieve it. But our considered moral judgments tell us that this is just wrong. As a physician, you are obligated to do everything in your power to save Smith, provided that you can secure a reasonable quality of life for him.

At this point a rule-utilitarian might argue that we can avoid this problem by adopting their brand of consequentialism. If we were act-utilitarians we would have to kill Smith if we could produce the greatest total happiness by doing so. However, rule-utilitarianism requires us first to adopt the set of rules, which, if consistently followed, will produce the greatest total happiness. Surely a rule that requires physicians not to detract from the health of any of their patients will produce more total happiness than a rule that does not. Physicians generally produce much more happiness when they save their patients, and all of the rest of us are much more comfortable living in a society that abides by this rule. It would be very nerve-racking to enter the hospital if we thought that physicians might view us as expendable sources of organs for other patients. This seems like a promising approach to the problem. Nevertheless, it is just at this point that we might accuse a rule-utilitarian of irrationality. Certainly the surgeon should let everyone think that she is abiding by a code of ethics in which she attempts to save each patient. But suppose that she could sacrifice Smith to harvest his organs without arousing any suspicion whatsoever that she has done so. If the ultimate moral demand is to create the best possible state of affairs overall as judged from an impartial perspective, and she can meet this demand by surreptitiously sacrificing Smith to save the other patients, isn't it irrational for her not to do so?

Many other examples have been constructed in which consequentialist theories in general and utilitarian theories in particular seem to generate results that conflict with our most firmly held and carefully considered moral judgments. Suppose that a series of crimes have been committed in a given community and officials are convinced that the perpetrator has moved on to another area. Nevertheless, the members of the community do not believe that this is so. They are terribly fearful and upset, and will not be able to relax until someone has been convicted of the crimes and sent to jail. If some of the officials in this community could produce the greatest total welfare by framing and punishing an innocent person—someone who is down and out and has no job, friends, or relatives—then wouldn't it be incumbent on them to do so?

In general, it seems that consequentialist theories fail to respect the needs and rights of individuals. They require us to do whatever it takes to produce the best *overall* state of affairs, even if we ride roughshod over an individual's basic rights in the process. Of course consequentialists can claim that they consider all individual interests impartially when they determine what constitutes the best overall state of affairs. But it still seems wrong to kill a patient in order to use his organs to save others, or to punish an innocent person, or to do many of the other things that a consequentialist theory might logically require us to do.

Bernard Williams has pointed out that in addition to requiring us to do things that seem morally wrong, utilitarian theories require us to do too much. All of us have goals or projects that we care about deeply, and that help to define who we are as individuals. We may want to become excellent skiers, to climb certain mountains, to paint, to write poetry, to practice yoga, etc. But if we are always required to act in such a way that we produce the best overall state of affairs as judged from an impartial perspective, we may never get to pursue these projects. For example, it could easily be the case that you could produce the best results overall by donating all the money you would have spent skiing to famine relief, or by donating all of the time you would have spent practicing yoga to the volunteer program at the hospital. Again, consequentialist theories conflict with our basic moral intuitions in this regard. We may be morally required to do more than we typically do to help others, but intuitively we believe that a good portion of our lives should be ours to direct as we see fit. It just seems wrong to say that we are constantly under an obligation to do whatever would produce the best overall results as judged from an impartial perspective.

Consequentialists may respond to these objections by arguing that we have not thought carefully enough about what would actually produce the best results. Perhaps on more careful analysis, we would find that consequentialism does not yield these counterintuitive implications after all.

Notes

1. Gilbert Harman, *The Nature of Morality* (New York: Oxford UP, 1977) 3.
2. Harman 3-4.

8.

SELECTION FROM *UTILITARIANISM*

✿ ✿ ✿

JOHN STUART MILL

*The British philosopher John Stuart Mill (1806-73) was one of the most impor-
tant thinkers of the nineteenth century. In addition to writing on ethics and
social philosophy, he published works on logic, scientific method, and the nature
of mathematical knowledge, to name a few of the issues with which he was concerned. Mill improved significantly on Bentham's version of utilitarianism by
adding consideration of the quality of pleasure to the calculations of quantity of
pleasure. Some pleasures are, according to Mill, better or more worthwhile than
other pleasures, and Mill provides us with criteria for determining which of two
pleasures is better. Mill also replies to several objections to utilitarianism and
attempts to prove that the principle of utility is true.*

The creed which accepts as the foundation of morals "utility" or the "greatest happiness principle" holds that actions are right in proportion as they
tend to promote happiness; wrong as they tend to produce the reverse of
happiness. By happiness is intended pleasure and the absence of pain; by
unhappiness, pain and the privation of pleasure. To give a clear view of the
moral standard set up by the theory, much more requires to be said; in particular, what things it includes in the ideas of pain and pleasure, and to what
extent this is left an open question. But these supplementary explanations
do not affect the theory of life on which this theory of morality is grounded—namely, that pleasure and freedom from pain are the only things desirable as ends; and that all desirable things (which are as numerous in the
utilitarian as in any other scheme) are desirable either for pleasure inherent in themselves or as means to the promotion of pleasure and the prevention of pain.

Now such a theory of life excites in many minds, and among them in some
of the most estimable in feeling and purpose, inveterate dislike. To suppose
that life has (as they express it) no higher end than pleasure—no better and
nobler object of desire and pursuit—they designate as utterly mean and grov-
eling, as a doctrine worthy only of swine, to whom the followers of Epicurus
were, at a very early period, contemptuously likened; and modern holders of
the doctrine are occasionally made the subject of equally polite comparisons
by its German, French, and English assailants.

When thus attacked, the Epicureans have always answered that it is not they, but their accusers, who represent human nature in a degrading light, since the accusation supposes human beings to be capable of no pleasures except those of which swine are capable. If this supposition were true, the charge could not be gainsaid, but would then be no longer an imputation; for if the sources of pleasure were precisely the same to human beings and to swine, the rule of life which is good enough for the one would be good enough for the other. The comparison of the Epicurean life to that of beasts is felt as degrading, precisely because a beast's pleasures do not satisfy a human being's conceptions of happiness. Human beings have faculties more elevated than the animal appetites and, when once made conscious of them, do not regard anything as happiness which does not include their gratification. I do not indeed, consider the Epicureans to have been by any means faultless in drawing out their scheme of consequences from the utilitarian principle. To do this in any sufficient manner, many Stoic, as well as Christian, elements require to be included. But there is no known Epicurean theory of life which does not assign to the pleasures of the intellect, of the feelings and imagination, and of the moral sentiments a much higher value as pleasures than to those of mere sensation. It must be admitted, however, that utilitarian writers in general have placed the superiority of mental over bodily pleasures chiefly in the greater permanency, safety, uncostliness, etc., of the former—that is, in their circumstantial advantages rather than in their intrinsic nature. And on all these points utilitarians have fully proved their case; but they might have taken the other and, as it may be called, higher ground with entire consistency. It is quite compatible with the principle of utility to recognize the fact that some kinds of pleasures are more desirable and more valuable than others. It would be absurd that, while in estimating all other things quality is considered as well as quantity, the estimation of pleasure should be supposed to depend on quantity alone.

If I am asked what I mean by difference of quality in pleasures, or what makes one pleasure more valuable than another, merely as a pleasure, except its being greater in amount, there is but one possible answer. Of two pleasures, if there be one to which all or almost all who have experience of both give a decided preference, irrespective of any feeling of moral obligation to prefer it, that is the more desirable pleasure. If one of the two is, by those who are competently acquainted with both, placed so far above the other that they prefer it, even though knowing it to be attended with a greater amount of discontent, and would not resign it for any quantity of the other pleasure which their nature is capable of, we are justified in ascribing to the preferred enjoyment a superiority in quality so far outweighing quantity as to render it, in comparison, of small account.

Now it is an unquestionable fact that those who are equally acquainted with and equally capable of appreciating and enjoying both do give a most marked preference to the manner of existence which employs their higher faculties. Few human creatures would consent to be changed into any of the lower animals for a promise of the fullest allowance of a beast's pleasures; no intelligent human being would consent to be a fool, no instructed person would be an ignoramus, no person of feeling and conscience would be selfish and base, even though they should be persuaded that the fool, the dunce, or the rascal is better satisfied with his lot than they are with theirs. They would not resign what they possess more than he for the most complete satisfaction of all the desires which they have in common with him. If they ever fancy they would, it is only in cases of unhappiness so extreme that to escape from it they would exchange their lot for almost any other, however undesirable in their own eyes. A being of higher faculties requires more to make him happy, is capable probably of more acute suffering, and certainly accessible to it at more points, than one of an inferior type; but in spite of these liabilities, he can never really wish to sink into what he feels to be a lower grade of existence. We may give what explanation we please of this unwillingness; we may attribute it to pride, a name which is given indiscriminately to some of the most and to some of the least estimable feelings of which mankind are capable; we may refer it to the love of liberty and personal independence, an appeal to which was with the Stoics one of the most effective means for the inculcation of it; to the love of power or to the love of excitement, both of which do really enter into and contribute to it; but its most appropriate appellation is a sense of dignity, which all human beings possess in one form or other, and in some, though by no means in exact, proportion to their higher faculties, and which is so essential a part of the happiness of those in whom it is strong that nothing which conflicts with it could be otherwise than momentarily an object of desire to them. Whoever supposes that this preference takes place at a sacrifice of happiness—that the superior being, in anything like equal circumstances, is not happier than the inferior—confounds the two very different ideas of happiness and content. It is indisputable that the being whose capacities of enjoyment are low has the greatest chance of having them fully satisfied; and a highly endowed being will always feel that any happiness which he can look for, as the world is constituted, is imperfect. But he can learn to bear its imperfections, if they are at all bearable; and they will not make him envy the being who is indeed unconscious of the imperfections, but only because he feels not at all the good which those imperfections qualify. It is better to be a human being dissatisfied than a pig satisfied; better to be Socrates dissatisfied than a fool satisfied. And if the fool, or the pig, are of a different opinion, it is because they only know their own side of the question. The other party to the comparison knows both sides.

It may be objected that many who are capable of the higher pleasures occasionally, under the influence of temptation, postpone them to the lower. But this is quite compatible with a full appreciation of the intrinsic superiority of the higher. Men often, from infirmity of character, make their election for the nearer good, though they know it to be the less valuable; and this no less when the choice is between two bodily pleasures than when it is between bodily and mental. They pursue sensual indulgences to the injury of health, though perfectly aware that health is the greater good. It may be further objected that many who begin with youthful enthusiasm for everything noble, as they advance in years, sink into indolence and selfishness. But I do not believe that those who undergo this very common change voluntarily choose the lower description of pleasures in preference to the higher. I believe that, before they devote themselves exclusively to the one, they have already become incapable of the other. Capacity for the nobler feelings is in most natures a very tender plant, easily killed, not only by hostile influences, but by mere want of sustenance; and in the majority of young persons it speedily dies away if the occupations to which their position in life has devoted them, and the society into which it has thrown them, are not favorable to keeping that higher capacity in exercise. Men lose their high aspirations as they lose their intellectual tastes, because they have not time or opportunity for indulging them; and they addict themselves to inferior pleasures, not because they deliberately prefer them, but because they are either the only ones to which they have access or the only ones which they are any longer capable of enjoying. It may be questioned whether anyone who has remained equally susceptible to both classes of pleasures ever knowingly and calmly preferred the lower, though many, in all ages, have broken down in an ineffectual attempt to combine both.

From this verdict of the only competent judges, I apprehend there can be no appeal. On a question which is the best worth having of two pleasures, or which of two modes of existence is the most grateful to the feelings, apart from its moral attributes and from its consequences, the judgment of those who are qualified by knowledge of both, or, if they differ, that of the majority among them, must be admitted as final. And there needs be the less hesitation to accept this judgment respecting the quality of pleasures, since there is no other tribunal to be referred to even on the question of quantity. What means are there of determining which is the acutest of two pains, or the intensest of two pleasurable sensations, except the general suffrage of those who are familiar with both? Neither pains nor pleasures are homogeneous, and pain is always heterogeneous with pleasure. What is there to decide whether a particular pleasure is worth purchasing at the cost of a particular pain, except the feelings and judgment of the experienced? When, therefore, those feelings and judgment declare the pleasures derived from the higher faculties to be preferable *in kind*, apart from the question of intensity, to those of which the animal nature, disjoined from the higher faculties, is susceptible, they are entitled on this subject to the same regard.

I have dwelt on this point as being a necessary part of a perfectly just conception of utility or happiness considered as the directive rule of human conduct. But it is by no means an indispensable condition to the acceptance of the utilitarian standard; for that standard is not the agent's own greatest happiness, but the greatest amount of happiness altogether; and if it may possibly be doubted whether a noble character is always the happier for its nobleness, there can be no doubt that it makes other people happier, and that the world in general is immensely a gainer by it. Utilitarianism, therefore, could only attain its end by the general cultivation of nobleness of character, even if each individual were only benefited by the nobleness of others, and his own, so far as happiness is concerned, were a sheer deduction from the benefit. But the bare enunciation of such an absurdity as this last renders refutation superfluous.

According to the greatest happiness principle, as above explained, the ultimate end, with reference to and for the sake of which all other things are desirable—whether we are considering our own good or that of other people—is an existence exempt as far as possible from pain, and as rich as possible in enjoyments, both in point of quantity and quality; the test of quality and the rule for measuring it against quantity being the preference felt by those who, in their opportunities of experience, to which must be added their habits of self-consciousness and self-observation, are best furnished with the means of comparison. This, being according to the utilitarian opinion the end of human action, is necessarily also the standard of morality, which may accordingly be defined "the rules and precepts for human conduct," by the observance of which an existence such as has been described might be, to the greatest extent possible, secured to all mankind; and not to them only, but, so far as the nature of things admits to, to the whole sentient creation....

I must again repeat what the assailants of utilitarianism seldom have the justice to acknowledge, that the happiness which forms the utilitarian standard of what is right in conduct is not the agent's own happiness but that of all concerned. As between his own happiness and that of others, utilitarianism requires him to be as strictly impartial as a disinterested and benevolent spectator. In the golden rule of Jesus of Nazareth, we read the complete spirit of the ethics of utility. "To do as you would be done by," and "to love your neighbor as yourself," constitute the ideal perfection of utilitarian morality. As the means of making the nearest approach to this ideal, utility would enjoin, first, that laws and social arrangements should place the happiness or (as, speaking practically, it may be called) the interest of every individual as nearly as possible in harmony with the interest of the whole; and, secondly, that education and opinion, which have so vast a power over human character, should so use that power as to establish in the mind of every individual an indissoluble association between his own happiness and the good of the whole, especially between his own happiness and the practice of such modes of conduct, negative and positive, as regard for the universal happiness prescribes; so that not only he may be unable to conceive the possibility of happiness to himself, consistently with conduct opposed to the general good, but also that a direct impulse to promote the general good may be in every individual one of the habitual motives of action, and the sentiments connected therewith may fill a large and prominent place in every human being's sentient existence. If the impugners of the utilitarian morality represented it to their own minds in this its true character, I know not what recommendation possessed by any other morality they could possibly affirm to be wanting to it; what more beautiful or more exalted developments of human nature any other ethical system can be supposed to foster, or what springs of action, not accessible to the utilitarian, such systems rely on for giving effect to their mandates....

Of What Sort of Proof the Principle of Utility is Susceptible

It has already been remarked that questions of ultimate ends do not admit of proof, in the ordinary acceptation of the term. To be incapable of proof by reasoning is common to all first principles, to the first premises of our knowledge, as well as to those of our conduct. But the former, being matters of fact, may be the subject of a direct appeal to the faculties which judge of fact—namely, our senses and our internal consciousness. Can an appeal be made to the same faculties on questions of practical ends? Or by what other faculty is cognizance taken of them?

Questions about ends are, in other words, questions about what things are desirable. The utilitarian doctrine is that happiness is desirable, and the only thing desirable, as an end; all other things being only desirable as means to that end. What ought to be required of this doctrine, what conditions is it requisite that the doctrine should fulfill—to make good its claim to be believed?

The only proof capable of being given that an object is visible is that people actually see it. The only proof that a sound is audible is that people hear it; and so of the other sources of our experience. In like manner, I apprehend, the sole evidence it is possible to produce that anything is desirable is that people do actually desire it. If the end which the utilitarian doctrine proposes to itself were not, in theory and in practice, acknowledged to be an end, nothing could ever convince any person that it was so. No reason can be given why the general happiness is desirable, except that each person, so far as he believes it to be attainable, desires his own happiness. This, however, being a fact, we have not only all the proof which the case admits of, but all which it is possible to require, that happiness is a good, that each person's happiness is a good to that person, and the general happiness, therefore, a good to the aggregate of all persons. Happiness has made out its title as *one* of the ends of conduct and, consequently, one of the criteria of morality.

But it has not, by this alone, proved itself to be the sole criterion. To do that, it would seem, by the same rule, necessary to show, not only that people desire happiness, but that they never desire anything else. Now it is palpable that they do desire things which, in common language, are decidedly distinguished from happiness. They desire, for example, virtue and the absence of vice no less really than pleasure and the absence of pain. The desire of virtue is not as universal, but it is as authentic a fact as the desire of happiness. And hence the opponents of the utilitarian standard deem that they have a right to infer that there are other ends of human action besides happiness, and that happiness is not the standard of approbation and disapprobation.

But does the utilitarian doctrine deny that people desire virtue, or maintain that virtue is not a thing to be desired? The very reverse. It maintains not only that virtue is to be desired, but that it is to be desired disinterestedly, for itself. Whatever may be the opinion of utilitarian moralists as to the original conditions by which virtue is made virtue, however they may believe (as they do) that actions and dispositions are only virtuous because they promote another end than virtue, yet this being granted, and it having been decided, from considerations of this description, what *is* virtuous, they not only place virtue at the very head of the things which are good as means to the ultimate end, but they also recognize as a psychological fact the possibility of its being, to the individual, a good in itself, without looking to any end beyond it; and hold that the mind is not in a right state, not in a state conformable to utility, not in the state most conducive to the general happiness, unless it does love virtue in this manner—as a thing desirable in itself, even although, in the individual instance, it should not produce those other desirable consequences which it tends to produce, and on account of which it is held to be virtue. This opinion is not, in the smallest degree, a departure from the happiness principle. The ingredients of happiness are very various, and each of them is desirable in itself, and not merely when considered as swelling an aggregate. The principle of utility does not mean that any given pleasure, as music, for instance, or any given exemption from pain, as for example health, is to be looked upon as means to a collective something termed happiness, and to be desired on that account. They are desired and desirable in and for themselves; besides being means, they are a part of the end. Virtue, according to the utilitarian doctrine, is not naturally and originally part of the end, but it is capable of becoming so; and in those who live it disinterestedly it has become so, and is desired and cherished, not as a means to happiness, but as a part of their happiness.

To illustrate this further, we may remember that virtue is not the only thing originally a means, and which if it were not a means to anything else would be and remain indifferent, but which by association with what it is a means to comes to be desired for itself, and that too with the utmost intensity. What, for example, shall we say of the love of money? There is nothing originally more desirable about money than about any heap of glittering pebbles. Its worth is solely that of the things which it will buy; the desires for other things than itself, which it is a means of gratifying. Yet the love of money is not only one of the strongest moving forces of human life, but money is, in many cases, desired in and for itself—, the desire to possess it is often stronger than the desire to use it, and goes on increasing when all the desires which point to ends beyond it, to be compassed by it, are falling off. It may, then, be said truly that money is desired not for the sake of an end, but as part of the end. From being a means to happiness, it has come to be itself a principal ingredient of the individual's conception of happiness. The same may be said of the majority of the great objects of human life: power, for example, or fame, except that to each of these there is a certain amount of immediate pleasure annexed, which has at least the semblance of being naturally inherent in them—a thing which cannot be said of money. Still, however, the strongest natural attraction, both of power and of fame, is the immense aid they give to the attainment of our other wishes; and it is the strong association thus generated between them and all our objects of desire which gives to the direct desire of them the intensity it often assumes, so as in some characters to surpass in strength all other desires. In these cases the means have become a part of the end, and a more important part of it than any of the things which they are means to. What was once desired as an instrument for the attainment of happiness has come to be desired for its own sake. In being desired for its own sake it is, however, desired as *part* of happiness. The person is made, or thinks he would be made, happy by its mere possession; and is made unhappy by failure to obtain it. The desire of it is not a different thing from the desire of happiness any more than the love of music or the desire of health. They are included in happiness. They are some of the elements of which the desire of happiness is made up. Happiness is not an abstract idea but a concrete whole; and these are some of its parts. And the utilitarian standard sanctions and approves their being so. Life would be a poor thing, very ill provided with sources of happiness, if there were not this provision of nature by which things originally indifferent, but conducive to, or otherwise associated with, the satisfaction of our primitive desires, become in themselves sources of pleasure more valuable than the primitive pleasures, both in permanency, in the space of human existence that they are capable of covering, and even in intensity.

Virtue, according to the utilitarian conception, is a good of this description. There was no original desire of it, or motive to it, save its conduciveness to pleasure, and especially to protection from pain. But through the association thus formed it may be felt a good in itself, and desired as such with as great intensity as any other good; and with this difference between it and the love of money, of power, or of fame—that all of these may, and often do, render the individual noxious to the other members of the society to which he belongs, whereas there is nothing which makes him so much a blessing to them as the cultivation of the disinterested love of virtue. And consequently, the utilitarian standard, while it tolerates and approves those other acquired desires, up to the point beyond which they would be more injurious to the general happiness than promotive of it, enjoins and requires the cultivation of the love of virtue up to the greatest strength possible, as being above all things important to the general happiness.

It results from the preceding considerations that there is in reality nothing desired except happiness. Whatever is desired otherwise than as a means to some end beyond itself, and ultimately to happiness, is desired as itself a part of happiness, and is not desired for itself until it has become so. Those who desire virtue for its own sake desire it either because the consciousness of it is a pleasure, or because the consciousness of being without it is a pain, or for both reasons united; as in truth the pleasure and pain seldom exist separately, but almost always together—the same person feeling pleasure in the degree of virtue attained, and pain in not having attained more. If one of these gave him no pleasure, and the other no pain, he would not love or desire virtue, or would desire it only for the other benefits which it might produce to himself or to persons whom he cared for ...

9.
TWO CONCEPTS OF RULES

✾ ✾ ✾

JOHN RAWLS

John Rawls (1921-2002) was a professor of philosophy at Harvard University and one of the leading moral and political philosophers of our time. His best known work, A Theory of Justice, is considered to be one of the primary texts of political philosophy. In A Theory of Justice, Rawls attempts to refute utilitarianism and to develop an alternative theory of justice. (A selection from this book will appear in Chapter 7.) However, in his earlier article printed below, "Two Concepts of Rules," he argues that the utilitarian position is actually stronger than most people recognize. If we distinguish carefully between a summary conception of rules and a practice conception of rules, utilitarians will have a stronger response to one of the central objections raised against their theory.

In this paper[1] I want to show the importance of the distinction between justifying a practice[2] and justifying a particular action falling under it, and I want to explain the logical basis of this distinction and how it is possible to miss its significance. While the distinction has frequently been made,[3] and is now becoming commonplace, there remains the task of explaining the tendency either to overlook it altogether, or to fail to appreciate its importance.

To show the importance of the distinction I am going to defend utilitarianism against those objections which have traditionally been made against it in connection with punishment and the obligation to keep promises. I hope to show that if one uses the distinction in question then one can state utilitarianism in a way which makes it a better explication of our considered moral judgments than traditional objections would seem to admit.[4] Thus the importance of the distinction is shown by the way it strengthens the utilitarian view regardless of whether that view is completely defensible or not.

To explain how the significance of the distinction may be overlooked, I am going to discuss two conceptions of rules. One of these conceptions conceals the importance of distinguishing between the justification of a rule or practice and the justification of a particular action falling under it. The other conception makes it clear why this distinction must be made and what is its logical basis.

1

The subject of punishment, in the sense of attaching legal penalties to the violation of legal rules, has always been a troubling moral question.[5] The trouble about it has not been that people disagree as to whether or not punishment is justifiable. Most people have held that, freed from certain abuses, it is an acceptable institution. Only a few have rejected punishment entirely, which is rather surprising when one considers all that can be said against it. The difficulty is with the justification of punishment: various arguments for it have been given by moral philosophers, but so far none of them has won any sort of general acceptance; no justification is without those who detest it. I hope to show that the use of the aforementioned distinction enables one to state the utilitarian view in a way which allows for the sound points of its critics.

For our purposes we may say that there are two justifications of punishment. What we may call the retributive view is that punishment is justified on the grounds that wrongdoing merits punishment. It is morally fitting that a person who does wrong should suffer in proportion to his wrongdoing. That a criminal should be punished follows from his guilt, and the severity of the appropriate punishment depends on the depravity of his act. The state of affairs where a wrongdoer suffers punishment is morally better than the state of affairs where he does not; and it is better irrespective of any of the consequences of punishing him.

What we may call the utilitarian view holds that on the principle that bygones are bygones and that only future consequences are material to present decisions, punishment is justifiable only by reference to the probable consequences of maintaining it as one of the devices of the social order. Wrongs committed in the past are, as such, not relevant considerations for deciding what to do. If punishment can be shown to promote effectively the interest of society it is justifiable, otherwise it is not.

I have stated these two competing views very roughly to make one feel the conflict between them: one feels the force of *both* arguments and one wonders how they can be reconciled. From my introductory remarks it is obvious that the resolution which I am going to propose is that in this case one must distinguish between justifying a practice as a system of rules to be applied and enforced, and justifying a particular action which falls under these rules; utilitarian arguments are appropriate with regard to questions about practices, while retributive arguments fit the application of particular rules to particular cases.

We might try to get clear about this distinction by imagining how a father might answer the question of his son. Suppose the son asks, "Why was J put in jail yesterday?" The father answers, "Because he robbed the bank at B. He was duly tried and found guilty. That's why he was put in jail yesterday." But suppose the son had asked a different question, namely, "Why do people put other people in jail?" Then the father might answer, "To protect good people from bad people" or "To stop people from doing things that would make it uneasy for all of us; for otherwise we wouldn't be able to go to bed at night and sleep in peace." There are two very different questions here. One question emphasizes the proper name: it asks why J was punished rather than someone else, or it asks what he was punished for. The other question asks why we have the institution of punishment: why do people punish one another rather than, say, always forgiving one another?

Thus the father says in effect that a particular man is punished, rather than some other man, because he is guilty, and he is guilty because he broke the law (past tense). In his case the law looks back, the judge looks back, the jury looks back, and a penalty is visited upon him for something he did. That a man is to be punished, and what his punishment is to be, is settled by its being shown that he broke the law and that the law assigns that penalty for the violation of it.

On the other hand we have the institution of punishment itself, and recommend and accept various changes in it, because it is thought by the (ideal) legislator and by those to whom the law applies that, as a part of a system of law impartially applied from case to case arising under it, it will have the consequence, in the long run, of furthering the interests of society.

One can say, then, that the judge and the legislator stand in different positions and look in different directions: one to the past, the other to the future. The justification of what the judge does, *qua* judge, sounds like the retributive view; the justification of what the (ideal) legislator does, *qua* legislator, sounds like the utilitarian view. Thus both views have a point (this is as it should be since intelligent and sensitive persons have been on both sides of the argument); and one's initial confusion disappears once one sees that these views apply to persons holding different offices with different duties, and situated differently with respect to the system of rules that make up the criminal law.[6]

One might say, however, that the utilitarian view is more fundamental since it applies to a more fundamental office, for the judge carries out the legislator's will so far as he can determine it. Once the legislator decides to have laws and to assign penalties for their violation (as things are there must be both the law and the penalty) an institution is set up which involves a retributive conception of particular cases. It is part of the concept of the criminal law as a system of rules that the application and enforcement of these rules in particular cases should be justifiable by arguments of a retributive character. The decision whether or not to use law rather than some other mechanism of social control, and the decision as to what laws to have and what penalties to assign, be settled by utilitarian arguments; but if one decides to have laws then one has decided on something whose working in particular cases is retributive in form.[7]

The answer, then, to the confusion engendered by the two views of punishment is quite simple: one distinguishes two offices, that of the judge and that of the legislator, and one distinguishes their different stations with respect to the system of rules which make up the law; and then one notes that the different sorts of considerations which would usually be offered as reasons for what is done under the cover of these offices can be paired off with the competing justifications of punishment. One reconciles the two views by the time-honored device of making them apply to different situations.

But can it really be this simple? Well, this answer allows for the apparent intent of each side. Does a person who advocates the retributive view necessarily advocate, as an *institution*, legal machinery whose essential purpose is to set up and preserve a correspondence between moral turpitude and suffering? Surely not.[8] What retributionists have rightly insisted upon is that no man can be punished unless he is guilty, that is, unless he has broken the law. Their fundamental criticism of the utilitarian account is that, as they interpret it, it sanctions an innocent person's being punished (if one may call it that) for the benefit of society.

On the other hand, utilitarians agree that punishment is to be inflicted only for the violation of law. They regard this much as understood from the concept of punishment itself.[9] The point of the utilitarian account concerns the institution as a system of rules: utilitarianism seeks to limit its use by declaring it justifiable only if it can be shown to foster effectively the good of society. Historically it is a protest against the indiscriminate and ineffective use of the criminal law.[10] It seeks to dissuade us from assigning to penal institutions the improper, if not sacrilegious, task of matching suffering with moral turpitude. Like others, utilitarians want penal institutions designed so that, as far as humanly possible, only those who break the law run afoul of it. They hold that no official should have discretionary power to inflict penalties whenever he thinks it for the benefit of society; for on utilitarian grounds an institution granting such power could not be justified.[11]

The suggested way of reconciling the retributive and the utilitarian justifications of punishment seems to account for what both sides have wanted to say. There are, however, two further questions which arise, and I shall devote the remainder of this section to them.

First, will not a difference of opinion as to the proper criterion of just law make the proposed reconciliation unacceptable to retributionists? Will they not question whether, if the utilitarian principle is used as the criterion, it follows that those who have broken the law are guilty in a way which satisfies their demand that those punished deserve to be punished? To answer this difficulty, suppose that the rules of the criminal law are justified on utilitarian grounds (it is only for laws that meet his criterion that the utilitarian can be held responsible). Then it follows that the actions which the criminal law specifies as offenses are such that, if they were tolerated, terror and alarm would spread in society. Consequently, retributionists can only deny that those who are punished deserve to be punished if they deny that such actions are wrong. This they will not want to do.

The second question is whether utilitarianism doesn't justify too much. One pictures it as an engine of justification which, if consistently adopted, could be used to justify cruel and arbitrary institutions. Retributionists may be supposed to concede that utilitarians *intend* to reform the law and to make it more humane; that utilitarians do not *wish* to justify any such thing as punishment of the innocent; and that utilitarians may appeal to the fact that punishment presupposes guilt in the sense that by punishment one understands an institution attaching penalties to the infraction of legal rules, and therefore that it is logically absurd to suppose that utilitarians in justifying *punishment* might also have justified punishment (if we may call it that) of the innocent. The real question, however, is whether the utilitarian, in justifying punishment, hasn't used arguments which commit him to accepting the infliction of suffering on innocent persons if it is for the good of society (whether or not one calls this punishment). More generally, isn't the utilitarian committed in principle to accepting many practices which he, as a morally sensitive person, wouldn't want to accept? Retributionists are inclined to hold that there is no way to stop the utilitarian principle from justifying too much except by adding to it a principle which distributes certain rights to individuals. Then the amended criterion is not the greatest benefit of society *simpliciter*, but the greatest benefit of society subject to the constraint that no one's rights may be violated. Now while I think that the classical utilitarians proposed a criterion of this more complicated sort, I do not want to argue that point here.[12] What I want to show is that there is *another* way of preventing the utilitarian principle from justifying too much, or at least of making it much less likely to do so: namely, by stating utilitarianism in a way which accounts for the distinction between the justification of an institution and the justification of a particular action falling under it.

I begin by defining the institution of punishment as follows: a person is said to suffer punishment whenever he is legally deprived of some of the normal rights of a citizen on the ground that he has violated a rule of law, the violation having been established by trial according to the due process of law, provided that the deprivation is carried out by the recognized legal authorities of the state, that the rule of law clearly specifies both the offense and the attached penalty, that the courts construe statutes strictly, and that the statute was on the books prior to the time of the offense.[13] This definition specifies what I shall understand by punishment. The question is whether utilitarian arguments may be found to justify institutions widely different from this and such as one would find cruel and arbitrary.

This question is best answered, I think, by taking up a particular accusation. Consider the following from Carritt:

... the utilitarian must hold that we are justified in inflicting pain always and only to prevent worse pain or bring about greater happiness. This, then, is all we need to consider in so-called punishment, which must be purely preventive. But if some kind of very cruel crime becomes common, and none of the criminals can be caught, it might be highly expedient, as an example, to hang an innocent man, if a charge against him could be so framed that he were universally thought guilty; indeed this would only fail to be an ideal instance of utilitarian "punishment" because the victim himself would not have been so likely as a real felon to commit such a crime in the future; in all other respects it would be perfectly deterrent and therefore felicific.[14]

Carritt is trying to show that there are occasions when a utilitarian argument would justify taking an action which would be generally condemned; and thus that utilitarianism justifies too much. But the failure of Carritt's argument lies in the fact that he makes no distinction between the justification of the general system of rules which constitutes penal institutions and the justification of particular applications of these rules to particular cases by the various officials whose job it is to administer them. This becomes perfectly clear when one asks who the "we" are of whom Carritt speaks. Who is this who has a sort of absolute authority on particular occasions to decide that an innocent man shall be "punished" if everyone can be convinced that he is guilty? Is this person the legislator, or the judge, or the body of private citizens, or what? It is utterly crucial to know who is to decide such matters, and by what authority, for all of this must be written into the rules of the institution. Until one knows these things one doesn't know what the institution is whose justification is being challenged; and as the utilitarian principle applies to the institution one doesn't know whether it is justifiable on utilitarian grounds or not.

Once this is understood it is clear what the countermove to Carritt's argument is. One must describe more carefully what the *institution* is which his example suggests, and then ask oneself whether or not it is likely that having this institution would be for the benefit of society in the long run. One must not content oneself with the vague thought that, when it's a question of *this* case, it would be a good thing if *somebody* did something even if an innocent person were to suffer.

Try to imagine, then, an institution (which we may call "telishment") which is such that the officials set up by it have authority to arrange a trial for the condemnation of an innocent man whenever they are of the opinion that doing so would be in the best interests of society. The discretion of officials is limited, however, by the rule that they may not condemn an innocent man to undergo such an ordeal unless there is, at the time, a wave of offenses similar to that with which they charge him and telish him for. We may imagine that the officials having the discretionary authority are the judges of the higher courts in consultation with the chief of police, the minister of justice, and a committee of the legislature.

Once one realizes that one is involved in setting up an *institution*, one sees that the hazards are very great. For example, what check is there on the officials? How is one to tell whether or not their actions are authorized? How is one to limit the risks involved in allowing such systematic deception? How is one to avoid giving anything short of complete discretion to the authorities to telish anyone they like? In addition to these considerations, it is obvious that people will come to have a very different attitude towards their penal system when telishment is adjoined to it. They will be uncertain as to whether a convicted man has been punished or telished. They will wonder whether or not they should feel sorry for him. They will wonder whether the same fate won't at any time fall on them. If one pictures how such an institution would actually work, and the enormous risks involved in it, it seems clear that it would serve no useful purpose. A utilitarian justification for this institution is most unlikely.

It happens in general that as one drops off the defining features of punishment one ends up with an institution whose utilitarian justification is highly doubtful. One reason for this is that punishment works like a kind of price system: by altering the prices one has to pay for the performance of actions it supplies a motive for avoiding some actions and doing others. The defining features are essential if punishment is to work in this way; so that an institution which lacks these features, e.g., an institution which is set up to "punish" the innocent, is likely to have about as much point as a price system (if one may call it that) where the prices of things change at random from day to day and one learns the price of something after one has agreed to buy it.[15]

If one is careful to apply the utilitarian principle to the institution which is to authorize particular actions, then there is *less* danger of its justifying too much. Carritt's example gains plausibility by its indefiniteness and by its concentration on the particular case. His argument will only hold if it can be shown that there are utilitarian arguments which justify an institution whose publicly ascertainable offices and powers are such as to permit officials to exercise that kind of discretion in particular cases. But the requirement of having to build the arbitrary features of the particular decision into the institutional practice makes the justification much less likely to go through.

2

I shall now consider the question of promises. The objection to utilitarianism in connection with promises seems to be this: it is believed that on the utilitarian view when a person makes a promise the only ground upon which he should keep it, if he should keep it, is that by keeping it he will realize the most good on the whole. So that if one asks the question "Why should I keep my promise?" the utilitarian answer is understood to be that doing so in *this* case will have the best consequences. And this answer is said, quite rightly, to conflict with the way in which the obligation to keep promises is regarded.

Now of course critics of utilitarianism are not unaware that one defense sometimes attributed to utilitarians is the consideration involving the practice of promisekeeping.[16] In this connection they are supposed to argue something like this: it must be admitted that we feel strictly about keeping promises, more strictly than it might seem our view can account for. But when we consider the matter carefully it is always necessary to take into account the effect which our action will have on the practice of making promises. The promisor must weigh, not only the effects of breaking his promise on the particular case, but also the effect which his breaking his promise will have on the practice itself. Since the practice is of great utilitarian value, and since breaking one's promise always seriously damages it, one will seldom be justified in breaking one's promise. If we view our individual promises in the wider context of the practice of promising itself we can account for the strictness of the obligation to keep promises. There is always one very strong utilitarian consideration in favor of keeping them, and this will ensure that when the question arises as to whether or not to keep a promise it will usually turn out that one should, even where the facts of the particular case taken by itself would seem to justify one's breaking it. In this way the strictness with which we view the obligation to keep promises is accounted for.

Ross has criticized this defense as follows:[17] however great the value of the practice of promising, on utilitarian grounds, there must be some value which is greater, and one can imagine it to be obtainable by breaking a promise. Therefore there might be a case where the promisor could argue that breaking his promise was justified as leading to a better state of affairs on the whole. And the promisor could argue in this way no matter how slight the advantage won by breaking the promise. If one were to challenge the promisor his defense would be that what he did was best on the whole in view of all the utilitarian considerations, which in this case *include* the importance of the practice. Ross feels that such a defense would be unacceptable. I think he is right insofar as he is protesting against the appeal to consequences in general and without further explanation. Yet it is extremely difficult to weigh the force of Ross's argument. The kind of case imagined seems unrealistic and one feels that it needs to be described. One is inclined to think it would either turn out that such a case came under an exception defined by the practice itself, in which case there would not be an appeal to consequences in general on the particular case, or it would happen that the circumstances were so peculiar that the conditions which the practice presupposes no longer obtained. But certainly Ross is right in thinking that it strikes us as wrong for a person to defend breaking a promise by a general appeal to consequences.

For a general utilitarian defense is not open to the promisor: it is not one of the defenses allowed by the practice of making promises.

Ross gives two further counterarguments.[18] First, he holds that it overestimates the damage done to the practice of promising by a failure to keep a promise. One who breaks a promise harms his own name certainly, but it isn't clear that a broken promise always damages the practice itself sufficiently to account for the strictness of the obligation. Second, and more important, I think, he raises the question of what one is to say of a promise which isn't known to have been made except to the promisor and the promisee, as in the case of a promise a son makes to his dying father concerning the handling of the estate.[19] In this sort of case the consideration relating to the practice doesn't weigh on the promisor at all, and yet one feels that this sort of promise is as binding as other promises. The question of the effect which breaking it has on the practice seems irrelevant. The only consequence seems to be that one can break the promise without running any risk of being censured; but the obligation itself seems not the least weakened. Hence it is doubtful whether the effect on the practice ever weighs in the particular case; certainly it cannot account for the strictness of the obligation where it fails to obtain. It seems to follow that a utilitarian account of the obligation to keep promises cannot be successfully carried out.

From what I have said in connection with punishment, one can foresee what I am going to say about these arguments and counterarguments. They fail to make the distinction between the justification of a practice and the justification of a particular action falling under it, and therefore they fall into the mistake of taking it for granted that the promisor, like Carritt's official, is entitled without restriction to bring utilitarian considerations to bear in deciding whether to keep *his* promise. But if one considers what the practice of promising is one will see, I think, that it is such as not to allow this sort of general discretion to the promisor. Indeed, the point of the practice is to abdicate one's title to act in accordance with utilitarian and prudential considerations in order that the future may be tied down and plans coordinated in advance. There are obvious utilitarian advantages in having a practice which denies to the promisor, as a defense, any general appeal to the utilitarian principle in accordance with which the practice itself may be justified. There is nothing contradictory, or surprising, in this: utilitarian (or aesthetic) reasons might properly be given in arguing that the game of chess, or baseball, is satisfactory just as it is, or in arguing that it should be changed in various respects, but a player in a game cannot properly appeal to such considerations as reasons for his making one move rather than another. It is a mistake to think that if the practice is justified on utilitarian grounds then the promisor must have complete liberty to use utilitarian arguments to decide whether or not to keep his promise. The practice forbids this general defense; and it is a purpose of the practice to do this. Therefore what the above arguments presuppose—the idea that if the utilitarian view is accepted then the promisor is bound if, and only if, the application of the utilitarian principle to his own case shows that keeping it is best on the whole—is false. The promisor is bound because he promised: weighing the case on its merits is not open to him.[20]

Is this to say that in particular cases one cannot deliberate whether or not to keep one's promise? Of course not. But to do so is to deliberate whether the various excuses, exceptions and defenses, which are understood by, and which constitute an important part of, the practice, apply to one's own case.[21] Various defenses for not keeping one's promise are allowed, but among them there isn't the one that, on general utilitarian grounds, the promisor (truly) thought his action best on the whole, even though there may be the defense that the consequences of keeping one's promise would have been *extremely* severe. While there are too many complexities here to consider all the necessary details, one can see that the general defense isn't allowed if one asks the following question: what would one say of someone who, when asked why he broke his promise, replied simply that breaking it was best on the whole? Assuming that his reply is sincere, and that his belief was reasonable (i.e., one need not consider the possibility that he was mistaken), I think that one would question whether or not he knows what it means to say "I promise" (in the appropriate circumstances). It would be said of someone who used this excuse without further explanation that he didn't understand what defenses the practice, which defines a promise, allows to him. If a child were to use this excuse one would correct him; for it is part of the way one is taught the concept of a promise to be corrected if one uses this excuse. The point of having the practice would be lost if the practice did allow this excuse.

It is no doubt part of the utilitarian view that every practice should admit the defense that the consequences of abiding by it would have been extremely severe; and utilitarians would be inclined to hold that some reliance on people's good sense and some concession to hard cases is necessary. They would hold that a practice is justified by serving the interests of those who take part in it; and as with any set of rules there is understood a background of circumstances under which it is expected to be applied and which need not—indeed which cannot—be fully stated. Should these circumstances change, then even if there is no rule which provides for the case, it may still be in accordance with the practice that one be released from one's obligation. But this sort of defense allowed by a practice must not be confused with the general option to weigh each particular case on utilitarian grounds which critics of utilitarianism have thought it necessarily to involve.

The concern which utilitarianism raises by its justification of punishment is that it may justify too much. The question in connection with promises is different: it is how utilitarianism can account for the obligation to keep promises at all. One feels that the recognized obligation to keep one's promise and utilitarianism are incompatible. And to be sure, they are incompatible if one interprets the utilitarian view as necessarily holding that each person has complete liberty to weigh every particular action on general utilitarian grounds. But must one interpret utilitarianism in this way? I hope to show that, in the sorts of cases I have discussed, one cannot interpret it in this way.

3

So far I have tried to show the importance of the distinction between the justification of a practice and the justification of a particular action falling under it by indicating how this distinction might be used to defend utilitarianism against two long-standing objections. One might be tempted to close the discussion at this point by saying that utilitarian considerations should be understood as applying to practices in the first instance and not to particular actions falling under them except insofar as the practices admit of it. One might say that in this modified form it is a better account of our considered moral opinions and let it go at that. But to stop here would be to neglect the interesting question as to how one can fail to appreciate the significance of this rather obvious distinction and can take it for granted that utilitarianism has the consequence that particular cases may always be decided on general utilitarian grounds.[22] I want to argue that this mistake may be connected with misconceiving the logical status of the rules of practices; and to show this I am going to examine two conceptions of rules; two ways of placing them within the utilitarian theory.

The conception which conceals from us the significance of the distinction I am going to call the summary view. It regards rules in the following way: one supposes that each person decides what he shall do in particular cases by applying the utilitarian principle; one supposes further that different people will decide the same particular case in the same way and that there will be recurrences of cases similar to those previously decided. Thus it will happen that in cases of certain kinds the same decision will be made either by the same person at different times or by different persons at the same time. If a case occurs frequently enough one supposes that a rule is formulated to cover that sort of case. I have called this conception the summary view because rules are pictured as summaries of past decisions arrived at by the *direct* application of the utilitarian principle to particular cases. Rules are regarded as reports that cases of a certain sort have been found on *other* grounds to be properly decided in a certain way (although, of course, they do not say this).

There are several things to notice about this way of placing rules within the utilitarian theory.[23]

1. The point of having rules derives from the fact that similar cases tend to recur and that one can decide cases more quickly if one records past decisions in the form of rules. If similar cases didn't recur, one would be required to apply the utilitarian principle directly, case by case, and rules reporting past decisions would be of no use.

2. The decisions made on particular cases are logically prior to rules. Since rules gain their point from the need to apply the utilitarian principle to many similar cases, it follows that a particular case (or several cases similar to it) may exist whether or not there is a rule covering that case. We are pictured as recognizing particular cases prior to there being a rule which covers them, for it is only if we meet with a number of cases of a certain sort that we formulate a rule. Thus we are able to describe a particular case as a particular case of the requisite sort whether there is a rule regarding *that* sort of case or not. Put another way: what the *A*'s and the *B*'s refer to in rules of the form "Whenever *A* do *B*" may be described as *A*'s and *B*'s whether or not there is the rule "Whenever *A* do *B*," or whether or not there is any body of rules which makes up a practice of which that rule is a part.

To illustrate this consider a rule, or maxim, which could arise in this way: suppose that a person is trying to decide whether to tell someone who is fatally ill what his illness is when he has been asked to do so. Suppose the person to reflect and then decide, on utilitarian grounds, that he should not answer truthfully; and suppose that on the basis of this and other like occasions he formulates a rule to the effect that when asked by someone fatally ill what his illness is, one should not tell him. The point to notice is that someone's being fatally ill and asking what his illness is, and someone's telling him, are things that can be described as such whether or not there is this rule. The performance of the action to which the rule refers doesn't require the stage-setting of a practice of which this rule is a part. This is what is meant by saying that on the summary view particular cases are logically prior to rules.

3. Each person is in principle always entitled to reconsider the correctness of a rule and to question whether or not it is proper to follow it in a particular case. As rules are guides and aids, one may ask whether in past decisions there might not have been a mistake in applying the utilitarian principle to get the rule in question, and wonder whether or not it is best in this case. The reason for rules is that people are not able to apply the utilitarian principle effortlessly and flawlessly; there is need to save time and to post a guide. On this view a society of rational utilitarians would be a society without rules in which each person applied the utilitarian principle directly and smoothly, and without error, case by case. On the other hand, ours is a society in which rules are formulated to serve as aids in reaching these ideally rational decisions on particular cases, guides which have been built up and tested by the experience of generations. If one applies this view to rules, one is interpreting them as maxims, as "rules of thumb"; and it is doubtful that anything to which the summary

conception did apply would be called a *rule*. Arguing as if one regarded rules in this way is a mistake one makes while doing philosophy.

4. The concept of *a general* rule takes the following form. One is pictured as estimating on what percentage of the cases likely to arise a given rule may be relied upon to express the correct decision, that is, the decision that would be arrived at if one were to correctly apply the utilitarian principle case by case. If one estimates that by and large the rule will give the correct decision, or if one estimates that the likelihood of making a mistake by applying the utilitarian principle directly on one's own is greater than the likelihood of making a mistake by following the rule, and if these considerations held of persons generally, then one would be justified in urging its adoption as a general rule. In this way *general* rules might be accounted for on the summary view. It will still make sense, however, to speak of applying the utilitarian principle case by case, for it was by trying to foresee the results of doing this that one got the initial estimates upon which acceptance of the rule depends. That one is taking a rule in accordance with the summary conception will show itself in the naturalness with which one speaks of the rule as a guide, or as a maxim, or as a generalization from experience, and as something to be laid aside in extraordinary cases where there is no assurance that the generalization will hold and the case must therefore be treated on its merits. Thus there goes with this conception the notion of a particular exception which renders a rule suspect on a particular occasion.

The other conception of rules I will call the practice conception. On this view rules are pictured as defining a practice. Practices are set up for various reasons, but one of them is that in many areas of conduct each person's deciding what to do on utilitarian grounds case by case leads to confusion, and that the attempt to coordinate behavior by trying to foresee how others will act is bound to fail. As an alternative one realizes that what is required is the establishment of a practice, the specification of a new form of activity; and from this one sees that a practice necessarily involves the abdication of full liberty to act on utilitarian and prudential grounds. It is the mark of a practice that being taught how to engage in it involves being instructed in the rules which define it, and that appeal is made to those rules to correct the behavior of those engaged in it. Those engaged in a practice recognize the rules as defining it. The rules cannot be taken as simply describing how those engaged in the practice in fact behave: it is not simply that they act as if they were obeying the rules. Thus it is essential to the notion of a practice that the rules are publicly known and understood as definitive; and it is essential also that the rules of a practice can be taught and can be acted upon to yield a coherent practice. On this conception, then, rules are not generalizations from the decisions of individuals applying the utilitarian principle directly and independently to recurrent particular cases. On the contrary, rules define a practice and are themselves the subject of the utilitarian principle.

To show the important differences between this way of fitting rules into the utilitarian theory and the previous way, I shall consider the differences between the two conceptions on the points previously discussed.

1. In contrast with the summary view, the rules of practices are logically prior to particular cases. This is so because there cannot be a particular case of an action falling under a rule of a practice unless there is the practice. This can be made clearer as follows: in a practice there are rules setting up offices, specifying certain forms of action appropriate to various offices, establishing penalties for the breach of rules, and so on. We may think of the rules of a practice as defining offices, moves, and offenses. Now what is meant by saying that the practice is logically prior to particular cases is this: given any rule which specifies a form of action (a move), a particular action which would be taken as falling under this rule given that there is the practice would not be *described* as that sort of action unless there was the practice. In the case of actions specified by practices it is logically impossible to perform them outside the stage-setting provided by those practices, for unless there is the practice, and unless the requisite proprieties are fulfilled, whatever one does, whatever movements one makes, will fail to count as a form of action which the practice specifies. What one does will be described in some *other* way.

One may illustrate this point from the game of baseball. Many of the actions one performs in a game of baseball one can do by oneself or with others whether there is the game or not. For example, one can throw a ball, run, or swing a peculiarly shaped piece of wood. But one cannot steal a base, or strike out, or draw a walk, or make an error, or balk; although one can do certain things which appear to resemble these actions such as sliding into a bag, missing a grounder and so on. Striking out, stealing a base, balking, etc., are all actions which can only happen in a game. No matter what a person did, what he did would not be described as stealing a base or striking out or drawing a walk unless he could also be described as playing baseball, and for him to be doing this presupposes the rule-like practice which constitutes the game. The practice is logically prior to particular cases: unless there is the practice the terms referring to actions specified by it lack a sense.[24]

2. The practice view leads to an entirely different conception of the authority which each person has to decide on the propriety of following a rule in particular cases. To engage in a practice, to perform those actions specified by a practice, means to follow the appropriate rules. If one wants to do an action which a certain practice specifies then there is no way to do it except to follow the rules which define it. Therefore, it doesn't make sense for a person to raise the question whether or not a rule of a practice correctly applies to *his* case where the action he contemplates is a form of action defined by a practice. If someone were to raise such a question, he would simply show that he didn't understand the situation in which he was acting. If one wants to perform an action specified by a practice, the only legitimate question concerns the nature of the practice itself ("How do I go about making a will?").

This point is illustrated by the behavior expected of a player in games. If one wants to play a game, one doesn't treat the rules of the game as guides as to what is best in particular cases. In a game of baseball if a batter were to ask "Can I have four strikes?" it would be assumed that he was asking what the rule was; and if, when told what the rule was, he were to say that he meant that on this occasion he thought it would be best on the whole for him to have four strikes rather than three, this would be most kindly taken as a joke. One might contend that baseball would be a better game if four strikes were allowed instead of three; but one cannot picture the rules as guides to what is best on the whole in particular cases, and question their applicability to particular cases as particular cases.

3. and 4. To complete the four points of comparison with the summary conception, it is clear from what has been said that rules of practices are not guides to help one decide particular cases correctly as judged by some higher ethical principle. And neither the quasi-statistical notion of generality, nor the notion of a particular exception, can apply to the rules of practices. A more or less general rule of a practice must be a rule which according to the structure of the practice applies to more or fewer of the kinds of cases arising under it; or it must be a rule which is more or less basic to the understanding of the practice. Again, a particular case cannot be an exception to a rule of a practice. An exception is rather a qualification or a further specification of the rule.

It follows from what we have said about the practice conception of rules that if a person is engaged in a practice, and if he is asked why *he* does what *he* does, or if he is asked to defend what he does, then his explanation, or defense, lies in referring the questioner to the practice. He cannot say of *his* action, if it is an action specified by a practice, that he does it rather than some other because he thinks it is best on the whole.[25] When a man engaged in a practice is queried about his action he must assume that the questioner either doesn't know that he is engaged in it ("Why are you in a hurry to pay him?" "I promised to pay him today") or doesn't know what the practice is. One doesn't so much justify one's particular action as explain, or show, that it is in accordance with the practice. The reason for this is that it is only against the stage-setting of the practice that one's particular action is described as it is. Only by reference to the practice can one say what one is doing. To explain or to defend one's own action, as a particular action, one fits it into the practice which defines it. If this is not accepted it's a sign that a different question is being raised as to whether one is justified in accepting the practice, or in tolerating it. When the challenge is to the practice, citing the rules (saying what the practice is) is naturally to no avail. But when the challenge is to the particular action defined by the practice, there is nothing one can do but refer to the rules. Concerning particular actions there is only a question for one who isn't clear as to what the practice is, or who doesn't know that it is being engaged in. This is to be contrasted with the case of a maxim which may be taken as pointing to the correct decision on the case as decided on *other* grounds, and so giving a challenge on the case a sense by having it question whether these other grounds really support the decision on this case.

If one compares the two conceptions of rules I have discussed, one can see how the summary conception misses the significance of the distinction between justifying a practice and justifying actions falling under it. On this view rules are regarded as guides whose purpose it is to indicate the ideally rational decision on the given particular case which the flawless application of the utilitarian principle would yield. One has, in principle, full option to use the guides or to discard them as the situation warrants without one's moral office being altered in any way: whether one discards the rules or not, one always holds the office of a rational person seeking case by case to realize the best on the whole. But on the practice conception, if one holds an office defined by a practice then questions regarding one's actions in this office are settled by reference to the rules which define the practice. If one seeks to question these rules, then one's office undergoes a fundamental change: one then assumes the office of one empowered to change and criticize the rules, or the office of a reformer, and so on. The summary conception does away with the distinction of offices and the various forms of argument appropriate to each. On that conception there is one office and so no offices at all. It therefore obscures the fact that the utilitarian principle must, in the case of actions and offices defined by a practice, apply to the practice, so that general utilitarian arguments are not available to those who act in offices so defined.[26]

Some qualifications are necessary in what I have said. First, I may have talked of the summary and the practice conceptions of rules as if only one of them could be true of rules, and if true of any rules, then necessarily true of *all* rules. I do not, of course, mean this. (It is the critics of utilitarianism who make this mistake insofar as their arguments against utilitarianism presuppose a summary conception of the rules of practices.) Some rules will fit one conception, some rules the other; and so there are rules of practices (rules in the strict sense), and maxims and "rules of thumb."

Secondly, there are further distinctions that can be made in classifying rules, distinctions which should be made if one were considering other questions. The distinctions which I have drawn are those most relevant for the rather special matter I have discussed, and are not intended to be exhaustive.

Finally, there will be many border-line cases about which it will be difficult, if not impossible, to decide which conception of rules is applicable. One expects border-line cases with any concept, and they are especially likely in connection with such involved concepts as those of a practice, institution, game, rule, and so on. Wittgenstein has shown how fluid these notions are.[27] What I have done is to emphasize and sharpen two conceptions for the limited purpose of this paper.

4

What I have tried to show by distinguishing between two conceptions of rules is that there is a way of regarding rules which allows the option to consider particular cases on general utilitarian grounds; whereas there is another conception which does not admit of such discretion except insofar as the rules themselves authorize it. I want to suggest that the tendency while doing philosophy to picture rules in accordance with the summary conception is what may have blinded moral philosophers to the significance of the distinction between justifying a practice and justifying a particular action falling under it; and it does so by misrepresenting the logical force of the reference to the rules in the case of a challenge to a particular action falling under a practice, and by obscuring the fact that where there is a practice, it is the practice itself that must be the subject of the utilitarian principle.

It is surely no accident that two of the traditional test cases of utilitarianism, punishment and promises, are clear cases of practices. Under the influence of the summary conception it is natural to suppose that the officials of a penal system, and one who has made a promise, may decide what to do in particular cases on utilitarian grounds. One fails to see that a general discretion to decide particular cases on utilitarian grounds is incompatible with the concept of a practice; and that what discretion one does have is itself defined by the practice (e.g., a judge may have discretion to determine the penalty within certain limits). The traditional objections to utilitarianism which I have discussed presuppose the attribution to judges, and to those who have made promises, of a plenitude of moral authority to decide particular cases on utilitarian grounds. But once one fits utilitarianism together with the notion of a practice, and notes that punishment and promising are practices, then one sees that this attribution is logically precluded.

That punishment and promising are practices is beyond question. In the case of promising this is shown by the fact that the form of words "I promise" is a performative utterance which presupposes the stage-setting of the practice and the proprieties defined by it. Saying the words "I promise" will only be promising given the existence of the practice. It would be absurd to interpret the rules about promising in accordance with the summary conception. It is absurd to say, for example, that the rule that promises should be kept could have arisen from its being found in past cases to be best on the whole to keep one's promise; for unless there were already the understanding that one keeps one's promises as part of the practice itself there couldn't have been any cases of promising.

It must, of course, be granted that the rules defining promising are not codified, and that one's conception of what they are necessarily depends on one's moral training. Therefore it is likely that there is considerable variation in the way people understand the practice, and room for argument as to how it is best set up. For example, differences as to how strictly various defenses are to be taken, or just what defenses are available, are likely to arise amongst persons with different backgrounds. But irrespective of these variations it belongs to the concept of the practice of promising that the general utilitarian defense is not available to the promisor. That this is so accounts for the force of the traditional objection which I have discussed. And the point I wish to make is that when one fits the utilitarian view together with the practice conception of rules, as one must in the appropriate cases, then there is nothing in that view which entails that there must be such a defense, either in the practice of promising, or in any other practice.

Punishment is also a clear case. There are many actions in the sequence of events which constitute someone's being punished which presuppose a practice. One can see this by considering the definition of punishment which I gave when discussing Carritt's criticism of utilitarianism. The definition there stated refers to such things as the normal rights of a citizen, rules of law, due process of law, trials and courts of law, statutes, etc., none of which can exist outside the elaborate stage-setting of a legal system. It is also the case that many of the actions for which people are punished presuppose practices. For example, one is punished for stealing, for trespassing and the like, which presuppose the institution of property. It is impossible to say what punishment is, or to describe a particular instance of it, without referring to offices, actions, and offenses specified by practices. Punishment is a move in an elaborate legal game and presupposes the complex of practices which make up the legal order. The same thing is true of the less formal sorts of punishment: a parent or guardian or someone in proper authority may punish a child, but no one else can.

There is one mistaken interpretation of what I have been saying which it is worthwhile to warn against. One might think that the use I am making of the distinction between justifying a practice and justifying the particular actions falling under it involves one in a definite social and political attitude in that it leads to a kind of conservatism. It might seem that I am saying that for each person the social practices of his society provide the standard of justification for his actions; therefore let each person abide by them and his conduct will be justified.

This interpretation is entirely wrong. The point I have been making is rather a logical point. To be sure, it has consequences in matters of ethical theory; but in itself it leads to no particular social or political attitude. It is simply that where a form of action is specified by a practice there is no justification possible of the particular action of a particular person save by reference to the practice. In such cases then action is what it is in virtue of the practice and to explain it is to refer to the practice. There is no inference whatsoever to be drawn with respect to whether or not one should accept the practices of one's society. One can be as radical as one likes but in the case of actions specified by practices the objects of one's radicalism must be the social practices and people's acceptance of them.

I have tried to show that when we fit the utilitarian view together with the practice conception of rules, where this conception is appropriate,[28] we can formulate it in a way which saves it from several traditional objections. I have further tried to show how the logical force of the distinction between justifying a practice and justifying an action falling under it is connected with the practice conception of rules and cannot be understood as long as one regards the rules of practices in accordance with the summary view. Why, when doing philosophy, one may be inclined to so regard them, I have not discussed. The reasons for this are evidently very deep and would require another paper.

Notes

1. This is a revision of a paper given at the Harvard Philosophy Club on April 30, 1954 ...
2. I use the word "practice" throughout as a sort of technical term meaning any form of activity specified by a system of rules which defines offices, roles, moves, penalties, defenses, and so on, and which gives the activity its structure. As examples one may think of games and rituals, trials and parliaments.
3. The distinction is central to Hume's discussion of justice in A *Treatise of Human Nature*, Bk. III, pt. II, esp. secs. 2-4. It is clearly stated by John Austin in the second lecture of *Lectures on Jurisprudence* (4th ed.; London, 1873), i, 116ff. (1st ed., 1832). Also it may be argued that J.S. Mill took it for granted in *Utilitarianism*; on this point cf. J.0. Urmson, "The Interpretation of the Moral Philosophy of J.S. Mill," *Philosophical Quarterly*, vol. iii (1953). In addition to the arguments given by Urmson there are several clear statements of the distinction in A *System of Logic* (8th ed.; London, 1872), Bk. VI, ch. xii pars. 2, 3, 7. The distinction is fundamental to J.D. Mabbott's important paper, "Punishment," *Mind*, n.s., vol. xlviii (April, 1939). More recently the distinction has been stated with particular emphasis by S.E. Toulmin in *The Place of Reason in Ethics* (Cambridge, 1950), see esp. ch. xi, where it plays a major part in his account of moral reasoning. Toulmin doesn't explain the basis of the distinction, nor how one might overlook its importance, as I try to in this paper, and in my review of his book *(Philosophical Review*, vol. lx [October, 1951]) as some of my criticisms show, I failed to understand the force of it. See also H.D. Aiken, "The Levels of Moral Discourse," *Ethics*, vol. lxii (1952); A.M. Quinton, "Punishment," *Analysis*, vol. xiv (June, 1954); and P.H. Nowell-Smith, *Ethics* (London, 1954), pp.. 236-39, 272-73.
4. On the concept of explication see the author's paper, *Philosophical Review*, vol. lx (April, 1951).
5. While this paper was being revised, Quinton's appeared; footnote 3 supra. There are several respects in which my remarks are similar to his. Yet as I consider some

further questions and rely on somewhat different arguments, I have retained the discussion of punishment and promises together as two test cases for utilitarianism.

6. Not the fact that different sorts of arguments are suited to different offices. One way of taking the differences between ethical theories is to regard them as accounts of the reasons expected in different offices.

7. On this connection see Mabbott, op. cit., pp. 163-64.

8. On this point see Sir David Ross, *The Right and the Good* (Oxford, 1930), pp. 57-60.

9. See Hobbes's definition of punishment in *Leviathan*, ch. xxviii; and Bentham's definition in *The Principle of Morals and Legislation*, ch. xii, par. 36, ch. xv, par. 28, and in *The Rationale of Punishment* (London, 1830), Bk. I, ch. i. They could agree with Bradley that: "Punishment is punishment only when it is deserved. We pay the penalty, because we owe it, and for no other reason; and if punishment is inflicted for any other reason whatever than because it is merited by wrong, it is a gross immorality, a crying injustice, an abominable crime, and not what it pretends to be." *Ethical Studies* (2nd ed.; Oxford, 1927), pp. 26-27. Certainly by definition it isn't what it pretends to be. The innocent can only be punished by mistake; deliberate "punishment" of the innocent necessarily involves fraud.

10. Cf. Leon Radzinowicz, A *History of English Criminal Law: The Movement for Reform 1750-1833* (London, 1948), esp. ch. xi on Bentham.

11. Bentham discusses how corresponding to a punitory provision of a criminal law there is another provision which stands to it as an antagonist and which needs a name as much as the punitory. He calls it, as one might expect, the *anaetiosostic*, and of it he says: "The punishment of guilt is the object of the former one: the preservation of innocence that of the latter." In the same connection he asserts that it is never thought fit to give the judge the option of deciding whether a thief (that is, a person whom he believes to be a thief, for the judge's belief is what the question must always turn upon) should hang or not, and so the law writes the provision: "The judge shall not cause a thief to be hanged unless he have been duly convicted and sentenced in course of law" (*The Limits of Jurisprudence Defined*, ed. C.W. Everett [New York, 1945], pp. 238-39).

12. By the classical utilitarians I understand Hobbes, Bentham, J.S. Mill, and Sidgwick.

13. All these features of punishment are mentioned by Hobbes; cf. *Leviathan*, ch. xxviii.

14. *Ethical and Political Thinking* (Oxford, 1947), p. 65.

15. The analogy with the price system suggests an answer to the question how utilitarian considerations ensure that punishment is proportional to the offense. It is interesting to note that Sir David Ross, after making the distinction between justifying a penal law and justifying a particular application of it, and after stating that utilitarian considerations have a large place in determining the former, still holds back from accepting the utilitarian justification of punishment on the grounds that justice requires that punishment be proportional to the offense,

and that utilitarianism is unable to account for this. Cf. *The Right and the Good,* pp. 61-62. I do not claim that utilitarianism can account for this requirement as Sir David might wish, but it happens, nevertheless, that if utilitarian considerations are followed penalties will be proportional to offenses in this sense: the order of offenses according to seriousness can be paired off with the order of penalties according to severity. Also the absolute level of penalties will be as low as possible. This follows from the assumption that people are rational (i.e., that they are able to take into account the "prices" the state puts on actions), the utilitarian rule that a penal system should provide a motive for preferring the less serious offense, and the principle that punishment as such is an evil. All this was carefully worked out by Bentham in *The Principles of Morals and Legislation,* chs. xiii-xv.

16. Ross, *The Right and the Good,* pp. 37-39, and *Foundations of Ethics* (Oxford, 1930), pp. 92-94. I know of no utilitarian who has used this argument except W.A. Pickard-Cambridge in "Two Problems about Duty," *Mind,* n.s., xli (April, 1932), 153-57, although the argument goes with G.K. Moore's version of utilitarianism in *Principia Ethica* (Cambridge, 1903). To my knowledge it does not appear in the classical utilitarians; and if one interprets their view correctly this is no accident.

17. Ross, *The Right and the Good,* pp. 38-39.

18. Ross, ibid, p. 39. The case of the nonpublic promise is discussed again in *Foundations of Ethics,* pp. 95-96, 104-05. It occurs also in Mabbott, "Punishment," op. cit., pp. 155-57, and in A.I. Melden, "Two Comments on Utilitarianism," *Philosophical Review,* lx (October, 1951), 519-23, which discusses Carritt's example in *Ethical and Political Thinking,* p. 64.

19. Ross's example is described simply as that of two men dying alone where one makes a promise to the other. Carritt's example (cf. n. 17 supra) [Note 1. Ed] is that of two men at the North Pole. The example in the text is more realistic and is similar to Mabbott's. Another example is that of being told something in confidence by one who subsequently dies. Such cases need not be "desert-island arguments" as Nowell-Smith seems to believe (cf. his *Ethics,* pp. 239-44).

20. What I have said in this paragraph seems to me to coincide with Hume's important discussion in the *Treatise of Human Nature,* Bk. III, pt. II, sec. 5; and also sec. 6, par. 8.

21. For a discussion of these, see H. Sidgwick, *The Methods of Ethics* (6th ed.; London, 1901), Bk. III, ch.vi.

22. They were among the leading economists and political theorists of their day, and they were not infrequently reformers interested in practical affairs. So far as I can see it is not until Moore that the doctrine is expressly stated in this way. See, for example, *Principia Ethica,* p. 147, where it is said that the statement "I am morally bound to perform this action" is identical with the statement "*This* action will produce the greatest possible amount of good in the Universe" (my italics). It is important to remember that those whom I have called the classical utilitarians were largely interested in social institutions. Utilitarianism historically goes together with a coherent view of society, and is not simply an ethical theory, much

less an attempt at philosophical analysis in the modern sense. The utilitarian principle was quite naturally thought of, and used, as a criterion for judging social institutions (practices) and as a basis for urging reforms. It is not clear, therefore, how far it is necessary to amend utilitarianism in its classical form. For a discussion of utilitarianism as an integral part of a theory of society, see L. Robbins, *The Theory of Economic Policy in English Classical Political Economy* (London, 1952).

23.   This footnote should be read after sec. 3 and presupposes what I have said there. It provides a few references to statements by leading utilitarians of the summary conception. In general it appears that when they discussed the logical features of rules the summary conception prevailed and that it was typical of the way they talked about moral rules. I cite a rather lengthy group of passages from Austin as a full illustration.

John Austin in his *Lectures on Jurisprudence* meets the objection that deciding in accordance with the utilitarian principle case by case is impractical by saying that this is a misinterpretation of utilitarianism. According to the utilitarian view "... our conduct would conform to *rules* inferred from the tendencies of actions, but would not be determined by a direct resort to the principle of general utility. Utility would be the test of our conduct, ultimately, but not immediately: the immediate test of the rules to which our conduct would conform, but not the immediate test of specific or individual actions. Our rules would be fashioned on utility; our conduct, on our rules" (vol. 1, p. 116). As to how one decides on the tendency of an action he says: "If we would try the tendency of a specific or individual act, we must not contemplate the act as if it were single and insulated, but must look at the class of acts to which it belongs. We must suppose that acts of the class were generally done or omitted, and consider the probable effect upon the general happiness or good. We must guess the consequences which would follow, if the class of acts were general; and also the consequences which would follow, if they were generally omitted. We must then compare the consequences on the positive and negative sides, and determine on which of the two the *balance* of advantage lies.... If we truly try the tendency of a specific or individual act, we try the tendency of the class to which that act belongs. The *particular* conclusion which we draw, with regard to the single act, implies a *general* conclusion embracing all similar acts.... To the rules thus inferred, and lodged in the memory, our conduct would conform *immediately* if it were truly adjusted to utility" (ibid., p. 117). One might think that Austin meets the objection by stating the practice conception of rules; and perhaps he did intend to. But it is not clear that he has stated this conception. Is the generality he refers to of the statistical sort? This is suggested by the notion of tendency. Or does he refer to the utility of setting up a practice? I don't know; but what suggests the summary view is his subsequent remarks. He says: "To consider the specific consequences of single or individual acts, would *seldom* [my italics] consist with that ultimate principle" (ibid., p. 117). But would one ever do this? He continues: "... this being admitted, the necessity of pausing and calculating, which the objection in question supposes, is an imagined necessity. To preface each act or forbearance by a conjecture and comparison of consequences, were clearly *superfluous* [my italics] and mischievous. It were clearly superfluous, inasmuch as the *result of that process* [my italics] would be embodied in a known *rule*. It were clearly mischievous, inasmuch as the *true* result would be expressed by that rule, whilst the process would probably be faulty, if it were done on the spur of the occasion" (ibid., pp. 117-18). He goes on: "If our experience and observation of particulars were not *generalized,* our experience and observation of particulars would seldom avail us in *practice....* The inferences suggested to our minds by repeated experience and observation are, therefore, drawn into *principles,* or compressed into *maxims.* These we carry about us ready for us ... and apply to individual cases promptly ... without reverting to the process by which they were obtained; or without recalling, and arraying before our minds, the numerous and intricate considerations of which they are *handy abridgments* [my italics].... True theory is a *compendium* of particular truths.... Speaking then, generally, human conduct is inevitably *guided* [my italics] by *rules,* or by *principles* or *maxims*" (ibid., pp. 117-18). I need not trouble to show how all these remarks incline to the summary view. Further, when Austin comes to deal with cases "of comparatively rare occurrence" he holds that specific considerations may outweigh the general. "Looking at the reasons from which we had inferred the rule, it were absurd to think it inflexible. We should therefore dismiss the *rule,* resort directly to the *principle* upon which our rules were fashioned; and calculate *specific* consequences to the best of our knowledge and ability" (ibid., pp. 120-121). Austin's view is interesting because it shows how one may come close to the practice conception and then slide away from it.

In *A System of Logic,* Bk. VI, ch. xii, par. 2, Mill distinguishes clearly between the position of judge and legislator and in doing so suggests the distinction between the two concepts of rules. However, he distinguishes the two positions to illustrate the difference between cases where one is to apply a rule already established and cases where one must formulate a rule to govern subsequent conduct. It's the latter case that interests him and he takes the "maxim of policy" of a legislator as typical of rules. In par. 3 the summary conception is very clearly stated. For example, he says of rules of conduct that they should be taken provisionally, as they are made for the most numerous cases. He says that they "point out" the manner in which it is least perilous to act; they serve as an "admonition" that a certain mode of conduct has been found suited to the most common occurrences. In *Utilitarianism,* ch. ii, par. 24, the summary conception appears in Mill's answer to the same objection Austin considered. Here he speaks of rules as "corollaries" from the principle of utility; these "secondary" rules are compared to "landmarks" and "direction-posts." They are based on long experience and so make it unnecessary to apply the utilitarian principle to each case. In par. 25 Mill refers to the task of the utilitarian principle in adjudicating between competing moral rules. He talks here as if one then applies the utilitarian principle directly to the particular case. On the practice view one would rather use the principle to decide which of the ways that make the practice consistent is the best. It should be noted that while in par. 10 Mill's definition of utilitarianism makes the utilitarian principle apply to morality, i.e., to the rules and precepts of human conduct, the definition in par. 2 uses the phrase "actions are right in *proportion* as they *tend* to promote happiness" [my italics] and this inclines towards the summary view. In the last paragraph of the essay "On the Definition of Political Economy," *Westminster Review* (October, 1836), Mill says that it is only in art, as distinguished from science, that one can properly speak of exceptions. In a question of practice, if something is fit to be done "in the majority of cases" then it is made the rule. "We may ... in talking of art *unobjectionably* speak of the *rule* and the *exception*, meaning by the rule the cases in which there exists a preponderance ... of inducements for acting in a particular way; and by the exception, the cases in which the preponderance is on the contrary side." These remarks, too, suggest the summary view.

In Moore's *Principia Ethica*, ch. v, there is a complicated and difficult discussion of moral rules. I will not examine it here except to express my suspicion that the summary conception prevails. To be sure, Moore speaks frequently of the utility of rules as generally followed, and of actions as generally practiced, but it is possible that these passages fit the statistical notion of generality which the summary conception allows. This conception is suggested by Moore's taking the utilitarian principle as applying directly to particular actions (pp. 147-48) and by his notion of a rule as something indicating which of the few alternatives likely to occur to anyone will generally produce a greater total good in the immediate future (p. 154). He talks of an "ethical law" as a prediction, and as a generalization (pp. 146, 155). The summary conception is also suggested by his discussion of exceptions (pp, 162-63) and of the force of examples of breaching a rule (pp. 163-64).

24. One might feel that it is a mistake to say that a practice is logically prior to the forms of action it specifies on the grounds that if there were never any instances of actions falling under a practice then we should be strongly inclined to say that there wasn't the practice either. Blue-prints for a practice do not make a practice. That there is a practice entails that there are instances of people having been engaged and now being engaged in it (with suitable qualifications). This is correct, but it doesn't hurt the claim that any given particular instance of a form of action specified by a practice presupposes the practice. This isn't so on the summary picture, as each instance must be "there" prior to the rules, so to speak, as something from which one gets the rule by applying the utilitarian principle to it directly.

25. A philosophical joke (in the mouth of Jeremy Bentham): "When I run to the other wicket after my partner has struck a good ball I do so because it is best on the whole."

26. How do these remarks apply to the case of the promise known only to father and son? Well, at first sight the son certainly holds the office of promisor, and so he isn't allowed by the practice to weigh the particular case on general utilitarian grounds. Suppose instead that he wishes to consider himself in the office of one

empowered to criticize and change the practice, leaving aside the question as to his right to move from his previously assumed office to another. Then he may consider utilitarian arguments as applied to the practice; but once he does this he will see that there are such arguments for not allowing a general utilitarian defense in the practice for this sort of case. For to do so would make it impossible to ask for and to give a kind of promise which one often wants to be able to ask for and to give. Therefore he will not want to change the practice, and so as a promisor he has no option but to keep his promise.

27. *Philosophical Investigations* (Oxford, 1953), I, pars. 65-71, for example.

28. As I have already stated, it is not always easy to say where the conception is appropriate. Nor do I care to discuss at this point the general sorts of cases to which it does apply except to say that one should not take it for granted that it applies to many so-called "moral rules." It is my feeling that relatively few actions of the moral life are defined by practices and that the practice conception is more relevant to understanding legal and legal-like arguments than it is to the more complex sort of moral arguments. Utilitarianism must be fitted to different conceptions of rules depending on the case, and no doubt the failure to do this has been one source of difficulty in interpreting it correctly.

10.

THE EXPERIENCE MACHINE

❦ ❦ ❦

ROBERT NOZICK

Robert Nozick (1938-2002) was a professor of philosophy at Harvard Universi-
ty. Although he was best known for his work in social and political philosophy,
he contributed to other areas of philosophy as well. In the following selection from
his book Anarchy, State and Utopia, *Nozick argues that it is not the case that*
only pleasure matters to us. If that were so, we would have excellent reason to be
hooked up to an experience machine that would cause us to have all of our
favourite sensations. But, Nozick argues, few of us would agree to be connected
to such a machine.

There are also substantial puzzles when we ask what matters other than how
people's experiences feel "from the inside." Suppose there were an experience
machine that would give you any experience you desired. Superduper neu-
ropsychologists could stimulate your brain so that you would think and feel
you were writing a great novel, or making a friend, or reading an interesting
book. All the time you would be floating in a tank, with electrodes attached
to your brain. Should you plug into this machine for life, preprogramming
your life's experiences? If you are worried about missing out on desirable
experiences, we can suppose that business enterprises have researched thoroughly the lives of many others. You can pick and choose from their large
library or smorgasbord of such experiences, selecting your life's experiences
for, say, the next two years. After two years have passed, you will have ten min-
utes or ten hours out of the tank, to select the experiences of your *next* two
years. Of course, while in the tank you won't know that you're there; you'll
think it's all actually happening. Others can also plug in to have the experiences they want, so there's no need to stay unplugged to serve them. (Ignore
problems such as who will service the machines if everyone plugs in.) Would
you plug in? *What else can matter to us, other than how our lives feel from the inside?*
Nor should you refrain because of the few moments of distress between the
moment you've decided and the moment you're plugged. What's a few
moments of distress compared to a lifetime of bliss (if that's what you
choose), and why feel any distress at all if your decision is the best one?

What does matter to us in addition to our experiences? First, we want to *do*
certain things, and not just have the experience of doing them. In the case of

certain experiences, it is only because first we want to do the actions that we want the experiences of doing them or thinking we've done them. (But why do we want to do the activities rather than merely to experience them?) A second reason for not plugging in is that we want to *be* a certain way, to be a certain sort of person. Someone floating in a tank is an indeterminate blob. There is no answer to the question of what a person is like who has long been in the tank. Is he courageous, kind, intelligent, witty, loving? It's not merely that it's difficult to tell; there's no way he is. Plugging into the machine is a kind of suicide. It will seem to some, trapped by a picture, that nothing about what we are like can matter except as it gets reflected in our experiences. But should it be surprising that what *we are* is important to us? Why should we be concerned only with how our time is filled, but not with what we are?

Thirdly, plugging into an experience machine limits us to a man-made reality, to a world no deeper or more important than that which people can construct. There is no *actual* contact with any deeper reality, though the experience of it can be simulated. Many persons desire to leave themselves open to such contact and to a plumbing of deeper significance.[1] This clarifies the intensity of the conflict over psychoactive drugs, which some view as mere local experience machines, and others view as avenues to a deeper reality; what some view as equivalent to surrender to the experience machine, others view as following one of the reasons *not* to surrender!

We learn that something matters to us in addition to experience by imagining an experience machine and then realizing that we would not use it. We can continue to imagine a sequence of machines each designed to fill lacks suggested for the earlier machines. For example, since the experience machine doesn't meet our desire to *be* a certain way, imagine a transformation machine which transforms us into whatever sort of person we'd like to be (compatible with our staying us). Surely one would not use the transformation machine to become as one would wish, and thereupon plug into the experience machine![2] So something matters in addition to one's experiences *and* what one is like. Nor is the reason merely that one's experiences are unconnected with what one is like. For the experience machine might be limited to provide only experiences possible to the sort of person plugged in. Is it that we want to make a difference in the world? Consider then the result machine, which produces in the world any result you would produce and injects your vector input into any joint activity. We shall not pursue here the fascinating details of these or other machines. What is most disturbing about them is their living of our lives for us. Is it misguided to search for particular additional functions beyond the competence of machines to do for us? Perhaps what we desire is to live (an active verb) ourselves, in contact with reality. (And this, machines cannot do for us.) Without elaborating on the implications of this, which I believe connect surprisingly with issues about free will and causal accounts of knowledge, we need merely note the intricacy of the question of what matters *for people* other than their experiences. Until one finds a satisfactory answer, and determines that this answer does not *also* apply to animals, one cannot reasonably claim that only the felt experiences of animals limit what we may do to them.

Notes

1. Traditional religious views differ on the *point of* contact with a transcendent reality. Some say that contact yields eternal bliss or Nirvana, but they have not distinguished this sufficiently from merely a *very* long run on the experience machine. Others think it is intrinsically desirable to do the will of a higher being which created us all, though presumably no one would think this if we discovered we had been created as an object of amusement by some superpowerful child from another galaxy or dimension. Still others imagine an eventual merging with a higher reality, leaving unclear its desirability, or where that merging leaves *us*.

2. Some wouldn't use the transformation machine at all; it seems like *cheating*. But the one-time use of the transformation machine would not remove all challenges; there would still be obstacles for the new us to overcome, a new plateau from which to strive even higher. And is this plateau any the less earned or deserved than that provided by genetic endowment and early childhood environment? But if the transformation machine could be used indefinitely often, so that we could accomplish anything by pushing a button to transform ourselves into someone who could do it easily, there would remain no limits we *need* to strain against or try to transcend. Would there be anything left to *do*? *Do* some theological views place God outside of time because an omniscient omnipotent being couldn't fill up his days?

11.
RICH AND POOR

✿ ✿ ✿

PETER SINGER

Peter Singer is professor of philosophy at Princeton University. He has written extensively on social and political issues and has been a strong advocate of animal rights. In the following selection from Practical Ethics, *Singer argues that we have an obligation to assist those who are hungry. His argument rests on the principle that if it is in our power to prevent something bad from happening, without thereby sacrificing anything of comparable moral significance, then we ought to do it. However, utilitarians may be more readily inclined to accept Singer's principle than non-utilitarians.*

Some Facts About Poverty

... Consider these facts: by the most cautious estimates, 400 million people lack the calories, protein, vitamins, and minerals needed to sustain their bodies and minds in a healthy state. Millions are constantly hungry; others suffer from deficiency diseases and from infections they would be able to resist on a better diet. Children are the worst affected. According to one study, 14 million children under five die every year from the combined effects of malnutrition and infection. In some districts half the children born can be expected to die before their fifth birthday.

Nor is lack of food the only hardship of the poor. To give a broader picture, Robert McNamara, when president of the World Bank, suggested the term "absolute poverty." The poverty we are familiar with in industrialised nations is relative poverty—meaning that some citizens are poor, relative to the wealth enjoyed by their neighbours. People living in relative poverty in Australia might be quite comfortably off by comparison with pensioners in Britain, and British pensioners are not poor in comparison with the poverty that exists in Mali or Ethiopia. Absolute poverty, on the other hand, is poverty by any standard. In McNamara's words:

> Poverty at the absolute level ... is life at the very margin of existence. The absolute poor are severely deprived human beings struggling to survive in a set of squalid and degraded circumstances almost beyond the power of our sophisticated imaginations and privileged circumstances to conceive.

Compared to those fortunate enough to live in developed countries, individuals in the poorest nations have:
  An infant mortality rate eight times higher
  A life expectancy one-third lower;
  An adult literacy rate 60 per cent less;
  A nutritional level, for one out of every two in the population, below acceptable standards;
  And for millions of infants, less protein than is sufficient to permit optimum development of the brain.

McNamara has summed up absolute poverty as "a condition of life so characterised by malnutrition, illiteracy, disease, squalid surroundings, high infant mortality and low life expectancy as to be beneath any reasonable definition of human decency."

Absolute poverty is, as McNamara has said, responsible for the loss of countless lives, especially among infants and young children. When absolute poverty does not cause death, it still causes misery of a kind not often seen in the affluent nations. Malnutrition in young children stunts both physical and mental development. According to the United Nations Development Programme, 180 million children under the age of five suffer from serious malnutrition. Millions of people on poor diets suffer from deficiency diseases, like goitre, or blindness caused by a lack of vitamin A. The food value of what the poor eat is further reduced by parasites such as hookworm and ringworm, which are endemic in conditions of poor sanitation and health education.

Death and disease apart, absolute poverty remains a miserable condition of life, with inadequate food, shelter, clothing, sanitation, health services, and education. The Worldwatch Institute estimates that as many as 1.2 billion people—or 23 per cent of the world's population—live in absolute poverty. For the purposes of this estimate, absolute poverty is defined as "the lack of sufficient income in cash or kind to meet the most basic biological needs for food, clothing, and shelter." Absolute poverty is probably the principal cause of human misery today.

Some Facts About Wealth

This is the background situation, the situation that prevails on our planet all the time. It does not make headlines. People died from malnutrition and related diseases yesterday, and more will die tomorrow. The occasional droughts, cyclones, earthquakes, and floods that take the lives of tens of thousands in one place and at one time are more newsworthy. They add greatly to the total amount of human suffering; but it is wrong to assume that when there are no major calamities reported, all is well.

The problem is not that the world cannot produce enough to feed and shelter its people. People in the poor countries consume, on average, 180 kilos of grain a year, while North Americans average around 900 kilos. The difference is caused by the fact that in the rich countries we feed most of our grain to animals, converting it into meat, milk, and eggs. Because this is a highly inefficient process, people in rich countries are responsible for the consumption of far more food than those in poor countries who eat few animal products. If we stopped feeding animals on grains and soybeans, the amount of food saved would—if distributed to those who need it—be more than enough to end hunger throughout the world.

These facts about animal food do not mean that we can easily solve the world food problem by cutting down on animal products, but they show that the problem is essentially one of distribution rather than production. The world does produce enough food. Moreover, the poorer nations themselves could produce far more if they made more use of improved agricultural techniques.

So why are people hungry? Poor people cannot afford to buy grain grown by farmers in the richer nations. Poor farmers cannot afford to buy improved seeds, or fertilisers, or the machinery needed for drilling wells and pumping water. Only by transferring some of the wealth of the rich nations to the poor can the situation be changed.

That this wealth exists is clear. Against the picture of absolute poverty that McNamara has painted, one might pose a picture of "absolute affluence." Those who are absolutely affluent are not necessarily affluent by comparison with their neighbours, but they are affluent by any reasonable definition of human needs. This means that they have more income than they need to provide themselves adequately with all the basic necessities of life. After buying (either directly or through their taxes) food, shelter, clothing, basic health services, and education, the absolutely affluent are still able to spend money on luxuries. The absolutely affluent choose their food for the pleasures of the palate, not to stop hunger; they buy new clothes to look good, not to keep warm; they move house to be in a better neighbourhood or have a playroom for the children, not to keep out the rain; and after all this there is still money to spend on stereo systems, video-cameras, and overseas holidays.

At this stage I am making no ethical judgments about absolute affluence, merely pointing out that it exists. Its defining characteristic is a significant amount of income above the level necessary to provide for the basic human needs of oneself and one's dependents. By this standard, the majority of citizens of Western Europe, North America, Japan, Australia, New Zealand, and the oil-rich Middle Eastern states are all absolutely affluent. To quote McNamara once more: "The average citizen of a developed country enjoys wealth beyond the wildest dreams of the one billion people in countries with per capita incomes under $200." These, therefore, are the countries—and individuals—who have wealth that they could, without threatening their own basic welfare, transfer to the absolutely poor.

At present, very little is being transferred. Only Sweden, the Netherlands, Norway, and some of the oil-exporting Arab states have reached the modest target, set by the United Nations, of 0.7 per cent of gross national product (GNP). Britain gives 0.31 per cent of its GNP in official development assistance and a small additional amount in unofficial aid from voluntary organisations. The total comes to about £2 per month per person, and compares with 5.5 per cent of GNP spent on alcohol, and 3 per cent on tobacco. Other, even wealthier nations, give little more: Germany gives 0.41 per cent and Japan 0.32 per cent. The United States gives a mere 0.15 per cent of its GNP.

The Moral Equivalent of Murder?

If these are the facts, we cannot avoid concluding that by not giving more than we do, people in rich countries are allowing those in poor countries to suffer from absolute poverty, with consequent malnutrition, ill health, and death. This is not a conclusion that applies only to governments. It applies to each absolutely affluent individual, for each of us has the opportunity to do something about the situation; for instance, to give our time or money to voluntary organisations like Oxfam, Care, War on Want, Freedom from Hunger, Community Aid Abroad, and so on. If, then, allowing someone to die is not intrinsically different from killing someone, it would seem that we are all murderers.

Is this verdict too harsh? Many will reject it as self-evidently absurd. They would sooner take it as showing that allowing to die cannot be equivalent to killing than as showing that living in an affluent style without contributing to an overseas aid agency is ethically equivalent to going over to Ethiopia and shooting a few peasants. And no doubt, put as bluntly as that, the verdict is too harsh.

There are several significant differences between spending money on luxuries instead of using it to save lives, and deliberately shooting people.

First, the motivation will normally be different. Those who deliberately shoot others go out of their way to kill; they presumably want their victims dead, from malice, sadism, or some equally unpleasant motive. A person who buys a new stereo system presumably wants to enhance her enjoyment of music—not in itself a terrible thing. At worst, spending money on luxuries instead of giving it away indicates selfishness and indifference to the sufferings of others, characteristics that may be undesirable but are not comparable with actual malice or similar motives.

Second, it is not difficult for most of us to act in accordance with a rule against killing people: it is, on the other hand, very difficult to obey a rule that commands us to save all the lives we can. To live a comfortable, or even luxurious life it is not necessary to kill anyone; but it is necessary to allow some to die whom we might have saved, for the money that we need to live comfortably could have been given away. Thus the duty to avoid killing is much easier to discharge completely than the duty to save. Saving every life we could would mean cutting our standard of living down to the bare essentials needed to keep us alive.[1] To discharge this duty completely would require a degree of moral heroism utterly different from that required by mere avoidance of killing.

A third difference is the greater certainty of the outcome of shooting when compared with not giving aid. If I point a loaded gun at someone at close range and pull the trigger, it is virtually certain that the person will be killed; whereas the money that I could give might be spent on a project that turns out to be unsuccessful and helps no one.

Fourth, when people are shot there are identifiable individuals who have been harmed. We can point to them and to their grieving families. When I buy my stereo system, I cannot know who my money would have saved if I had given it away. In a time of famine I may see dead bodies and grieving families on television reports, and I might not doubt that my money would have saved some of them; even then it is impossible to point to a body and say that had I not bought the stereo, that person would have survived.

Fifth, it might be said that the plight of the hungry is not my doing, and so I cannot be held responsible for it. The starving would have been starving if I had never existed. If I kill, however, I am responsible for my victims' deaths, for those people would not have died if I had not killed them.

These differences need not shake our previous conclusion that there is no intrinsic difference between killing and allowing to die. They are extrinsic differences, that is, differences normally but not necessarily associated with the distinction between killing and allowing to die. We can imagine cases in which someone allows another to die for malicious or sadistic reasons; we can imagine a world in which there are so few people needing assistance, and they are so easy to assist, that our duty not to allow people to die is as easily discharged as our duty not to kill; we can imagine situations in which the outcome of not helping is as sure as shooting; we can imagine cases in which we can identify the person we allow to die. We can even imagine a case of allowing to die in which, if I had not existed, the person would not have died—for instance, a case in which if I had not been in a position to help (though I don't help) someone else would have been in my position and would have helped....

To explain our conventional ethical attitudes is not to justify them. Do the five differences not only explain, but also justify, our attitudes? Let us consider them one by one:

1. Take the lack of an identifiable victim first. Suppose that I am a travelling salesperson, selling tinned food, and I learn that a batch of tins contains

a contaminant, the known effect of which, when consumed, is to double the risk that the consumer will die from stomach cancer. Suppose I continue to sell the tins. My decision may have no identifiable victims. Some of those who eat the food will die from cancer. The proportion of consumers dying in this way will be twice that of the community at large, but who among the consumers died because they ate what I sold, and who would have contracted the disease anyway? It is impossible to tell; but surely this impossibility makes my decision no less reprehensible than it would have been had the contaminant had more readily detectable, though equally fatal, effects.

2. The lack of certainty that by giving money I could save a life does reduce the wrongness of not giving, by comparison with deliberate killing; but it is insufficient to show that not giving is acceptable conduct. The motorist who speeds through pedestrian crossings, heedless of anyone who might be on them, is not a murderer. She may never actually hit a pedestrian; yet what she does is very wrong indeed.

3. The notion of responsibility for acts rather than omissions is more puzzling. On the one hand, we feel ourselves to be under a greater obligation to help those whose misfortunes we have caused. (It is for this reason that advocates of overseas aid often argue that Western nations have created the poverty of third world nations, through forms of economic exploitation that go back to the colonial system.) On the other hand, any consequentialist would insist that we are responsible for all the consequences of our actions, and if a consequence of my spending money on a luxury item is that someone dies, I am responsible for that death. It is true that the person would have died even if I had never existed, but what is the relevance of that? The fact is that I do exist, and the consequentialist will say that our responsibilities derive from the world as it is, not as it might have been.

One way of making sense of the non-consequentialist view of responsibility is by basing it on a theory of rights of the kind proposed by John Locke or, more recently, Robert Nozick. If everyone has a right to life, and this right is a right *against* others who might threaten my life, but not a right to assistance from others when my life is in danger, then we can understand the feeling that we are responsible for acting to kill but not for omitting to save. The former violates the rights of others, the latter does not.

Should we accept such a theory of rights? If we build up our theory of rights by imagining, as Locke and Nozick do, individuals living independently from each other in a "state of nature," it may seem natural to adopt a conception of rights in which as long as each leaves the other alone, no rights are violated. I might, on this view, quite properly have maintained my independent existence if I had wished to do so. So if I do not make you any worse off than you would have been if I had had nothing at all to do with you, how can I have violated your rights? But why start from such an unhistorical, abstract and ultimately inexplicable idea as an independent individual? Our ancestors were—like other primates—social beings long before they were human beings, and could not have developed the abilities and capacities of human beings if they had not been social beings first. In any case, we are not, now, isolated individuals. So why should we assume that rights must be restricted to rights against interference? We might, instead, adopt the view that taking rights to life seriously is incompatible with standing by and watching people die when one could easily save them.

4. What of the difference in motivation? That a person does not positively wish for the death of another lessens the severity of the blame she deserves; but not by as much as our present attitudes to giving aid suggest. The behaviour of the speeding motorist is again comparable, for such motorists usually have no desire at all to kill anyone. They merely enjoy speeding and are indifferent to the consequences. Despite their lack of malice, those who kill with cars deserve not only blame but also severe punishment.

5. Finally, the fact that to avoid killing people is normally not difficult, whereas to save all one possibly could save is heroic, must make an important difference to our attitude to failure to do what the respective principles demand. Not to kill is a minimum standard of acceptable conduct we can require of everyone; to save all one possibly could is not something that can realistically be required, especially not in societies accustomed to giving as little as ours do. Given the generally accepted standards, people who give, say, $1,000 a year to an overseas aid organisation are more aptly praised for above average generosity than blamed for giving less than they might. The appropriateness of praise and blame is, however, a separate issue from the rightness or wrongness of actions. The former evaluates the agent: the latter evaluates the action. Perhaps many people who give $1,000 really ought to give at least $5,000, but to blame them for not giving more could be counterproductive. It might make them feel that what is required is too demanding, and if one is going to be blamed anyway, one might as well not give anything at all.

(That an ethic that put saving all one possibly can on the same footing as not killing would be an ethic for saints or heroes should not lead us to assume that the alternative must be an ethic that makes it obligatory not to kill, but puts us under no obligation to save anyone. There are positions in between these extremes, as we shall soon see.)

Here is a summary of the five differences that normally exist between killing and allowing to die, in the context of absolute poverty and overseas aid. The lack of an identifiable victim is of no moral significance, though it may play an important role in explaining our attitudes. The idea that we are directly responsible for those we kill, but not for those we do not help, depends on a questionable notion of responsibility and may need to be based on a controversial theory of rights. Differences in certainty and motivation are ethically significant, and show that not aiding the poor is not to be condemned as murdering them; it could, however, be on a par with killing some-

one as a result of reckless driving, which is serious enough. Finally the difficulty of completely discharging the duty of saving all one possibly can makes
it inappropriate to blame those who fall short of this target as we blame those
who kill; but this does not show that the act itself is less serious. Nor does it
indicate anything about those who, far from saving all they possibly can, make
no effort to save anyone.

These conclusions suggest a new approach. Instead of attempting to deal
with the contrast between affluence and poverty by comparing not saving
with deliberate killing, let us consider afresh whether we have an obligation
to assist those whose lives are in danger, and if so, how this obligation applies
to the present world situation.

The Obligation to Assist

The Argument for an Obligation to Assist

The path from the library at my university to the humanities lecture theatre
passes a shallow ornamental pond. Suppose that on my way to give a lecture
I notice that a small child has fallen in and is in danger of drowning. Would
anyone deny that I ought to wade in and pull the child out? This will mean
getting my clothes muddy and either cancelling my lecture or delaying it
until I can find something dry to change into; but compared with the avoidable death of a child this is insignificant.

A plausible principle that would support the judgment that I ought to pull
the child out is this: if it is in our power to prevent something very bad from
happening, without thereby sacrificing anything of comparable moral significance, we ought to do it. This principle seems uncontroversial. It will obviously win the assent of consequentialists; but non-consequentialists should
accept it too, because the injunction to prevent what is bad applies only when
nothing comparably significant is at stake. Thus the principle cannot lead to
the kinds of actions of which non-consequentialists strongly disapprove—serious violations of individual rights, injustice, broken promises, and so on. If
non-consequentialists regard any of these as comparable in moral significance to the bad thing that is to be prevented, they will automatically regard
the principle as not applying in those cases in which the bad thing can only
be prevented by violating rights, doing injustice, breaking promises, or whatever else is at stake. Most non-consequentialists hold that we ought to prevent
what is bad and promote what is good. Their dispute with consequentialists
lies in their insistence that this is not the sole ultimate ethical principle: that
it is an ethical principle is not denied by any plausible ethical theory.

Nevertheless the uncontroversial appearance of the principle that we
ought to prevent what is bad when we can do so without sacrificing anything

of comparable moral significance is deceptive. If it were taken seriously and acted upon, our lives and our world would be fundamentally changed. For the principle applies, not just to rare situations in which one can save a child from a pond, but to the everyday situation in which we can assist those living in absolute poverty. In saying this I assume that absolute poverty, with its hunger and malnutrition, lack of shelter, illiteracy, disease, high infant mortality, and low life expectancy, is a bad thing. And I assume that it is within the power of the affluent to reduce absolute poverty, without sacrificing anything of comparable moral significance. If these two assumptions and the principle we have been discussing are correct, we have an obligation to help those in absolute poverty that is no less strong than our obligation to rescue a drowning child from a pond. Not to help would be wrong, whether or not it is intrinsically equivalent to killing. Helping is not, as conventionally thought, a charitable act that it is praiseworthy to do, but not wrong to omit; it is something that everyone ought to do.

This is the argument for an obligation to assist. Set out more formally, it would look like this.

First premise: If we can prevent something bad without sacrificing anything of comparable significance, we ought to do it.
Second premise: Absolute poverty is bad.
Third premise: There is some absolute poverty we can prevent without sacrificing anything of comparable moral significance.
Conclusion: We ought to prevent some absolute poverty.

The first premise is the substantive moral premise on which the argument rests, and I have tried to show that it can be accepted by people who hold a variety of ethical positions.

The second premise is unlikely to be challenged. Absolute poverty is, as McNamara put it, "beneath any reasonable definition of human decency" and it would be hard to find a plausible ethical view that did not regard it as a bad thing.

The third premise is more controversial, even though it is cautiously framed. It claims only that some absolute poverty can be prevented without the sacrifice of anything of comparable moral significance. It thus avoids the objection that any aid I can give is just "drops in the ocean" for the point is not whether my personal contribution will make any noticeable impression on world poverty as a whole (of course it won't) but whether it will prevent some poverty. This is all the argument needs to sustain its conclusion, since the second premise says that any absolute poverty is bad, and not merely the total amount of absolute poverty. If without sacrificing anything of comparable moral significance we can provide just one family with the means to raise itself out of absolute poverty, the third premise is vindicated.

I have left the notion of moral significance unexamined in order to show that the argument does not depend on any specific values or ethical principles. I think the third premise is true for most people living in industrialised nations, on any defensible view of what is morally significant. Our affluence means that we have income we can dispose of without giving up the basic necessities of life, and we can use this income to reduce absolute poverty. Just how much we will think ourselves obliged to give up will depend on what we consider to be of comparable moral significance to the poverty we could prevent: stylish clothes, expensive dinners, a sophisticated stereo system, overseas holidays, a (second?) car, a larger house, private schools for our children, and so on. For a utilitarian, none of these is likely to be of comparable significance to the reduction of absolute poverty; and those who are not utilitarians surely must, if they subscribe to the principle of universalisability, accept that at least some of these things are of far less moral significance than the absolute poverty that could be prevented by the money they cost. So the third premise seems to be true on any plausible ethical view— although the precise amount of absolute poverty that can be prevented before anything of moral significance is sacrificed will vary according to the ethical view one accepts.

Objections to the Argument

Taking care of our own. Anyone who has worked to increase overseas aid will have come across the argument that we should look after those near us, our families, and then the poor in our own country, before we think about poverty in distant places.

No doubt we do instinctively prefer to help those who are close to us. Few could stand by and watch a child drown; many can ignore a famine in Africa. But the question is not what we usually do, but what we ought to do, and it is difficult to see any sound moral justification for the view that distance, or community membership, makes a crucial difference to our obligations.

Consider, for instance, racial affinities. Should people of European origin help poor Europeans before helping poor Africans? Most of us would reject such a suggestion out of hand ... people's need for food has nothing to do with their race, and if Africans need food more than Europeans, it would be a violation of the principle of equal consideration to give preference to Europeans.

The same point applies to citizenship or nationhood. Every affluent nation has some relatively poor citizens, but absolute poverty is limited largely to the poor nations. Those living on the streets of Calcutta, or in the drought-prone Sahel region of Africa, are experiencing poverty unknown in the West. Under these circumstances it would be wrong to decide that only those fortunate enough to be citizens of our own community will share our abundance.

We feel obligations of kinship more strongly than those of citizenship. Which parents could give away their last bowl of rice if their own children were starving? To do so would seem unnatural, contrary to our nature as biologically evolved beings—although whether it would be wrong is another question altogether. In any case, we are not faced with that situation, but with one in which our own children are well-fed, well-clothed, well-educated, and would now like new bikes, a stereo set, or their own car. In these circumstances any special obligations we might have to our children have been fulfilled, and the needs of strangers make a stronger claim upon us.

The element of truth in the view that we should first take care of our own, lies in the advantage of a recognised system of responsibilities. When families and local communities look after their own poorer members, ties of affection and personal relationships achieve ends that would otherwise require a large, impersonal bureaucracy. Hence it would be absurd to propose that from now on we all regard ourselves as equally responsible for the welfare of everyone in the world; but the argument for an obligation to assist does not propose that. It applies only when some are in absolute poverty, and others can help without sacrificing anything of comparable moral significance. To allow one's own kin to sink into absolute poverty would be to sacrifice something of comparable significance; and before that point had been reached, the breakdown of the system of family and community responsibility would be a factor to weigh the balance in favour of a small degree of preference for family and community. This small degree of preference is, however, decisively outweighed by existing discrepancies in wealth and property.

Property rights. Do people have a right to private property, a right that contradicts the view that they are under an obligation to give some of their wealth away to those in absolute poverty? According to some theories of rights (for instance, Robert Nozick's), provided one has acquired one's property without the use of unjust means like force and fraud, one may be entitled to enormous wealth while others starve. This individualistic conception of rights is in contrast to other views, like the early Christian doctrine to be found in the works of Thomas Aquinas, which holds that since property exists for the satisfaction of human needs, "whatever a man has in superabundance is owed, of natural right, to the poor for their sustenance." A socialist would also, of course, see wealth as belonging to the community rather than the individual, while utilitarians, whether socialist or not, would be prepared to override property rights to prevent great evils.

Does the argument for an obligation to assist others therefore presuppose one of these other theories of property rights, and not an individualistic theory like Nozick's? Not necessarily. A theory of property rights can insist on our *right* to retain wealth without pronouncing on whether the rich *ought* to give to the poor. Nozick, for example, rejects the use of compulsory means like taxation to redistribute income, but suggests that we can achieve the ends we deem morally desirable by voluntary means. So Nozick would reject the claim that rich people have an "obligation" to give to the poor, in so far as this implies that the poor have a right to our aid, but might accept that giving is something we ought to do and failing to give, though within one's rights, is wrong—for there is more to an ethical life than respecting the rights of others.

The argument for an obligation to assist can survive, with only minor modifications, even if we accept an individualistic theory of property rights. In any case, however, I do not think we should accept such a theory. It leaves too much to chance to be an acceptable ethical view. For instance, those whose forefathers happened to inhabit some sandy wastes around the Persian Gulf are now fabulously wealthy, because oil lay under those sands; while those whose forefathers settled on better land south of the Sahara live in absolute poverty, because of drought and bad harvests. Can this distribution be acceptable from an impartial point of view? If we imagine ourselves about to begin life as a citizen of either Bahrain or Chad—but we do not know which—would we accept the principle that citizens of Bahrain are under no obligation to assist people living in Chad?

Population and the ethics of triage. Perhaps the most serious objection to the argument that we have an obligation to assist is that since the major cause of absolute poverty is overpopulation, helping those now in poverty will only ensure that yet more people are born to live in poverty in the future.

In its most extreme form, this objection is taken to show that we should adopt a policy of "triage." The term comes from medical policies adopted in wartime. With too few doctors to cope with all the casualties, the wounded were divided into three categories: those who would probably survive without medical assistance, those who might survive if they received assistance, but otherwise probably would not, and those who even with medical assistance probably would not survive. Only those in the middle category were given medical assistance. The idea, of course, was to use limited medical resources as effectively as possible. For those in the first category, medical treatment was not strictly necessary; for those in the third category, it was likely to be useless. It has been suggested that we should apply the same policies to countries, according to their prospects of becoming self-sustaining. We would not aid countries that even without our help will soon be able to feed their populations. We would not aid countries that, even with our help, will not be able to limit their population to a level they can feed. We would aid those countries where our help might make the difference between success and failure in bringing food and population into balance.

Advocates of this theory are understandably reluctant to give a complete list of the countries they would place into the "hopeless" category; Bangladesh has been cited as an example, and so have some of the countries of the Sahel region of Africa. Adopting the policy of triage would, then, mean cutting off assistance to these countries and allowing famine, disease, and natural disasters to reduce the population of those countries to the level at which they can provide adequately for all.

In support of this view Garrett Hardin has offered a metaphor: we in the rich nations are like the occupants of a crowded lifeboat adrift in a sea full of drowning people. If we try to save the drowning by bringing them aboard, our boat will be overloaded and we shall all drown. Since it is better that some survive than none, we should leave the others to drown. In the world today, according to Hardin, "lifeboat ethics" apply. The rich should leave the poor to starve, for otherwise the poor will drag the rich down with them.

Against this view, some writers have argued that overpopulation is a myth. The world produces ample food to feed its population, and could, according to some estimates, feed ten times as many. People are hungry not because there are too many but because of inequitable land distribution, the manipulation of third world economies by the developed nations, wastage of food in the West, and so on.

Putting aside the controversial issue of the extent to which food production might one day be increased, it is true, as we have already seen, that the world now produces enough to feed its inhabitants—the amount lost by being fed to animals itself being enough to meet existing grain shortages. Nevertheless population growth cannot be ignored. Bangladesh could, with land reform and using better techniques, feed its present population of 115 million; but by the year 2000, according to United Nations Population Division estimates, its population will be 150 million. The enormous effort that will have to go into feeding an extra 35 million people, all added to the population within a decade, means that Bangladesh must develop at full speed to stay where it is. Other low-income countries are in similar situations. By the end of the century, Ethiopia's population is expected to rise from 49 to 66 million; Somalia's from 7 to 9 million, India's from 853 to 1041 million, Zaire's from 35 to 49 million.[2]

What will happen if the world population continues to grow? It cannot do so indefinitely. It will be checked by a decline in birth rates or a rise in death rates. Those who advocate triage are proposing that we allow the population growth of some countries to be checked by a rise in death rates—that is, by increased malnutrition, and related diseases; by widespread famines; by increased infant mortality; and by epidemics of infectious diseases.

The consequences of triage on this scale are so horrible that we are inclined to reject it without further argument. How could we sit by our television sets, watching millions starve while we do nothing? Would not that be the end of all notions of human equality and respect for human life? (Those who attack the proposals for legalising euthanasia, ... saying that these proposals will weaken respect for human life, would surely do better to object to the idea that we should reduce or end our overseas aid programs, for that proposal, if implemented, would be responsible for a far greater loss of human life.) Don't people have a right to our assistance, irrespective of the consequences?

Anyone whose initial reaction to triage was not one of repugnance would be an unpleasant sort of person. Yet initial reactions based on strong feelings are not always reliable guides. Advocates of triage are rightly concerned with the long-term consequences of our actions. They say that helping the poor and starving now merely ensures more poor and starving in the future. When our capacity to help is finally unable to cope—as one day it must be—the suffering will be greater than it would be if we stopped helping now. If this is correct, there is nothing we can do to prevent absolute starvation and poverty, in the long run, and so we have no obligation to assist. Nor does it seem reasonable to hold that under these circumstances people have a right to our assistance. If we do accept such a right, irrespective of the consequences, we are saying that, in Hardin's metaphor, we should continue to haul the drowning into our lifeboat until the boat sinks and we all drown.

If triage is to be rejected it must be tackled on its own ground, within the framework of consequentialist ethics. Here it is vulnerable. Any consequentialist ethics must take probability of outcome into account. A course of action that will certainly produce some benefit is to be preferred to an alternative course that may lead to a slightly larger benefit, but is equally likely to result in no benefit at all. Only if the greater magnitude of the uncertain benefit outweighs its uncertainty should we choose it. Better one certain unit of benefit than a 10 per cent chance of five units; but better a 50 per cent chance of three units than a single certain unit. The same principle applies when we are trying to avoid evils.

The policy of triage involves a certain, very great evil: population control by famine and disease. Tens of millions would die slowly. Hundreds of millions would continue to live in absolute poverty, at the very margin of existence. Against this prospect, advocates of the policy place a possible evil that is greater still: the same process of famine and disease, taking place in, say, fifty years' time, when the world's population may be three times its present level, and the number who will die from famine, or struggle on in absolute poverty, will be that much greater. The question is: how probable is this forecast that continued assistance now will lead to greater disasters in the future?

Forecasts of population growth are notoriously fallible, and theories about the factors that affect it remain speculative. One theory, at least as plausible as any other, is that countries pass through a "demographic transition" as their standard of living rises. When people are very poor and have no access to modern medicine their fertility is high, but population is kept in check by high death rates. The introduction of sanitation, modern medical techniques, and other improvements reduces the death rate, but initially has little effect on the birth rate. Then population grows rapidly. Some poor countries, especially in sub-Saharan Africa, are now in this phase. If standards of living continue to rise, however, couples begin to realise that to have the same number of children surviving to maturity as in the past, they do not need to give birth to as many children as their parents did. The need for children to provide economic support in old age diminishes. Improved education and the emancipation and employment of women also reduce the birth-rate, and so population growth begins to level off. Most rich nations have reached this stage, and their populations are growing only very slowly, if at all.

If this theory is right, there is an alternative to the disasters accepted as inevitable by supporters of triage. We can assist poor countries to raise the living standards of the poorest members of their population. We can encourage the governments of these countries to enact land reform measures, improve education, and liberate women from a purely child-bearing role. We can also help other countries to make contraception and sterilisation widely available. There is a fair chance that these measures will hasten the onset of the demographic transition and bring population growth down to a manageable level. According to United Nations estimates, in 1965 the average woman in the third world gave birth to six children, and only 8 per cent were using some form of contraception; by 1991 the average number of children had dropped to just below four, and more than half the women in the third world were taking contraceptive measures. Notable successes in encouraging the use of contraception had occurred in Thailand, Indonesia, Mexico, Colombia, Brazil, and Bangladesh. This achievement reflected a relatively low expenditure in developing countries—considering the size and significance of the problem—of $3 billion annually, with only 20 per cent of this sum coming from developed nations. So expenditure in this area seems likely to be highly cost-effective. Success cannot be guaranteed; but the evidence suggests that we can reduce population growth by improving economic security and education, and making contraceptives more widely available. This prospect makes triage ethically unacceptable. We cannot allow millions to die from starvation and disease when there is a reasonable probability that population can be brought under control without such horrors.

Population growth is therefore not a reason against giving overseas aid, although it should make us think about the kind of aid to give. Instead of food handouts, it may be better to give aid that leads to a slowing of population growth. This may mean agricultural assistance for the rural poor, or assistance with education, or the provision of contraceptive services. Whatever kind of aid proves most effective in specific circumstances, the obligation to assist is not reduced.

One awkward question remains. What should we do about a poor and already overpopulated country that, for religious or nationalistic reasons, restricts the use of contraceptives and refuses to slow its population growth? Should we nevertheless offer development assistance? Or should we make our offer conditional on effective steps being taken to reduce the birth-rate? To the latter course, some would object that putting conditions on aid is an attempt to impose our own ideas on independent sovereign nations. So it is— but is this imposition unjustifiable? If the argument for an obligation to assist is sound, we have an obligation to reduce absolute poverty; but we have no obligation to make sacrifices that, to the best of our knowledge, have no prospect of reducing poverty in the long run. Hence we have no obligation to assist countries whose governments have policies that will make our aid ineffective. This could be very harsh on poor citizens of these countries—for they may have no say in the government's policies—but we will help more people in the long run by using our resources where they are most effective. (The same principles may apply, incidentally, to countries that refuse to take other steps that could make assistance effective—like refusing to reform systems of land holding that impose intolerable burdens on poor tenant farmers.)

Leaving it to the government. We often hear that overseas aid should be a government responsibility, not left to privately run charities. Giving privately, it is said, allows the government to escape its responsibilities.

Since increasing government aid is the surest way of making a significant increase to the total amount of aid given, I would agree that the governments of affluent nations should give much more genuine, no-strings-attached, aid than they give now. Less than one-sixth of one per cent of GNP is a scandalously small amount for a nation as wealthy as the United States to give. Even the official UN target of 0.7 per cent seems much less than affluent nations can and should give—though it is a target few have reached. But is this a reason against each of us giving what we can privately, through voluntary agencies? To believe that it is seems to assume that the more people there are who give through voluntary agencies, the less likely it is that the government will do its part. Is this plausible? The opposite view—that if no one gives voluntarily the government will assume that its citizens are not in favour of overseas aid, and will cut its programme accordingly—is more reasonable. In any case, unless there is a definite probability that by refusing to give we would be helping to bring about an increase in government assistance, refusing to give privately is wrong for the same reason that triage is wrong: it is a refusal to prevent a definite evil for the sake of a very uncertain gain. The onus of showing how a refusal to give privately will make the government give more is on those who refuse to give.

This is not to say that giving privately is enough. Certainly we should campaign for entirely new standards for both public and private overseas aid. We should also work for fairer trading arrangements between rich and poor countries, and less domination of the economies of poor countries by multinational corporations more concerned about producing profits for shareholders back home than food for the local poor. Perhaps it is more important to be politically active in the interests of the poor than to give to them one-self—but why not do both? Unfortunately, many use the view that overseas aid is the government's responsibility as a reason against giving, but not as a rea-son for being politically active.

Too high a standard? The final objection to the argument for an obligation to assist is that it sets a standard so high that none but a saint could attain it. This objection comes in at least three versions. The first maintains that, human nature being what it is, we cannot achieve so high a standard, and since it is absurd to say that we ought to do what we cannot do, we must reject the claim that we ought to give so much. The second version asserts that even if we could achieve so high a standard, to do so would be undesirable. The third version of the objection is that to set so high a standard is undesirable because it will be perceived as too difficult to reach, and will discourage many from even attempting to do so.

Those who put forward the first version of the objection are often influ-enced by the fact that we have evolved from a natural process in which those with a high degree of concern for their own interests, or the interests of their offspring and kin, can be expected to leave more descendants in future generations, and eventually to completely replace any who are entirely altruistic. Thus the biologist Garrett Hardin has argued, in support of his "lifeboat ethics," that altruism can only exist "on a small scale, over the short term, and within small, intimate groups"; while Richard Dawkins has written, in his provocative book *The Selfish Gene:* "Much as we might wish to believe otherwise, universal love and the welfare of the species as a whole are concepts which simply do not make evolutionary sense." I have already noted, in discussing the objection that we should first take care of our own, the very strong tendency for partiality in human beings. We nat-urally have a stronger desire to further our own interests, and those of our close kin, than we have to further the interests of strangers. What this means is that we would be foolish to expect widespread conformity to a standard that demands impartial concern, and for that reason it would scarcely be appropriate or feasible to condemn all those who fail to reach such a standard. Yet to act impartially, though it might be very difficult, is not impossible. The commonly quoted assertion that "ought" implies "can" is a reason for rejecting such moral judgments as "You ought to have saved all the people from the sinking ship," when in fact if you had taken one more person into the lifeboat, it would have sunk and you would not have saved any. In that situation, it is absurd to say that you ought to have done what you could not possibly do. When we have money to spend on luxuries and others are starving, however, it is clear that we can all give much more than we do give, and we can therefore all come closer to the impartial stan-dard proposed in this chapter. Nor is there, as we approach closer to this standard, any barrier beyond which we cannot go. For that reason there is no basis for saying that the impartial standard is mistaken because "ought" implies "can" and we cannot be impartial.

The second version of the objection has been put by several philosophers during the past decade, among them Susan Wolf in a forceful article entitled "Moral Saints." Wolf argues that if we all took the kind of moral stance defended in this chapter, we would have to do without a great deal that makes life interesting: opera, gourmet cooking, elegant clothes, and professional sport, for a start. The kind of life we come to see as ethically required of us would be a single-minded pursuit of the overall good, lacking that broad diversity of interests and activities that, on a less demanding view, can be part of our ideal of a good life for a human being. To this, however, one can respond that while the rich and varied life that Wolf upholds as an ideal may be the most desirable form of life for a human being in a world of plenty, it is wrong to assume that it remains a good life in a world in which buying luxuries for oneself means accepting the continued avoidable suffering of others. A doctor faced with hundreds of injured victims of a train crash can scarcely think it defensible to treat fifty of them and then go to the opera, on the grounds that going to the opera is part of a well-rounded human life. The life-or-death needs of others must take priority. Perhaps we are like the doctor in that we live in a time when we all have an opportunity to help to mitigate a disaster.

Associated with this second version of the objection is the claim that an impartial ethic of the kind advocated here makes it impossible to have serious personal relationships based on love and friendship; these relationships are, of their nature, partial. We put the interests of our loved ones, our family, and our friends ahead of those of strangers; if we did not do so, would these relationships survive? I have already indicated, in the response I gave when considering the objection that we should first take care of our own, that there is a place, within an impartially grounded moral framework, for recognising some degree of partiality for kin, and the same can be said for other close personal relationships. Clearly, for most people, personal relationships are among the necessities of a flourishing life, and to give them up would be to sacrifice something of great moral significance. Hence no such sacrifice is required by the principle for which I am here arguing.

The third version of the objection asks: might it not be counterproductive to demand that people give up so much? Might not people say: "As I can't do what is morally required anyway, I won't bother to give at all." If, however, we were to set a more realistic standard, people might make a genuine effort to reach it. Thus setting a lower standard might actually result in more aid being given.

It is important to get the status of this third version of the objection clear. Its accuracy as a prediction of human behaviour is quite compatible with the argument that we are obliged to give to the point at which by giving more we sacrifice something of comparable moral significance. What would follow from the objection is that public advocacy of this standard of giving is undesirable. It would mean that in order to do the maximum to reduce absolute poverty, we should advocate a standard lower than the amount we think people really ought to give. Of course we ourselves—those of us who accept the original argument, with its higher standard—would know that we ought to do more than we publicly propose people ought to do, and we might actually give more than we urge others to give. There is no inconsistency here, since in both our private and our public behaviour we are trying to do what will most reduce absolute poverty.

For a consequentialist, this apparent conflict between public and private morality is always a possibility, and not in itself an indication that the underlying principle is wrong. The consequences of a principle are one thing, the consequences of publicly advocating it another. A variant of this idea is already acknowledged by the distinction between the intuitive and critical levels of morality ... If we think of principles that are suitable for the intuitive level of morality as those that should be generally advocated, these are the principles that, when advocated, will give rise to the best consequences. Where overseas aid is concerned, those will be the principles that lead to the largest amount being given by the affluent to the poor.

Is it true that the standard set by our argument is so high as to be counterproductive? There is not much evidence to go by, but discussions of the argument, with students and others have led me to think it might be. Yet, the conventionally accepted standard—a few coins in a collection tin when one is waved under your nose—is obviously far too low. What level should we advocate? Any figure will be arbitrary, but there may be something to be said for a round percentage of one's income like, say, 10 per cent—more than a token donation, yet not so high as to be beyond all but saints. (This figure has the additional advantage of being reminiscent of the ancient tithe, or tenth, that was traditionally given to the church, whose responsibilities included care of the poor in one's local community. Perhaps the idea can be revived and applied to the global community.) Some families, of course, will find 10 per cent a considerable strain on their finances. Others may be able to give more without difficulty. No figure should be advocated as a rigid minimum or maximum; but it seems safe to advocate that those earning average or above average incomes in affluent societies, unless they have an unusually large number of dependents or other special needs, ought to give a tenth of their income to reducing absolute poverty. By any reasonable ethical standards this is the minimum we ought to do, and we do wrong if we do less.

Notes

1. Strictly, we would need to cut down to the minimum level compatible with earning the income which, after providing for our needs, left us most to give away. Thus if my present position earns me, say, $40,000 a year, but requires me to spend $5,000 a year on dressing respectably and maintaining a car, I cannot save more people by giving away the car and clothes if that will mean taking a job that, although it does not involve me in these expenses, earns me only $20,000.
2. Ominously, in the twelve years that have passed between editions of this book, the signs are that the situation is becoming even worse than was then predicted. In 1979 Bangladesh had a population of 80 million and it was predicted that by 2000 its population would reach 146 million; Ethiopia's was only 29 million, and was predicted to reach 54 million; and India's was 620 million and predicted to reach 958 million.

CHAPTER FIVE

DEONTOLOGY

INTRODUCTION

Deontological theories have a fundamentally different structure from consequentialist theories. As we saw in the last section, consequentialists hold that the good is a more fundamental moral concept than the right. Deontologists hold the opposite position: the right is a more fundamental concept than the good. Rather than identifying the best possible results and telling us to perform whatever actions will lead to these results, deontological theories tell us that certain actions themselves are right and others are wrong regardless of the consequences. We cannot legitimately pursue even the best results in just any way we choose. The ends do not justify the means. Some actions are simply intrinsically wrong, and we ought not perform them even in pursuit of the most noble or outstanding consequences.

In the last chapter, we saw that consequentialist theories have certain advantages. They generally offer the benefit of theoretical simplicity by giving us one fundamental moral principle in reference to which we can determine what we ought to do. Further, it seems that most of us use consequentialist reasoning at least part of the time. If given the choice between saving five people in an emergency situation or ignoring five to save one, we would generally choose to save the five, and for consequentialist reasons. And finally, the basic consequentialist claim that we should always try to produce the best results overall as judged from an impartial perspective has strong intuitive plausibility. However, we also saw that consequentialist theories may have the significant disadvantage of running afoul of our firmly held considered moral judgments. If you are a surgeon and have a number of patients who will die without organ transplants, and another patient, Smith, who can be restored to health but happens to be a perfect match for all your patients who need transplants, you may be able to produce the best results overall by killing Smith surreptitiously and harvesting his organs to save the others. But this course of action just seems wrong to most people. Our considered moral judgments tell us that Smith has a basic right to be treated in good faith and restored to health.

In general, deontological moral theories perform significantly better than consequentialist theories in accounting for our considered moral judgments. Kant's second formulation of the categorical imperative tells us that we must always act in such a way that we treat humanity, whether in our own person or in the person of any other, never merely as a means but also always at the same time as an end. This moral principle tells us that it is clearly wrong to kill Smith or to allow him to die) so that we can use his organs to save other patients. Even if the result of saving the other patients is very good, we cannot pursue this result by killing Smith. We cannot use him as a mere means to achieve our own ends, however worthwhile those ends may be. Deontological theories, then, tend to incorporate much more respect for individual rights than consequentialist theories. Unlike consequentialist theories, they do not allow us to ride roughshod over the most fundamental interests of individuals in an attempt to bring about a particular state of affairs.

Deontological theories also capture our intuitions that certain things that have happened in the past are morally relevant. Consequentialist theories are strictly forward-looking theories. They look forward from the time of the decision at issue to see how we can bring about the best possible results in the future. Deontological theories allow that backward-looking considerations can have moral significance. To take an example developed by W.D. Ross, suppose that you have made a promise to someone. It now happens that you could produce 1001 units of happiness if you break the promise, but only 1000 units of happiness if you keep the promise. A strict consequentialist will look only at the number of units of happiness you can achieve in the future, all things considered, and may therefore tell you to break the promise. Intuitively, it seems seriously wrong to break a promise for such a frivolous reason. The fact that you have made a promise in the past cannot simply be dismissed because you want to bring about the slightly better results you could achieve in the future by breaking it. On the other hand, Kant holds that deceiving persons or making false promises to them constitutes using them as a mere means to our own ends, and that it is simply wrong. Likewise, deontological theories will not allow us to punish innocent persons even if we can promote general welfare in the future by doing so. Backward-looking considerations of desert are morally significant to the deontologist. It is simply wrong to punish someone who does not deserve punishment, even if we could produce good consequences in the future by doing so.

Further, deontological theories are structured in such a way that they can accommodate our important moral conviction that our lives are largely our own to lead. Consequentialist theories hold that we must always attempt to bring about the best results overall, as judged from an impartial perspective. As Bernard Williams has pointed out, this theoretical structure can leave us with very little room to pursue our own projects and life plans. If we must always behave in this manner, it is possible at any time that other people's interests should be pursued at the expense of our own projects. We can imagine that situations of this sort may occur on a regular basis, and that therefore our lives may be extensively constrained by other people's needs. In contrast, deontological theories do not insist that we remain continuously committed to attempting to bring about certain results. Instead they articulate specific constraints on our actions, and allow us the freedom to pursue our own goals as long as we operate within these constraints.

Deontologists can also challenge the claim that consequentialist theories are more intuitively plausible than deontological theories. Initially, it does seem plausible to say that we ought to try to bring about the best results overall, as judged from an impartial perspective. But John Rawls has pointed out that there is no individual who ever experiences the best overall results. There is no being who ever experiences the sum total of happiness in the world, and no being who benefits from the sum total of preference satisfaction. As individuals, we each experience our own lives separately. Therefore a deontological theory which insists that we respect every individual may well be more intuitively plausible than a consequentialist theory that requires us to sacrifice the basic interests of some individuals in order to generate a state of affairs that will never be experienced, as a whole, by any individual person.

Nevertheless, the consequentialist might claim to have the last word in this debate. For situations in which the stakes are extremely high, we tend to revert to consequentialist reasoning. For example, during World War II much of the Western world considered it absolutely imperative to defeat Adolf Hitler. Many individual's lives were sacrificed to achieve this end, and many moral rules were broken. Although we would not consider it justifiable to abandon all moral constraints in defeating Hitler, it is not clear to what extent we would be willing to follow the constraints set out by deontological theories in this situation, or in any situation in which what is at stake is sufficiently serious. The dire global consequences of unrestrained human population growth and consumption may raise this type of ethical challenge for us in the near future.

12.

SELECTION FROM *THE FOUNDATIONS OF*
THE METAPHYSICS OF MORALS

✳ ✳ ✳

IMMANUEL KANT

Immanuel Kant (1724-1804) is one of the greatest philosophers of all time, and he made major contributions to virtually every area of philosophy. The following is a selection from The Foundations of the Metaphysics of Morals, *in which he outlines his ethical system. At the centre of his system is the claim that moral laws are categorical and not contingent on our sentiments and desires. They are necessary laws that hold for all rational beings. Moral acts are to be judged not by their consequences, but rather by the principle on which the person acted.*

First Section

Transition from the Common Rational Knowledge of Morality to the Philosophical

Nothing can possibly be conceived in the world, or even out of it, which can be called good without qualification, except a *good will.* Intelligence, wit, judgment, and the other *talents* of the mind, however they may be named, or courage, resolution, perseverance, as qualities of temperament, are undoubtedly good and desirable in many respects; but these gifts of nature may also become extremely bad and mischievous if the will which is to make use of them, and which, therefore, constitutes what is called *character,* is not good. It is the same with the *gifts of fortune.* Power, riches, honor, even health, and the general well-being and contentment with one's condition which is called *happiness,* inspire pride, and often presumption, if there is not a good will to correct the influence of these on the mind, and with this also to rectify the whole principle of acting, and adapt it to its end. The sight of a being who is not adorned with a single feature of a pure and good will, enjoying unbroken prosperity, can never give pleasure to an impartial rational spectator. Thus a good will appears to constitute the indispensable condition even of being worthy of happiness.

There are even some qualities which are of service to this good will itself, and may facilitate its actions, yet which have no intrinsic unconditional value, but always presuppose a good will, and this qualifies the esteem that we just-ly have for them, and does not permit us to regard them as absolutely good. Moderation in the affections and passions, self-control, and calm deliberation are not only good in many respects, but even seem to constitute part of the intrinsic worth of the person; but they are far deserving to be called good without qualification, although they have been so unconditionally praised by the ancients. For without the principles of a good will, they may become extremely bad; and the coolness of a villain not only makes him far more dangerous, but also directly makes him more abominable in our eyes than he would have been without it.

A good will is good not because of what it performs or effects, not by its aptness for the attainment of some proposed end, but simply by virtue of the volition—that is, it is good in itself, and considered by itself is to be esteemed much higher than all that can be brought about by it in favor of any inclination, nay, even of the sum-total of all inclinations. Even if it should happen that, owing to special disfavor of fortune, or the niggardly provision of a step-motherly nature, this will should wholly lack power to accomplish its purpose, if with its greatest efforts it should yet achieve nothing, and there should remain only the good will (not, to be sure, a mere wish, but the summoning of all means in our power), then, like a jewel, it would still shine by its own light, as a thing which has its whole value in itself. Its usefulness or fruitless-ness can neither add to nor take away anything from this value. It would be, as it were, only the setting to enable us to handle it the more conveniently in common commerce, or to attract to it the attention of those who are not yet connoisseurs, but not to recommend it to true connoisseurs, or to determine its value.

There is, however, something so strange in this idea of the absolute value of the mere will, in which no account is taken of its utility, that notwithstanding the thorough assent of even common reason to the idea, yet a suspicion must arise that it may perhaps really be the product of mere high-flown fancy, and that we may have misunderstood the purpose of nature in assigning reason as the governor of our will. Therefore we will examine this idea from this point of view....

We have then to develop the notion of a will which deserves to be highly esteemed for itself, and is good without a view to anything further, a notion which exists already in the sound natural understanding, requiring rather to be cleared up than to be taught, and which in estimating the value of our actions always takes the first place and constitutes the condition of all the rest. In order to do this, we will take the notion of duty, which includes that of a good will, although implying certain subjective restrictions and hin-drances. These, however, far from concealing it or rendering it unrecogniz-able, rather bring it out by contrast and make it shine forth so much the brighter.

I omit here all actions which are already recognized as inconsistent with duty, although they may be useful for this or that purpose, for with these the question whether they are done from *duty* cannot arise at all, since they even conflict with it. I also set aside those actions which really conform to duty, but to which men have *no* direct *inclination*, performing them because they are impelled thereto by some other inclination. For in this case we can readily distinguish whether the action which agrees with duty is done from *duty* or from a selfish view. It is much harder to make this distinction when the action accords with duty, and the subject has besides a *direct* inclination to it. For example, it is always a matter of duty that a dealer should not overcharge an inexperienced purchaser; and wherever there is much commerce the prudent tradesman does not overcharge, but keeps a fixed price for everyone, so that a child buys of him as well as any other. Men are thus *honestly* served; but this is not enough to make us believe that the tradesman has so acted from duty and from principles of honesty; his own advantage required it; it is out of the question in this case to suppose that he might besides have a direct inclination in favor of the buyers, so that, as it were, from love he should give no advantage to one over another. Accordingly the action was done neither from duty nor from direct inclination, but merely with a selfish view.

On the other hand, it is a duty to maintain one's life; and, in addition, everyone has also a direct inclination to do so. But on this account the often anxious care which most men take for it has no intrinsic worth, and their maxim has no moral import. They preserve their life *as duty requires*, no doubt, but not *because duty requires*. On the other hand, if adversity and hopeless sorrow have completely taken away the relish for life, if the unfortunate one, strong in mind, indignant at his fate rather than desponding or dejected, wishes for death, and yet preserves his life without loving it— not from inclination or fear, but from duty—then his maxim has a moral worth.

To be beneficent when we can is a duty; and besides this, there are many minds so sympathetically constituted that, without any other motive of vanity or self-interest, they find a pleasure in spreading joy around them, and can take delight in the satisfaction of others so far as it is their own work. But I maintain that in such a case an action of this kind, however proper, however amiable it may be, has nevertheless no true moral worth, but is on a level with other inclinations, for example, the inclination to honor, which, if it is happily directed to that which is in fact of public utility and accordant with duty, and consequently honorable, deserves praise and encouragement, but not esteem. For the maxim lacks the moral import, namely, that such actions be done *from duty*, not from inclination. Put the case that the mind of that philanthropist was clouded by sorrow of his own, extinguishing all sympathy with the lot of others, and that while he still has the power to benefit others in distress, he is not touched by their trouble because he is absorbed with his own; and now suppose that he tears himself out of this dead insensibility and performs the action without any inclination to it, but simply from duty, then first has his action its genuine moral worth. Further still, if nature has put little sympathy in the heart of this or that man, if he, supposed to be an upright man, is by temperament cold and indifferent to the sufferings of others, perhaps because in respect of his own he is provided with the special gift of patience and fortitude, and supposes, or even requires, that others should have the same—and such a man would certainly not be the meanest product of nature—but if nature had not specially framed him for a philanthropist, would he not still find in himself a source from whence to give himself a far higher worth than that of a good-natured temperament could be? Unquestionably. It is just in this that the moral worth of the character is brought out which is incomparably the highest of all, namely, that he is beneficent, not from inclination, but from duty....

... That an action done from duty derives its moral worth, *not from the purpose* which is to be attained by it, but from the maxim by which it is determined, and therefore does not depend on the realization of the object of the action, but merely on the *principle of volition* by which the action has taken place, without regard to any object of desire. It is clear from what precedes that the purposes which we may have in view in our actions, or their effects regarded as ends and springs of the will, cannot give to actions any unconditional or moral worth. In what, then, can their worth lie if it is not to consist in the will and in reference to its expected effect? It cannot lie anywhere but in the *principle of the will* without regard to the ends which can be attained by the action. For the will stands between its *a priori* principle, which is formal, and its *a posteriori* spring, which is material, as between two roads, and as it must be determined by something, it follows that it must be determined by the formal principle of volition when an action is done from duty, in which case every material principle has been withdrawn from it.

... *Duty is the necessity of acting from respect for the law.* I may have *inclination* for an object as the effect of my proposed action, but I cannot have *respect* for it just for this reason that it is an effect and not an energy of will. Similarly, I cannot have respect for inclination, whether my own or another's; I can at most, if my own, approve it; if another's, sometimes even love it, that is, look on it as favorable to my own interest. It is only what is connected with my will as a principle, by no means as an effect—what does not subserve my inclination, but overpowers it, or at least in case of choice excludes it from its calculation—in other words, simply the law of itself, which can be an object of respect, and hence a command. Now an action done from duty must wholly exclude the influence of inclination, and with it every object of the will, so that nothing remains which can determine the will except objectively the *law*, and subjectively *pure respect* for this practical law, and consequently the maxim[1] that I should follow this law even to the thwarting of all my inclinations.

Thus the moral worth of an action does not lie in the effect expected from it, nor in any principle of action which requires to borrow its motive from this expected effect. For all these effects—agreeableness of one's condition, and even the promotion of the happiness of others—could have been also brought about by other causes, so that for this there would have been no need of the will of a rational being; whereas it is in this alone that the supreme and unconditional good can be found. The pre-eminent good which we call moral can therefore consist in nothing else than *the conception of law* in itself, *which certainly is only possible in a rational being*, in so far as this conception, and not the expected effect, determines the will. This is a good which is already present in the person who acts accordingly, and we have not to wait for it to appear first in the result.[2]

But what sort of law can that be the conception of which must determine the will, even without paying any regard to the effect expected from it, in order that this will may be called good absolutely and without qualification? As I have deprived the will of every impulse which could arise to it from obedience to any law, there remains nothing but the universal conformity of its actions to law in general, which alone is to serve the will as a principle, that is, I am never to act otherwise than *so that I could also will that my maxim should become a universal law*. Here, now, it is the simple conformity to law in general, without assuming any particular law applicable to certain actions, that serves the will as its principle, and must so serve it if duty is not to be a vain delusion and a chimerical notion. The common reason of men in its practical judgments perfectly coincides with this, and always has in view the principle here suggested....

Second Section

Transition from Popular Moral Philosophy to the Metaphysic of Morals

... Everything in nature works according to laws. Rational beings alone have the faculty of acting according to *the conception* of laws—that is, according to principles, that is, have a *will*. Since the deduction of actions from principles requires *reason*, the will is nothing but practical reason. If reason infallibly determines the will, then the actions of such a being which are recognized as objectively necessary are subjectively necessary also, that is, the will is a faculty to choose *that only* which reason independent of inclination recognizes as practically necessary, that is, as good. But if reason of itself does not sufficiently determine the will, if the latter is subject also to subjective conditions (particular impulses) which do not always coincide with the objective conditions, in a word, if the will does not *in itself* completely accord with reason (which is actually the case with men), then the actions which objectively are recognized as necessary are subjectively contingent, and the determination of such a will according to objective laws is *obligation*, that is to say, the relation of the objective laws to a will that is not thoroughly good is conceived as the determination of the will of a rational being by principles of reason, but which the will from its nature does not of necessity follow.

The conception of an objective principle, in so far as it is obligatory for a will, is called a command (of reason), and the formula of the command is called an Imperative.

All imperatives are expressed by the word *ought* [or *shall*], and thereby indicate the relation of an objective law of reason to a will which from its subjective constitution is not necessarily determined by it (an obligation). They say that something would be good to do or to forbear, but they say it to a will which does not always do a thing because it is conceived to be good to do it. That is practically *good*, however, which determines the will by means of the conceptions of reason, and consequently not from subjective causes, but objectively, that is, on principles which are valid for every rational being as such. It is distinguished from the *pleasant* as that which influences the will only by means of sensation from merely subjective causes, valid only for the sense of this or that one, and not as a principle of reason which holds for every one.[3]

A perfectly good will would therefore be equally subject to objective laws (viz., laws of good), but could not be conceived as *obliged* thereby to act lawfully, because of itself from its subjective constitution it can only be determined by the conception of good. Therefore no imperatives hold for the Divine will, or in general for a *holy* will; *ought* is here out of place because the volition is already of itself necessarily in unison with the law. Therefore imperatives are only formulae to express the relation of objective laws of all volition to the subjective imperfection of the will of this or that rational being, for example, the human will.

Now all *imperatives* command either *hypothetically* or *categorically*. The former represent the practical necessity of a possible action as means to something else that is willed (or at least which one might possibly will). The categorical imperative would be that which represented an action as necessary of itself without reference to another end, that is, as objectively necessary.

Since every practical law represents a possible action as good, and on this account, for a subject who is practically determinable by reason as necessary, all imperatives are formulae determining an action which is necessary according to the principle of a will good in some respects. If now the action is good only as a means *to something else*, then the imperative is *hypothetical*; if it is conceived as good *in itself* and consequently as being necessarily the principle of a will which of itself conforms to reason, then it is *categorical*.

Thus the imperative declares what action possible by me would be good, and presents the practical rule in relation to a will which does not forthwith perform an action simply because it is good, whether because the subject does not always know that it is good, or because, even if it knows this, yet its maxims might be opposed to the objective principles of practical reason.

Accordingly the hypothetical imperative only says that the action is good for some purpose, *possible* or *actual.* In the first case it is a *problematical,* in the second an *assertorial* practical principle. The categorical imperative which declares an action to be objectively necessary in itself without reference to any purpose, that is, without any other end, is valid as an *apodictic* (practical) principle.

Whatever is possible only by the power of some rational being may also be conceived as a possible purpose of some will; and therefore the principles of action as regards the means necessary to attain some possible purpose are in fact infinitely numerous. All sciences have a practical part consisting of problems expressing that some end is possible for us, and of imperatives directing how it may be attained. These may, therefore, be called in general imperatives of *skill.* Here there is no question whether the end is rational and good, but only what one must do in order to attain it. The precepts for the physician to make his patient thoroughly healthy, and for a poisoner to ensure certain death, are of equal value in this respect, that each serves to effect its purpose perfectly. Since in early youth it cannot be known what ends are likely to occur to us in the course of life, parents seek to have their children taught a *great many things*, and provide for their *skill* in the use of means for all sorts of arbitrary ends, of none of which can they determine whether it may not perhaps hereafter be an object to their pupil, but which it is at all events *possible* that he might aim at; and this anxiety is so great that they commonly neglect to form and correct their judgment on the value of the things which may be chosen as ends.

There is *one* end, however, which may be assumed to be actually such to all rational beings (so far as imperatives apply to them, viz., as dependent beings), and, therefore, one purpose which they not merely *may* have, but which we may with certainty assume that they all actually *have* by a natural necessity, and this is *happiness,* The hypothetical imperative which expresses the practical necessity of an action as means to the advancement of happiness is *assertorial.* We are not to present it as necessary for an uncertain and merely possible purpose, but for a purpose which we may presuppose with certainty and *a priori* in every man, because it belongs to his being. Now skill in the choice of means to his own greatest well-being may be called *prudence*,[4] in the narrowest sense. And thus the imperative which refers to the choice of means to one's own happiness, that is, the precept of prudence, is still always *hypothetical;* the action is not commanded absolutely, but only as means to another purpose.

Finally, there is an imperative which commands a certain conduct immediately, without having as its condition any other purpose to be attained by it. This imperative is *categorical.* It concerns not the matter of the action, or its intended result, but its form and the principle of which it is itself a result; and what is essentially good in it consists in the mental disposition, let the consequence be what it may. This imperative may be called that of *morality,*....

When I conceive a hypothetical imperative, in general I do not know beforehand what it will contain until I am given the condition. But when I conceive a categorical imperative, I know at once what it contains. For as the imperative contains besides the law only the necessity that the maxims[5] shall conform to this law, while the law contains no conditions restricting it, there remains nothing but the general statement that the maxim of the action should conform to a universal law, and it is this conformity alone that the imperative properly represents as necessary.

There is therefore but one categorical imperative, namely, this: *Act only on that maxim whereby thou canst at the same time will that it should become a universal law.*

Now if all imperatives of duty can be deduced from this one imperative as from their principle, then, although it should remain undecided whether what is called duty is not merely a vain notion, yet at least we shall be able to show what we understand by it and what this notion means.

Since the universality of the law according to which effects are produced constitutes what is properly called *nature* in the most general sense (as to form)—that is, the existence of things so far as it is determined by general laws—the imperative of duty may be expressed thus: *Act as if the maxim of thy action were to become by thy will a universal law of nature.*

We will now enumerate a few duties, adopting the usual division of them into duties to ourselves and to others, and into perfect and imperfect duties.[6]

1. A man reduced to despair by a series of misfortunes feels wearied of life, but is still so far in possession of his reason that he can ask himself whether it would not be contrary to his duty to himself to take his own life. Now he inquires whether the maxim of his action could become a universal law of nature. His maxim is: From self-love I adopt it as a principle to shorten my life when its longer duration is likely to bring more evil than satisfaction. It is asked then simply whether this principle founded on self-love can become a universal law of nature. Now we see at once that a system of nature of which it should be a law to destroy life by means of the very feeling whose special nature it is to impel to the improvement of life would contradict itself, and therefore could not exist as a system of nature; hence that maxim cannot possibly exist as a universal law of nature, and consequently would be wholly inconsistent with the supreme principle of all duty.

2. Another finds himself forced by necessity to borrow money. He knows that he will not be able to repay it, but sees also that nothing will be lent to him unless he promises stoutly to repay it in a definite time. He desires to make this promise, but he has still so much conscience as to ask himself: Is it not unlawful and inconsistent with duty to get out of a difficulty in this way? Suppose, however, that he resolves to do so, then the maxim of his action would be expressed thus: When I think myself in want of money, I will borrow money and promise to repay it, although I know that I never can do so. Now this principle of self-love or of one's own advantage may perhaps be consistent with my whole future welfare; but the question now is, Is it right? I change then the suggestion of self-love into a universal law, and state the question thus: How would it be if my maxim were a universal law? Then I see at once that it could never hold as a universal law of nature, but would necessarily contradict itself. For supposing it to be a universal law that everyone when he thinks himself in a difficulty should be able to promise whatever he pleases, with the purpose of not keeping his promise, the promise itself would become impossible, as well as the end that one might have in view in it, since no one would consider that anything was promised to him, but would ridicule all such statements as vain pretenses.

3. A third finds in himself a talent which with the help of some culture might make him a useful man in many respects. But he finds himself in comfortable circumstances and prefers to indulge in pleasure rather than to take pains in enlarging and improving his happy natural capacities. He asks, however, whether his maxim of neglect of his natural gifts, besides agreeing with his inclination to indulgence, agrees also with what is called duty. He sees then that a system of nature could indeed subsist with such a universal law, although men (like the South Sea islanders) should let their talents rest and resolve to devote their lives merely to idleness, amusement, and propagation of their species—in a word, to enjoyment; but he cannot possibly *will* that this should be a universal law of nature, or be implanted in us as such by a natural instinct. For, as a rational being, he necessarily wills that his faculties be developed, since they serve him, and have been given him, for all sorts of possible purposes.

4. A fourth, who is in prosperity, while he sees that others have to contend with great wretchedness and that he could help them, thinks: What concern is it of mine? Let everyone be as happy as Heaven pleases, or as he can make himself; I will take nothing from him nor even envy him, only I do not wish to contribute anything to his welfare or to his assistance in distress! Now no doubt, if such a mode of thinking were a universal law, the human race might very well subsist, and doubtless even better than in a state in which everyone talks of sympathy and good-will, or even takes care occasionally to put it into practice, but, on the other side, also cheats when he can, betrays the rights of men, or otherwise violates them. But although it is possible that a universal

law of nature might exist in accordance with that maxim, it is impossible to *will* that such a principle should have the universal validity of a law of nature. For a will which resolved this would contradict itself, inasmuch as many cases might occur in which one would have the need of the love and sympathy of others, and in which, by such a law of nature, sprung from his own will, he would deprive himself of all hope of the aid he desires.

These are a few of the many actual duties, or at least what we regard as such, which obviously fall into two classes on the one principle that we have laid down. We must be *able to will* that a maxim of our action should be a universal law. This is the canon of the moral appreciation of the action generally. Some actions are of such a character that their maxim cannot without contradiction be even *conceived* as a universal law of nature, far from it being possible that we should *will* that it *should* be so. In others, this intrinsic impossibility is not found, but still it is impossible to *will* that their maxim should be raised to the universality of a law of nature, since such a will would contradict itself. It is easily seen the former violate strict or rigorous (inflexible) duty; the latter only laxer (meritorious) duty. Thus it has been completely shown by these examples how all duties depend as regards the nature of the obligation (not the object of the action) on the same principle.

If now we attend to ourselves on occasion of any transgression of duty, we shall find that we in fact do not will that our maxim should be a universal law, for that is impossible for us; on the contrary, we will that the opposite should remain a universal law, only we assume the liberty of making an *exception* in our own favor or (just for this time only) in favor of our inclination. Consequently, if we considered all cases from one and the same point of view, namely, that of reason, we should find a contradiction in our own will, namely, that a certain principle should be objectively necessary as a universal law, and yet subjectively should not be universal, but admit of exceptions. As, however, we at one moment regard our action from the point of view of a will wholly conformed to reason, and then again look at the same action from the point of view of a will affected by inclination, there is not really any contradiction, but an antagonism of inclination to the precept of reason, whereby the universality of the principle is changed into a mere generality, so that the practical principle of reason shall meet the maxim half way. Now, although this cannot be justified in our own impartial judgment, yet it proves that we do really recognize the validity of the categorical imperative and (with all respect for it) only allow ourselves a few exceptions which we think unimportant and forced from us....

The will is conceived as a faculty of determining oneself to action *in accordance with the conception of certain laws*. And such a faculty can be found only in rational beings. Now that which serves the will as the objective ground of its self-determination is the *end*, and if this is assigned by reason alone, it must hold for all rational beings. On the other hand, that which merely contains the ground of possibility of the action of which the effect is the end, this is called the *means*. The subjective ground of the desire is the *spring*, the objective ground of the volition is the motive; hence the distinction between subjective ends which rest on springs, and objective ends which depend on motives valid for every rational being. Practical principles are *formal* when they abstract from all subjective ends; they are *material* when they assume these, and therefore particular, springs of action. The ends which a rational being proposes to himself at pleasure as *effects* of his actions (material ends) are all only relative, for it is only their relation to the particular desires of the subject that gives them their worth, which therefore cannot furnish principles universal and necessary for all rational beings and for every volition, that is to say, practical laws, Hence all these relative ends can give rise only to hypothetical imperatives.

Supposing, however, that there were something *whose existence* has *in itself* an absolute worth, something which, being *an end in itself*, could be a source of definite laws, then in this and this alone would lie the source of a possible categorical imperative, that is, a practical law.

Now I say: man and generally any rational being *exists* as an end in himself, *not merely as a means* to be arbitrarily used by this or that will, but in all his actions, whether they concern himself or other rational beings, must be always regarded at the same time as an end. All objects of the inclinations have only a conditional worth; for if the inclinations and the wants founded on them did not exist, then their object would be without value. But the inclinations themselves, being sources of want, are so far from having an absolute worth for which they should be desired that, on the contrary, it must be the universal wish of every rational being to be wholly free from them. Thus the worth of any object which is *to be acquired* by our action is always conditional. Beings whose existence depends not on our will but on nature's, have nevertheless, if they are nonrational beings, only a relative value as means, and are therefore called *things*; rational beings, on the contrary, are called *persons*, because their very nature points them out as ends in themselves, that is, as something which must not be used merely as means, and so far therefore restricts freedom of action (and is an object of respect). These, therefore, are not merely subjective ends whose existence has a worth *for us* as an effect of our action, but *objective ends*, that is, things whose existence is an end in itself—an end, moreover, for which no other can be substituted, which they should subserve *merely* as means, for otherwise nothing whatever would possess *absolute worth*; but if all worth were conditioned and therefore contingent, then there would be no supreme practical principle of reason whatever.

If then there is a supreme practical principle or, in respect of the human will, a categorical imperative, it must be one which, being drawn from the conception of that which is necessarily an end for everyone because it is *an end in itself*, constitutes an *objective* principle of will, and can therefore serve as a universal practical law. The foundation of this principle is: *rational nature exists as an end in itself.* Man necessarily conceives his own existence as being so; so far then this is a *subjective* principle of human actions. But every other rational being regards its existence similarly, just on the same rational principle that holds for me;[7] so that it is at the same time an objective principle from which as a supreme practical law all laws of the will must be capable of being deduced. Accordingly the practical imperative will be as follows: So *act as to treat humanity, whether in thine own person or in that of any other, in every case as an end withal, never as means only.* We will now inquire whether this can be practically carried out.

To abide by the previous examples:

First, under the head of necessary duty to oneself. He who contemplates suicide should ask himself whether his action can be consistent with the idea of humanity *as an end in itself*. If he destroys himself in order to escape from painful circumstances, he uses a person merely as *a mean* to maintain a tolerable condition up to the end of life. But a man is not a thing, that is to say, something which can be used merely as means, but must in all his actions be always considered as an end in himself. I cannot, therefore, dispose in any way of a man in my own person so as to mutilate him, to damage or kill him. (It belongs to ethics proper to define this principle more precisely, so as to avoid all misunderstanding, for example, as to the amputation of the limbs in order to preserve myself; as to exposing my life to danger with a view to preserve it, etc. This question is therefore omitted here.)

Secondly, as regards necessary duties, or those of strict obligation, towards others: He who is thinking of making a lying promise to others will see at once that he would be using another man *merely as a mean*, without the latter containing at the same time the end in himself. For he whom I propose by such a promise to use for my own purposes cannot possibly assent to my mode of acting towards him, and therefore cannot himself contain the end of this action. This violation of the principle of humanity in other men is more obvious if we take in examples of attacks on the freedom and property of others. For then it is clear that he who transgresses the rights of men intends to use the person of others merely as means, without considering that as rational beings they ought always to be esteemed also as ends, that is, as beings who must be capable of containing in themselves the end of the very same action.[8]

Thirdly, as regards contingent (meritorious) duties to oneself. It is not enough that the action does not violate humanity in our own person as an end in itself, it must also *harmonize with* it. Now there are in humanity capacities of greater perfection which belong to the end that nature has in view in regard to humanity in ourselves as the subject; to neglect these might perhaps be consistent with the *maintenance* of humanity as an end in itself, but not with the *advancement* of this end.

Fourthly, as regards meritorious duties towards others: The natural end which all men have is their own happiness. Now humanity might indeed subsist although no one should contribute anything to the happiness of others, provided he did not intentionally withdraw anything from it; but after all, this would only harmonize negatively, not positively, with *humanity as an end in itself,* if everyone does not also endeavor, as far as in him lies, to forward the ends of others. For the ends of any subject which is an end in himself ought as far as possible to be *my* ends also, if that conception is to have its *full* effect with me.

This principle that humanity and generally every rational nature is *an end in itself* (which is the supreme limiting condition of every man's freedom of action), is not borrowed from experience, *first,* because it is universal, applying as it does to all rational beings whatever, and experience is not capable of determining anything about them; *secondly,* because it does not present humanity as an end to men (subjectively), that is, as an object which men do of themselves actually adopt as an end; but as an objective end which must as a law constitute the supreme limiting condition of all our subjective ends, let them be what we will; it must therefore spring from pure reason. In fact the objective principle of all practical legislation lies (according to the first principle) in *the rule* and its form of universality which makes it capable of being a law (say, for example, a law of nature); but the *subjective* principle is in the *end;* now by the second principle, the subject of all ends is each rational being inasmuch as it is an end in itself. Hence follows the third practical principle of the will, which is the ultimate condition of its harmony with the universal practical reason, viz., the idea of *the will of every rational being as a universally legislative will.*

On this principle all maxims are rejected which are inconsistent with the will being itself universal legislator. Thus the will is not subject to the law, but so subject that it must be regarded *as itself giving the law,* and on this ground only subject to the law (of which it can regard itself as the author).

In the previous imperatives, namely, that based on the conception of the conformity of actions to general laws, as in a *physical system of nature,* and that based on the universal *prerogative* of rational beings as *ends* in themselves— these imperatives just because they were conceived as categorical excluded from any share in their authority all admixture of any interest as a spring of action; they were, however, only *assumed* to be categorical, because such an assumption was necessary to explain the conception of duty. But we could not prove independently that there are practical propositions which command categorically, nor can it be proved in this section; one thing, however, could be done, namely, to indicate in the imperative itself, by some determinate expression, that in the case of volition from duty all interest is renounced, which is the specific criterion of categorical as distinguished from hypothetical imperatives. This is done in the present (third) formula of the principle, namely, in the idea of the will of every rational being as a *universally legislating will.*

For although a will *which is subject to laws* may be attached to this law by means of an interest, yet a will which is itself a supreme lawgiver, so far as it is such, cannot possibly depend on any interest, since a will so dependent would itself still need another law restricting the interest of its self-love by the condition that it should be valid as universal law.

Thus the *principle* that every human will is *a will which in all its maxims gives universal laws,*[9] provided it be otherwise justified, would be very *well adapted* to be the categorical imperative, in this respect, namely, that just because of the idea of universal legislation it *is not based on any interest,* and therefore it alone among all possible imperatives can be *unconditional.* Or still better, converting the proposition, if there is a categorical imperative (that is, a law for the will of every rational being), it can only command that everything be done from maxims of one's will regarded as a will which could at the same time will that it should itself give universal laws, for in that case only the practical principle and the imperative which it obeys are unconditional, since they cannot be based on any interest.

Looking back now on all previous attempts to discover the principle of morality, we need not wonder why they all failed. It was seen that man was bound to laws by duty, but it was not observed that the laws to which he is subject are *only those of his own giving,* though at the same time they are *universal,* and that he is only bound to act in conformity with his own will—a will, however, which is designed by nature to give universal laws. For when one has conceived man only as a subject to a law (no matter what), then this law required some interest, either by way of attraction or constraint, since it did not originate as a law from his own will, but this will was according to a law obliged by *something else* to act in a certain manner. Now by this necessary consequence all the labor spent in finding a supreme principle of *duty* was irrevocably lost. For men never elicited duty, but only a necessity of acting from a certain interest. Whether this interest was private or otherwise, in any case the imperative must be conditional, and could not by any means be capable of being a moral command. I will therefore call this the principle of *Autonomy* of the will, in contrast with every other which I accordingly reckon as *Heteronomy.*

The conception of every rational being as one which must consider itself as giving in all the maxims of its will universal laws, so as to judge itself and its actions from this point of view—this conception leads to another which depends on it and is very fruitful, namely, that of a *kingdom of ends.*

By a "kingdom" I understand the union of different rational beings in a system by common laws. Now since it is by laws that ends are determined as regards their universal validity, hence, if we abstract from the personal differences of rational beings, and likewise from all the content of their private ends, we shall be able to conceive all ends combined in a systematic whole (including both rational beings as ends in themselves, and also the special ends which each may propose to himself), that is to say, we can conceive a kingdom of ends, which on the preceding principles is possible.

For all rational beings come under the *law* that each of them must treat itself and all others *never merely as means*, but in every case *at the same time as ends in themselves*. Hence results a systematic union of rational beings by common objective laws, that is, a kingdom which may be called a kingdom of ends, since what these laws have in view is just the relation of these beings to one another as ends and means. It is certainly only an ideal.

A rational being belongs as a *member* to the kingdom of ends when, although giving universal laws in it, he is also himself subject to these laws. He belongs to it *as sovereign* when, while giving laws, he is not subject to the will of any other.

A rational being must always regard himself as giving laws either as member or as sovereign in a kingdom of ends which is rendered possible by the freedom of will. He cannot, however, maintain the latter position merely by the maxims of his will, but only in case he is a completely independent being without wants and with unrestricted power adequate to his will.

Morality consists then in the reference of all action to the legislation which alone can render a kingdom of ends possible. This legislation must be capable of existing in every rational being, and of emanating from his will, so that the principle of this will is never to act on any maxim which could not without contradiction be also a universal law, and accordingly always so to act *that the will could at the same time regard itself as giving in its maxims universal laws*. If now the maxims of rational beings are not by their own nature coincident with this objective principle, then the necessity of acting on it is called practical necessitation, that is, *duty*. Duty does not apply to the sovereign in the kingdom of ends, but it does to every member of it and to all in the same degree.

The practical necessity of acting on this principle, that is, duty, does not rest at all on feelings, impulses, or inclinations, but solely on the relation of rational beings to one another, a relation in which the will of a rational being must always be regarded as *legislative*, since otherwise it could not be conceived as *an end in itself*. Reason then refers every maxim of the will, regarding it as legislating universally, to every other will and also to every action towards oneself; and this not on account of any other practical motive or any future advantage, but from the idea of the *dignity* of a rational being, obeying no law but that which he himself also gives.

In the kingdom of ends everything has either *value* or *dignity*. Whatever has a value can be replaced by something else which is *equivalent*; whatever, on the other hand, is above all value, and therefore admits of no equivalent, has a dignity.

Whatever has reference to the general inclinations and wants of mankind has a *market value*; whatever, without presupposing a want, corresponds to a certain taste, that is, to a satisfaction in the mere purposeless play of our faculties, has a *fancy value*; but that which constitutes the condition under which alone anything can be an end in itself, that has not merely a relative worth, that is, value, but an intrinsic worth, that is, *dignity*.

Now morality is the condition under which alone a rational being can be an end in himself, since by this alone it is possible that he should be a legislating member in the kingdom of ends. Thus morality, and humanity as capable of it, is that which alone has dignity. Skill and diligence in labor have a market value; wit, lively imagination, and humor have fancy value; on the other hand, fidelity to promises, benevolence from principle (not from instinct), have an intrinsic worth. Neither nature nor art contains anything which in default of these it could put in their place, for their worth consists not in the effects which spring from them, not in the use and advantage which they secure, but in the disposition of the mind, that is, the maxims of the will which are ready to manifest themselves in such actions, even though they should not have the desired effect. These actions also need no recommendation from any subjective taste or sentiment, that they may be looked on with immediate favor and satisfaction; they need no immediate propension or feeling for them; they exhibit the will that performs them as an object of an immediate respect, and nothing but reason is required to *impose* them on the will; not to *flatter* it into them, which, in the case of duties, would be a contradiction. This estimation therefore shows that the worth of such a disposition is dignity, and places it infinitely above all value, with which it cannot for a moment be brought into comparison or competition without as it were violating its sanctity....

Now such a kingdom of ends would be actually realized by means of maxims conforming to the canon which the categorical imperative prescribes to all rational beings, *if they were universally followed*. But although a rational being, even if he punctually follows this maxim himself, cannot reckon upon all others being therefore true to the same, nor expect that the kingdom of nature and its orderly arrangements shall be in harmony with him as a fitting member, so as to form a kingdom of ends to which he himself contributes, that is to say, that it shall favor his expectation of happiness, still that law: Act according to the maxims of a member of a merely possible kingdom of ends legislating in it universally, remains in its full force inasmuch as it commands categorically.

Notes

1. A maxim is the subjective principle of volition. The objective principle (i.e., that which would also serve subjectively as a practical principle to all rational beings if reason had full power over the faculty of desire) is the practical law.

2. It might be here objected to me that I take refuge behind the word respect in an obscure feeling, instead of giving a distinct solution of the question by a concept of the reason. But although respect is a feeling, it is not a feeling received through influence, but is self-wrought by a rational concept, and, therefore, is specifically distinct from all feelings of the former kind, which may be referred either to inclination or fear. What I recognize immediately as a law for me, I recognize with respect. This merely signifies the consciousness that my will is subordinate to a law, without the intervention of other influences on my sense. The immediate determination of the will by the law, and the consciousness of this, is called respect, so that this is regarded as an effect of the law on the subject, and not as the cause of it. Respect is properly the conception of a worth which thwarts my self-love. Accordingly it is something which is considered neither as an object of inclination nor of fear, although it has something analogous to both. The object of respect is the law only, that is, the law which we impose on ourselves, and yet recognize as necessary in itself. As a law, we are subjected to it without consulting self-love; as imposed by us on ourselves, it is a result of our will. In the former aspect it has an analogy to fear, in the latter to inclination. Respect for a person is properly only respect for the law (of honesty, etc.) of which he gives us an example. Since we also look on the improvement of our talents as a duty, we consider that we see in a person of talents, as it were, the example of a law (viz., to become like him in this by exercise), and this constitutes our respect. All so-called moral interest consists simply in respect for the law.

3. The dependence of the desires on sensations is called inclination, and this accordingly always indicates a want. The dependence of a contingently determinable will on principles of reason is called an *interest*. This, therefore, is found only in the case of a dependent will which does not always of itself conform to reason; in the Divine will we cannot conceive any interest. But the human will can also *take an interest* in a thing without therefore acting from interest. The former signifies the practical interest in the action, the latter the pathological in the object of the action. The former indicates only dependence of the will on principles of reason in themselves; the second, dependence on principles of reason for the sake of inclination, reason supplying only the practical rules how the requirement of the inclination may be satisfied. In the first case the action interests me; in the second the object of the action (because it is pleasant to me). We have seen in the first section that in an action done from duty we must look not to the interest in the object, but only to that in the action itself, and in its rational principle (viz., the law).

4. The word *prudence* is taken in two senses: in the one it may bear the name of knowledge of the world, in the other that of private prudence. The former is a man's ability to influence others so as to use them for his own purposes. The latter is the sagacity to combine all these purposes for his own lasting benefit. This latter is properly that to which the value even of the former is reduced, and when

a man is prudent in the former sense, but not in the latter, we might say of him that he is clever and cunning, but, on the whole, imprudent.

5. A "maxim" is a subjective principle of action, and must be distinguished from the *objective principle*, namely, practical law. The former contains the practical rule set by reason according to the conditions of the subject (often its ignorance or its inclinations), so that it is the principle on which the subject acts; but the law is the objective principle valid for every rational being, and is the principle on which it ought to act—that is an imperative.

6. It must be noted here that I reserve the division of duties for a future *metaphysic of morals*; so that I give it here only as an arbitrary one (in order to arrange my examples). For the rest, I understand by a perfect duty one that admits no exception in favor of inclination, and then I have not merely external but also internal perfect duties. This is contrary to the use of the word adopted in the schools; but I do not intend to justify it here, as it is all one for my purpose whether it is admitted or not.

7. This proposition is here stated as a postulate. The ground of it will be found in the concluding section.

8. Let it not be thought that the common: *quod tibi non vis fieri, etc.*, could serve here as the rule or principle. For it is only a deduction from the former, though with several limitations; it cannot be a universal law, for it does not contain the principle of duties to oneself, nor of the duties of benevolence to others (for many a one would gladly consent that others should not benefit him, provided only that he might be excused from showing benevolence to them), nor finally that of duties of strict obligation to one another, for on this principle the criminal might argue against the judge who punishes him, and so on.

9. I may be excused from adducing examples to elucidate this principle as those which have already been used to elucidate the categorical imperative and its formula would all serve for the like purpose here.

13.
A SIMPLIFIED VERSION OF KANT'S ETHICS
PERPLEXITIES OF FAMINE AND WORLD HUNGER

❋ ❋ ❋

ONORA O'NEILL

Onora O'Neill is a professor of philosophy at the University of Cambridge, and is a well known British philosopher. In the following selection O'Neill provides an interpretation of Kant's "End in Itself" formulation of the Categorical Imperative. She then outlines a Kantian approach to the issues of famine and poverty and compares it to a utilitarian approach to the same issues.

A Simplified Account of Kant's Ethic

Kant's theory is frequently and misleadingly assimilated to theories of human rights. It is, in fact, a theory of human obligations; therefore it is wider in scope than a theory of human rights. (Not all obligations generate corresponding rights.) Kant does not, however, try to generate a set of precise rules defining human obligations in all possible circumstances; instead, he attempts to provide a set of *principles of obligation* that can be used as the starting points for moral reasoning in actual contexts of action. The primary focus of Kantian ethics is, then, on *action* rather than either *results*, as in utilitarian thinking, or *entitlements*, as in theories that make human rights their fundamental category. Morality requires action of certain sorts. But to know *what* sort of action is required (or forbidden) in which circumstances, we should not look just at the expected results of action or at others' supposed entitlements but, in the first instance, at the nature of the proposed actions themselves.

When we engage in moral reasoning, we often need go no further than to refer to some quite specific principle or tradition. We may say to one another, or to ourselves, things like "It would be hypocritical to pretend that our good fortune is achieved without harm to the Third World" or "Redistributive taxation shouldn't cross national boundaries." But when these specific claims are challenged, we may find ourselves pushed to justify or reject or modify them. Such moral debate, on Kant's account, rests on appeals to what he calls the *Supreme Principle of Morality*, which can (he thinks) be used to work out more specific principles of obligation. This principle, the famous Categorical

Imperative, plays the same role in Kantian thinking that the Greatest Happiness Principle plays in utilitarian thought.

A second reason why Kant's moral thought often appears difficult is that he offers a number of different versions of this principle, that he claims are equivalent, but which look very different. A straightforward way in which to simplify Kantian moral thought is to concentrate on just one of these formulations of the Categorical Imperative. For present purposes I shall choose the version to which he gives the sonorous name of *The Formula of the End in Itself*.

The Formula of the End in Itself

The "Formula of the End in Itself" runs as follows:

> Act in such a way that you always treat humanity, whether in your own person or in the person of any other, never simply as a means but always at the same time as an end.

To understand this principle we need in the first place to understand what Kant means by the term *maxim*. The maxim of an act or policy or activity is the *underlying principle* of the act, policy or activity, by which other, more superficial aspects of action are guided. Very often interpretations of Kant have supposed that maxims can only be the (underlying) intentions of individual human agents. If that were the case it would limit the usefulness of Kantian modes of moral thought in dealing with world hunger and famine problems. For it is clear enough that individual action (while often important) cannot deal with all the problems of Third World poverty. A moral theory that addresses *only* individual actors does not have adequate scope for discussing famine problems. As we have seen, one of the main attractions of utilitarianism as an approach to Third World poverty was that its scope is so broad: it can be applied with equal appropriateness to the practical deliberations of individuals, of institutions and groups, and even of nation states and international agencies. Kantian ethical thinking can be interpreted (though it usually isn't) to have equally broad scope.

Since maxims are *underlying* principles of action, they may not always be obvious either to the individuals or institutions whose maxims they are, or to others. We can determine what the underlying principles of some activity or institution are only by seeing the patterns made by various more superficial aspects of acts, policies and activities. Only those principles that would generate that pattern of activity are maxims of action. Sometimes more than one principle might lie behind a given pattern of activity, and we may be unsure what the maxim of the act was. For example, we might wonder (as Kant does) how to tell whether somebody gives change accurately only out of concern to have an honest reputation or whether he or she would do so anyhow. In such cases we can sometimes set up an "isolation test"—for example, a situation in which it would be open to somebody to be dishonest without any chance of a damaged reputation. But quite often we can't set up any such situation and may be to some extent unsure which maxim lies behind a given act. Usually we have to rely on whatever individual actors tell us about their maxims of action and on what policymakers or social scientists may tell us about the underlying principles of institutional or group action. What they tell us may well be mistaken. While mistakes can be reduced by care and thoughtfulness, there is no guarantee that we can always work out which maxim of action should be scrutinized in the light of the Categorical Imperative.

It is helpful to think of some examples of maxims that might be used to guide action in contexts where poverty and the risk of famine are issues. Somebody who contributes to famine-relief work or advocates development might have an underlying principle such as, "Try to help reduce the risk or severity of world hunger." This commitment might be reflected in varied surface action in varied situations. In one context a gift of money might be relevant; in another some political activity such as lobbying for or against certain types of aid and trade might express the same underlying commitment. Sometimes superficial aspects of action may seem at variance with the underlying maxim they in fact express. For example, if there is reason to think that indiscriminate food aid damages the agricultural economy of the area to which food is given, then the maxim of seeking to relieve famine might be expressed in action aimed at limiting the extent of food aid. More lavish use of food aid might *seem* to treat the needy more generously, but if in fact it will damage their medium- or long-term economic prospects, then it is not (contrary to superficial appearances) aimed at improving and securing their access to subsistence. On a Kantian theory, the basis for judging action should be its *fundamental* principle or policy, and superficially similar acts may be judged morally very different. Regulating food aid in order to drive up prices and profit from them is one matter; regulating food aid in order to enable local farmers to sell their crops and to stay in the business of growing food quite another.

When we want to work out whether a proposed act or policy is morally required we should not, on Kant's view, try to find out whether it would produce more happiness than other available acts. Rather we should see whether the act or policy is required by, or ruled out by, or merely compatible with maxims that avoid using others as mere means and maxims that treat others as ends in themselves. These two aspects of Kantian duty can each be spelled out and shown to have determinate implications for acts and policies that may affect the risk and course of famines.

Using Others as Mere Means

We use others as *mere means* if what we do reflects some maxim *to which they could not in principle consent*. Kant does not suggest that there is anything wrong about using someone as a means. Evidently every cooperative scheme of action does this. A government that agrees to provide free or subsidized food to famine-relief agencies both uses and is used by the agencies; a peasant who sells food in a local market both uses and is used by those who buy it. In such examples each party to the transaction can and does consent to take part in that transaction. Kant would say that the parties to such transactions use one another but do not use one another as *mere* means. Each party assumes that the other has its own maxims of action and is not just a thing or prop to be used or manipulated.

But there are other cases where one party to an arrangement or transaction not only uses the other but does so in ways that could only be done on the basis of a fundamental principle or maxim to which the other could not in principle consent. If a false promise is given, the party that accepts the promise is not just used but used as a mere means, because it is *impossible* for consent to be given to the fundamental principle or project of deception that must guide every false promise, whatever its surface character. Those who accept false promises *must* be kept ignorant of the underlying principle or maxim on which the "undertaking" is based. If this isn't kept concealed, the attempted promise will either be rejected or will not be a *false* promise at all. In false promising the deceived party becomes, as it were, a prop or tool—a *mere* means—in the false promisor's scheme. Action based on any such maxim of deception would be wrong in Kantian terms, whether it is a matter of a breach of treaty obligations, of contractual undertakings, or of accepted and relied upon modes of interaction. Maxims of deception *standardly* use others as mere means, and acts that could only be based on such maxims are unjust.

Another standard way of using others as mere means is by coercing them. Coercers, like deceivers, standardly don't give others the possibility of dissenting from what they propose to do. In deception, "consent" is spurious because it is given to a principle that couldn't be the underlying principle of *that* act at all; but the principle governing coercion may be brutally plain. Here any "consent" given is spurious because there was no option *but* to consent. If a rich or powerful landowner or nation threatens a poorer or more vulnerable person, group, or nation with some intolerable difficulty unless a concession is made, the more vulnerable party is denied a genuine choice between consent and dissent. While the boundary that divides coercion from mere bargaining and negotiation varies and is therefore often hard to discern, we have no doubt about the clearer cases. Maxims of coercion may threaten physical force, seizure of possessions, destruction of opportunities, or any other harm that the coerced party is thought to be unable to absorb without grave injury or danger. A moneylender in a Third World village who threatens not to make or renew an indispensable loan, without which survival until the next harvest would be impossible, uses the peasant as mere means. The peasant does not have the possibility of genuinely consenting to the "offer he can't refuse." The outward form of some coercive transactions may *look* like ordinary commercial dealings: but we know very well that some action that is superficially of this sort is based on maxims of coercion. To avoid coercion, action must be governed by maxims that the other party can choose to refuse and is not bound to accept. The more vulnerable the other party in any transaction or negotiation, the less their scope for refusal, and the more demanding it is likely to be to ensure that action is noncoercive.

In Kant's view, acts done on maxims that coerce or deceive others, so therefore cannot in principle have the consent of those others, are wrong. When individuals or institutions, or nation states act in ways that can only be based on such maxims they fail in their duty. They treat the parties who are either deceived or coerced unjustly. To avoid unjust action it is not enough to observe the outward forms of free agreement and cooperation; it is also essential to see that the weaker party to any arrangement has a genuine option to refuse the fundamental character of the proposal.

Treating Others as Ends in Themselves

For Kant, as for utilitarians, justice is only one part of duty. We may fail in our duty, even when we don't use anyone as mere means (by deception or coercion), if we fail to treat others as "ends in themselves." To treat others as "Ends in Themselves" we must not only avoid using them as mere means but also treat them as rational and autonomous beings with their own maxims. If human beings were *wholly* rational and autonomous then, on a Kantian view, duty would require only that they not use one another as mere means. But, as Kant repeatedly stressed, but later Kantians have often forgotten, human beings are *finite* rational beings. They are finite in several ways.

First, human beings are not ideal rational calculators. We *standardly* have neither a complete list of the actions possible in a given situation nor more than a partial view of their likely consequences. In addition, abilities to assess and to use available information are usually quite limited.

Second, these cognitive limitations are *standardly* complemented by limited autonomy. Human action is limited not only by various sorts of physical barrier and inability but by further sorts of (mutual or asymmetrical) dependence. To treat one another as ends in themselves such beings have to base their action on principles that do not undermine but rather sustain and

extend one another's capacities for autonomous action. A central requirement for doing so is to share and support one another's ends and activities at
least to some extent. Since finite rational beings cannot generally achieve
their aims without some help and support from others, a general refusal of
help and support amounts to failure to treat others as rational and
autonomous beings, that is as ends in themselves. Hence Kantian principles
require us not only to act justly, that is in accordance with maxims that don't
coerce or deceive others, but also to avoid manipulation and to lend some
support to others' plans and activities. Since famine, great poverty and pow-
erlessness all undercut the possibility of autonomous action, and the requirement of treating others as ends in themselves demands that Kantians standardly act to support the possibility of autonomous action where it is most
vulnerable, Kantians are required to do what they can to avert, reduce, and
remedy famine. On a Kantian view, beneficence is as indispensable as justice
in human lives.

Justice and Beneficence in Kant's Thought

Kant is often thought to hold that justice is morally required, but beneficence
is morally less important. He does indeed, like Mill, speak of justice as a *perfect duty* and of beneficence as an *imperfect duty*. But he does not mean by this
that beneficence is any less a duty; rather, he holds that it has (unlike justice)
to be selective. We cannot share or even support *all* others' maxims *all* of the
time. Hence support for others' autonomy is always selective. By contrast we
can make all action and institutions conform fundamentally to standards of
nondeception and noncoercion. Kant's understanding of the distinction
between perfect and imperfect duties differs from Mill's. In a Kantian perspective justice isn't a matter of the core requirements for beneficence, as in
Mill's theory, and beneficence isn't just an attractive but optional moral
embellishment of just arrangements (as tends to be assumed in most theories
that take human rights as fundamental).

Justice to the Vulnerable in Kantian Thinking

For Kantians, justice requires action that conforms (at least outwardly) to
what could be done in a given situation while acting on maxims neither of
deception nor of coercion. Since anyone hungry or destitute is more than
usually vulnerable to deception and coercion, the possibilities and tempta-
tions to injustice are then especially strong.

Examples are easily suggested. I shall begin with some situations that might
arise for somebody who happened to be part of a famine-stricken population.

Where shortage of food is being dealt with by a reasonably fair rationing scheme, any mode of cheating to get more than one's allocated share involves using some others and is unjust. Equally, taking advantage of others' desperation to profiteer—for example, selling food at colossal prices or making loans on the security of others' future livelihood, when these are "offers they can't refuse"—constitutes coercion and so uses others as mere means and is unjust. Transactions that have the outward form of normal commercial dealing may be coercive when one party is desperate. Equally, forms of corruption that work by deception—such as bribing officials to gain special benefits from development schemes, or deceiving others about their entitlements—use others unjustly. Such requirements are far from trivial and frequently violated in hard times; acting justly in such conditions may involve risking one's own life and livelihood and require the greatest courage.

It is not so immediately obvious what justice, Kantianly conceived, requires of agents and agencies who are remote from destitution. Might it not be sufficient to argue that those of us fortunate enough to live in the developed world are far from famine and destitution, so if we do nothing but go about our usual business will successfully avoid injustice to the destitute? This conclusion has often been reached by those who take an abstract view of rationality and forget the limits of human rationality and autonomy. In such perspectives it can seem that there is nothing more to just action than meeting the formal requirements of nondeception and noncoercion in our dealings with one another. But once we remember the limitations of human rationality and autonomy, and the particular ways in which they are limited for those living close to the margins of subsistence, we can see that mere conformity to ordinary standards of commercial honesty and political bargaining is not enough for justice toward the destitute. If international agreements themselves can constitute "offers that cannot be refused" by the government of a poor country, or if the concessions required for investment by a transnational corporation or a development project reflect the desperation of recipients rather than an appropriate contribution to the project, then (however benevolent the motives of some parties) the weaker party to such agreements is used by the stronger.

In the earlier days of European colonial penetration of the now underdeveloped world it was evident enough that some of the ways in which "agreements" were made with native peoples were in fact deceptive or coercive or both. "Sales" of land by those who had no grasp of market practices and "cession of sovereignty" by those whose forms of life were prepolitical constitute only spurious consent to the agreements struck. But it is not only in these original forms of bargaining between powerful and powerless that injustice is frequent. There are many contemporary examples. For example, if capital investment (private or governmental) in a poorer country requires the receiving country to contribute disproportionately to the maintenance of a developed, urban "enclave" economy that offers little local employment but lavish standards of life for a small number of (possibly expatriate) "experts," while guaranteeing long-term exemption from local taxation for the investors, then we may doubt that the agreement could have been struck without the element of coercion provided by the desperation of the weaker party. Or if a trade agreement extracts political advantages (such as military bases) that are incompatible with the fundamental political interests of the country concerned, we may judge that at least some leaders of that country have been "bought" in a sense that is not consonant with ordinary commercial practice.

Even when the actions of those who are party to an agreement don't reflect a fundamental principle of coercion or deception, the agreement may alter the life circumstances and prospects of third parties in ways to which they patently could not have not consented. For example, a system of food aid and imports agreed upon by the government of a Third World country and certain developed countries or international agencies may give the elite of that Third World country access to subsidized grain. If that grain is then used to control the urban population and also produces destitution among peasants (who used to grow food for that urban population), then those who are newly destitute probably have not been offered any opening or possibility of refusing their new and worsened conditions of life. If a policy is imposed, those affected *cannot* have been given a chance to refuse it: had the chance been there, they would either have assented (and so the policy would not have been *imposed*) or refused (and so proceeding with the policy would have been evidently coercive).

Beneficence to the Vulnerable in Kantian Thinking

In Kantian moral reasoning, the basis for beneficent action is that we cannot, without it, treat others of limited rationality and autonomy as ends in themselves. This is not to say that Kantian beneficence won't make others happier, for it will do so whenever they would be happier if (more) capable of autonomous action, but that happiness secured by purely paternalistic means, or at the cost (for example) of manipulating others' desires, will not count as beneficent in the Kantian picture. Clearly the vulnerable position of those who lack the very means of life, and their severely curtailed possibilities for autonomous action, offer many different ways in which it might be possible for others to act beneficently. Where the means of life are meager, almost any material or organizational advance may help extend possibilities for autonomy. Individual or institutional action that aims to advance economic or social development can proceed on many routes. The provision of clean water, of improved agricultural techniques, of better grain storage systems, or of adequate means of local transport may all help transform material prospects. Equally, help in the development of new forms of social organization—whether peasant self-help groups, urban cooperatives, medical and contraceptive services, or improvements in education or in the position of women—may help to extend possibilities for autonomous action. Kantian thinking does not provide a means by which all possible projects of this sort could be listed and ranked. But where some activity helps secure possibilities for autonomous action for more people, or is likely to achieve a permanent improvement in the position of the most vulnerable, or is one that can be done with more reliable success, this provides reason for furthering that project rather than alternatives.

Clearly the alleviation of need must rank far ahead of the furthering of happiness in the Kantian picture. I might make my friends very happy by throwing extravagant parties: but this would probably not increase anybody's possibility for autonomous action to any great extent. But the sorts of development-oriented changes that have just been mentioned may *transform* the possibilities for action of some. Since famine and the risk of famine are always and evidently highly damaging to human autonomy, any action that helps avoid or reduce famine must have a strong claim on any Kantian who is thinking through what beneficence requires. Depending on circumstances, such action may have to take the form of individual contribution to famine relief and development organizations, of individual or collective effort to influence the trade and aid policies of developed countries, or of attempts to influence the activities of those Third World elites for whom development does not seem to be an urgent priority. Some activities can best be undertaken by private citizens of developed countries; others are best approached by those who work for governments, international agencies, or transnational corporations. Perhaps the most dramatic possibilities to act for a just or an unjust, a beneficent or selfish future belongs to those who hold positions of influence within the Third World. But wherever we find ourselves, our duties are not, on the Kantian picture, limited to those close at hand. Duties of justice arise whenever there is some involvement between parties—and in the modern world this is never lacking. Duties of beneficence arise whenever destitution puts the possibility of autonomous action in question for the more vulnerable. When famines were not only far away, but nothing could be done to relieve them, beneficence or charity may well have begun—and stayed—at home. In a global village, the moral significance of distance has shrunk, and we may be able to affect the capacities for autonomous action of those who are far away.

The Scope of Kantian Deliberations about Famine and Hunger

In many ways Kantian moral reasoning is less ambitious than utilitarian moral reasoning. It does not propose a process of moral reasoning that can (in principle) rank *all* possible actions or all possible institutional arrangements from the happiness-maximizing "right" action or institution downward. It aims rather to offer a pattern of reasoning by which we can identify whether *proposed action or institutional arrangements* would be just or unjust, beneficent or lacking in beneficence. While *some* knowledge of causal connections is needed for Kantian reasoning, it is far less sensitive than is utilitarian reasoning to gaps in our causal knowledge. The conclusions reached about particular proposals for action or about institutional arrangements will not hold for all time, but be relevant for the contexts for which action is proposed. For example, if it is judged that some institution—say the World Bank—provides, under present circumstances, a just approach to certain development problems, it will not follow that under all other circumstances such an institution would be part of a just approach. There may be other institutional arrangements that are also just; and there may be other circumstances under which the institutional structure of the World Bank would be shown to be in some ways deceptive or coercive and so unjust.

These points show us that Kantian deliberations about famine and hunger can lead only to conclusions that are useful in determinate contexts. This, however, is standardly what we need to know for action, whether individual or institutional. We do not need to be able to generate a complete list of available actions in order to determine whether proposed lines of action are not unjust and whether any are beneficent. Kantian patterns of moral reasoning cannot be guaranteed to identify the optimal course of action in a situation. They provide methods neither for listing nor for ranking all possible proposals for action. But any line of action that is considered can be checked.

The reason this pattern of reasoning will not show any action or arrangement the most beneficent one available is that the Kantian picture of beneficence is less mathematically structured than the utilitarian one. It judges beneficence by its overall contribution to the prospects for human autonomy and not by the quantity of happiness expected to result. To the extent that the autonomous pursuit of goals is what Mill called "one of the principal ingredients of human happiness" (but only to that extent), the requirements of Kantian and of utilitarian beneficence will coincide. But whenever expected happiness is not a function of the scope for autonomous action, the two accounts of beneficent action diverge. For utilitarians, paternalistic imposition of, for example, certain forms of aid and development assistance need not be wrong and may even be required. But for Kantians, whose beneficence should secure others' possibilities for autonomous action, the case for paternalistic imposition of aid or development projects without the recipients' involvement must always be questionable.

In terms of some categories in which development projects are discussed, utilitarian reasoning may well endorse "top-down" aid and development projects which override whatever capacities for autonomous choice and action the poor of a certain area now have in the hopes of securing a happier future. If the calculations work out in a certain way, utilitarians may even think a "generation of sacrifice"—or of forced labor or of imposed population-control policies not only permissible but mandated. In their darkest Malthusian moments some utilitarians have thought that average happiness might best be maximized not by improving the lot of the poor but by minimizing their numbers, and so have advocated policies of "benign neglect" of the poorest and most desperate. Kantian patterns of reasoning are likely to endorse less global and less autonomy-overriding aid and development projects; they are not likely to endorse neglect or abandoning of those who are most vulnerable and lacking in autonomy. If the aim of beneficence is to keep or put others in a position to act for themselves, then emphasis must be placed on "bottom-up" projects, which from the start draw on, foster, and establish indigenous capacities and practices of self-help and local action.

14.
HUMAN CLONING: A KANTIAN APPROACH

❧ ❧ ❧

PHILIP KITCHER

Philip Kitcher is a professor of philosophy at Columbia University, having previously taught philosophy for several years at the University of California, San Diego. He is well known for his work in philosophy of science (especially philosophy of biology) and philosophy of mathematics, and for the connections he draws between these fields and central questions in ethics, metaphysics, and epistemology. The following selection is from his book, The Lives to Come: The Genetic Revolution and Human Possibilities. *Kitcher applies Kant's "End in Itself" formulation of the Categorical Imperative to the issue of reproductive cloning. He examines three cases in which reproductive cloning may be morally acceptable. On Kitcher's approach, to determine the morality of reproductive cloning we must look at the details of a particular case to determine if we are violating the cloned person's autonomy or using him as a mere means to our own ends.*

"Researchers Astounded" is not the typical phraseology of a headline on the front page of the *New York Times* (February 23, 1997). Lamb number 6LL3, better known as Dolly, took the world by surprise, sparking debate about the proper uses of biotechnology and inspiring predictable public fantasies (and predictable jokes). Recognizing that what is possible today with sheep will probably be feasible with human beings tomorrow, commentators speculated about the legitimacy of cloning Pavarotti or Einstein, about the chances that a demented dictator might produce an army of supersoldiers, and about the future of basketball in a world where the Boston Larry Birds play against the Chicago Michael Jordans. Polls showed that Mother Teresa was the most popular choice for person-to-be-cloned, although a film star (Michelle Pfeiffer) was not far behind, and Bill Clinton and Hillary Clinton obtained some support....

If cloning human beings is undertaken in the hope of generating a particular kind of person, a person whose standards of what matters in life are imposed from without, then it is morally repugnant, not because it involves biological tinkering but because it is continuous with other ways of interfering with human autonomy that we ought to resist. Human cloning would provide new ways of committing old moral errors. To discover whether or not there are morally permissible cases of cloning, we need to see if this objectionable feature can be removed, if there are situations in which the intention of the prospective parents is properly focused on the quality of human lives but in which cloning represents the only option for them. Three scenarios come immediately to mind.

The case of the dying child. Imagine a couple, whose only son is slowly dying. If the child were provided with a kidney transplant within the next ten years, he would recover and be able to lead a normal life. Unfortunately, neither parent is able to supply a compatible organ, and it is known that individuals with kidneys that could be successfully transplanted are extremely rare. However, if a brother were produced by cloning, then it would be possible to use one of his kidneys to save the life of the elder son. Supposing that the technology of cloning human beings has become sufficiently reliable to give the couple a very high probability of successfully producing a son with the same complement of nuclear genes, is it permissible for them to do so?

The case of the grieving widow. A woman's much-loved husband has been killed in a car crash. As the result of the same crash, the couple's only daughter lies in a coma, with irreversible brain damage, and she will surely die in a matter of months. The widow is no longer able to bear children. Should she be allowed to have the nuclear DNA from one of her daughter's cells inserted in an egg supplied by another woman, and to have a clone of her child produced through surrogate motherhood?

The case of the loving lesbians. A lesbian couple, devoted to one another for many years, wish to produce a child. Because they would like the child to be biologically connected to each of them, they request that a cell nucleus from one of them be inserted in an egg from the other, and that the embryo be implanted in the woman who donated the egg. (Here, one of the women would be nuclear mother and the other would be both egg mother and womb mother.) Should their request be accepted?

In all of these instances, ... there is no blatant attempt to impose the plan of a new life, to interfere with a child's own conception of what is valuable. Yet there are lingering concerns that need to be addressed. The first scenario, and to a lesser extent the second, arouses suspicion that children are being subordinated to special adult purposes and projects. Turning ... to one of the ... great influences on contemporary moral theory, Immanuel Kant, we can formulate the worry as a different question about respecting the autonomy of the child: Can these cases be reconciled with the injunction "to treat humanity whether in your own person or in that of another, always as an end and never as a means only"?

It is quite possible that the parents in the case of the dying child would have intentions that flout that principle. They have no desire for another child. They are desperate to save the son they have, and if they could only find an appropriate organ to transplant, they would be delighted to do that; for them the younger brother would simply be a cache of resources, something to be used in saving the really important life. Presumably, if the brother were born and the transplant did not succeed, they would regard that as a failure. Yet the parental attitudes do not have to be so stark and callous (and, in the instances in which parents have actually contemplated bearing a child to save an older sibling, it is quite clear that they are much more complex). Suppose we imagine that the parents plan to have another child in any case, that they are committed to loving and cherishing the child for his or her own sake. What can be the harm in planning that child's birth so as to allow their firstborn to live?

The moral quality of what is done plainly depends on the parental attitudes, specifically on whether or not they have the proper concern for the younger boy's well-being, independently of his being able to save his elder brother. Ironically, their love for him may be manifested most clearly if the project goes awry and the first child dies. Although that love might equally be present in cases where the elder son survives, reflective parents will probably always wonder whether it is untinged by the desire to find some means of saving the first-born—and, of course, the younger boy is likely to entertain worries of a similar nature. He would by no means be the first child to feel himself a second-class substitute, in this case either a helpmeet or a possible replacement for someone loved in his own right.

Similarly, the grieving widow might be motivated solely by desire to forge some link with the happy past, so that the child produced by cloning would be valuable because she was genetically close to the dead (having the same nuclear DNA as her sister, DNA that derives from the widow and her dead husband). If so, another person is being treated as a means to understandable, but morbid, ends. On the other hand, perhaps the widow is primarily moved by the desire for another child, and the prospect of cloning simply reflects the common attitude of many (though not all) parents who prize biological connection to their offspring. However, as in the case of the dying child, the participants, if they are at all reflective, are bound to wonder about the mixture of attitudes surrounding the production of a life so intimately connected to the past.

The case of the loving lesbians is the purest of the three, for here we seem to have a precise analogue of the situation in which heterosexual couples find themselves. Cloning would enable the devoted pair to have a child biologically related to both of them. There is no question of imposing some particular plan on the nascent life, even the minimal one of hoping to save another child or to serve as a reminder of the dead, but simply the wish to have a child who is their own, the expression of their mutual love. If human cloning is ever defensible, it will be in contexts like this.

During past decades, medicine has allowed many couples to overcome reproductive problems and to have biological children. The development of techniques of assisted reproduction responds to the sense that couples who have problems with infertility have been deprived of something that it is quite reasonable for people to value, and that various kinds of manipulations with human cells are legitimate responses to their frustrations. Yet serious issues remain. How close an approximation to the normal circumstances of reproduction and the normal genetic connections should we strive to achieve? How should the benefits of restoring reproduction be weighed against possible risks of the techniques? Both kinds of questions arise with respect to our scenarios.

Lesbian couples already have an option to produce a child who will be biologically related to both. If an egg from one of them is fertilized with sperm (supplied, say, by a male relative of the other) and the resultant embryo is implanted in the womb of the woman who did not give the egg, then both have a biological connection to the child (one is egg mother, the other womb mother). That method of reproduction might even seem preferable, diminishing any sense of burden that the child might feel because of special biological closeness to one of the mothers and allowing for the possibility of having children of either sex. The grieving widow might turn to existing techniques of assisted reproduction and rear a child conceived from artificial insemination of one of her daughter's eggs. In either case, cloning would create a closer biological connection—but should that extra degree of relationship be assigned particularly high value?

My discussion of all three scenarios also depends on assuming that human cloning works smoothly, that there are no worrisome risks that the pregnancy will go awry, producing a child whose development is seriously disrupted. Dolly, remember, was one success out of 277 tries, and we can suppose that early ventures in human cloning would have an appreciable rate of failure. We cannot know yet whether the development of technology for cloning human beings would simply involve the death of early embryos, or whether, along the way, researchers would generate malformed fetuses and, from time to time, children with problems undetectable before birth. During the next few years, we shall certainly come to know much more about the biological processes involved in cloning mammals, and the information we acquire may make it possible to undertake human cloning with confidence that any breakdowns will occur early in development (before there is a person with rights). Meanwhile, we can hope that the continuing transformation of our genetic knowledge will provide improved methods of transplantation, and thus bring relief to parents whose children die for lack of compatible organs.

Should human cloning be banned? Until we have much more extensive and detailed knowledge of how cloning can be achieved (and what the potential problems are) in a variety of mammalian species, there is no warrant for trying to perform Wilmut's clever trick on ourselves. I have suggested that there are some few circumstances in which human cloning might be morally permissible, but, in at least two of these, there are genuine concerns about attitudes to the nascent life, while, in the third, alternative techniques, already available, offer almost as good a response to the underlying predicament. Perhaps, when cloning techniques have become routine in non-human mammalian biology, we may acknowledge human cloning as appropriate relief for the parents of dying children, for grieving widows, and for loving lesbians. For now, however, we do best to try to help them in other ways....

At the first stages of the Human Genome Project, James Watson argued for the assignment of funds to study the "ethical, legal, and social implications" of the purely scientific research. Watson explicitly drew the analogy with the original development of nuclear technology, recommending that, this time, scientific and social change might go hand in hand. Almost a decade later, the mapping and sequencing are advancing faster than most people had anticipated—and the affluent nations remain almost where they were in terms of supplying the social backdrop that will put the genetic knowledge to proper use. That is not for lack of numerous expert studies that outline the potential problems and that propose ways of overcoming them. Much has been written. Little has been done. In the United States we still lack the most basic means of averting genetic discrimination, to wit universal health coverage, but Britain and even the continental European nations are little better placed to cope with what is coming.

The belated response to cloning is of a piece with a general failure to translate clear moral directives into regulations and policies. Dolly is a highly visible symbol, but behind her is a broad array of moral issues that citizens of affluent societies seem to prefer to leave in the shadows. However strongly we feel about the plight of loving lesbians, grieving widows, or even couples whose children are dying, deciding the legitimate employment of human cloning in dealing with their troubles is not our most urgent problem. Those who think that working out the proper limits of human cloning is the big issue are suffering from moral myopia.

General moral principles provide us with an obligation to improve the quality of human lives, where we have the opportunity to do so, and developments in biotechnology provide opportunities and challenges. If we took the principles seriously, we would be led to demand serious investment in programs to improve the lives of the young, the disabled, and the socially disadvantaged. That is not quite what is going on in the "civilized" world. Making demands for social investment seems quixotic, especially at a time when, in America, funds for poor children and disabled people who are out of work are being slashed, and when, in other affluent countries, there is serious questioning of the responsibilities of societies to their citizens. Yet the application of patronizing adjectives does nothing to undermine the legitimacy of the demands. What is truly shameful is not that the response to possibilities of cloning came so late, nor that it has been confused, but the common reluctance of all the affluent nations to think through the implications of time-honored moral principles and to design a coherent use of the new genetic information and technology for human well-being.

CHAPTER SIX

MORAL PLURALISM

INTRODUCTION

Moral pluralism is a position that has become influential in recent years. There are two basic types of moral pluralism. Some theorists, specifically some of those who endorse deontological moral theories, believe that there is a plurality of moral principles which are all equally fundamental. None of these principles can be subsumed under or explained in terms of another. This type of pluralism is pluralism about moral principles. The other type of moral pluralism is pluralism about values. This second type of pluralism holds that there is a plurality of values, none of which can be explained in terms of the others. For example, the values of friendship, pleasure, spiritual development, adventure, security, and so on, are simply different values that cannot be explained in terms of one another, or in terms of an overarching value. Therefore they are incommensurable. There is no master value in terms of which we can compare them. The position that is opposed to pluralism is monism. Monists about moral principles hold that there is a single, overarching moral principle, from which more specific moral principles or conclusions can be derived. Monists about value hold that there is a single, master value in terms of which we can explain everything else that is valuable. For example, a theorist of this sort might hold that happiness is the master value, and that other things are valuable because they contribute to happiness. If we adopt a position of this sort, then values are commensurable. We can compare them in terms of how well or extensively they contribute to happiness. Let us consider each of these kinds of pluralism in turn.

Immanuel Kant's moral theory, found in Chapter Five of this book, can be understood as a monistic moral theory. Although Kant gave three formulations of the categorical imperative, he believed they were three different ways of expressing the same moral principle. If he is correct, then he offers a single moral principle from which other moral principles and conclusions can be derived. W.D. Ross, on the other hand, presents us with several different "*prima facie* duties," which are duties that would apply if there were no other countervailing moral considerations. Ross believes that these *prima facie* duties will often come into conflict, and when they do, there is no overarching moral principle that tells us how the conflict should be resolved. Instead, when two or more such duties come into conflict, we must consider both the *prima facie* duties involved and the circumstances of the case very carefully. We must then use our judgment to determine which of the duties is more compelling in the particular case at hand, or in other words, what we ought to do in this case all things considered. There is no way to be absolutely certain that we have resolved the case correctly, although in some cases we will have a high degree of confidence that we have done so. For example, suppose that I promise a child that on Tuesday I will take her out on some rocks that overhang the ocean, but on this day there happens to be a violent storm that makes venturing out on these rocks very treacherous. In this case my *prima facie* duty to keep my promises will come into conflict with my *prima facie* duty not to harm the child. By reflecting on these duties and the circumstances of my choice, I will see that the second duty is much more compelling in this case. In another set of circumstances, however, the duty to keep my promise may be the more compelling of conflicting *prima facie* duties.

Critics of this type of moral pluralism will point out that a theory of this sort leaves a wide range of our moral thought unspecified. They will argue that the point of constructing moral theories in the first place is that we are often unsure of our judgment in particular cases. If we were very confident that we could always intuit or apprehend what is morally right in any given situation, there would be little point in constructing moral theories, or indeed, in engaging in the study of ethics at all. The truth is, however, that we are often uncertain and confused about what we ought to do, and further, we often disagree with one another about the correct action to take in a given situation, the right public policy to adopt, the right laws to pass, and so on. Ideally, our moral theories would help us to move beyond our individual judgments to tell us which decisions are right *and why*. Monists will argue that a single overarching moral principle will provide us with the guidance we need to resolve our difficult and contentious moral issues. Further, a moral theory based on a single principle of this sort will have the virtue of theoretical simplicity. A single, overarching moral principle will have a great deal of explanatory power, and will be less likely than the more narrow principles endorsed by the pluralist to be ad hoc, or to constitute an accidental generalization of our considered moral judgments.

Pluralists like Ross can respond that the ultimate test of the adequacy of a moral theory is that it encompasses our firmly held moral convictions. Ross argues that these convictions are the "data" with which we work in ethics, just as our empirical observations are the data we work with in science. Although the monist's moral theory is simpler than the pluralist's, the simplicity of a theory is secondary in importance to the extent to which the theory accounts for the data. As David Schmidtz has pointed out, a periodic table that listed only four elements (or perhaps even only one element) would be simpler than the periodic table we now accept, but it would be nowhere near as adequate.[1] Likewise Newton's theory is quite a bit simpler than Einstein's special and general theories of relativity. Nevertheless, Einstein's theory is more adequate than Newton's because it performs better than Newton's in accounting for the data. Moral pluralists can point out that there have been serious objections raised against all the overarching moral principles proposed by those who have advanced our most prominent monistic moral theories, and suggest that their more complex moral theories provide a more accurate account of our most firmly held moral convictions.

Further, moral pluralists can point out that sometimes two or more moral principles *converge* on a particular moral issue (such as global warming) rather than coming into conflict with one another. In cases of this sort, each moral principle seems to carry some weight, and the indicated resolution to the moral problem seems to be very strong. Perhaps when a number of equally fundamental moral principles point to the same course of action, the pluralist is better able to explain the moral importance of adopting this course of action than the monist.

The second kind of moral pluralism is pluralism about values. A values pluralist holds that there are a plurality of values that often come into conflict in life, and that none of these values can be reduced to or explained in terms of each other, or in terms of a fundamental master value. There is an important sense, then, in which these values are incommensurable. Because these values cannot be reduced to or explained in terms of a single value, there is no established continuum on which we can compare the relative worth of these values. Theorists of this sort also hold that there is no authoritative moral standard, such as a single moral principle, in reference to which we can assess these values. Moral pluralists of this type again argue that although a monistic account of value is simpler, the pluralistic position provides a more accurate account of our moral experience. Our moral lives are complex, and a moment's reflection on our actual moral experience shows that we often struggle to choose between conflicting and apparently incommensurable values. For example, we may struggle for a long time with a choice between a job that we find to be very meaningful and a job that would provide us with much more financial security, or with a choice between spending more time with our families and excelling in our chosen careers. Further, moral pluralists point out that even after we have thought very carefully and made a decision of this sort, we may feel some regret for the opportunity we passed by in order to realize our preferred value. Pluralists take this phenomenon as evidence of the fact that these competing values cannot be reduced to or explained in terms of a single fundamental value. If they could be reduced to a single value, our choices could be made simply by determining which option would create more of this fundamental value, and then we would have no regrets about the option we passed by. For example, if I have a choice between two fifteen-month certificates of deposit, one of which has an interest rate of 3.5 and one of which has an interest rate of 4.0, I will clearly choose the second, and I will have no regrets whatsoever about letting go of the first. The only value at stake here is money, and clearly I would prefer to have more money rather than less.

The central question faced by values pluralists is whether we can ever make a rational choice between values that come into conflict. If there is a plurality of values and these values are incommensurable, then it is not clear that such a rational choice can be made. Yet we like to think of ourselves as behaving rationally as we attempt to lead a moral life. It would be disconcerting for us to believe or discover that some of our most significant choices in life are completely arbitrary. One way for a values pluralist to respond to this question is to argue that we can appeal to something other than a fundamental value in making a rational choice between incommensurable values. This is the strategy employed by John Kekes. He suggests that we can appeal to the basic or minimal requirements of human welfare in making these decisions, and that proceeding in this manner is rationally justifiable.

When the pluralist appeals to judgment in deciding which of many principles or values is the strongest in a particular situation, she need not assume that everyone is equally capable of sorting through the alternatives. Some people may well have better moral judgment than others, if we understand moral judgment to be the capacity to weigh and balance competing moral considerations. Even if there is no algorithm to apply in determining when one moral consideration overrides another, it seems clear that some people make better moral decisions than others. Those who have thought long and hard about moral problems and how to solve them are probably better than average at identifying various duties and values and assessing their relative importance. If so, then these persons provide a resource for the rest of us in developing our moral thought.

Note

1. David Schmidtz, *Elements of Justice* (Cambridge, New York: Cambridge UP, 2006) 4.

15.
WHAT MAKES RIGHT ACTS RIGHT?

❋ ❋ ❋

W.D. ROSS

Sir William Davis Ross (1877-1971) was provost of Oriel College, Oxford University. The following is a selection from The Right and the Good, *in which Ross defends ethical intuitionism. He argues against utilitarianism without dismissing entirely the importance of consequences, and emphasizes prima facie duties as action-guiding principles. Unlike Kant's formulations of the Categorical Imperative, Ross's prima facie duties are not absolute duties. Instead, one prima facie duty, such as the duty to keep a promise, can be overridden by another prima facie duty, such as the duty to render aid.*

The real point at issue between hedonism and utilitarianism on the one hand and their opponents on the other is not whether "right" means "productive of so and so"; for it cannot with any plausibility be maintained that it does. The point at issue is that to which we now pass, viz. whether there is any general character which makes right acts right, and if so, what it is. Among the main historical attempts to state a single characteristic of all right actions which is the foundation of their rightness are those made by egoism and utilitarianism. But I do not propose to discuss these, not because the subject is unimportant, but because it has been dealt with so often and so well already, and because there has come to be so much agreement among moral philosophers that neither of these theories is satisfactory. A much more attractive theory has been put forward by Professor Moore: that what makes actions right is that they are productive of more *good* than could have been produced by any other action open to the agent.[1]

This theory is in fact the culmination of all the attempts to base rightness on productivity of some sort of result. The first form this attempt takes is the attempt to base rightness on conduciveness to the advantage or pleasure of the agent. This theory comes to grief over the fact, which stares us in the face, that a great part of duty consists in an observance of the rights and a furtherance of the interests of others, whatever the cost to ourselves may be. Plato and others may be right in holding that a regard for the rights of others never in the long run involves a loss of happiness for the agent, that "the just life profits a man." But this, even if true, is irrelevant to the rightness of the act. As soon as a man does an action *because* he thinks he will promote his own interests thereby, he is acting not from a sense of its rightness but from self-interest.

To the egoistic theory hedonistic utilitarianism supplies a much-needed amendment. It points out correctly that the fact that a certain pleasure will be enjoyed by the agent is no reason why he *ought* to bring it into being rather than an equal or greater pleasure to be enjoyed by another, though, human nature being what it is, it makes it not unlikely that he *will* try to bring it into being. But hedonistic utilitarianism in its turn needs a correction. On reflection it seems clear that pleasure is not the only thing in life that we think good in itself, that for instance we think the possession of a good character, or an intelligent understanding of the world, as good or better. A great advance is made by the substitution of "productive of the greatest good" for "productive of the greatest pleasure."

Not only is this theory more attractive than hedonistic utilitarianism, but its logical relation to that theory is such that the latter could not be true unless *it* were true, while it might be true though hedonistic utilitarianism were not. It is in fact one of the logical bases of hedonistic utilitarianism. For the view that what produces the maximum pleasure is right has for its bases the views (1) that what produces the maximum good is right, and (2) that pleasure is the only thing good in itself. If they were not assuming that what produces the maximum *good* is right, the utilitarians' attempt to show that pleasure is the only thing good in itself, which is in fact the point they take most pains to establish, would have been quite irrelevant to their attempt to prove that only what produces the maximum *pleasure is* right. If, therefore, it can be shown that productivity of the maximum good is not what makes all right actions right, we shall *a fortiori* have refuted hedonistic utilitarianism.

When a plain man fulfils a promise because he thinks he ought to do so, it seems clear that he does so with no thought of its total consequences, still less with any opinion that these are likely to be the best possible. He thinks in fact much more of the past than of the future. What makes him think it right to act in a certain way is the fact that he has promised to do so—that and, usually, nothing more. That his act will produce the best possible consequences is not his reason for calling it right. What lends colour to the theory we are examining, then, is not the actions (which form probably a great majority of our actions) in which some such reflection as "I have promised" is the only reason we give ourselves for thinking a certain action right, but the exceptional cases in which the consequences of fulfilling a promise (for instance) would be so disastrous to others that we judge it right not to do so. It must of course be admitted that such cases exist. If I have promised to meet a friend at a particular time for some trivial purpose, I should certainly think myself justified in breaking my engagement if by doing so I could prevent a serious accident or bring relief to the victims of one. And the supporters of the view we are examining hold that my thinking so is due to my thinking that I shall bring more good into existence by the one action than by the other. A different account may, however, be given of the matter, an account which will, I believe, show itself to be the true one. It may be said that besides the duty of fulfilling promises I have and recognize a duty of relieving distress,[2] and that when I think it right to do the latter at the cost of not doing the former, it is not because I think I shall produce more good thereby but because I think it the duty which is in the circumstances more of a duty. This account surely corresponds much more closely with what we really think in such a situation. If, so far as I can see, I could bring equal amounts of good into being by fulfilling my promise and by helping some one to whom I had made no promise, I should not hesitate to regard the former as my duty. Yet on the view that what is right is right because it is productive of the most good I should not so regard it.

There are two theories, each in its way simple, that offer a solution of such cases of conscience. One is the view of Kant, that there are certain duties of perfect obligation, such as those of fulfilling promises, of paying debts, of telling the truth, which admit of no exception whatever in favour of duties of imperfect obligation, such as that of relieving distress. The other is the view of, for instance, Professor Moore and Dr. Rashdall, that there is only the duty of producing good, and that all "conflicts of duties" should be resolved by asking "by which action will most good be produced?" But it is more important that our theory fit the facts than that it be simple, and the account we have given above corresponds (it seems to me) better than either of the simpler theories with what we really think, viz. that normally promise-keeping, for example, should come before benevolence, but that when and only when the good to be produced by the benevolent act is very great and the promise comparatively trivial, the act of benevolence becomes our duty.

In fact the theory of "ideal utilitarianism," if I may for brevity refer so to the theory of Professor Moore, seems to simplify unduly our relations to our fellows. It says, in effect, that the only morally significant relation in which my neighbours stand to me is that of being possible beneficiaries by my action.[3] They do stand in this relation to me, and this relation is morally significant. But they may also stand to me in the relation of promisee to promisor, of creditor to debtor, of wife to husband, of child to parent, of friend to friend, of fellow countryman to fellow countryman, and the like; and each of these relations is the foundation of a *prima facie* duty, which is more or less incumbent on me according to the circumstances of the case. When I am in a situation, as perhaps I always am, in which more than one of these *prima facie* duties is incumbent on me, what I have to do is to study the situation as fully as I can until I form the considered opinion (it is never more) that in the circumstances one of them is more incumbent than any other; then I am bound to think that to do this *prima facie* duty is my duty *sans phrase* in the situation.

I suggest *"prima facie* duty" or "conditional duty" as a brief way of referring to the characteristic (quite distinct from that of being a duty proper) which an act has, in virtue of being of a certain kind (e.g., the keeping of a promise), of being an act which would be a duty proper if it were not at the same time of another kind which is morally significant. Whether an act is a duty proper or actual duty depends on *all* the morally significant kinds it is an instance of. The phrase *"prima facie* duty" must be apologized for, since (1) it suggests that what we are speaking of is a certain kind of duty, whereas it is in fact not a duty, but something related in a special way to duty. Strictly speaking, we want not a phrase in which duty is qualified by an adjective, but a separate noun. (2) *"Prima" facie* suggests that one is speaking only of an appearance which a moral situation presents at first sight, and which may turn out to be illusory; whereas what I am speaking of is an objective fact involved in the nature of the situation, or more strictly in an element of its nature, though not, as duty proper does, arising from its *whole* nature. I can, however, think of no term which fully meets the case. "Claim" has been suggested by Professor Prichard. The word "claim" has the advantage of being quite a familiar one in this connexion, and it seems to cover much of the ground. It would be quite natural to say, "a person to whom I have made a promise has a claim on me," and also, "a person whose distress I could relieve (at the cost of breaking the promise) has a claim on me." But (1) while "claim" is appropriate from *their* point of view, we want a word to express the corresponding fact from the agent's point of view—the fact of his being subject to claims that can be made against him; and ordinary language provides us with no such correlative to "claim." And (2) (what is more important) "claim" seems inevitably to suggest two persons, one of whom might make a claim on the other; and while this covers the ground of social duty, it is inappropriate in the case of that important part of duty which is the duty of cultivating a certain kind of character in oneself. It would be artificial, I think, and at any rate metaphorical, to say that one's character has a claim on oneself.

There is nothing arbitrary about these *prima facie* duties. Each rests on a definite circumstance which cannot seriously be held to be without moral significance. Of *prima facie* duties I suggest, without claiming completeness or finality for it, the following division.[4]

(1) Some duties rest on previous acts of my own. These duties seem to include two kinds, (*a*) those resting on a promise or what may fairly be called an implicit promise, such as the implicit undertaking not to tell lies which seems to be implied in the act of entering into conversation (at any rate by civilized men), or of writing books that purport to be history and not fiction. These may be called the duties of fidelity. (*b*) Those resting on a previous wrongful act. These may be called the duties of reparation. (2) Some rest on previous acts of other men, i.e., services done by them to me. These may be loosely described as the duties of gratitude.[5] (3) Some rest on the fact or pos-

sibility of a distribution of pleasure or happiness (or of the means thereto) which is not in accordance with the merit of the persons concerned; in such cases there arises a duty to upset or prevent such a distribution. These are the duties of justice. (4) Some rest on the mere fact that there are other beings in the world whose condition we can make better in respect of virtue, or of intelligence, or of pleasure. These are the duties of beneficence. (5) Some rest on the fact that we can improve our own condition in respect of virtue or of intelligence. These are the duties of self-improvement. (6) I think that we should distinguish from (4) the duties that may be summed up under the title of "not injuring others." No doubt to injure others is incidentally to fail to do them good; but it seems to me clear that non-maleficence is apprehended as a duty distinct from that of beneficence, and as a duty of a more stringent character. It will be noticed that this alone among the types of duty has been stated in a negative way. An attempt might no doubt be made to state this duty, like the others, in a positive way. It might be said that it is really the duty to prevent ourselves from acting either from an inclination to harm others or from an inclination to seek our own pleasure, in doing which we should incidentally harm them. But on reflection it seems clear that the primary duty here is the duty not to harm others, this being a duty whether or not we have an inclination that if followed would lead to our harming them; and that when we have such an inclination the primary duty not to harm others gives rise to a consequential duty to resist the inclination. The recognition of this duty of non-maleficence is the first step on the way to the recognition of the duty of beneficence, and that accounts for the prominence of the commands "thou shalt not kill," "thou shalt not commit adultery," "thou shalt not steal," "thou shalt not bear false witness" in so early a code as the Decalogue. But even when we have come to recognize the duty of beneficence, it appears to me that the duty of non-maleficence is recognized as a distinct one, and as *prima facie* more binding. We should not in general consider it justifiable to kill one person in order to keep another alive, or to steal from one in order to give alms to another.

The essential defect of the "ideal utilitarian" theory is that it ignores, or at least does not do full justice to, the highly personal character of duty. If the only duty is to produce the maximum of good, the question who is to have the good—whether it is myself, or my benefactor, or a person to whom I have made a promise to confer that good on him, or a mere fellow man to whom I stand in no such special relation—should make no difference to my having a duty to produce that good. But we are all in fact sure that it makes a vast difference.

One or two other comments must be made on this provisional list of the divisions of duty. (1) The nomenclature is not strictly correct. For by "fidelity" or "gratitude" we mean, strictly, certain states of motivation; and, as I have urged, it is not our duty to have certain motives, but to do certain acts. By "fidelity," for instance, is meant, strictly, the disposition to fulfil promises and implicit promises *because we have made them.* We have no general word to cover the actual fulfilment of promises and implicit promises *irrespective of motive*; and I use "fidelity," loosely but perhaps conveniently, to fill this gap. So too I use "gratitude" for the returning of services, irrespective of motive. The term "justice" is not so much confined, in ordinary usage, to a certain state of motivation, for we should often talk of a man as acting justly even when we did not think his motive was the wish to do what was just simply for the sake of doing so. Less apology is therefore needed for our use of "justice" in this sense. And I have used the word "beneficence" rather than "benevolence," in order to emphasize the fact that it is our duty to do certain things, and not to do them from certain motives.

(2) If the objection be made, that this catalogue of the main types of duty is an unsystematic one resting on no logical principle, it may be replied, first, that it makes no claim to being ultimate. It is a *prima facie* classification of the duties which reflection on our moral convictions seems actually to reveal. And if these convictions are, as I would claim that they are, of the nature of knowledge, and if I have not misstated them, the list will be a list of authentic conditional duties, correct as far as it goes though not necessarily complete. The list of *goods* put forward by the rival theory is reached by exactly the same method—the only sound one in the circumstances—viz. that of direct reflection on what we really think. Loyalty to the facts is worth more than a symmetrical architectonic or a hastily reached simplicity. If further reflection discovers a perfect logical basis for this or for a better classification, so much the better.

(3) It may, again, be objected that our theory that there are these various and often conflicting types of *prima facie* duty leaves us with no principle upon which to discern what is our actual duty in particular circumstances. But this objection is not one which the rival theory is in a position to bring forward. For when we have to choose between the production of two heterogeneous goods, say knowledge and pleasure, the "ideal utilitarian" theory can only fall back on an opinion, for which no logical basis can be offered, that one of the goods is the greater; and this is no better than a similar opinion that one of two duties is the more urgent. And again, when we consider the infinite variety of the effects of our actions in the way of pleasure, it must surely be admitted that the claim which *hedonism* sometimes makes, that it offers a readily applicable criterion of right conduct, is quite illusory.

I am unwilling, however, to content myself with an *argument ad hominem,* and I would contend that in principle there is no reason to anticipate that every act that is our duty is so for one and the same reason. Why should two sets of circumstances, or one set of circumstances, *not* possess different characteristics, any one of which makes a certain act our *prima facie* duty? When I ask what it is that makes me in certain cases sure that I have a *prima facie* duty to do so and so, I find that it lies in the fact that I have made a promise; when I ask the same question in another case, I find the answer lies in the fact that I have done a wrong. And if on reflection I find (as I think I do) that neither of these reasons is reducible to the other, I must not on any *a priori* ground assume that such a reduction is possible.

An attempt may be made to arrange in a more systematic way the main types of duty which we have indicated. In the first place it seems self-evident that if there are things that are intrinsically good, it is *prima facie* a duty to bring them into existence rather than not to do so, and to bring as much of them into existence as possible. It will be argued ... that there are three main things that are intrinsically good—virtue, knowledge, and, with certain limitations, pleasure. And since a given virtuous disposition, for instance, is equally good whether it is realized in myself or in another, it seems to be my duty to bring it into existence whether in myself or in another. So too with a given piece of knowledge.

The case of pleasure is difficult; for while we clearly recognize a duty to produce pleasure for others, it is by no means so clear that we recognize a duty to produce pleasure for ourselves. This appears to arise from the following facts. The thought of an act as our duty is one that presupposes a certain amount of reflection about the act; and for that reason does not normally arise in connexion with acts towards which we are already impelled by another strong impulse. So far, the cause of our not thinking of the promotion of our own pleasure as a duty is analogous to the cause which usually prevents a highly sympathetic person from thinking of the promotion of the pleasure of others as a duty. He is impelled so strongly by direct interest in the well-being of others towards promoting their pleasure that he does not stop to ask whether it is his duty to promote it; and we are all impelled so strongly towards the promotion of our own pleasure that we do not stop to ask whether it is a duty or not. But there is a further reason why even when we stop to think about the matter it does not usually present itself as a duty: viz. that, since the performance of most of our duties involves the giving up of some pleasure that we desire, the doing of duty and the getting of pleasure for ourselves come by a natural association of ideas to be thought of as incompatible things. This association of ideas is in the main salutary in its operation, since it puts a check on what but for it would be much too strong, the tendency to pursue one's own pleasure without thought of other considerations. Yet if pleasure is good, it seems in the long run clear that it is right to get it for ourselves as well as to produce it for others, when this does not involve the failure to discharge some more stringent *prima facie* duty. The question is a very difficult one, but it seems that this conclusion can be denied only on one or other of three grounds: (1) that pleasure is not *prima facie* good (i.e., good when it is neither the actualization of a bad disposition nor undeserved), (2) that there is no *prima facie* duty to produce as much

that is good as we can, or (3) that though there is a *prima facie* duty to produce other things that are good, there is no *prima facie* duty to produce pleasure which will be enjoyed by ourselves. I give reasons later[6] for not accepting the first contention. The second hardly admits of argument but seems to
me plainly false. The third seems plausible only if we hold that an act that is
pleasant or brings pleasure to ourselves must for that reason not be a duty;
and this would lead to paradoxical consequences, such as that if a man
enjoys giving pleasure to others or working for their moral improvement, it
cannot be his duty to do so. Yet it seems to be a very stubborn fact, that in
our ordinary consciousness we are not aware of a duty to get pleasure for
ourselves; and by way of partial explanation of this I may add that though, as
I think, one's own pleasure is a good and there is a duty to produce it, it is
only if we *think* of our own pleasure not as simply our own pleasure, but as
an objective good, something that an impartial spectator would approve,
that we can think of the getting it as a duty; and we do not habitually think
of it in this way.

If these contentions are right, what we have called the duty of beneficence
and the duty of self-improvement rest on the same ground. No different principles of duty are involved in the two cases. If we feel a special responsibility
for improving our own character rather than that of others, it is not because
a special principle is involved, but because we are aware that the one is more
under our control than the other. It was on this ground that Kant expressed
the practical law of duty in the form "seek to make yourself good and other
people happy." He was so persuaded of the internality of virtue that he
regarded any attempt by one person to produce virtue in another as bound
to produce, at most, only a counterfeit of virtue, the doing of externally right
acts not from the true principle of virtuous action but out of regard to another person. It must be admitted that one man cannot compel another to be
virtuous; compulsory virtue would just not be virtue. But experience clearly
shows that Kant overshoots the mark when he contends that one man cannot
do anything to *promote* virtue in another, to bring such influences to bear
upon him that his own response to them is more likely to be virtuous than his
response to other influences would have been. And our duty to do this is not
different in kind from our duty to improve our own characters.

It is equally clear, and clear at an earlier stage of moral development, that
if there are things that are bad in themselves we ought, *prima facie*, not to
bring them upon others; and on this fact rests the duty of non-maleficence.

The duty of justice is particularly complicated, and the word is used to
cover things which are really very different—things such as the payment
of debts, the reparation of injuries done by oneself to another, and the
bringing about of a distribution of happiness between other people in
proportion to merit. I use the word to denote only the last of these three.
... I shall try to show that besides the three (comparatively) simple goods,

virtue, knowledge, and pleasure, there is a more complex good, not reducible to these, consisting in the proportionment of happiness to virtue. The bringing of this about is a duty which we owe to all men alike, though it may be reinforced by special responsibilities that we have undertaken to particular men. This, therefore, with beneficence and self-improvement, comes under the general principle that we should produce as much good as possible, though the good here involved is different in kind from any other.

But besides this general obligation, there are special obligations. These may arise, in the first place, incidentally, from acts which were not essentially meant to create such an obligation, but which nevertheless create it. From the nature of the case such acts may be of two kinds—the infliction of injuries on others, and the acceptance of benefits from them. It seems clear that these put us under a special obligation to other men, and that only these acts can do so incidentally. From these arise the twin duties of reparation and gratitude.

And finally there are special obligations arising from acts the very intention of which, when they were done, was to put us under such an obligation. The name for such acts is "promises"; the name is wide enough if we are willing to include under it implicit promises, i.e., modes of behaviour in which without explicit verbal promise we intentionally create an expectation that we can be counted on to behave in a certain way in the interest of another person.

These seem to be, in principle, all the ways in which *prima facie* duties arise. In actual experience they are compounded together in highly complex ways. Thus, for example, the duty of obeying the laws of one's country arises partly (as Socrates contends in the *Crito*) from the duty of gratitude for the benefits one has received from it; partly from the implicit promise to obey which seems to be involved in permanent residence in a country whose laws we know we are *expected* to obey, and still more clearly involved when we ourselves invoke the protection of its laws (this is the truth underlying the doctrine of the social contract); and partly (if we are fortunate in our country) from the fact that its laws are potent instruments for the general good.

Or again, the sense of a general obligation to bring about (so far as we can) a just apportionment of happiness to merit is often greatly reinforced by the fact that many of the existing injustices are due to a social and economic system which we have, not indeed created, but taken part in and assented to; the duty of justice is then reinforced by the duty of reparation.

It is necessary to say something by way of clearing up the relation between *prima facie* duties and the actual or absolute duty to do one particular act in particular circumstances. If, as almost all moralists except Kant are agreed, and as most plain men think, it is sometimes right to tell a lie or to break a promise, it must be maintained that there is a difference between *prima facie* duty and actual or absolute duty. When we think ourselves justified in break-ing, and indeed morally obliged to break, a promise in order to relieve some one's distress, we do not for a moment cease to recognize a *prima facie* duty to keep our promise, and this leads us to feel, not indeed shame or repen-tance, but certainly compunction, for behaving as we do; we recognize, fur-ther, that it is our duty to make up somehow to the promisee for the break-ing of the promise. We have to distinguish from the characteristic of being our duty that of tending to be our duty. Any act that we do contains various elements in virtue of which it falls under various categories. In virtue of being the breaking of a promise, for instance, it tends to be wrong; in virtue of being an instance of relieving distress it tends to be right. Tendency to be one's duty may be called a parti-resultant attribute, i.e., one which belongs to an act in virtue of some one component in its nature. *Being* one's duty is a toti-resultant attribute, one which belongs to an act in virtue of its whole nature and of nothing less than this.[7] This distinction between parti-resul-tant and toti-resultant attributes is one which we shall meet in another con-text also.[8]

Another instance of the same distinction may be found in the operation of natural laws. *Qua* subject to the force of gravitation towards some other body, each body tends to move in a particular direction with a particular velocity; but its actual movement depends on *all* the forces to which it is sub-ject. It is only by recognizing this distinction that we can preserve the absoluteness of laws of nature, and only by recognizing a corresponding dis-tinction that we can preserve the absoluteness of the general principles of morality. But an important difference between the two cases must be point-ed out. When we say that in virtue of gravitation a body tends to move in a certain way, we are referring to a causal influence actually exercised on it by another body or other bodies. When we say that in virtue of being deliber-ately untrue a certain remark tends to be wrong, we are referring to no causal relation, to no relation that involves succession in time, but to such a relation as connects the various attributes of a mathematical figure. And if the word "tendency" is thought to suggest too much a causal relation, it is better to talk of certain types of act as being *prima facie* right or wrong (or of different persons as having different and possibly conflicting claims upon us), than of their tending to be right or wrong.

Something should be said of the relation between our apprehension of the *prima facie* rightness of certain types of act and our mental attitude towards particular acts. It is proper to use the word "apprehension" in the former case and not in the latter. That an act, *qua* fulfilling a promise, or *qua* effecting a just distribution of good, or *qua* returning services rendered, or *qua* promoting the good of others, or *qua* promoting the virtue or insight of the agent, is *prima facie* right, is self-evident; not in the sense that it is evident from the beginning of our lives, or as soon as we attend to the proposition for the first time, but in the sense that when we have reached sufficient mental maturity and have given sufficient attention to the proposition it is evident without any need of proof, or of evidence beyond itself. It is self-evident just as a mathematical axiom, or the validity of a form of inference, is evident. The moral order expressed in these propositions is just as much part of the fundamental nature of the universe (and, we may add, of any possible universe in which there were moral agents at all) as is the spatial or numerical structure expressed in the axioms of geometry or arithmetic. In our confidence that these propositions are true there is involved the same trust in our reason that is involved in our confidence in mathematics; and we should have no justification for trusting it in the latter sphere and distrusting it in the former. In both cases we are dealing with propositions that cannot be proved, but that just as certainly need no proof.

Some of these general principles of *prima facie* duty may appear to be open to criticism. It may be thought, for example, that the principle of returning good for good is a falling off from the Christian principle, generally and rightly recognized as expressing the highest morality, of returning good for evil. To this it may be replied that I do not suggest that there is a principle commanding us to return good for good and forbidding us to return good for evil, and that I do suggest that there is a positive duty to seek the good of all men. What I maintain is that an act in which good is returned for good is recognized as *specially* binding on us just because it is of that character, and that *ceteris paribus* any one would think it his duty to help his benefactors rather than his enemies, if he could not do both; just as it is generally recognized that *ceteris paribus* we should pay our debts rather than give our money in charity, when we cannot do both. A benefactor is not only a man, calling for our effort on his behalf on that ground, but also our benefactor, calling for our *special* effort on *that* ground.

Our judgements about our actual duty in concrete situations have none of the certainty that attaches to our recognition of the general principles of duty. A statement is certain, i.e., is an expression of knowledge, only in one or other of two cases: when it is either self-evident, or a valid conclusion from self-evident premises. And our judgements about our particular duties have neither of these characters. (1) They are not self-evident. Where a possible act is seen to have two characteristics, in virtue of one of which it is *prima facie* right, and in virtue of the other *prima facie* wrong, we are (I think) well aware that we are not certain whether we ought or ought not to do it; that whether we do it or not, we are taking a moral risk. We come in the long run, after consideration, to think one duty more pressing than the other, but we do not feel certain that it is so. And though we do not always recognize that a possible act has two such characteristics, and though there *may* be cases in which it has not, we are never certain that any particular possible act has not, and therefore never certain that it is right, nor certain that it is wrong. For, to go no further in the analysis, it is enough to point out that any particular act will in all probability in the course of time contribute to the bringing about of good or of evil for many human beings, and thus have a *prima facie* rightness or wrongness of which we know nothing. (2) Again, our judgements about our particular duties are not logical conclusions from self-evident premises. The only possible premises would be the general principles stating their *prima facie* rightness or wrongness *qua* having the different characteristics they do have; and even if we could (as we cannot) apprehend the extent to which an act will tend on the one hand, for example, to bring about advantages for our benefactors, and on the other hand to bring about disadvantages for fellow men who are not our benefactors, there is no principle by which we can draw the conclusion that it is on the whole right or on the whole wrong. In this respect the judgement as to the rightness of a particular act is just like the judgement as to the beauty of a particular natural object or work of art. A poem is, for instance, in respect of certain qualities beautiful and in respect of certain others not beautiful; and our judgement as to the degree of beauty it possesses on the whole is never reached by logical reasoning from the apprehension of its particular beauties or particular defects. Both in this and in the moral case we have more or less probable opinions which are not logically justified conclusions from the general principles that are recognized as self-evident.

There is therefore much truth in the description of the right act as a fortunate act. If we cannot be certain that it is right, it is our good fortune if the act we do is the right act. This consideration does not, however, make the doing of our duty a mere matter of chance. There is a parallel here between the doing of duty and the doing of what will be to our personal advantage. We never *know* what act will in the long run be to our advantage. Yet it is certain that we are more likely in general to secure our advantage if we estimate to the best of our ability the probable tendencies of our actions in this respect, than if we act on caprice. And similarly we are more likely to do our duty if we reflect to the best of our ability on the *prima facie* rightness or wrongness of various possible acts in virtue of the characteristics we perceive them to have, than if we act without reflection. With this greater likelihood we must be content.

Many people would be inclined to say that the right act for me is not that whose general nature I have been describing, viz. that which if I were omniscient I should see to be my duty, but that which on all the evidence available to me I should think to be my duty. But suppose that from the state of partial knowledge in which I think act *A* to be my duty, I could pass to a state of perfect knowledge in which I saw act *B* to be my duty, should I not say "act *B* was the right act for me to do"? I should no doubt add "though I am not to be blamed for doing act *A*." But in adding this, am I not passing from the question "what is right" to the question "what is morally good"? At the same time I am not making the *full* passage from the one notion to the other; for in order that the act should be morally good, or an act I am not to be blamed for doing, it must not merely be the act which it is reasonable for me to think my duty; it must also be done for that reason, or from some other morally good motive. Thus the conception of the right act as the act which it is reasonable for me to think my duty is an unsatisfactory compromise between the true notion of the right act and the notion of the morally good action.

The general principles of duty are obviously not self-evident from the beginning of our lives. How do they come to be so? The answer is, that they come to be self-evident to us just as mathematical axioms do. We find by experience that this couple of matches and that couple make four matches, that this couple of balls on a wire and that couple make four balls: and by reflection on these and similar discoveries we come to see that it is of the nature of two and two to make four. In a precisely similar way, we see the *prima facie* rightness of an act which would be the fulfilment of a particular promise, and of another which would be the fulfilment of another promise, and when we have reached sufficient maturity to think in general terms, we apprehend *prima facie* rightness to belong to the nature of any fulfilment of promise. What comes first in time is the apprehension of the self-evident *prima facie* rightness of an individual act of a particular type. From this we come by reflection to apprehend the self-evident general principle of *prima facie* duty. From this, too, perhaps along with the apprehension of the self-evident *prima facie* rightness of the same act in virtue of its having another characteristic as well, and perhaps in spite of the apprehension of its *prima facie* wrongness in virtue of its having some third characteristic, we come to believe something not self-evident at all, but an object of probable opinion, viz. that this particular act is (not *prima facie* but) actually right.

In this respect there is an important difference between rightness and mathematical properties. A triangle which is isosceles necessarily has two of its angles equal, whatever other characteristics the triangle may have—whatever, for instance, be its area, or the size of its third angle. The equality of the two angles is a parti-resultant attribute.[9] And the same is true of all mathematical attributes. It is true, I may add, of *prima facie* rightness. But no act is ever, in virtue of falling under some general description, necessarily actually right; its rightness depends on its whole nature[10] and not on any element in it. The reason is that no mathematical object (no figure, for instance, or angle) ever has two characteristics that tend to give it opposite resultant characteristics, while moral acts often (as every one knows) and indeed always (as on reflection we must admit) have different characteristics that tend to make them at the same time *prima facie* right and *prima facie* wrong; there is probably no act, for instance, which does good to any one without doing harm to some one else, and *vice versa.*

Supposing it to be agreed, as I think on reflection it must, that no one *means by* "right" just "productive of the best possible consequences," or "optimific," the attributes "right" and "optimific" might stand in either of two kinds of relation to each other. (1) They might be so related that we could apprehend *a priori*, either immediately or deductively, that any act that is optimific is right and any act that is right is optimific, as we can apprehend that any triangle that is equilateral is equiangular and *vice versa.* Professor Moore's view is, I think, that the coextensiveness of "right" and "optimific" is apprehended immediately.[11] He rejects the possibility of any proof of it. Or (2) the two attributes might be such that the question whether they are invariably connected had to be answered by means of an inductive inquiry. Now at first sight it might seem as if the constant connexion of the two attributes could be immediately apprehended. It might seem absurd to suggest that it could be right for any one to do an act which would produce consequences less good than those which would be produced by some other act in his power. Yet a little thought will convince us that this is not absurd. The type of case in which it is easiest to see that this is so is, perhaps, that in which one has made a promise. In such a case we all think that *prima facie* it is our duty to fulfil the promise irrespective of the precise goodness of the total consequences. And though we do not think it is necessarily our actual or absolute duty to do so, we are far from thinking that any, even the slightest, gain in the value of the total consequences will necessarily justify us in doing something else instead. Suppose, to simplify the case by abstraction, that the fulfilment of a promise to A would produce 1,000 units of good[12] for him, but that by doing some other act I could produce 1,001 units of good for B, to whom I have made no promise, the other consequences of the two acts being of equal value; should we really think it self-evident that it was our duty to do the second act and not the first? I think not. We should, I fancy, hold that only a much greater disparity of value between the total consequences would justify us in failing to discharge our *prima facie* duty to A. After all, a promise is a promise, and is not to be treated so lightly as the theory we are examining would imply. What, exactly, a promise is, is not so easy to determine, but we are surely agreed that it constitutes a serious moral limitation to our freedom of action. To produce the 1,001 units of good for B rather than fulfil our promise to A would be to take, not perhaps our duty as philanthropists too seriously, but certainly our duty as makers of promises too lightly.

Or consider another phase of the same problem. If I have promised to confer on A a particular benefit containing 1,000 units of good, is it self-evident that if by doing some different act I could produce 1,001 units of good for A himself (the other consequences of the two acts being supposed equal in value), it would be right for me to do so? Again, I think not. Apart from my general *prima facie* duty to do A what good I can, I have another *prima facie* duty to do him the particular service I have promised to do him, and this is not to be set aside in consequence of a disparity of good of the order of 1,001 to 1,000 though a much greater disparity might justify me in so doing.

Or again, suppose that *A* is a very good and *B* a very bad man, should I then, even when I have made no promise, think it self-evidently right to produce 1,001 units of good for *B* rather than 1,000 for *A*? Surely not. I should be sensible of a *prima facie* duty of justice, i.e., of producing a distribution of goods in proportion to merit, which is not outweighed by such a slight disparity in the total goods to be produced.

Such instances—and they might easily be added to—make it clear that there is no self-evident connexion between the attributes "right" and "optimific." The theory we are examining has a certain attractiveness when applied to our decision that a particular act is our duty (though I have tried to show that it does not agree with our actual moral judgements even here). But it is not even plausible when applied to our recognition of *prima facie* duty. For if it were self-evident that the right coincides with the optimific, it should be self-evident that what is *prima facie* right is *prima facie* optimific. But whereas we are certain that keeping a promise is *prima facie* right, we are not certain that it is *prima facie* optimific (though we are perhaps certain that it is *prima facie* bonific). Our certainty that it is *prima facie* right depends not on its consequences but on its being the fulfilment of a promise. The theory we are examining involves too much difference between the evident ground of our conviction about *prima facie* duty and the alleged ground of our conviction about actual duty.

The coextensiveness of the right and the optimific is, then, not self-evident. And I can see no way of proving it deductively; nor, so far as I know, has any one tried to do so. There remains the question whether it can be established inductively. Such an inquiry, to be conclusive, would have to be very thorough and extensive. We should have to take a large variety of the acts which we, to the best of our ability, judge to be right. We should have to trace as far as possible their consequences, not only for the persons directly affected but also for those indirectly affected, and to these no limit can be set. To make our inquiry thoroughly conclusive, we should have to do what we cannot do, viz. trace these consequences into an unending future. And even to make it reasonably conclusive, we should have to trace them far into the future. It is clear that the most we could possibly say is that a large variety of typical acts that are judged right appear, so far as we can trace their consequences, to produce more good than any other acts possible to the agents in the circumstances. And such a result falls far short of proving the constant connexion of the two attributes. But it is surely clear that no inductive inquiry justifying even this result has ever been carried through. The advocates of utilitarian systems have been so much persuaded either of the identity or of the self-evident connexion of the attributes "right" and "optimific" (or "felicific") that they have not attempted even such an inductive inquiry as is possible. And in view of the enormous complexity of the task and the inevitable inconclusiveness of the result, it is worth no one's while to make the attempt. What, after all, would be gained by it? If, as I have tried to show, for an act to be right and to be optimific are not the same thing, and an act's being optimific is not even the ground of its being right, then if we could ask ourselves (though the question is really unmeaning) which we ought to do, right acts because they are right or optimific acts because they are optimific, our answer must be "the former." If they are optimific as well as right, that is interesting but not morally important; if not, we still ought to do them (which is only another way of saying that they *are* the right acts), and the question whether they are optimific has no importance for moral theory.

There is one direction in which a fairly serious attempt has been made to show the connexion of the attributes "right" and "optimific." One of the most evident facts of our moral consciousness is the sense which we have of the sanctity of promises, a sense which does not, on the face of it, involve the thought that one will be bringing more good into existence by fulfilling the promise than by breaking it. It is plain, I think, that in our normal thought we consider that the fact that we have made a promise is in itself sufficient to create a duty of keeping it, the sense of duty resting on remembrance of the past promise and not on thoughts of the future consequences of its fulfilment. Utilitarianism tries to show that this is not so, that the sanctity of promises rests on the good consequences of the fulfilment of them and the bad consequences of their non-fulfilment. It does so in this way: it points out that when you break a promise you not only fail to confer a certain advantage on your promisee but you diminish his confidence, and indirectly the confidence of others, in the fulfilment of promises. You thus strike a blow at one of the devices that have been found most useful in the relations between man and man—the device on which, for example, the whole system of commercial credit rests—and you tend to bring about a state of things wherein each man, being entirely unable to rely on the keeping of promises by others, will have to do everything for himself, to the enormous impoverishment of human well-being.

To put the matter otherwise, utilitarians say that when a promise ought to be kept it is because the total good to be produced by keeping it is greater than the total good to be produced by breaking it, the former including as its main element the maintenance and strengthening of general mutual confidence, and the latter being greatly diminished by a weakening of this confidence. They say, in fact, that the case I put some pages back[13] never arises— the case in which by fulfilling a promise I shall bring into being 1,000 units of good for my promisee, and by breaking it 1,001 units of good for some one else, the other effects of the two acts being of equal value. The other effects, they say, never are of equal value. By keeping my promise I am helping to strengthen the system of mutual confidence; by breaking it I am helping to weaken this; so that really the first act produces $1,000+x$ units of good, and the second $1,001-y$ units, and the difference between $+x$ and $-y$ is enough to outweigh the slight superiority in the *immediate* effects of the second act. In answer to this it may be pointed out that there must be *some* amount of good that exceeds the difference between $+x$ and $-y$ (i.e., exceeds $x+y$); say, $x+y+z$. Let us suppose the *immediate* good effects of the second act to be assessed not at $1,000$ but at $1,000+x+y+z$. Then its *net* good effects are $1,000+x+z$, i.e., greater than those of the fulfilment of the promise; and the utilitarian is bound to say forthwith that the promise should be broken. Now, we may ask whether that is really the way we think about promises? Do we really think that the production of the slightest balance of good, no matter who will enjoy it, by the breach of a promise frees us from the obligation to keep our promise? We need not doubt that a system by which promises are made and kept is one that has great advantages for the general well-being. But that is not the whole truth. To make a promise is not merely to adapt an ingenious device for promoting the general well-being; it is to put oneself in a new relation to one person in particular, a relation which creates a specifically new *prima facie* duty to him, not reducible to the duty of promoting the general well-being of society. By all means let us try to foresee the net good effects of keeping one's promise and the net good effects of breaking it, but even if we assess the first at $1,000+x$ and the second at $1,000+x+z$, the question still remains whether it is not our duty to fulfil the promise. It may be suspected, too, that the effect of a single keeping or breaking of a promise in strengthening or weakening the fabric of mutual confidence is greatly exaggerated by the theory we are examining. And if we suppose two men dying together alone, do we think that the duty of one to fulfil before he dies a promise he has made to the other would be extinguished by the fact that neither act would have any effect on the general confidence? Any one who holds this may be suspected of not having reflected on what a promise is.

I conclude that the attributes "right" and "optimific" are not identical, and that we do not know either by intuition, by deduction, or by induction that they coincide in their application, still less that the latter is the foundation of the former. It must be added, however, that if we are ever under no special obligation such as that of fidelity to a promisee or of gratitude to a benefactor, we ought to do what will produce most good; and that even when we are under a special obligation the tendency of acts to promote general good is one of the main factors in determining whether they are right.

In what has preceded, a good deal of use has been made of what we really think about moral questions; a certain theory has been rejected because it does not agree with what we really think. It might be said that this is in principle wrong; that we should not be content to expound what our present moral consciousness tells us but should aim at a criticism of our existing moral consciousness in the light of theory. Now I do not doubt that the moral consciousness of men has in detail undergone a good deal of modification as regards the things we think right, at the hands of moral theory. But if we are told, for instance, that we should give up our view that there is a special obligatoriness attaching to the keeping of promises because it is self-evident that the only duty is to produce as much good as possible, we have to ask ourselves whether we really, when we reflect, *are* convinced that this is self-evident, and whether we really *can* get rid of our view that promise-keeping has a bindingness independent of productiveness of maximum good. In my own experience I find that I cannot, in spite of a very genuine attempt to do so; and I venture to think that most people will find the same, and that just because they cannot lose the sense of special obligation, they cannot accept as self-evident, or even as true, the theory which would require them to do so. In fact it seems, on reflection, self-evident that a promise, simply as such, is something that *prima facie* ought to be kept, and it does *not*, on reflection, seem self-evident that production of maximum good is the only thing that makes an act obligatory. And to ask us to give up at the bidding of a theory our actual apprehension of what is right and what is wrong seems like asking people to repudiate their actual experience of beauty, at the bidding of a theory which says "only that which satisfies such and such conditions can be beautiful." If what I have called our actual apprehension is (as I would maintain that it is) truly an apprehension, i.e., an instance of knowledge, the request is nothing less than absurd.

I would maintain, in fact, that what we are apt to describe as "what we think" about moral questions contains a considerable amount that we do not think but know, and that this forms the standard by reference to which the truth of any moral theory has to be tested, instead of having itself to be tested by reference to any theory. I hope that I have in what precedes indicated what in my view these elements of knowledge are that are involved in our ordinary moral consciousness.

It would be a mistake to found a natural science on "what we really think," i.e., on what reasonably thoughtful and well-educated people think about the subjects of the science before they have studied them scientifically. For such opinions are interpretations, and often misinterpretations, of sense-experience; and the man of science must appeal from these to sense-experience itself, which furnishes his real data. In ethics no such appeal is possible. We have no more direct way of access to the facts about rightness and goodness and about what things are right or good, than by thinking about them; the moral convictions of thoughtful and well-educated people are the data of ethics just as sense-perceptions are the data of a natural science. Just as some of the latter have to be rejected as illusory, so have some of the former; but as the latter are rejected only when they are in conflict with other more accurate sense-perceptions, the former are rejected only when they are in conflict with other convictions which stand better the test of reflection. The existing body of moral convictions of the best people is the cumulative product of the moral reflection of many generations, which has developed an extremely delicate power of appreciation of moral distinctions; and this the theorist cannot afford to treat with anything other than the greatest respect. The verdicts of the moral consciousness of the best people are the foundation on which he must build; though he must first compare them with one another and eliminate any contradictions they may contain.

It is worth while to try to state more definitely the nature of the acts that are right. We may try to state first what (if anything) is the universal nature of *all* acts that are right. It is obvious that any of the acts that we do has countless effects, directly or indirectly, on countless people, and the probability is that any act, however right it be, will have adverse effects (though these may be very trivial) on some innocent people. Similarly, any wrong act will probably have beneficial effects on some deserving people. Every act therefore, viewed in some aspects, will be *prima facie* right, and viewed in others, *prima facie* wrong, and right acts can be distinguished from wrong acts only as being those which, of all those possible for the agent in the circumstances, have the greatest balance of *prima facie* rightness, in those respects in which they are *prima facie* right, over their *prima facie* wrongness, in those respects in which they are *prima facie* wrong—*prima facie* rightness and wrongness being understood in the sense previously explained. For the estimation of the comparative stringency of these *prima facie* obligations no general rules can, so far as I can see, be laid down. We can only say that a great deal of stringency belongs to the duties of "perfect obligation"—the duties of keeping our promises, of repairing wrongs we have done, and of returning the equivalent of services we have received. For the rest, ϵv $\tau \eta$ $\alpha \iota \sigma \theta \eta \sigma \epsilon \iota \xi.$[14] This sense of our particular duty in particular circumstances, preceded and informed by the fullest reflection we can bestow on the act in all its bearings, is highly fallible, but it is the only guide we have to our duty.

When we turn to consider the nature of individual right acts, the first point to which attention should be called is that any act may be correctly described in an indefinite, and in principle infinite, number of ways. An act is the production of a change in the state of affairs (if we ignore, for simplicity's sake, the comparatively few cases in which it is the maintenance of an existing state of affairs; cases which, I think, raise no special difficulty). Now the only changes we can *directly* produce are changes in our own bodies or in our own minds. But these are not, as such, what as a rule we think it our duty to produce. Consider some comparatively simple act, such as telling the truth or fulfilling a promise. In the first case what I produce directly is movements of my vocal organs. But what I think it my duty to produce is a true view in some one else's mind about some fact, and between my movement of my vocal organs and this result there intervenes a series of physical events and events in his mind. Again, in the second case, I may have promised, for instance, to return a book to a friend. I may be able, by a series of movements of my legs and hands, to place it in his hands. But what I am just as likely to do, and to think I have done my duty in doing, is to send it by a messenger or to hand it to his servant or to send it by post; and in each of these cases what I *do* directly is worthless in itself and is connected by a series of intermediate links with what I do think it is my duty to bring about, viz. his receiving what I have promised to return to him. This being so, it *seems* as if what I *do* has no obligatoriness in itself and as if one or other of three accounts should be given of the matter, each of which makes rightness not belong to what I do, considered in its own nature.

(1) One of them would be that what is obligatory is not *doing* anything in the natural sense of producing any change in the state of affairs, but *aiming at* something—at, for instance, my friend's reception of the book. But this account will not do. For *(a)* to aim at something is to act from a motive consisting of the wish to bring that thing about. But we have seen[15] that motive never forms part of the content of our duty; if anything is certain about morals, that, I think, is certain. And *(b)* if I have promised to return the book to my friend, I obviously do not fulfil my promise and do my duty merely by aiming at his receiving the book; I must see that he actually receives it. (2) A more plausible account is that which says I must do that which is likely to produce the result. But this account is open to the second of these objections, and probably also to the first. For in the first place, however likely my act may seem, even on careful consideration, and even however likely it may in fact be, to produce the result, if it does not produce it I have not done what I promised to do, i.e., have not done my duty. And secondly, when it is said that I ought to do what is likely to produce the result, what is *probably* meant is that I ought to do a certain thing as a result of the wish to produce a certain result, and of the thought that my act is likely to produce it; and this again introduces motive into the content of duty. (3) Much the most plausible of the three accounts is that which says, "I ought to do that which will actually produce a certain result." This escapes objection *(b)*. Whether it escapes objection *(a)* or not depends on what exactly is meant. If it is meant that I ought to do a certain thing from the wish to produce a certain result and the thought that it will do so, the account is still open to objection *(a)*. But if it is meant simply that I ought to do a certain thing, and that the reason why I ought to do it is that it will produce a certain result, objection *(a)* is avoided. Now this account in its second form is that which utilitarianism gives. It says what is right are certain acts, not certain acts motivated in a certain way; and it says that acts are never right by their own nature but by virtue of the goodness of their actual results. And this account is, I think, clearly nearer the truth than one

which makes the rightness of an act depend on the goodness of either the *intended* or the *likely* results.

Nevertheless, this account appears not to be the true one. For it implies that what we consider right or our duty is what we do *directly*. It is this, e.g., the packing up and posting of the book, that derives its moral significance not from its own nature but from its consequences. But this is *not* what we should describe, strictly, as our duty; our duty is to fulfil our promise, i.e., to put the book into our friend's possession. This we consider obligatory in its own nature, just because it is a fulfilment of promise, and not because of *its* consequences. But, it might be replied by the utilitarian, I do not do this; I only do something that leads up to this, and what I do has no moral significance in itself but only because of its consequences. In answer to this, however, we may point out that a cause produces not only its immediate, but also its remote consequences, and the latter no less than the former. I, therefore, not only produce the immediate movements of parts of my body but also my friend's reception of the book, which results from these. Or, if this be objected to on the grounds that I can hardly be said to have produced my friend's reception of the book when I have packed and posted it, owing to the time that has still to elapse before he receives it, and that to say I have produced the result hardly does justice to the part played by the Post Office, we may at least say that I have *secured* my friend's reception of the book. What I do is as truly describable in this way as by saying that it is the packing and posting of a book. (It is equally truly describable in many other ways; e.g., I have provided a few moments' employment for Post Office officials. But this is irrelevant to the argument.) And if we ask ourselves whether it is *qua* the packing and posting of a book, or *qua* the securing of my friend's getting what I have promised to return to him, that my action is right, it is clear that it is in the second capacity that it is right; and in this capacity, the only capacity in which it is right, it is right by its own nature and not because of its consequences.

This account may no doubt be objected to, on the ground that we are ignoring the freedom of will of the other agents—the sorter and the postman, for instance—who are equally responsible for the result. Society, it may be said, is not like a machine, in which event follows event by rigorous necessity. Some one may, for instance, in the exercise of his freedom of will, steal the book on the way. But it is to be observed that I have excluded that case, and any similar case. I am dealing with the case in which I secure my friend's receiving the book; and if he does not receive it I have not secured his receiving it. If on the other hand the book reaches its destination, that alone shows that, the system of things being what it is, the trains by which the book travels and the railway lines along which it travels being such as they are and subject to the laws they are subject to, the postal officials who handle it being such as they are, having the motives they have and being subject to the psychological laws they are subject to, my posting the book was the one further thing which was sufficient to procure my friend's receiving it. If it had not been sufficient, the result would not have followed. The attainment of the result proves the sufficiency of the means. The objection in fact rests on the supposition that there can be unmotived action, i.e., an event without a cause, and may be refuted by reflection on the universality of the law of causation.

It is equally true that non-attainment of the result proves the insufficiency of the means. If the book had been destroyed in a railway accident or stolen by a dishonest postman, that would prove that my immediate act was not sufficient to produce the desired result. We get the curious consequence that however carelessly I pack or dispatch the book, if it comes to hand I have done my duty, and however carefully I have acted, if the book does not come to hand I have not done my duty. Success and failure are the only test, and a sufficient test, of the performance of duty. Of course, I should deserve more praise in the second case than in the first; but that is an entirely different question; we must not mix up the question of right and wrong with that of the morally good and the morally bad. And that our conclusion is not as strange as at first sight it might seem is shown by the fact that if the carelessly dispatched book comes to hand, it is not my duty to send another copy, while if the carefully dispatched book does not come to hand I must send another copy to replace it. In the first case I have not my duty still to do, which shows that I have done it; in the second I have it still to do, which shows that I have not done it.

We have reached the result that my act is right *qua* being an ensuring of one of the particular states of affairs of which it is an ensuring, viz., in the case we have taken, of my friend's receiving the book I have promised to return to him. But this answer requires some correction; for it refers only to the *prima facie* rightness of my act. If to be a fulfilment of promise were a sufficient ground of the rightness of an act, all fulfilments of promises would be right, whereas it seems clear that there are cases in which some other *prima facie* duty overrides the *prima facie* duty of fulfilling a promise. The more correct answer would be that the ground of the actual rightness of the act is that, of all acts possible for the agent in the circumstances, it is that whose *prima facie* rightness in the respects in which it is *prima facie* right most outweighs its *prima facie* wrongness in any respects in which it is *prima facie* wrong. But since its *prima facie* rightness is mainly due to its being a fulfilment of promise, we may call its being so the salient element in the ground of its rightness.

Subject to this qualification, then, it is as being the production (or if we prefer the word, the securing or ensuring) of the reception by my friend of what I have promised him (or in other words as the fulfilment of my promise) that my act is right. It is not right as a packing and posting of a book. The packing and posting of the book is only incidentally right, right only because it is a fulfilment of promise, which is what is directly or essentially right.

Our duty, then, is not to do certain things which will produce certain results. Our acts, at any rate our acts of special obligation, are not right because they will produce certain results—which is the view common to all forms of utilitarianism. To say that is to say that in the case in question what is essentially right is to pack and post a book, whereas what is essentially right is to secure the possession by my friend of what I have promised to return to him. An act is not right because it, being one thing, produces good results different from itself; it is right because it is itself the production of a certain state of affairs. Such production is right in itself, apart from any consequence.

But, it might be said, this analysis applies only to acts of special obligation; the utilitarian account still holds good for the acts in which we are not under a special obligation to any person or set of persons but only under that of augmenting the general good. Now merely to have established that there *are* special obligations to do certain things irrespective of their consequences would be already to have made a considerable breach in the utilitarian walls; for according to utilitarianism there is no such thing, there is only the single obligation to promote the general good. But, further, on reflection it is clear that just as (in the case we have taken) my act is not only the packing and posting of a book but the fulfilling of a promise, and just as it is in the latter capacity and not in the former that it is my duty, so an act whereby I augment the general good is not only, let us say, the writing of a begging letter on behalf of a hospital, but the producing (or ensuring) of whatever good ensues therefrom, and it is in the latter capacity and not in the former that it is right, if it *is* right. That which is right is right not because it is an act, one thing, which will produce another thing, an increase of the general welfare, but because it is itself the producing of an increase in the general welfare. Or, to qualify this in the necessary way, its being the production of an increase in the general welfare is the salient element in the ground of its rightness. Just as before we were led to recognize the *prima facie* rightness of the fulfilment of promises, we are now led to recognize the *prima facie* rightness of promoting the general welfare. In both cases we have to recognize the *intrinsic* rightness of a certain type of act, not depending on its consequences but on its own nature.

Notes

1. I take the theory which, as I have tried to show, seems to be put forward in *Ethics* rather than the earlier and less plausible theory put forward in *Principia Ethica*. For the difference, cf. my pp. 8-11 [for this and other page references in these Notes, refer to W.D. Ross, *The Right and the Good* (Oxford UP, 1930)].

2. These are not strictly speaking duties, but things that tend to be our duty, or *prima facie* duties. Cf. pp. 19-20.

3. Some will think it, apart from other considerations, a sufficient refutation of this view to point out that I also stand in that relation to myself, so that for this view the distinction of oneself from others is morally insignificant.

4. I should make it plain at this stage that I am *assuming* the correctness of some of our main convictions as to *prima facie* duties, or, more strictly, am claiming that we *know* them to be true. To me it seems as self-evident as anything could be, that to make a promise, for instance, is to create a moral claim on us in someone else. Many readers will perhaps say that they do not know this to be true. If so, I certainly cannot prove it to them; I can only ask them to reflect again, in the hope that they will ultimately agree that they also know it to be true. The main moral convictions of the plain man seem to me to be, not opinions which it is for philosophy to prove or disprove, but knowledge from the start; and in my own case I seem to find little difficulty in distinguishing these essential convictions from other moral convictions which I also have, which are merely fallible opinions based on an imperfect study of the working for good or evil of certain institutions or types of action.

5. For a needed correction of this statement, cf. pp. 22-23.

6. pp. 135-38.

7. But cf. the qualification in p. 33, n.2.

8. Cf pp. 122-23.

9. Cf. pp. 28, 122-23.

10. To avoid complicating unduly the statement of the general view I am putting forward, I have here rather overstated it. Any act is the origination of a great variety of things many of which make no difference to its rightness or wrongness. But there are always many elements in its nature (i.e., in what it is the origination of) that make a difference to its rightness or wrongness, and no element in its nature can be dismissed without consideration as indifferent.

11. *Ethics*, 181. [G.E. Moore, *Ethics* (Cambridge UP, 1903)].

12. I am assuming that good is objectively quantitative (cf. pp. 142-44), but not that we can accurately assign an exact quantitative measure to it. Since it is of a definite amount, we can make the supposition that its amount is so-and-so, though we cannot with any confidence *assert* that it is.

13. p. 34.

14. "The decision rests with perception." Arist. *Nic. Eth.* 1109b23, 1126b4.

15. pp. 5-6.

16.
Pluralism and the Value of Life

John Kekes

John Kekes is professor emeritus of philosophy at the State University of New York at Albany. He has published several books on ethics, including The Morality of Pluralism. *As an advocate of moral pluralism, Kekes argues that we hold many incommensurable values in life, that these values can and do come into conflict with each other, and that there are no authoritative standards for resolving these value conflicts. Nevertheless, in the selection below he suggests that these conflicts may reasonably be resolved by an appeal to the basic or minimal requirements of human welfare.*

As an initial approximation, pluralism may be understood as the combination of four theses. First, there are many incommensurable values whose realization is required for living a good life. Second, these values often conflict with each other, and, as a result, the realization of some excludes the realization of others. Third, there is no authoritative standard that could be appealed to to resolve such conflicts, because there is also a plurality of standards; consequently, no single standard would be always acceptable to all fully informed and reasonable people. Fourth, there are, nevertheless, reasonable ways of resolving conflicts among incommensurable values.

The purpose of this essay is to defend pluralism by contrasting it with the less satisfactory alternatives of monism and relativism and by showing how it can handle conflicts involving the value of life. One reason for concentrating on the value of life is that it is particularly resistant to a pluralistic interpretation. It may be thought either that life takes precedence over all other values that may conflict with it, or that if not even life does that, then all conflict-resolutions are ultimately arbitrary. It seems, therefore, that either monism or relativism is correct, and there is therefore no room left for pluralism. What seems to be true, however, is not—or so it will be argued.

I. Pluralism versus Monism and Relativism

Pluralism is that rare thing: a genuinely new approach to thinking about values. Its novelty, of course, does not preclude historical anticipations; various passages in the writings of Aristotle, Michel de Montaigne, David Hume, John

Stuart Mill, and William James readily lend themselves to pluralistic interpretation. Yet there exists no authoritative formulation of pluralism, although Isaiah Berlin and Michael Oakeshott began to struggle with the task in the 1940s and 1950s. By now, pluralism has become a recognizable label; nevertheless, it remains less than clear why those who are usually included under its heading are included.[1] We may well doubt, however, whether at this early stage of development an authoritative formulation of pluralism is either possible or desirable. In any case, none will be attempted here. We shall begin by sketching one version of pluralism, but it must be emphasized that no claim to finality, general acceptance, or sufficient detail is made on its behalf. In the interest of brevity, it will be referred to as "pluralism," but it should be understood that there are other versions as well.

Pluralism, then, is a theory about values. The point of view from which pluralists approach values is that of human beings trying to live a good life. The central thesis of pluralism is that there are many reasonable conceptions of a good life and many reasonable values upon whose realization good lives depend. These conceptions and values are often so related, however, that the realization of one excludes the realization of another. Consequently, conflicts among reasonable conceptions of a good life and among reasonable values must be recognized as unavoidable features of an adequate understanding of morality and politics. Pluralists believe that living a good life must be essentially concerned with coping with these conflicts, but doing so is formidably difficult because the conflicts are often caused by the incompatibility and incommensurability of the values whose realization is regarded as essential.

The incompatibility of values is partly due to qualities intrinsic to the conflicting values. Because of these qualities, the realization of one value may totally or proportionally exclude the realization of the other. Habitual gourmandizing and asceticism are totally incompatible, while a lifelong commitment to both political activism and solitude are proportionally so. The incompatibility of values, therefore, derives at least in part from the nature of the values, rather than from our attitude toward them. For the favorable attitude of some people toward both of the incompatible values does not make them compatible. Their compatibility depends also on whether or not the intrinsic qualities of the values exclude each other. But the intrinsic qualities of some values are only partly responsible for their incompatibility. Another part is contributed by human nature. It is only for beings like us that the intrinsic qualities of some values are incompatible. If gourmandizing did not give us pleasure, it would not be incompatible with asceticism. And if split personalities were normal for us, then we could combine solitude and political activism.

It is worth noting, if only in passing, that the incompatibility of values, created by the conjunction of qualities intrinsic to them and qualities intrinsic to human nature, constitutes a further reason for regarding at least some values as objective. For their incompatibility shows that prizing them is not merely a matter of having a favorable attitude toward them, but that we prize them also because our favorable attitudes are toward qualities intrinsic to the values which it is reasonable or unreasonable for beings like us to prize.

The basic idea of incommensurability is that there are some things so unalike as to exclude any reasonable comparison between them. Square roots and insults, smells and puns, canasta and telescopes are utterly disparate, and they seem to exclude any common measure by which we could evaluate their respective merits or demerits. That this is so is not usually troublesome, because there is scarcely a need to compare them. It is otherwise, however, with values. It often happens that we want to realize incompatible values, and it becomes important to compare them so that we can choose among them in a reasonable manner. But if incompatible values are also incommensurable, then reasonable comparisons among them become problematic.

There are three main reasons why pluralists suppose that values are incommensurable. First, it does not seem to them that there exists a highest value, such as happiness, to which all other values could always be reasonably subordinated and with reference to which all other values could be authoritatively ranked. Second, they are also dubious about there being some medium, such as money, in terms of which all the different values could be expressed, quantified, and compared in a way that all reasonable people would accept. And third, they are similarly skeptical about claims made on behalf of some one or some few canonical principles, such as Kant's categorical imperative, which could be appealed to in resolving conflicts among values to the satisfaction of all reasonable people.

Incommensurability and incompatibility are logically distinct notions. Incommensurable values need not be incompatible, and if they are not, then they can, and often do, coexist in a life. Patriotism and spelunking are incommensurable, but not incompatible. If values were merely incommensurable, without being incompatible, it would not be hard to reconcile them, for we should only have to develop sufficiently capacious conceptions of a good life to include all the incommensurable values we want to realize. The reason why this strategy cannot work is that many values are not only incommensurable but also incompatible. Consequently, they cannot all be fully realized in even the most receptively rich conception of a good life. Moral conflicts of the relevant type occur precisely because we want to realize both incompatible and incommensurable values.

Nor need incompatible values be incommensurable. We often want to realize two readily comparable yet mutually exclusive values. If I wanted to be alone for a few days, I could go camping or visit a strange city, but not both; or, if I wanted to improve my finances, I could cautiously husband my resources or make risky but possibly lucrative investments, but the more I do of one, the less I could do of the other. Pluralists are committed to the conjunction of two claims: moral conflicts are frequent, and many of them are due to our wanting to realize incompatible and incommensurable values.

We may express the conclusion pluralists draw from the incommensurability and incompatibility of values positively, by saying that reasonable commitment to values should be conditional, as well as negatively, by saying that it is unreasonable to regard any value as being always overriding. The possibility that conditionality excludes and overridingness hinges on is that of resolving conflicts among values in a way that would *always* command the assent of *all* fully reasonable people. As it has been succinctly put: "There is no consideration of any kind that overrides all other considerations in all conceivable circumstances."[2]

Pluralists, of course, do not deny that many conflicts among values can be resolved by appealing to some reasonable ranking of the values in question. Such rankings are acknowledged by pluralists to be both possible and desirable. The point they insist on is that just as there is a plurality of equally reasonable conceptions of a good life and of values, so also there is a plurality of equally reasonable rankings of them. According to pluralists, reason does not require commitment to some one highest value, or to some medium for comparing values, or to some one or few authoritative principles. On the contrary, reason allows people to commit themselves to any one of a plurality of equally reasonable values, ranking schemes, or principles.

Pluralism is intended to occupy the middle ground between two other theories about the nature of values: monism and relativism. Monists are committed to there being some overriding value, but they need not suppose that it is a single value; their commitment may be to some small number of values, principles, or ranking schemes on the basis of which values could be compared in a way that all reasonable people would find compelling.

A value is overriding, then, if it meets two conditions: in conflicts it always defeats the claims of any other value, and the only justification for violating it on any particular occasion is that by the violation its realization would be generally served. For instance, if life were an overriding value, then in conflicts with freedom or justice life would always take precedence; furthermore, the only justification for taking a life would then be to preserve other lives.[3]

In contrast with overriding values, there are conditional values; their claims may be defeated by the conflicting claim of some other value. We may define "conditional" values as nonoverriding values. If life were a conditional value, then in conflicts with freedom (e.g., is life worth living under tyranny?) or justice (e.g., should lives be risked in resisting injustice?), the claims of life could be defeated by the claims of these other values.

Pluralists are opposed to monism because they reject the idea of there being an overriding value. It makes no difference to this rejection whether the overriding value is thought to be single or a combination of a few values, whether it is a principle or principles, or whether it is a simple or a complex ranking scheme. It is the very idea of there being some evaluative consideration that should *always* take precedence over *all* other evaluative considerations that pluralists oppose.

Yet pluralists see, as well as monists do, that if values are incompatible and incommensurable, then they will conflict, and all conceptions of a good life require that there be some reasonable resolution of these conflicts. Pluralists and monists therefore agree about the need for reasonable conflict-resolution; their disagreement concerns the question of whether it can be based on some overriding value.[4]

The other theory about values that pluralists reject is relativism. Relativists agree with pluralists about there being no overriding values, about all values being conditional, about the plurality of incompatible and incommensurable values, about the like plurality of principles and organizing schemes, and about the need for conflict-resolution. But relativists go beyond pluralism and think that all conditional values are conventional in character. They regard all values merely as the products of the customs, practices, and beliefs which happened to have developed in a particular tradition, and they deny that any value can carry epistemological or moral authority outside of its traditional context. Relativists may concede that reason has a role to play in settling conflicts among values, but, according to them, reason is confined to play that role *within* particular traditions. There is no reasonable way of settling conflicts *between* values belonging to different traditions, because what counts as reasonable is itself a product of particular traditions.[5]

Pluralists disagree because they believe that there is a context-independent ground to which we can reasonably appeal in settling conflicts between incompatible and incommensurable values, even if the values are conditional and the conflicts occur in the context of different traditions. At the same time, pluralists and relativists may join in their opposition to the monistic commitment to an overriding value. Similarly, pluralists and monists may agree in opposing the relativistic denial of a context-independent ground for resolving conflicts, even as they disagree about basing an overriding value on that ground.

The central idea that pluralists aim to develop and defend against both monists and relativists is that there is a context-independent ground for settling conflicts among conditional values that would be acceptable to all sufficiently informed and reasonable people. Relativists reject pluralism because they deny that there is a ground answering this description. And monists reject pluralism because, while they think that the ground pluralists appeal to exists, they also think that on its basis some values can be shown to be overriding, and not merely conditional. One consequence of this dispute is that pluralists must always argue on two fronts: against relativists, to whom they must show the existence of a context-independent ground for resolving conflicts among conditional values; and against monists, to whom they must show that only conditional and not overriding values can be based on this ground.

The context-independent ground required by the pluralistic thesis is constituted of the minimum requirements of human welfare. These requirements are set by universally human, historically constant, and culturally invariant needs created by human nature. Many of these needs are physiological: for food, shelter, rest, and so forth; other needs are psychological: for companionship, hope, the absence of horror and terror in one's life, and the like; yet other needs are social: for some order and predictability in one's society, for security, for some respect, and so on. Let us call the satisfaction of these basic human needs "primary values," in contrast with "secondary values." Secondary values derive from the satisfaction of needs that vary with traditions and conceptions of a good life. We can say, then, that the minimum requirements of human welfare are met by the realization of primary values. Let us call the rules, customs, and principles protecting people in their pursuit of primary values "deep conventions." It follows, then, that any morally acceptable tradition must protect people belonging to it by deep conventions.[6]

The pluralistic claim for the universality, constancy, and invariance of primary values concerns only the bare fact *that* human welfare requires their enjoyment. It is readily acknowledged by pluralists—indeed it is part of their thesis—that there are vast historical, cultural, and individual differences about *how* primary values are enjoyed. Correspondingly, the pluralistic claim is that any morally acceptable tradition must uphold deep conventions, although it is further acknowledged and insisted upon that the range of cases covered by particular deep conventions may vary from one tradition to another.

We can now state more sharply the dispute that pluralists have with relativists and monists. As pluralists see it, relativists fail to recognize that there are primary values and that they need to be protected by deep conventions. These values and conventions will command the assent of all sufficiently informed and reasonable people because they protect the minimum requirements of human welfare regardless of what conceptions of good life and what other values are recognized in any particular tradition. Primary values thus constitute a context-independent ground for settling some conflicts among some values.

There are two reasons why the existence of this context-independent ground does not support the monistic claim that we are entitled to regard primary values as overriding. First, primary values may conflict with each other. Even if the claims of primary values always overrode the conflicting claims of secondary values, this could not be true of the conflicting claims of primary values. Second, the claims of primary values are conditional on their contribution to the realization of the agents' conception of a good life. But agents may reasonably judge in adverse circumstances that they are prevented from realizing their conceptions, and so they may judge as well that they have no good reason to recognize the claims of primary values. If people have no hope of a good life, then they will not be convinced by the claims of a value based on its necessity to a good life. It is for these reasons that pluralists regard even primary values as conditional.

It should be remembered that this account is only of one version of pluralism and that it is no more than a sketchy description without supporting arguments. The full case for pluralism cannot be made in a single essay.[7] What will be done instead is to show how both monistic and relativistic arguments fail and the pluralistic argument succeeds about one value which has perhaps the strongest claim to being primary: the value of life.

II. Life as a Primary Value

There can be no serious doubt in anyone's mind that life is one of the most likely candidates for being a primary value. It is unclear, however, what precisely this claim implies.[8] There is much cant about the sanctity of life. Albert Schweitzer, for instance, tells us that "[t]he fundamental principle of ethics ... is reverence for life.... [R]everence for life contains within itself ... the commandment to love, and it calls for compassion for all creature life."[9] Does this mean that without reverence, love, and compassion for AIDS viruses, bedbugs, and turnips, we cannot be ethical? But perhaps Schweitzer should restrict his claim to human lives. The question, then, is whether this reverence, love, and compassion for human lives commit one to oppose suicide, just wars, capital punishment, abortion, motorcycle racing, sunbathing, overeating, and rock climbing?

There *are* strong reasons for regarding life as a primary value. But these reasons do not commit us to accepting the indefensible claim that life is an overriding value. In some circumstances, it is reasonable to give or to take a life. The problem is to specify the circumstances. Formulating the problem in this way has considerable importance. We are no longer asking *whether* the deep convention protecting life can be reasonably violated; we want to know rather *when* its violation may be reasonable.

We may approach the problem of specifying the circumstances in which it may be reasonable to give or to take a life by reflecting on our actual situation. What we find around us is a glaring discrepancy between rousing declarations and actual practice. Everybody knows that many lives would be saved if we lowered the speed limit, destroyed tobacco crops, sent drug addicts to concentration camps, discouraged mining, outlawed parachute jumping and Himalayan expeditions, and instituted such lifesaving measures as forcing fat people to lose weight, over-achievers to slow down, and the sedentary to take exercise.

Of course, we neither act on this knowledge nor advocate that others should do so; and if we tried either, a great howl would be heard throughout the land. The appropriate laws would be unenforceable, much as the lifesaving legislation establishing Prohibition in America was and the speed limit is. The reason for this is that although we value life, we also value other things. Freedom, justice, prosperity, adventure, privacy, free trade, civic harmony, and countless other values continually come into conflict with the value of life. As the examples just given show, the claims of these other values are routinely judged by a very large number of people to override the claims of life. If genuine moral commitments require corresponding action, then very few people indeed hold the commitment they avow to the sanctity of life, or to the right to life, or to life being inalienable, indefeasible, or imprescriptible.

The source of this discrepancy between avowed commitment and actual practice is not so much hypocrisy as lack of thought. People consult their conscience and passionately declare their attachment to something they regard as good, much as Schweitzer did. There is no reason to doubt the sincerity of many of these declarations. The trouble is that in the grip of moralistic fervor these people forget that they are also committed to other values, and that they cannot have all of them. The claims of conflicting values must be balanced against each other. As soon as this is realized, sincere commitment to some value must be supplemented by a reasoned account of how the conflicting claims of it and other values should be resolved. And that realization brings us to pluralism, the moral theory concerned with reasonable conflict-resolution among a plurality of values.

It may be objected to this description of our actual moral situation that, while it may be a correct account of how things are, the concern of moral theory is with how things ought to be. Our actual situation reflects our moral defects. But the lamentable aspects of our humanity no more tell against the merits of a moral theory than a prevalent form of sickness tells against the merits of a medical theory which proposes a treatment of it. It may be argued that the immorality, inconsistency, and confusion reflected by our actions not only fail as arguments against human life being an overriding value, but actually demonstrate the importance of reaffirming our commitment to it. The reasonable way to resolve the conflicting claims of life and other values is to recognize the overriding value of life. And that means the acceptance of some form of monism as opposed to pluralism.

In reply to this monistic argument, we need only to remember that what it is reasonable to value is not life itself, but a life with some duration and enjoyment, one that merits self-respect and some sense of accomplishment. It is a life that is judged to be at least acceptable by the person living it, rather than an intolerable burden. All of us can imagine circumstances in which we would not want to go on living. In doing so, we tacitly appeal to some values whose lack would make us lose the motivation to sustain our life. And this shows that the value we attribute to our own life is not always overriding. Furthermore, such judgments may reasonably be extended to lives other than our own: those involving, for instance, irreversible coma, excruciating pain and terminal illness, or gross indignities brought on by Alzheimer's disease.

It is important to add by way of necessary caution that the judgment that in some circumstances our own or someone else's life would not be worth living does not imply any particular action. What follows may be resignation, pity, self-deception, resentment, or religious conversion; or it may be suicide, euthanasia, or murder. The reasonableness of the judgment is one thing, the moral credentials of the response to the life reasonably judged not to be worth living is quite another. The pluralistic case appeals only to the possibility of the former.

If this is right, it follows from pluralism that in some contexts life may be reasonably taken or given up. And this begins to look suspiciously close to relativism. For relativists may agree that life is a primary value, but go on to insist that traditions may reasonably differ about the circumstances in which the deep convention protecting life may be defeated. Different traditions have different conventions about the appropriate ways of treating the old, infants, criminals, enemies, traitors, and so on. Each tradition may recognize life as a primary value, and yet legitimize widely different reasons for taking it. In the context of a tradition, the exposure of the old, infanticide, capital punishment, or death caused by torture or mutilation may be regarded as reasonable. As we move away from a monistic insistence on the overriding value of life, so we seem to move toward the relativistic view that any attitude toward life is reasonable in a given context, provided only that it is sanctioned by the prevailing tradition.

The problem for pluralists, therefore, is to arrest the movement that begins with the rejection of monism and ends with the acceptance of relativism. Or, to put the point in moral terms, the problem for pluralists is to show that if we give up the view that life is of overriding value, we still need not embrace the view that there is no reasonable prohibition against taking life that all traditions should recognize.

But it is useless to try to grapple with this problem in generalities. We shall consider, therefore, a concrete case which occurs in the context of a well-established tradition. It involves members of a society killing one of their own in a way that strikes our Western sensibility as exceptionally brutal. As we try to understand the tradition in the background, however, the killing will start to look less brutal. As a result, we shall find our attitude shifting back and forth between monistic moral imperialism and relativistic moral promiscuity. This will motivate us to seek a pluralistic position between them where it may be reasonable to rest our judgment.

III. The Morality of Live Burial

The case is a custom of the Dinka, a tribe of about a million people, living in Africa, in the southern Sudan. The custom no longer exists because the Sudanese authorities have outlawed it. The account of the custom and its significance for the Dinka comes from Godfrey Lienhardt, an ethnographer who lived with the Dinka; his book about them is widely regarded as an outstanding work.[10]

The custom is the live burial of the most important and respected religious and political leaders the Dinka have, the spear-masters. At the appropriate time, the Dinka dig a deep hole in the ground and, in the midst of various religious ceremonies, place the living spear-master into it. Then the assembled people throw cattle dung on the spear-master until it covers the hole in which he lies, except for a very narrow opening, and the spear-master slowly suffocates in the excrement which is piled on him (300-04). This seems to us a spectacularly gruesome form of murder, involving the illegitimate violation of a deep convention. But let us look further.

The appropriate time for the live burial is when the spear-master is quite old and feels the proximity of death. When that time comes is usually, although not invariably, announced by the spear-master himself. In most of the cases about which Lienhardt has information, the choice of the time, although never the method, of his death was left to the spear-master. He had known that he would die in this way ever since he became spear-master many years ago. The attitude of the Dinka toward the spear-master's death is also instructive. The "people should not mourn, but rather should be joyful.... For the ... master's people ... the human symbolic action involved in the 'artificial' burial must be seen to transform the experience of the leader's death into a concentrated public experience of vitality" (316-17). It should be noted as well that cattle dung is not a repulsive object for the Dinka. Their economy depends on cattle, and they believe that cattle dung has curative and restorative powers. The significance of throwing cattle dung on the spear-master is not that of heaping excrement on a moribund old man.

The heart of the matter, however, is the live burial itself. Why do the Dinka and the spear-masters themselves believe that spear-masters should not die a natural death? Lienhardt says: "'Life,' *wei*, is the same word in Dinka as that for breath.... *Wei* is something which living creatures have and which is the source of their animation, and more, the source of their vigorous animation. Life is therefore in creatures to a larger or smaller degree" (206). The reason why spear-masters are so important and respected is that they are "thought to have in them more life than is necessary to sustain them only, and thereby sustain the lives of their people and their cattle" (207). The Dinka believe that "[i]t is because the master of the fishing-spear's life is bound up with the vitality of his people that he must not ... die as other men die, for this would be the diminution of the vitality of all" (208).

The significance of the ceremony of live burial of the spear-master is that "[i]f he 'dies' like ordinary men, the 'life' of his people which is in his keeping goes with him.... What they [the Dinka] represent in contriving the death which they give him is the conservation of 'life' which they themselves receive from him" (316). Through the narrow opening left in the cattle dung under which they bury him, the life, or breath—the *wei*—of the spear-master leaves him and passes on to his people so that they can continue with their lives. "In his death, then, the Dinka master of the fishing-spear is made to represent to his people the survival with which masters of the fishing-spear are associated.... Notions of individual immortality mean little to non-Christian Dinka, but the assertion of collective immortality means much, and it is this which they make in the funeral ceremonies of their religious leaders" (318-19).

If we come to appreciate how the Dinka themselves see the live burial of the spear-master, then the moral significance we attribute to this violation of a deep convention will change from the initial uninformed judgment of regarding it as gruesome murder to a more sophisticated response. Live burial is clearly a violation of one minimum requirement of human welfare. But the Dinka believe that it is morally justified because it is necessary for the transmission of life from the spear-master to his people. Live burial for them is like donating blood or a kidney is for us, except that for the Dinka one person is the donor for all of them, while we proceed on a one-to-one basis. It is true that both blood or kidney donors and spear-masters suffer various degrees of injury, but it is in a good cause, and both the altruistic victims and the beneficiaries see it as such. So the live burial of the spear-master should be seen both as a morally commendable sacrifice made by good people and as a possible case where there may be good reasons for violating the deep convention protecting life.

Moreover, if we abstract from the perspective of the Dinka and ask from a point of view outside of their context about the moral credentials of live burial, then the answer still remains that, provided the underlying beliefs are true, live burial itself is morally justified. Without it, the vitality of the Dinka would be sapped, as would be the vitality of those who would have to do without the blood or the kidney they need.

Relativists will conclude from this case that what counts as a morally acceptable form of killing partly depends on the beliefs that form the background of the relevant actions. Since the background beliefs vary from context to context, so also must vary reasonable judgments of what counts as permissible killing. The pluralistic attempt to provide reasons which would carry weight outside of the context cannot succeed, according to relativists, because what counts as an acceptable reason depends on the tradition which prevails in the context.

This relativistic argument, however, rests on a failure to distinguish between how background beliefs affect the moral status of particular *actions* and the moral status of the *agents* who perform the actions. If the Dinka's beliefs about the transmission of life from the spear-master to the tribe are false, then, by the actions involved in the live burial, they are violating one minimum requirement of human welfare. But since they are not doing it knowingly and intentionally, their moral status as agents is quite different from what it would be if their violations were deliberate. Just exactly what that status is depends on the balance of reasons available to them for the continuation of the practice. The position of the Dinka in this respect is analogous to what our position would be if future medical research were to reveal that blood transfusion and kidney transplants are harmful to the recipients. Since we have no reason to think that now, and we have good reasons to think the opposite, we, as agents—like the Dinka, as agents—should not be blamed if future developments force a shift in the present weight of reasons.

None of this, however, affects the question of whether our actions, or the Dinka's, adversely affect human welfare. If we distinguish between the question of the extent to which *agents*, whose actions violate deep conventions due to reasonably held yet false beliefs, are blameworthy and the question of whether or not particular *actions* violate deep conventions, then it is the relativistic argument rather than the pluralistic one that fails. We can subject various actions to a context-independent moral evaluation by asking how they affect human welfare, and we can answer without thereby necessarily committing ourselves to praising or blaming the agents of the relevant actions. We can reasonably claim from a moral point of view independent of any tradition that a tradition in which rightly respected leaders are allowed to die a natural death is, in that respect, morally better than one in which they are buried alive under cattle dung. And we can make the claim without prejudice to the moral status of the people who perpetuate either tradition.

IV. Relativism Redux?

Let us, however, go a little deeper. Suppose that a reflective Dinka or an ethnographer responds to doubts about the Dinka's belief that life passes from the spear-master to the tribe by saying that what matters is the symbolic, not the literal, truth of their belief. The fact is, it may be said, that as a result of the ceremony the tribe *is* revitalized. The members of the tribe reaffirm their identity, the continuity of their tradition, their solidarity, and their determination to face adversity together; and that is as good as if *wei* actually passed from the suffocating spear-master to the tribe. The significance of this for the issue between relativism and pluralism is that if this claim were acceptable, then there would be a new reason for thinking that what justifies the violation of the deep convention protecting life depends on the context. Live burial would be justified in the Dinka context because it would be a sustaining part of the tradition upon which the good lives of the Dinka depend, while in another context, such as ours, live burial remains morally impermissible. The moral status of live burial depends, therefore, on the tradition in which it plays a part. Given this symbolic interpretation, it is a mistake, it will be said, to attempt to evaluate actions from a perspective external to the larger context in which they occur.

The pluralistic response to this modified relativistic claim is that while it is true that the moral evaluation of actions must take into account their context, it is false that reasonable evaluations must appeal to considerations that carry weight only in the tradition which provides the context. Contrary to the relativistic claim, the Dinka custom of live burial actually supports the pluralistic case.

To see why this is so, we need to focus on the nature of the relativistic argument. Relativists think that the reason why live burial is a justifiable violation of the deep convention protecting life is that for the Dinka it symbolically sustains life. By so thinking, relativists concede the fundamental point at issue, namely, that the Dinka think as we do about the value of life. It is precisely because they value life as highly as we do that they celebrate the spear-masters for sacrificing their lives. For the point of the sacrifices is to sustain the life of the tribe. The difference between our tradition and the Dinka's is not that the primary value we assign to life in our tradition is demoted to a secondary value in theirs. They and we agree about life being a primary value. What we disagree about is whether what they regard as a reasonable case for taking the lives of the spear-masters is indeed reasonable.

Nor is this disagreement closed to reasoned resolution. The relativistic argument concedes that the Dinka and we also agree about one good reason for taking a life, namely, that by taking it we protect many lives. If the Dinka were right in believing that the killing of the spear-master is the best way to sustain the life of the tribe, then we would have to agree with them about live burial being reasonable. Our disagreement with the Dinka is made possible only by the deeper agreement between them and us about the taking of a life being morally permissible if it is the best way of preventing the loss of many lives.

Reflection on the Dinka custom of live burial, which upon first encounter strikes us as a barbaric aberration, reveals two deeper levels on which the Dinka and we see eye to eye on moral matters. On the deepest level, the Dinka agree with us about the value of life. If they did not, they would not kill the spear-masters, since it is by killing them that they aim to protect life. On the next level, the Dinka also agree with us about one good reason for taking a life. If they did not, they would not celebrate the death of their respected leaders. Only on the third, morally much more superficial level do we have a disagreement with the Dinka. They think, and we do not, that live burial is a reasonable way of protecting life. But we should note, before turning to that disagreement, that it would be impossible to have it if we did not agree first on the two deeper levels, for the disagreement presupposes the agreements. We should note also that such plausibility as relativism has derives from its concentration on the more superficial disagreement, while ignoring the deeper agreement between us about the value of life and about one morally permissible reason for taking it.[11]

Let us now consider our disagreement. To begin with, if we interpret the Dinka's belief literally rather than symbolically, then we must regard it as simply false. Life does not pass from the mouth of a dying person to members of his tribe. If the Dinka case for killing the spear-masters rests on the belief that it does, then it is a bad case. The symbolic interpretation, however, cannot be so easily dismissed. The tribe is sustained by its members' belief that life passes from the spear-masters to them. To be sure, they are not sustained by their belief as food sustains them. But—arguably—psychological sustenance may be as important as its physical analogue. Yet while it is true that the Dinka derive psychological sustenance from their tradition, their tradition is complex and the ceremonies connected with the live burial of the spear-masters are only a small, although important, part of it. If they were deprived of that source of sustenance, they might still receive sustenance in other ways.

We know that this is so because the Dinka tradition has remained strong even after Sudanese authorities have outlawed live burial. Indeed, Lienhardt's study was written after the desuetude of the custom. The symbolic interpretation of the Dinka case, therefore, also falls short of making it morally acceptable, since the killing of the spear-masters cannot be justified on the grounds that it was required for the survival of the tribe. And since that was the reason why the burial was thought to be a justified violation of the deep convention protecting life, the symbolically interpreted case for live burial also fails. We must conclude that the Sudanese authorities acted reasonably in outlawing live burial.

This still leaves two loose ends. The first is how the Dinka themselves should think about the matter and the other is the moral status of the agents who perpetuated the morally unjustifiable custom. We have no information about how the Dinka actually think about it, but it is not hard to reconstruct how they are likely to think. No doubt, some will perceive in the prohibition of live burial a serious threat to their tradition; others will say that one must move with the times; yet others will attend to their cattle and let the local pundits worry about the matter; and perhaps some will celebrate it as a step in the march of progress. The reason why this reconstruction is so plausible is that we can readily put ourselves in the Dinka's position as we reflect on *our* range of attitudes toward changes in *our* traditions regarding, for instance, homosexuality, the waning of religious belief, or the availability of life-sustaining medical technology.

The second loose end is the question of what moral evaluation would be reasonable of the Dinka *agents*, not of their actions, who took part in what we now see as the morally unjustifiable live burial of the spear-masters. Their moral situation was that they believed themselves to have good reasons for acting as they did, but they were mistaken. Our moral evaluation of them must depend on how we answer the question of whether their mistake was culpable. Given that the custom has persisted in their tradition since time immemorial, that critical reflection on prevailing practices has not been part of the Dinka tradition, and that both the victims and their authorities had agreed about the value of the custom, it would be wrong to hold the Dinka culpable for perpetuating their morally objectionable custom. The appropriate concrete reaction to the whole situation is just what the Sudanese did: outlaw it, enforce the prohibition, and let that be the end of the matter.

V. Conclusion

Reflection on the custom of live burial permits us to conclude that the form of relativism we have been considering is mistaken. The strength of relativism, as we have interpreted it, is its insistence on the richness and variety of human possibilities and its reluctance to condemn moral possibilities from a point of view alien to them. These are useful and needed correctives of moral dogmatism. But relativists go too far. There *are* human differences, but they are *human* differences. Traditions allow different possibilities, but there is a limit to the differences among them because they are allowing moral possibilities for human beings. The Dinka and we, radical feminists and ayatollahs, Tibetan lamas and stockbrokers are all human beings, and therefore they are—we are—united at a deep level of our being. The minimum requirements of our welfare are the same. These requirements create a case for meeting them, and that case will be found persuasive by all reasonable people who pause to reflect on it. The case is simply that if we can, we should want the human enterprise to go on as well as possible. This is what morality is about. Of course, beyond this elementary yet deep level, significant differences emerge about how different traditions interpret the human enterprise going well. But these differences all occur on that third level which is so close to the surface: the level on which we disagree with the Dinka about live burial.

What relativists miss is that moral disagreements are possible only if there are moral agreements in the background. *Moral* disagreements presuppose that the parties to it are committed to morality, which on any view of the matter involves commitment to human welfare, and that they are also committed to the shared procedure of settling some moral disagreements by evaluating some of the conflicting values on the basis of their contribution to human welfare. Of course, disagreements need not be moral, and of course many moral disagreements are not open to being settled in this way. The appeal to the minimum requirements of human welfare makes only some conflicts tractable, while it leaves many other conflicts unresolved. But the commitment to morality, and thus to human welfare, is sufficient to establish that at least one form of relativism is mistaken. For one consequence of that commitment is that, contrary to relativism, it is not the case that moral disagreements may affect *all* moral judgments made within the contexts of differing traditions. If traditions are healthy, then there must be *some* agreement in the moral judgments that can reasonably be made within them. It is this layer of agreement, derived from our common humanity, that transcends particular traditions and constitutes the context-independent ground of some moral judgments. Pluralism allows for it, relativism does not, indeed it cannot, and that is a reason for preferring pluralism to relativism.

The argument of this essay has been directed mainly against relativism. It should be noted, however, that the moral agreement reasonable people will share about primary values, which constitute the context-independent ground of judgment, cannot be used to support monism. Primary values remain conditional, and do not become overriding, as monists suppose, for the two reasons given earlier. First, they are conditional on the commitment to living good lives. Lives may be so bad, however, as to exclude the possibility of ever becoming good, and then the value of life, as of any other value, may be reasonably overridden. Second, any primary value may conflict with some other primary value, and it is not possible to decide a priori how such conflicts are to be resolved. Sometimes the claims of life reasonably override the claims of freedom or justice; sometimes reason points the other way. Since pluralists recognize this possibility, while monists cannot do so and remain consistent, we have reason to prefer pluralism to monism as well.[12]

Notes

1. Annette Baier, Richard Brandt, Stuart Hampshire, Thomas Nagel, David Norton, Martha Nussbaum, Edmund Pincoffs, John Rawls, Richard Rorty, Michael Stocker, Peter Strawson, Charles Taylor, Michael Walzer, and Bernard Williams are all pluralists in some sense or another, although many deep disagreements divide them.
2. Stuart Hampshire, *Innocence and Experience* (Cambridge, MA: Harvard UP, 1989), p. 172.
3. The distinction between overriding and conditional values is not the same as the distinction between absolute and prima facie values. Overriding values may be prima facie because they may be justifiably violated in any particular case provided that that is the best way of protecting the value in general.
4. Some classical versions of monism are those of Plato, Kant, and John Stuart Mill, among others; contemporary versions have been defended by Alan Donagan, Alan Gewirth, R.M. Hare, and others.

5. Some classical versions of relativism are those of Protagoras, Montaigne, Giambattista Vico, and Johann Gottfried Herder, among others; contemporary versions have been defended by Clifford Geertz, Gilbert Harman, Joseph Margolis, Richard Rorty, Michael Walzer, and others.

6. This distinction between primary and secondary values needs much more explanation than it is possible to provide here. For further explanation, see the author's *Moral Tradition and Individuality* (Princeton: Princeton UP, 1989), ch. 1, and *Facing Evil* (Princeton UP, 1990), ch. 3.

7. Such a case is attempted in the author's *The Morality of Pluralism* (Princeton: Princeton UP, 1993).

8. For accounts of some of these controversies, see Jonathan Glover, *Causing Death and Saving Lives* (Harmondsworth: Penguin, 1977); Eike-Henner Kluge, *The Practice of Death* (New Haven: Yale UP, 1975); Daniel H. Labby, ed., *Life or Death* (Seattle: U of Washington P, 1968); and Bonnie Steinbock, ed., *Killing and Letting Die* (Englewood Cliffs, NJ: Prentice-Hall, 1980).

9. Albert Schweitzer, *The Teaching of Reverence for Life*, trans. R. and C. Winston (New York: Holt, Rineheart, and Winston, 1965), p. 26.

10. Godfrey Lienhardt, Divinity and *Experience: The Religion of the Dinka* (Oxford: Clarendon, 1961); page references to this book will be given in parentheses in the text below.

11. For a similar argument against relativism, see Renford Bambrough, *Moral Scepticism and Moral Knowledge* (London: Routledge, 1979).

12. This essay draws on material from chapters 3 and 7 of the author's *The Morality of Pluralism*.

17.
GLOBAL WARMING

❧ ❧ ❧

ROBERT HOOD

Robert Hood is Assistant Director in the Office of Public Health at the Florida Department of Health. He earned a doctorate in philosophy at Bowling Green State University and specializes in environmental ethics, public health ethics, and research ethics. Hood argues that although there are still uncertainties about various causes and effects of climate change, it is indisputable that it exists and is caused by human activity. He addresses three central questions about this phenomenon: whether industrialized nations who are causing climate change bear a greater responsibility to do something about this problem than other nations, whether current generations who are causing climate change have obligations to future generations, and whether humans have obligations to the environment itself. In each case Hood brings a plurality of moral considerations to bear on the questions at issue.

The purpose of this chapter is to review and clarify ethical issues concerning climate change. The greenhouse effect, first suggested by Swedish chemist Svante Arrhenius in 1896, refers to the ways so-called "greenhouse gases," chiefly carbon dioxide, methane, and water vapor, trap heat and keep the planet warm enough for life. The existence of the greenhouse effect is not at issue; rather, the ethical debate focuses on implications of increasing levels of greenhouse gases and global warming. The burning of fossil fuels since the Industrial Revolution is the chief cause of increased levels of greenhouse gases in the atmosphere. Since increased levels of greenhouse gases result in a variety of effects, not just increased warming, but also more severe weather, and changes in wind patterns and ocean currents, it is more accurate to use "climate change" to refer to all the effects of increasing levels of greenhouse gases.

The first section of this chapter will provide an overview of the problem of climate change. Then the next section will survey the science and explore some reasons for the uncertainty in climate science. The final section will explore ethical issues, such as questions of fairness between industrialized countries and less-developed countries, obligations to future generations, and questions about the nature and kind of obligations toward the environment itself.

Climate Change

Climate change has been the subject of impassioned debate, both by environmentalists and the mainstream public. On one side, environmentalists have worried that climate change is a threat of such magnitude that "conditions that are essential to life as we know it are now at risk" (Flavin, 1991: 79). Bill McKibben (1989) argues that climate change means the "end of nature" because by changing the climate we have "deprived nature of its independence" creating an artifact: "Summer is going extinct, replaced by something else that will be called 'summer' ... but it will not be summer, just as even the best prosthesis is not a leg" (McKibben, 1989: 59). In contrast, others have dismissed worries about climate change, denying them outright, or claiming that the crisis is not climate change but the politicization of science and environmental policy to suit the special interests of environmentalists (Bast et al., 1994; Simon, 1996). While these debates were largely limited to environmentalists, arguably it was the testimony of respected climate scientist James Hansen before the United States Congress in 1988 that made climate change an issue of mainstream public attention. He stated plainly that it is "time to stop waffling so much" and admit that "Global warming is here" (Stevens, 1999). This event resulted in widespread media coverage of climate change, including a decision by the editors of *Time* magazine to name the warming Earth as its "man of the year" for 1988.

It is interesting, given all of this, that environmental philosophers have said relatively little about climate change. There are only a handful of articles focusing solely on climate change in the major peer-reviewed journals in the field (Lemons, 1983; Jamieson, 1992; Kverndokk, 1995). It is possible that the limited discussion of climate change as such is due to the especially technical nature of the science, though this has not stopped environmental ethicists from wading into other technical debates concerning, for example, species extinction or the use of genetically modified organisms in agriculture. More likely it is because the ethical issues raised by climate change have been seen as instances of more general moral phenomena such as concern for future generations. As an example of this, Bryan Norton (1991) discusses climate change as just one example of a class of problems that he characterizes as "third generation" environmental problems. These problems differ from earlier environmental problems because they involve "apparently small risks of cataclysmic effects" (Norton, 1991: 210).

There are three features that distinguish climate change from earlier environmental problems. First, the extreme complexity of climate change, as well as that of other relatively new environmental problems, such as the storage of nuclear waste, makes identifying the causal processes difficult, technical, and generally open to uncertainty and dispute. The relatively long timeframes from increased emission of greenhouse gases to the effects of climate change, and the obscurity and complexity of the causal chains, make identifying and characterizing the effects of climate change particularly complex. This is compounded by the fact that there will be some good effects of climate change alongside the bad effects. A result of this uncertainty is that decisions may be made under conditions of less than perfect knowledge that have potentially catastrophic consequences. These uncertainties pose difficulties for policy-makers because of the potentially enormous negative consequences of failing to act on these problems. By the time there is complete scientific certainty about damage from climate change, or by the time the actual damage occurs, it will be too late to reverse the effects of climate change, which are expected to last for several centuries after greenhouse gas emissions are reduced.

A second feature of climate change concerns uncertainties about moral obligations and responsibilities. Those who enjoy the benefits of industrialization and the increased greenhouse gas emissions may not be the most affected by the results of climate change, a situation that raises questions about equity. Furthermore, some of the people who are most likely to be affected may not even be born yet; decisions are being made now which affect not only their lives but also the conditions of ecosystems in the future. The moral issues become more complex when questions are raised about obligations to the environment concerning climate change.

A third feature of climate change is that collective action is particularly important in understanding its dynamics. Collective action problems are those where individual actions may not be themselves harmful, but result in harms when coupled with the effects of others (Olson, 1965; Hardin, 1994). Climate change is a function not just of what any single individual or a single country does, but also of what other individuals or other countries do. Given that some uncertainty remains concerning the effects of climate change, some people will prefer to wait to act to mitigate these effects. Indeed, some may think it is not rational to act given the uncertainty; others may prefer to wait to see if the actions of other individuals or countries can eliminate the effects of climate change. In any case, the sooner reductions are made in the amounts of emissions then the lower the total amount of warming and the smaller the ecosystemic and economic effects.

Uncertainty Concerning the Science of Climate Change

Since much of the public debate has emphasized the uncertainty of the science, it is important to be clear about what is not in dispute concerning climate change and what remains to be discovered. The Intergovernmental Panel on Climate Change (IPCC), comprised of two thousand climate scientists, reported in 1995 that climate change existed and is caused by human activity. The most recent IPCC report indicates that there is "new and stronger evidence that most of the warming observed over the last 50 years is attributable to human activities" (Intergovernmental Panel on Climate Change, 2001). The number of scientists involved in this project and the rigorous analytical procedures used ensure that it reflects the consensus views of climate scientists. Moreover, the findings of the IPCC have been checked by the National Research Council at the request of the United States government. The National Research Council concluded that the evidence for climate change was stronger than that found by the IPCC, and concluded that "Temperatures are, in fact, rising" and that "Human activities are responsible for the increase" (Committee on the Science of Climate Change, National Research Council, 2001).

The understanding of climate change has broadened over time and now integrates more types of evidence, including observations as well as computer simulations of climate. Evidence for climate change comes from a variety of sources, including observations such as historical and current atmospheric and ocean temperature readings, studies of the atmosphere preserved in the polar ice sheets (ice-core data), shrinkage of glaciers, thawing of permafrost, and changes in the distribution and range of plants and animals and an increase in average global ocean levels. In addition to these observations of climate change, computer models are used to both understand and predict global climate change. Due to the increased understanding provided by this broad evidence, there is consensus among climate scientists that the world is warming and that other changes in climate are underway, and that the cause of climate change is human activities, particularly the burning of fossil fuels.

However, the effects of climate change on the world's ecosystems and economic systems are currently less well understood. The IPCC notes that the "stakes of climate change are high" and include additional warming, changes in the distribution and amounts of precipitation, change in the distribution and number of extreme climate events such as droughts and hurricanes, changes in the distribution of human and animal diseases, and sea-level rise. There is also uncertainty whether climate change might involve any threshold effects or feedback loops which could cause dramatic changes in ecosystems.

Currently, the area of greatest uncertainty about climate change concerns the effects of climate change on human societies. In general the social sciences indicate that climate change will not affect all human societies in the same way and to the same degree. The areas that are expected to be most affected by climate change have the least capacity to adapt and change because they lack education, information, wealth and resources, and management capacities.

There are several reasons why uncertainty exists in the science of climate change. Carl Cranor (1993) has explored the ways in which the presuppositions of environmental science incline it toward certain kinds of uncertainty. Although his work has looked at risks from environmental exposure to toxic chemicals, it can be extended to climate change. Environmental scientists begin with the presumption that greenhouse gases have no effects until these have been proved in appropriate ways. Demonstrating these properties often requires substantial technical sophistication, which is perhaps one reason why the hypothesis of global warming, first proposed in the late nineteenth century, took another century to be demonstrated. In addition, the disposition of environmental scientists is to avoid one kind of error (false positives) where their analysis mistakenly shows that emissions are associated with climate change when they are in fact not. Concern to avoid false positives potentially makes it more likely to commit another type of error, where a procedure mistakenly shows that emissions are not associated with climate change when they in fact are (false negatives). The burdens of proof against false positives reinforce protections for potentially climate-changing substances. The presumption in environmental science and regulation is that a product has no effect until proved otherwise, unlike the situation in the medical sciences where the presumption requires that substances be shown to be safe and effective before use.

A further complication is that the effects of greenhouse gases can have long latency periods, operate by obscure causal mechanisms, and may involve threshold effects where no effects are noticed until a certain concentration is reached. Greenhouse gases cause effects that are causally over-determined; that is, where a number of different causes may result in the same effect. For example, a species may become extinct because of climate change, but also because their habitat is reduced due to human actions, and any number of other potential reasons.

Another reason for uncertainty about climate change is that there is an asymmetry between information about the benefits of climate-changing substances and their adverse effects. For example, oil companies and auto companies have obvious incentives to understand the costs of producing their products but have less of an incentive to discover the potential environmental costs of pollution caused by their products. There are also asymmetries between developed countries, which produce most of the greenhouse emissions, and less-developed countries which are expected to bear the brunt of the effects.

Lastly, there are social reasons why there may appear to be more uncertainty than is actually the case. For example, climate scientist Richard Lindzen has asserted that climate research is "polluted with political rhetoric" and that increased emissions of greenhouse gases due to the burning of fossil fuels have about as much affect on global climate as when "a butterfly shuts its wings" (Grossman, 2001: 39). Understood as part of a scientific dialogue, his views are recognized as dissenting from majority opinion. Moreover, not all of his views dissent from the consensus opinion: he was a member of the National Research Council study that concluded that climate change is occurring and that its causes are due to human actions. However, the portrayal of climate science in the popular media can inadvertently give greater weight to such views than they have within the scientific community. Portraying the scientific debate as having two equal sides, and giving both views similar amounts of time, serves to over-emphasize disagreement and fails to recognize the degree to which the majority of climate scientists are in agreement about climate change.

In response to the ways in which environmental science is disposed to certain kinds of uncertainty, and in response to the fact that scientists are called upon by policy-makers for information and to make recommendations on climate change, some have advocated a "precautionary" approach to environmental science (Barrett and Raffensperger, 1999). Precautionary science is a view about how science should proceed in the light of uncertainty, and argues that in the face of scientific uncertainties people should refrain from actions that might harm the environment. In addition, this view suggests that the burden of proof for assuring the safety of an action falls upon those who practice it. There is debate about whether the precautionary approach involves a change in science, or whether it instead requires a commitment to normative values about the environment. Even if something like a precautionary approach to climate science would change standards of evidence or the use of science in policy, it is important to note that decisions still need to be made concerning how to prioritize environmental policy. Ethical issues will continue to exist even after the effects of climate change are well understood. It is to a discussion of the uncertainties concerning environmental values that I turn in the next section.

Uncertainties and the Ethics of Climate Change

It is standard in environmental ethics to distinguish between concern for other humans in our dealings with the environment and concern for the environment itself. The discussion that follows first reviews obligations toward other humans regarding climate change, and then discusses the more complex question about obligations to the environment itself. Since it is expected that climate change will not affect all people and all nations the same, one issue raised by climate change concerns equity and justice concerning the treatment of other people. Related to issues of equity toward existing people are issues of intergenerational equity due to the fact that most of the effects of climate change will have an impact upon people, species, and ecosystems in the future. Since climate change does not have the same effect on different ecosystems, and might have different effects even within a given ecosystem, a third moral issue about climate change raises questions of the way in which we characterize the harm to the environment as well as the nature of our obligations to the environment.

Running through all of the issues concerning the ethics of climate change is the question of what should be done when it is uncertain what morality requires (Lockhart, 2000). Until the science improves, the difficulties faced concerning whether to act, given the current uncertainty, will remain. There is abundant discussion of the justification of moral rules or principles—utilitarian justifications, deontological justifications, feminist justifications, and many others—but the treatment of priority questions has received less discussion. There is a similar diversity of justifications in environmental ethics (Hargrove, 2001). However, the issue of how to prioritize issues in environmental ethics needs to be explored in greater detail. For example, although it is possible to reduce greenhouse gas emissions by using nuclear power, this also comes with its own set of long-term and potentially global effects concerning disposal requirements for nuclear waste.

Climate change raises issues of equity and justice because it is expected that climate change will not affect all people or all countries the same. There are a number of approaches to equity, focusing on maximizing the greatest good for the greatest number, on minimizing the impact on the least fortunate, on determinations of who is most responsible, and on the allocation of property rights. In addition, it is possible to distinguish different aspects of equality, such as maintaining a fair process, ensuring fair outcomes, and ensuring fair opportunities. Some have argued that it may be possible to find a core set of concerns or a convergence of views by focusing on those who are the worst off (Dasgupta, 1993). Environmental pragmatists have emphasized that policy justifications will be stronger where there is a convergence of different theoretical views (Light and Katz, 1996). Trying to see whether a convergence of ethical views is possible concerning climate change is particularly helpful given the controversy over climate change.

Historically, land use practices concerning pollution involve norms of dilution and dispersion. So long as an individual's pollution is less than the capacity of the environment to absorb or dilute it, and so long as the pollution is not a nuisance, then there is generally not a moral problem. The ethical problem of climate change stems from the fact that the pollution of greenhouse gases exceeds what can be diluted and absorbed by the atmosphere. What might be called the default view concerning pollution is known as the "pollution principle," and states that the costs of pollution should be internalized into the costs of the product. This is based on the straightforward idea that if someone causes a problem, whether intentionally or not, they should, in the future, take steps not to cause the problem again. However, the pollution principle is "forward-looking" and does not address the problem of harmful effects of climate change due to emissions of greenhouse gases in the past.

Henry Shue (1999) has argued for obligations by industrialized countries to reduce greenhouse gas emissions in the future as well as to compensate other countries for harms involving past emissions. The argument is that it is mainly people in industrialized countries who have caused the problem. The industrialization that causes climate change creates problems for everyone on the planet, but only some people have received benefits from it. Even if unintended, industrialized countries have got benefits without paying for them—they have exacted a taking against non-industrialized countries. However, emissions of greenhouse gases are far from unintended. Industrialized countries have continued to produce greenhouse gas emissions long after it has been known that they cause climate change. Shue concludes that, to the extent that industrialized countries have made a greater contribution to the problem of climate change, then they have an obligation to "shoulder burdens that are unequal at least to the extent of the unfair advantage previously taken" (Shue, 1999: 534).

Second, Shue argues that people in industrialized countries have a greater ability to pay to fix the harms caused by global warming. Given the assumption that industrialized countries have managed to produce a surplus of individual wealth and non-industrialized countries are struggling to provide a basic minimum, then fairness requires those with greater ability to shoulder a greater portion of the burden. This point is controversial. But Shue suggests that if industrialized countries reject either of these requirements and argue that there is no general obligation to help less-developed countries, then "citizens of poor states ... have no general obligation to assist wealthy states in dealing with the environmental problems that the wealthy states' own industrial processes are producing" (Shue, 1999). If an industrialized country were to reject the argument about responsibility or the argument about ability to pay and assert that there is no obligation to help developed countries, then a less-developed country such as China has no obligation to help out the United States. If industrialized countries have an interest in avoiding harms from climate change, then they have an interest in less-developed countries developing their economies in ways that minimize the emissions of greenhouse gases. Consequently, as long as industrialized countries want help from less-developed countries to not exacerbate climate change, the industrialized countries are under obligations to help out the less-developed countries.

An additional argument could be made that if some countries can reduce their greenhouse gas emissions more efficiently and less expensively than others then, all things being equal, the less expensive options should be tried first (Claussen and McNeilly, 2000). This argument recognizes that there is a diminishing return on reducing greenhouse gas emissions for a given unit of investment. At this point it is useful to distinguish between assessing responsibilities for emissions in terms of each individual's contribution and in terms of each country's contribution. Sorting out the details of these issues is obviously technical, and has been the subject of negotiations of the United Nations Conferences on Global Climate Change.

Markets in emissions are advocated by free-market environmentalists, who think that market forces and the rule of law should govern environmental policy concerning climate change (Anderson and Leal, 2001). If property rights were granted to the atmosphere, then the use of more than the granted share would constitute an imposition on others' property. Market approaches suggest that those wishing to use more than their share would have to purchase rights from others. Since it is likely that the United States would use more than its share of property rights to the atmosphere, it would have to purchase the use of others' emission shares. It would appear that, even though the theoretical approaches of Shue and the free-market environmentalists differ, there nevertheless appears to be convergence about policy: industrialized countries such as the United States who are causing the problem are bound to compensate nonindustrialized countries.

In addition to equity among existing people, there is also the question of intergenerational equity or duties to future generations, who are expected to bear most of the harm from climate change. There is an extensive literature about duties to future generations (de Shalit, 1995). Standard theories of intergenerational equity have concluded that obligations to our children and their children are greater than obligations to people who might live in the very distant future. In contrast, environmentalists have generally held that there are obligations to distant future generations of people as well as to the future members of species and future ecosystems, and that if standard theories do not account for these obligations, then new theories are needed. Norton, for example, concludes that if standard theories of obligations to future generations prohibit "recognition of felt obligations to distant generations, then those theories are inadequate, by their essential nature" to deal with environmental problems such as climate change (Norton, 1991: 216). The problem of duties to future generations may be overemphasized, however. In large part, actions which will prevent harms to future generations also will lead to increased quality of life for the current generation. Developing alternative and cleaner energy sources and improving conservation efforts benefit those currently living as well as future generations (Bernstein et al., 2001).

This discussion is necessarily sketchy, and does not address a number of complexities. For example, it does not address the implications of different tolerances for risks: some people are more willing to take risks concerning the environment or to impose those risks on others (Shrader-Frechette, 1991). Nor does it address the sense of some environmentalists that the consumption that drives the production of greenhouse gases is itself morally wrong and inflicting unfair burdens on others currently living and on those in the future (Milbrath, 1993). Perhaps the most important omission of much discussion of climate change is the implications of climate change for other species and ecosystems.

Environmental ethicists should be in a position to contribute to the discussion of the ethical implications of climate change for other species and ecosystems, and the remainder of this chapter sketches some possibilities. There is a variety of ways of justifying the value of the environment as such. The most likely candidates to address obligations toward the environment concerning climate change are views that focus on obligations toward ecosystems and ecological processes rather than species of individual animals (Rolston, 1975; Scherer, 1988; Callicott, 1989). It is helpful to distinguish between different time-scales to evaluate the effects of climate change on species and ecosystems. From a very long-term perspective of tens of thousands of years to hundreds of thousands of years, there have been large numbers of species extinctions as well as the creation of new species. In the long run, since species will become extinct and new species will be created, the obligation is not so much to protect any particular species or community or ecosystem, but rather to protect overall biological diversity and the overall capacity of ecosystems to maintain themselves.

Obligations toward the environment in the short run are considerably more complex, and turn on questions of how to characterize harm to ecosystems and on questions of how to prioritize ecosystem management. Given the scientific consensus that currently there is continuing global loss of biological diversity, and assuming that there are not resources to save all species or protect all ecosystems equally, then the question in the short run is one of management priorities. Increasingly there is recognition of the need to identify "the kinds of biodiversity that are most significant to the ways ecosystems function" (Walker, 1992). Protecting those species that have a disproportionate effect on ecosystem function provides a way to prioritize management efforts. For example, it is possible to distinguish between so-called "driver" and "passenger" species in ecosystems on the grounds that ecological functions are disproportionately affected by the removal of some species (drivers), and that the loss of others (passengers) has relatively little effect on ecosystem function (Walker, 1992). Another model focuses on the disproportionate effect of some species on ecosystem function in terms of their habitat manipulations, in particular, the structural changes produced by certain organisms, so-called "ecosystem engineers" (Jones et al., 1994). Ecosystem engineers, including such diverse species as coral, beavers, and trees, all have disproportionate effects on ecosystem function by creating structures that other species can also use. That ecosystem engineers create goods and services for other species, and that their removal results in loss of ecosystem functions, are reasons for making their management a priority.

Another promising course of action is to explore ways in which climate change might have an impact upon the services that the environment provides to human communities in the short run. Recent literature on ecosystem management characterizes ecosystems as providing various goods and services, such as habitat, food, as well as a variety of services also of direct interest to human such as resource production and flood control. The idea here is to protect the capacities of ecosystems to provide ecosystem goods and services as a way of prioritizing management. To the extent that the interests of non-human species in ecosystems are frequently the same as those of humans, then protecting the capacity of ecosystems to provide goods and services in light of climate change is an example of a convergence between human and environmental ethics. To the extent that ecosystems are valuable because they provide ecosystem goods and services, and to the extent that climate change lowers this provision of ecosystem goods, then management should give priority to protecting these capacities by, among other things, reducing emission of greenhouse gases and climate change. As the effects of climate change continue, there will be an increasing need to think seriously about obligations to restore ecosystems and to protect biodiversity, if only to protect human interests (Gobster and Hull, 2000; Throop, 2000).

In conclusion, this chapter has noted that there is cultural uncertainty about the effects of climate change and a reluctance by some to commit to actions to limit greenhouse gas emissions. Given this uncertainty, it is likely that the most promising directions will focus on areas where there is a convergence between the ethics of concern for people in terms of equity and the ethics of concern for the environment for its own sake. In particular, perhaps the most promising area of convergence focuses on protecting and restoring those ecosystem goods and services that protect people from the effects of climate change, and those that protect biodiversity and the capacity of ecosystems to adapt to climate change.

References

Anderson, T. and Leal, D. (2001) *Free Market Environmentalism*. New York: Palgrave.

Barrett, K. and Raffensperger, C. (1999) "Precautionary Science." In C. Raffensperger and J. Tichner (eds.), *Protecting Public Health and the Environment: Implementing the Precautionary Principle*. Washington, DC: Island P.

Bast, J.L., Hill, P.J. et al. (1994) *Eco-Sanity: A Common-Sense Guide to Environmentalism*. Lanham, MD: Madison Books.

Bernstein, M., Hassell, S. et al. (2001) *May Cooler Tempers Prevail: Let Technology Reduce Hot Air over Global Warming*. RAND Corporation.

Callicott, J.B. (1989) *In Defense of the Land Ethic: Essays in Environmental Philosophy*. Albany, NY: State U of New York P.

Claussen, E. and McNeilly, L. (2000) *Equity and Global Climate Change: The Complex Elements of Global Fairness*, pp. 1-36. Pew Center on Global Climate Change.

Committee on the Science of Climate Change. National Research Council (2001) *Climate Change Science: An Analysis of Some Key Questions.* Washington, DC: National Academy of Science.

Cranor, C.F. (1993) *Regulating Toxic Substances: A Philosophy of Science and the Law.* New York: Oxford UP.

Dasgupta, P. (1993) *An Inquiry into Well-being and Destitution.* Oxford: Clarendon P.

de Shalit, A. (1995) *Why Posterity Matters: Environmental Policies and Future Generations.* New York: Routledge.

Flavin, C. (1991) "The Heat Is on: The Greenhouse Effect." In L. Brown (ed.), *The Worldwatch Reader on Global Environmental Issues*, pp. 75-94. New York: Norton.

Gobster, P.H. and Hull, R.B. (2000) *Restoring Nature: Perspectives from the Social Sciences and Humanities.* Washington, DC: Island P.

Grossman, D. (2001) "Dissent in the Maelstrom." *Scientific American*, November: 38-39.

Hardin, R. (1994) *Contested Communities* (unpublished manuscript).

Hargrove, E.C. (2001) *A Very Brief History of the Origins of Environmental Ethics for the Novice.* Center for Environmental Philosophy.

Intergovernmental Panel on Climate Change (2001) *Climate Change 2001: Synthesis Report.* Geneva: Switzerland: IPCC.

Jamieson, D. (1992) "Ethics, Public Policy, and Global Warming." *Science, Technology, and Human Values*, 17 (2): 139-53.

Jones, C.G., Lawton, J.H. et al. (1994) "Organisms as Ecosystem Engineers." *Oikos*, 69: 373-86.

Kverndokk, S. (1995) "Tradeable CO_2 Emission Permits: Initial Distribution as a Justice Problem." *Environmental Values*, 4(2): 129-48.

Lemons, J. (1983) "Atmospheric Carbon Dioxide: Environmental Ethics and Environmental Facts." *Environmental Ethics*, 5: 21-32.

Light, A. and Katz, E. (1996) *Environmental Pragmatism.* New York: Routledge.

Lockhart, T. (2000) *Moral Uncertainty and its Consequences.* New York: Oxford UP.

McKibben, B. (1989) *The End of Nature.* New York: Random House.

Milbrath, L.W. (1993) "Redefining the Good Life in a Sustainable Society." *Environmental Values*, 2(3): 261-70.

Norton, B. (1991) *Toward Unity among Environmentalists.* New York: Oxford UP.

Olson, M. (1965) *The Logic of Collective Action.* Cambridge, MA: Harvard UP.

Rolston, H.I. (1975) "Is There an Ecological Ethic?" *Ethics*, 85(2): 93-109.

Scherer, D. (1988) "A Disentropic Ethic." *The Monist*, 70 (October): 3-32.

Shrader-Frechette, K. (1991) *Risk and Rationality.* Berkeley, CA: U of California P.

Shue, H. (1999) "Global Environment and International Inequality." *International Affairs*, 75: 531-45.

Simon, J.L. (1996) *The Ultimate Resource 2.* Princeton, NJ: Princeton UP.

Stevens, W.K. (1999) "1998: Warmest Year of Past Millennium." *Science News*, 155 (March 20): 191.

Throop, W. (ed.) (2000) *Environmental Restoration: Ethics, Theory, and Practice.* Amherst: Humanity Books.

Walker, B.H. (1992) "Biodiversity and Ecological Redundancy." *Conservation Biology*, 6 (1): 18-23.

CHAPTER SEVEN

JUSTICE

INTRODUCTION

Justice is a centrally important concept in most nonconsequentialist moral theories. Such theories insist that there are certain constraints with which we must comply in our pursuit of any end or goal. These constraints often pertain to being just to individuals. As we have seen, nonconsequentialist moral theories often perform quite well in accounting for our moral intuitions. Intuitively, we believe that it is important from a moral point of view to comply with the demands of justice. However, there has been a good deal of controversy on the question of what the demands of justice are.

The concept of justice has both a formal element and a substantive element. The formal element is generally agreed upon. An action, policy, or institution is just when each individual is given his or her due. Like cases are to be treated in a like manner, and the same rule or set of rules is to apply to all. But this formal element of justice leaves a great deal unspecified. Each person is to be given his or her due, but how do we determine what individuals are due? Like cases are to be treated alike, but how do we determine relevant similarity, and how is any given case to be treated? And the same rules should be applied to all, but what should these rules be?

Consider the allocation of organs available for transplant. Currently organs are scarce, and must be allocated by some procedure that selects among patients who could benefit from them. We want this procedure to be just, but what would constitute a just allocation of organs? Should we transplant the organs into patients on a first come, first served basis, provided that medical criteria indicate a strong possibility of a successful graft? Should law-abiding citizens have priority over persons with serious criminal records? Should persons who have made substantial contributions to society be given priority over those who have not? Or should organs simply be sold to the highest bidder?

The distribution of wealth and income in a society raises similar problems. Does justice demand that wealth and income be distributed equally in any given society, or perhaps throughout the world? Does it demand that each person be allowed to control his or her own fate by making voluntary transactions in a free market economy? Or does it demand some other principle of allocation, such as "from each according to his ability; to each according to his need"? We can say that allocations should be made in accordance with a set of rules established in advance and made available to the public. We can add, in a democratic society, that the majority of people should agree on the rules. But while these points are important, they leave the central questions unanswered. It is possible to establish in advance and publicize an unjust set of rules, and it is also quite possible for a majority of persons to agree on a practice that is unjust. In order to answer the question of whether any given practice is just, we need a substantive theory of justice.

To date, there is little agreement on substantive theories of justice. Some of these theories are egalitarian. They hold that all persons have equal intrinsic worth and that they ought therefore to be treated with equal concern and respect. Others are inegalitarian. They hold that the intrinsic worth of persons varies according to one or more of their personal characteristics—most commonly moral merit. In this case we are not all owed equal concern and respect—some of us are owed more of these things than others. Inegalitarians challenge egalitarians to identify any characteristic held equally by all persons that could serve as a basis for the claim that we all have equal intrinsic worth and an equal moral status. Egalitarians have made a variety of responses here. Some claim that all persons possess rational autonomy or the capacity for moral agency. Some point out that all persons have the capacity to determine their own values and life plans, and then to be disappointed or fulfilled in terms of them. Some say simply that we are all equally the subjects of our own lives. Each of these positions would obviously have implications for who might be included or excluded from personhood.

In any case, there is substantial disagreement even among egalitarians of the same stripe on substantive principles of justice. John Rawls and Robert Nozick each agree that all persons have an equal moral status and ought to be treated with equal concern and respect. Nevertheless, they arrive at radically different positions on the issue of distribution of wealth and income. Rawls holds that we should first secure for each person the most extensive set of basic rights and liberties, compatible with like rights and liberties for all, and ensure that offices and positions are made available to all under conditions of fair equality of opportunity. Then wealth and income ought to be distributed equally, unless an inequality would be to the advantage of the least advantaged group. Nozick, on the other hand, holds that wealth and income should not be "distributed" at all. Each person is entitled to acquire unowned property if he "mixes his labor" with it and if there is as much and as good left for others. He is further entitled to any property he acquires through voluntary transactions with others, or as restitution for harm that they have wrongfully inflicted on him.

How might we adjudicate between these two positions? Each seems to have its own counterintuitive implications. In a society based on Nozick's theory, people who were genuinely unable to provide for themselves would die unless persons of means sought them out and volunteered to provide for them. Disabled persons would be entirely at the mercy of the goodwill of others. They would have no just claims to assistance from anyone. On Rawls's theory, each person would be given an equal share of wealth and income (unless an inequality would benefit the least advantaged group) regardless of how little she contributed and how little she exerted herself. An individual who wanted to work hard to advance her own life and achieve important aspects of her life plans would find it difficult to do so. She and others who were ambitious could make progress in this direction only by advancing the lives of all the people who were less ambitious than themselves.

It seems that each of these theories fails to secure important benefits for individuals. Nozick's theory fails to establish a minimally decent level of security for all individuals and Rawls's theory fails to secure for individuals the opportunity to make the most of their own lives by their own efforts. Perhaps, then, an egalitarian theory of justice could most plausibly be based on the following principle: Each individual ought to be secured the most fundamental interests in life compatible with like benefits for all, and no individual ought to be required to sacrifice an important interest so that others can benefit in less important ways. If this principle, or something like it, were accepted, then careful analysis would still be required to determine which interests persons have at stake in any given conflict situation. We would also have to carefully examine our values to determine which interests are most fundamental. These are typical of the difficulties that have confronted those trying to establish a substantive theory of justice.

18.

SELECTION FROM *A THEORY OF JUSTICE*

❧ ❧ ❧

JOHN RAWLS

The following selection is from Rawls's highly influential work, A Theory of
Justice. *Rawls argues that the principles of justice that govern the basic structure
of society are the principles that would be agreed upon in a hypothetical fair bargaining position, which he calls "the original position." In this excerpt he
describes the original position and shows how it would lead to agreement on two
basic principles of justice. The first principle grants each person an equal right to
the most extensive basic liberty compatible with similar liberty for others. The second requires that social and economic inequalities must exist only if they are to
everyone's advantage and attached to positions that are open to everyone under
conditions of fair equality of opportunity.*

The Main Idea of the Theory of Justice

My aim is to present a conception of justice which generalizes and carries to
a higher level of abstraction the familiar theory of the social contract as
found, say, in Locke, Rousseau, and Kant.[1] In order to do this we are not to
think of the original contract as one to enter a particular society or to set up
a particular form of government. Rather, the guiding idea is that the principles of justice for the basic structure of society are the object of the original
agreement. They are the principles that free and rational persons concerned
to further their own interests would accept in an initial position of equality as
defining the fundamental terms of their association. These principles are to
regulate all further agreements; they specify the kinds of social cooperation
that can be entered into and the forms of government that can be established. This way of regarding the principles of justice I shall call justice as
fairness.

Thus we are to imagine that those who engage in social cooperation
choose together, in one joint act, the principles which are to assign basic
rights and duties and to determine the division of social benefits. Men are to
decide in advance how they are to regulate their claims against one another
and what is to be the foundation charter of their society. Just as each person

must decide by rational reflection what constitutes his good, that is, the system of ends which it is rational for him to pursue, so a group of persons must decide once and for all what is to count among them as just and unjust. The choice which rational men would make in this hypothetical situation of equal liberty, assuming for the present that this choice problem has a solution, determines the principles of justice.

In justice as fairness the original position of equality corresponds to the state of nature in the traditional theory of the social contract. This original position is not, of course, thought of as an actual historical state of affairs, much less as a primitive condition of culture. It is understood as a purely hypothetical situation characterized so as to lead to a certain conception of justice.[2] Among the essential features of this situation is that no one knows his place in society, his class position or social status, nor does any one know his fortune in the distribution of natural assets and abilities, his intelligence, strength, and the like. I shall even assume that the parties do not know their conceptions of the good or their special psychological propensities. The principles of justice are chosen behind a veil of ignorance. This ensures that no one is advantaged or disadvantaged in the choice of principles by the outcome of natural chance or the contingency of social circumstances. Since all are similarly situated and no one is able to design principles to favor his particular condition, the principles of justice are the result of a fair agreement or bargain. For given the circumstances of the original position, the symmetry of everyone's relations to each other, this initial situation is fair between individuals as moral persons, that is, as rational beings with their own ends and capable, I shall assume, of a sense of justice. The original position is, one might say, the appropriate initial status quo, and thus the fundamental agreements reached in it are fair. This explains the propriety of the name "justice as fairness": it conveys the idea that the principles of justice are agreed to in an initial situation that is fair. The name does not mean that the concepts of justice and fairness are the same, any more than the phrase "poetry as metaphor" means that the concepts of poetry and metaphor are the same.

Justice as fairness begins, as I have said, with one of the most general of all choices which persons might make together, namely, with the choice of the first principles of a conception of justice which is to regulate all subsequent criticism and reform of institutions. Then, having chosen a conception of justice, we can suppose that they are to choose a constitution and a legislature to enact laws, and so on, all in accordance with the principles of justice initially agreed upon. Our social situation is just if it is such that by this sequence of hypothetical agreements we would have contracted into the general system of rules which defines it. Moreover, assuming that the original position does determine a set of principles (that is, that a particular concept of justice would be chosen), it will then be true that whenever social institutions satisfy these principles those engaged in them can say to one another that they are cooperating on terms to which they would agree if they were free and equal persons whose relations with respect to one another were fair. They could all view their arrangements as meeting the stipulations which they would acknowledge in an initial situation that embodies widely accepted and reasonable constraints on the choice of principles. The general recognition of this fact would provide the basis for a public acceptance of the corresponding principles of justice. No society can, of course, be a scheme of cooperation which men enter voluntarily in a literal sense; each person finds himself placed at birth in some particular position in some particular society, and the nature of this position materially affects his life prospects. Yet a society satisfying the principles of justice as fairness comes as close as a society can to being a voluntary scheme, for it meets the principles which free and equal persons would assent to under circumstances that are fair. In this sense its members are autonomous and the obligations they recognize self-imposed.

One feature of justice as fairness is to think of the parties in the initial situation as rational and mutually disinterested. This does not mean that the parties are egoists, that is, individuals with only certain kinds of interests, say in wealth, prestige, and domination. But they are conceived as not taking an interest in one another's interests. They are to presume that even their spiritual aims may be opposed, in the way that the aims of those of different religions may be opposed. Moreover, the concept of rationality must be interpreted as far as possible in the narrow sense, standard in economic theory, of taking the most effective means to given ends. I shall modify this concept to some extent, as explained later, but one must try to avoid introducing into it any controversial ethical elements. The initial situation must be characterized by stipulations that are widely accepted.

In working out the conception of justice as fairness one main task clearly is to determine which principles of justice would be chosen in the original position. To do this we must describe this situation in some detail and formulate with care the problem of choice which it presents. These matters I shall take up later. It may be observed, however, that once the principles of justice are thought of as arising from an original agreement in a situation of equality, it is an open question whether the principle of utility would be acknowledged. Offhand it hardly seems likely that persons who view themselves as equals, entitled to press their claims upon one another, would agree to a principle which may require lesser life prospects for some simply for the sake of a greater sum of advantages enjoyed by others. Since each desires to protect his interests, his capacity to advance his conception of the good, no one has a reason to acquiesce in an enduring loss for himself in order to bring about a greater net balance of satisfaction. In the absence of strong and lasting benevolent impulses, a rational man would not accept a basic structure merely because it maximized the algebraic sum of advantages irrespective of its permanent effects on his own basic rights and interests. Thus it seems that the principle of utility is incompatible with the conception of social cooperation among equals for mutual advantage. It appears to be inconsistent with the idea of reciprocity implicit in the notion of a well-ordered society. Or, at any rate, so I shall argue.

I shall maintain instead that the persons in the initial situation would choose two rather different principles: the first requires equality in the assignment of basic rights and duties, while the second holds that social and economic inequalities, for example inequalities of wealth and authority, are just only if they result in compensating benefits for everyone, and in particular for the least advantaged members of society. These principles rule out justifying institutions on the grounds that the hardships of some are offset by a greater good in the aggregate. It may be expedient but it is not just that some should have less in order that others may prosper. But there is no injustice in the greater benefits earned by a few provided that the situation of persons not so fortunate is thereby improved. The intuitive idea is that since everyone's well-being depends upon a scheme of cooperation without which no one could have a satisfactory life, the division of advantages should be such as to draw forth the willing cooperation of everyone taking part in it, including those less well situated. Yet this can be expected only if reasonable terms are proposed. The two principles mentioned seem to be a fair agreement on the basis of which those better endowed, or more fortunate in their social position, neither of which we can be said to deserve, could expect the willing cooperation of others when some workable scheme is a necessary condition of the welfare of all.[3] Once we decide to look for a conception of justice that nullifies the accidents of natural endowment and the contingencies of social circumstance as counters in the quest for political and economic advantage, we are led to these principles. They express the result of leaving aside those aspects of the social world that seem arbitrary from a moral point of view.

The problem of the choice of principles, however, is extremely difficult. I do not expect the answer I shall suggest to be convincing to everyone. It is, therefore, worth noting from the outset that justice as fairness, like other contract views, consists of two parts: (1) an interpretation of the initial situation and of the problem of choice posed there, and (2) a set of principles which, it is argued, would be agreed to. One may accept the first part of the theory (or some variant thereof), but not the other, and conversely. The concept of the initial contractual situation may seem reasonable although the particular principles proposed are rejected. To be sure, I want to maintain that the most appropriate conception of this situation does lead to principles of justice contrary to utilitarianism and perfectionism, and therefore that the contract doctrine provides an alternative to these views. Still, one may dispute this contention even though one grants that the contractarian method is a useful way of studying ethical theories and of setting forth their underlying assumptions.

Justice as fairness is an example of what I have called a contract theory. Now there may be an objection to the term "contract" and related expressions, but I think it will serve reasonably well. Many words have misleading connotations which at first are likely to confuse. The terms "utility" and "utilitarianism" are surely no exception. They too have unfortunate suggestions which hostile critics have been willing to exploit; yet they are clear enough for those prepared to study utilitarian doctrine. The same should be true of the term "contract" applied to moral theories. As I have mentioned, to understand it one has to keep in mind that it implies a certain level of abstraction. In particular, the content of the relevant agreement is not to enter a given society or to adopt a given form of government, but to accept certain moral principles. Moreover, the undertakings referred to are purely hypothetical: a contract view holds that certain principles would be accepted in a well-defined initial situation.

The merit of the contract terminology is that it conveys the idea that principles of justice may be conceived as principles that would be chosen by rational persons, and that in this way conceptions of justice may be explained and justified. The theory of justice is a part, perhaps the most significant part, of the theory of rational choice. Furthermore, principles of justice deal with conflicting claims upon the advantages won by social cooperation; they apply to the relations among several persons or groups. The word "contract" suggests this plurality as well as the condition that the appropriate division of advantages must be in accordance with principles acceptable to all parties. The condition of publicity for principles of justice is also connoted by the contract phraseology. Thus, if these principles are the outcome of an agreement, citizens have a knowledge of the principles that others follow. It is characteristic of contract theories to stress the public nature of political principles. Finally there is the long tradition of the contract doctrine. Expressing the tie with this line of thought helps to define ideas and accords with natural piety. There are then several advantages in the use of the term "contract." With due precautions taken, it should not be misleading.

A final remark. Justice as fairness is not a complete contract theory. For it is clear that the contractarian idea can be extended to the choice of more or less an entire ethical system, that is, to a system including principles for all the virtues and not only for justice. Now for the most part I shall consider only principles of justice and others closely related to them; I make no attempt to discuss the virtues in a systematic way. Obviously if justice as fairness succeeds reasonably well, a next step would be to study the more general view suggested by the name "rightness as fairness." But even this wider theory fails to embrace all moral relationships, since it would seem to include only our relations with other persons and to leave out of account how we are to conduct ourselves toward animals and the rest of nature. I do not contend that the contract notion offers a way to approach these questions, which are certainly of the first importance; and I shall have to put them aside. We must recognize the limited scope of justice as fairness and of the general type of view that it exemplifies. How far its conclusions must be revised once these other matters are understood cannot be decided in advance.

The Original Position and Justification

I have said that the original position is the appropriate initial status quo which insures that the fundamental agreements reached in it are fair. This fact yields the name "justice as fairness." It is clear, then, that I want to say that one conception of justice is more reasonable than another, or justifiable with respect to it, if rational persons in the initial situation would choose its principles over those of the other for the role of justice. Conceptions of justice are to be ranked by their acceptability to persons so circumstanced. Understood in this way the question of justification is settled by working out a problem of deliberation: we have to ascertain which principles it would be rational to adopt given the contractual situation. This connects the theory of justice with the theory of rational choice.

If this view of the problem of justification is to succeed, we must, of course, describe in some detail the nature of this choice problem. A problem of rational decision has a definite answer only if we know the beliefs and interests of the parties, their relations with respect to one another, the alternatives between which they are to choose, the procedure whereby they make up their minds, and so on. As the circumstances are presented in different ways, correspondingly different principles are accepted. The concept of the original position, as I shall refer to it, is that of the most philosophically favored interpretation of this initial choice situation for the purposes of a theory of justice.

But how are we to decide what is the most favored interpretation? I assume, for one thing, that there is a broad measure of agreement that principles of justice should be chosen under certain conditions. To justify a particular description of the initial situation one shows that it incorporates these commonly shared presumptions. One argues from widely accepted but weak premises to more specific conclusions. Each of the presumptions should by itself be natural and plausible; some of them may seem innocuous or even trivial. The aim of the contract approach is to establish that taken together they impose significant bounds on acceptable principles of justice. The ideal outcome would be that these conditions determine a unique set of principles; but I shall be satisfied if they suffice to rank the main traditional conceptions of social justice.

One should not be misled, then, by the somewhat unusual conditions which characterize the original position. The idea here is simply to make vivid to ourselves the restrictions that it seems reasonable to impose on arguments for principles of justice, and therefore on these principles themselves. Thus it seems reasonable and generally acceptable that no one should be advantaged or disadvantaged by natural fortune or social circumstances in the choice of principles. It also seems widely agreed that it should be impossible to tailor principles to the circumstances of one's own case. We should ensure further that particular inclinations and aspirations, and persons' conceptions of their good, do not affect the principles adopted. The aim is to rule out those principles that it would be rational to propose for acceptance, however little the chance of success, only if one knew certain things that are irrelevant from the standpoint of justice. For example, if a man knew that he was wealthy, he might find it rational to advance the principle that various taxes for welfare measures be counted unjust; if he knew that he was poor, he would be most likely to propose the contrary principle. To represent the desired restrictions one imagines a situation in which everyone is deprived of this sort of information. One excludes the knowledge of those contingencies which sets men at odds and allows them to be guided by their prejudices. In this manner the veil of ignorance is arrived at in a natural way. This concept should cause no difficulty if we keep in mind the constraints on arguments that it is meant to express. At any time we can enter the original position, so to speak, simply by following a certain procedure, namely, by arguing for principles of justice in accordance with these restrictions.

It seems reasonable to suppose that the parties in the original position are equal. That is, all have the same rights in the procedure for choosing principles; each can make proposals, submit reasons for their acceptance, and so on. Obviously the purpose of these conditions is to represent equality between human beings as moral persons, as creatures having a conception of their good and capable of a sense of justice. The basis of equality is taken to be similar in these two respects. Systems of ends are not ranked in value; and each man is presumed to have the requisite ability to understand and to act upon whatever principles are adopted. Together with the veil of ignorance, these conditions define the principles of justice as those which rational persons concerned to advance their interests would consent to as equals when none are known to be advantaged or disadvantaged by social and natural contingencies.

There is, however, another side to justifying a particular description of the original position. This is to see if the principles which would be chosen match our considered convictions of justice or extend them in an acceptable way. We can note whether applying these principles would lead us to make the same judgments about the basic structure of society which we now make intuitively and in which we have the greatest confidence; or whether, in cases where our present judgments are in doubt and given with hesitation, these principles offer a resolution which we can affirm on reflection. There are questions which we feel sure must be answered in a certain way. For example, we are confident that religious intolerance and racial discrimination are unjust. We think that we have examined these things with care and have reached what we believe is an impartial judgment not likely to be distorted by an excessive attention to our own interests. These convictions are provisional fixed points which we presume any conceptions of justice must fit. But we have much less assurance as to what is the correct distribution of wealth and authority. Here we may be looking for a way to remove our doubts. We can check an interpretation of the initial situation, then, by the capacity of its principles to accommodate our firmest convictions and to provide guidance where guidance is needed.

In searching for the most favored description of this situation we work from both ends. We begin by describing it so that it represents generally shared and preferably weak conditions. We then see if these conditions are strong enough to yield a significant set of principles. If not, we look for further premises equally reasonable. But if so, and these principles match our considered convictions of justice, then so far well and good. But presumably there will be discrepancies. In this case we have a choice. We can either modify the account of the initial situation or we can revise our existing judgments, for even the judgments we take provisionally as fixed points are liable to revision. By going back and forth, sometimes altering the conditions of the contractual circumstances, at others withdrawing our judgments and conforming them to principle, I assume that eventually we shall find a description of the initial situation that both expresses reasonable conditions and yields principles which match our considered judgments duly pruned and adjusted. This state of affairs I refer to as reflective equilibrium.[4] It is an equilibrium because at last our principles and judgments coincide; and it is reflective since we know to what principles our judgments conform and the premises of their derivation. At the moment everything is in order. But this equilibrium is not necessarily stable. It is liable to be upset by further examination of the conditions which should be imposed on the contractual situation and by particular cases which may lead us to revise our judgments. Yet for the time being we have done what we can to render coherent and to justify our convictions of social justice. We have reached a conception of the original position.

I shall not, of course, actually work through this process. Still, we may think of the interpretation of the original position that I shall present as the result of such a hypothetical course of reflection. It represents the attempt to accommodate within one scheme both reasonable philosophical conditions on principles as well as our considered judgments of justice. In arriving at the favored interpretation of the initial situation there is no point at which an appeal is made to self-evidence in the traditional sense either of general conceptions or of particular convictions. I do not claim for the principles of justice proposed that they are necessary truths or derivable from such truths. A conception of justice cannot be deduced from self-evident premises or conditions on principles; instead, its justification is a matter of the mutual support of many considerations, of everything fitting together into one coherent view.

A final comment. We shall want to say that certain principles of justice are justified because they would be agreed to in an initial situation of equality. I have emphasized that this original position is purely hypothetical. It is natural to ask why, if this agreement is never actually entered into, we should take any interest in these principles, moral or otherwise. The answer is that the conditions embodied in the description of the original position are ones that we do in fact accept. Or if we do not, then perhaps we can be persuaded to do so by philosophical reflection. Each aspect of the contractual situation can be given supporting grounds. Thus what we shall do is to collect together into one conception a number of conditions on principles that we are ready upon due consideration to recognize as reasonable. These constraints express what we are prepared to regard as limits on fair terms of social cooperation. One way to look at the idea of the original position, therefore, is to see it as an expository device which sums up the meaning of these conditions and helps us to extract their consequences. On the other hand, this conception is also an intuitive notion that suggests its own elaboration, so that led on by it we are drawn to define more clearly the standpoint from which we can best interpret moral relationships. We need a conception that enables us to envision our objective from afar: the intuitive notion of the original position is to do this for us....

Two Principles of Justice

I shall now state in a provisional form the two principles of justice that I believe would be chosen in the original position. In this section I wish to make only the most general comments, and therefore the first formulation of these principles is tentative. As we go on I shall run through several formulations and approximate step by step the final statement to be given much later [in the book]. I believe that doing this allows the exposition to proceed in a natural way.

The first statement of the two principles reads as follows.

First: each person is to have an equal right to the most extensive basic liberty compatible with a similar liberty for others.

Second: social and economic inequalities are to be arranged so that they are both (a) reasonably expected to be to everyone's advantage, and (b) attached to positions and offices open to all.

By way of general comment, these principles primarily apply, as I have said, to the basic structure of society. They are to govern the assignment of rights and duties and to regulate the distribution of social and economic advantages. As their formulation suggests, these principles presuppose that the social structure can be divided into two more or less distinct parts, the first principle applying to the one, the second to the other. They distinguish between those aspects of the social system that define and secure the equal liberties of citizenship and those that specify and establish social and economic inequalities. The basic liberties of citizens are roughly speaking, political liberty (the right to vote and to be eligible for public office) together with freedom of speech and assembly; liberty of conscience and freedom of thought; freedom of the person along with the right to hold (personal) property; and freedom from arbitrary arrest and seizure as defined by the concept of the rule of law. These liberties are all required to be equal by the first principle, since citizens of a just society are to have the same basic rights.

The second principle applies, in the first approximation, to the distribution of income and wealth and to the design of organizations that make use of differences in authority and responsibility, or chains of command. While the distribution of wealth and income need not be equal, it must be to everyone's advantage, and at the same time, positions of authority and offices of command must be accessible to all. One applies the second principle by holding positions open, and then, subject to this constraint, arranges social and economic inequalities so that everyone benefits.

These principles are to be arranged in a serial order with the first principle prior to the second. This ordering means that a departure from the institutions of equal liberty required by the first principle cannot be justified by, or compensated for, by greater social and economic advantages. The distribution of wealth and income, and the hierarchies of authority, must be consistent with both the liberties of equal citizenship and equality of opportunity.

It is clear that these principles are rather specific in their content, and their acceptance rests on certain assumptions that I must eventually try to explain and justify. A theory of justice depends upon a theory of society in ways that will become evident as we proceed. For the present, it should be observed that the two principles (and this holds for all formulations) are a special case of a more general conception of justice that can be expressed as follows.

All social values—liberty and opportunity, income and wealth, and the bases of self-respect—are to be distributed equally unless an unequal distribution of any, or all, of these values is to everyone's advantage.

Injustice then, is simply inequalities that are not to the benefit of all. Of course, this conception is extremely vague and requires interpretation.

As a first step, suppose that the basic structure of society distributes certain primary goods, that is, things that every rational man is presumed to want. These goods normally have a use whatever a person's rational plan of life. For simplicity, assume that the chief primary goods at the disposition of society are rights and liberties, powers and opportunities, income and wealth. ... These are the social primary goods. Other primary goods such as health and vigor, intelligence and imagination, are natural goods; although their possession is influenced by the basic structure, they are not so directly under its control. Imagine, then, a hypothetical initial arrangement in which all the social primary goods are equally distributed: everyone has similar rights and duties, and income and wealth are evenly shared. This state of affairs provides a benchmark for judging improvements. If certain inequalities of wealth and organizational powers would make everyone better off than in this hypothetical starting situation, then they accord with the general conception.

Now it is possible, at least theoretically, that by giving up some of their fundamental liberties men are sufficiently compensated by the resulting social and economic gains. The general conception of justice imposes no restrictions on what sort of inequalities are permissible; it only requires that everyone's position be improved. We need not suppose anything so drastic as consenting to a condition of slavery. Imagine instead that men forgo certain political rights when the economic returns are significant and their capacity to influence the course of policy by the exercise of these rights would be marginal in any case. It is this kind of exchange which the two principles as stated rule out; being arranged in serial order they do not permit exchanges between basic liberties and economic and social gains. The serial ordering of principles expresses an underlying preference among primary social goods. When this preference is rational, so likewise is the choice of these principles in this order.

In developing justice as fairness I shall, for the most part, leave aside the general conception of justice and examine instead the special case of the two principles in serial order. The advantage of this procedure is that from the first the matter of priorities is recognized and an effort made to find principles to deal with it. One is led to attend throughout to the conditions under which the acknowledgement of the absolute weight of liberty with respect to social and economic advantages, as defined by the lexical order of the two principles, would be reasonable. Offhand, this ranking appears extreme and too special a case to be of much interest; but there is more justification for it than would appear at first sight. Or at any rate, so I shall maintain. Furthermore, the distinction between fundamental rights and liberties and economic and social benefits marks a difference among primary social goods that one should try to exploit. It suggests an important division in the social system. Of course, the distinctions drawn and the ordering proposed are bound to be at best only approximations. There are surely circumstances in which they fail. But it is essential to depict clearly the main lines of a reasonable concept of justice; and under many conditions anyway, the two principles in serial order may serve well enough. When necessary we can fall back on the more general conception.

The fact that the two principles apply to institutions has certain consequences. Several points illustrate this. First of all, the rights and liberties referred to by these principles are those which are defined by the public rules of the basic structure. Whether men are free is determined by the rights and duties established by the major institutions of society. Liberty is a certain pattern of social forms. The first principle simply requires that certain sorts of rules, those defining basic liberties, apply to everyone equally and that they allow the most extensive liberty compatible with a like liberty for all. The only reason for circumscribing the rights defining liberty and making men's freedom less extensive than it might otherwise be is that these equal rights as institutionally defined would interfere with one another.

Another thing to bear in mind is that when principles mention persons, or require that everyone gain from an inequality, the reference is to representative persons holding the various social positions, or offices, or whatever, established by the basic structure. Thus in applying the second principle I assume that it is possible to assign an expectation of well-being to representative individuals holding these positions. This expectation indicates their life prospects as viewed from their social station. In general, the expectations of representative persons depend upon the distribution of rights and duties throughout the basic structure. When this changes, expectations change. I assume, then, that expectations are connected: by raising the prospects of the representative man in one position we presumably increase or decrease the prospects of representative men in other positions. Since it applies to institutional forms, the second principle (or rather the first part of it) refers to the expectations of representative individuals. As I shall discuss below, neither principle applies to distributions of particular goods to particular individuals who may be identified by their proper names. The situation where someone is considering how to allocate certain commodities to needy persons who are known to him is not within the scope of the principles. They are meant to regulate basic institutional arrangements. We must not assume that there is much similarity from the standpoint of justice between an administrative allotment of goods to specific persons and the appropriate design of society. Our common-sense intuitions for the former may be a poor guide to the latter.

Now the second principle insists that each person benefit from permissible inequalities in the basic structure. This means that it must be reasonable for each relevant representative man defined by this structure, when he views it as a going concern, to prefer his prospects with the inequality to his prospects without it. One is not allowed to justify differences in income or organizational powers on the ground that the disadvantages of those in one position are outweighed by the greater advantages of those in another. Much less can infringements of liberty be counterbalanced in this way. Applied to the basic structure, the principle of utility would have us maximize the sum of expectations of representative men (weighted by the number of persons they represent, on the classical view); and this would permit us to compensate for the losses of some by the gains of others. Instead, the two principles require that everyone benefit from economic and social inequalities. It is obvious, however, that there are indefinitely many ways in which all may be advantaged when the initial arrangement of equality is taken as a benchmark. How then are we to choose among these possibilities? The principles must be specified so that they yield a determinate conclusion. I now turn to this problem....

The Reasoning Leading to the Two Principles of Justice

In this section I take up the choice between the two principles of justice and the principle of average utility. Determining the rational preference between these two options is perhaps the central problem in developing the conception of justice as fairness as a viable alternative to the utilitarian tradition. I shall begin in this section by presenting some intuitive remarks favoring the two principles. I shall also discuss briefly the qualitative structure of the argument that needs to be made if the case for these principles is to be conclusive.

It will be recalled that the general conception of justice as fairness requires that all primary social goods be distributed equally unless an unequal distribution would be to everyone's advantage. No restrictions are placed on exchanges of these goods and therefore a lesser liberty can be compensated for by greater social and economic benefits. Now looking at the situation from the standpoint of one person selected arbitrarily, there is no way for him to win special advantages for himself. Nor, on the other hand, are there grounds for his acquiescing in special disadvantages. Since it is not reasonable for him to expect more than an equal share in the division of social goods, and since it is not rational for him to agree to less, the sensible thing for him to do is to acknowledge as the first principle of justice one requiring an equal distribution. Indeed, this principle is so obvious that we would expect it to occur to anyone immediately.

Thus, the parties start with a principle establishing equal liberty for all, including equality of opportunity, as well as an equal distribution of income and wealth. But there is no reason why this acknowledgment should be final. If there are inequalities in the basic structure that work to make everyone better off in comparison with the benchmark of initial equality, why not permit them? The immediate gain which a greater equality might allow can be regarded as intelligently invested in view of its future return. If, for example, these inequalities set up various incentives which succeed in eliciting more productive efforts, a person in the original position may look upon them as necessary to cover the costs of training and to encourage effective performance. One might think that ideally individuals should want to serve one another. But since the parties are assumed not to take an interest in one another's interests, their acceptance of these inequalities is only the acceptance of the relations in which men stand in the circumstances of justice. They have no grounds for complaining of one another's motives. A person in the original position would, therefore, concede the justice of these inequalities. Indeed, it would be shortsighted of him not to do so. He would hesitate to agree to these regularities only if he would be dejected by the bare knowledge or perception that others were better situated; and I have assumed that the parties decide as if they are not moved by envy. In order to make the principle regulating inequalities determinate, one looks at the system from the standpoint of the least advantaged representative person. Inequalities are permissible when they maximize, or at least all contribute to, the long-term expectations of the least fortunate group in society.

Now this general conception imposes no constraints on what sorts of inequalities are allowed, whereas the special conception, by putting the two principles in serial order (with the necessary adjustments in meaning), forbids exchanges between basic liberties and economic and social benefits. I shall not try to justify this ordering here. But roughly, the idea underlying this ordering is that if the parties assume that their basic liberties can be effectively exercised, they will not exchange a lesser liberty for an improvement in economic well-being. It is only when social conditions do not allow the effective establishment of these rights that one can concede their limitation; and these restrictions can be granted only to the extent that they are necessary to prepare the way for a free society. The denial of equal liberty can be defended only if it is necessary to raise the level of civilization so that in due course these freedoms can be enjoyed. Thus in adopting a serial order we are in effect making a special assumption in the original position, namely, that the parties know that the conditions of their society, whatever they are, admit the effective realization of the equal liberties. The serial ordering of the two principles of justice eventually comes to be reasonable if the general conception is consistently followed. This lexical ranking is the long-run tendency of the general view. For the most part I shall assume that the requisite circumstances for the serial order obtain.

It seems clear from these remarks that the two principles are at least a plausible conception of justice. The question, though, is how one is to argue for them more systematically. Now there are several things to do. One can work out their consequences for institutions and note their implications for fundamental social policy. In this way they are tested by a comparison with our considered judgments of justice. ... But one can also try to find arguments in their favor that are decisive from the standpoint of the original position. In order to see how this might be done, it is useful as a heuristic device to think of the two principles as the maximin solution to the problem of social justice. There is an analogy between the two principles and the maximin rule for choice under uncertainty.[5] This is evident from the fact that the two principles are those a person would choose for the design of a society in which his enemy is to assign him his place. The maximin rule tells us to rank alternatives by their worst possible outcomes: we are to adopt the alternative the worst outcome of which is superior to the worst outcomes of the others. The persons in the original position do not, of course, assume that their initial place in society is decided by a malevolent opponent. As I note below, they should not reason from false premises. The veil of ignorance does not violate this idea, since an absence of information is not misinformation. But that the two principles of justice would be chosen if the parties were forced to protect themselves against such a contingency explains the sense in which this conception is the maximin solution. And this analogy suggests that if the original position has been described so that it is rational for the parties to adopt the conservative attitude expressed by this rule, a conclusive argument can indeed be constructed for these principles. Clearly the maximin rule is not, in general, a suitable guide for choices under uncertainty. But it is attractive in situations marked by certain special features. My aim, then, is to show that a good case can be made for the two principles based on the fact that the original position manifests these features to the fullest possible degree, carrying them to the limit, so to speak.

Decisions	Circumstances		
	c_1	c_2	c_3
d_1	-7	8	12
d_2	-8	7	14
d_3	5	6	8

Consider the gain-and-loss table shown here. It represents the gains and losses for a situation which is not a game of strategy. There is no one playing against the person making the decision; instead he is faced with several possible circumstances which may or may not obtain. Which circumstances happen to exist does not depend upon what the person choosing decides or whether he announces his moves in advance. The numbers in the table are monetary values (in hundreds of dollars) in comparison with some initial situation. The gain (g) depends upon the individual's decision (d) and the circumstances (c). Thus g = f (d, c). Assuming that there are three possible decisions and three possible circumstances, we might have this gain-and-loss table.

The maximin rule requires that we make the third decision. For in this case the worst that can happen is that one gains 500 dollars, which is better than the worst for the other actions. If we adopt one of these we may lose either 800 or 700 dollars. Thus, the choice of d, maximizes f (d, c) for that value of c, which for a given d, minimizes f. The term "maximin" means the maximum minimorum; and the rule directs our attention to the worst that can happen under any proposed course of action, and directs us to decide in the light of that.

Now there appear to be three chief features of situations that give plausibility to this unusual rule.[6] First, since the rule takes no account of the likelihoods of the possible circumstances, there must be some reason for sharply discounting estimates of these probabilities. Offhand, the most natural rule of choice would seem to be to compute the expectation of monetary gain for each decision and then to adopt the course of action with the highest prospect. (This expectation is defined as follows: let us suppose that g_{ij} represents the numbers in the gain-and-loss table, where i is the row index and j is the column index; and let p_j, j = 1, 2, 3, be the likelihoods of the circumstances, with $\Sigma p_j = 1$. Then the expectation for the ith decision is equal to $\Sigma p_i g_{ij}$.) Thus it must be, for example, that the situation is one in which a knowledge of likelihoods is impossible, or at best extremely insecure. In this case it is unreasonable not to be skeptical of probabilistic calculations unless there is no other way out, particularly if the decision is a fundamental one that needs to be justified to others.

The second feature that suggests the maximin rule is the following: the person choosing has a conception of the good such that he cares very little, if anything, for what he might gain above the minimum stipend that he can, in fact, be sure of by following the maximin rule. It is not worthwhile for him to take a chance for the sake of a further advantage, especially when it may turn out that he loses much that is important to him. This last provision brings in the third feature, namely, that the rejected alternatives have outcomes that one can hardly accept. The situation involves grave risks. Of course these features work most effectively in combination. The paradigm situation for following the maximin rule is when all three features are realized to the highest degree. This rule does not, then, generally apply, nor of course is it self-evident. Rather, it is a maxim, a rule of thumb, that comes into its own in special circumstances. Its application depends upon the qualitative structure of possible gains and losses in relation to one's conception of the good, all this against a background in which it is reasonable to discount conjectural estimates of likelihoods.

It should be noted, as comments on the gain-and-loss table say, that the entries in the table represent monetary values and not utilities. This difference is significant since for one thing computing expectations on the basis of such objective values is not the same thing as computing expected utility and may lead to different results. The essential point though is that in justice as fairness the parties do not know their conception of the good and cannot estimate their utility in the ordinary sense. In any case, we want to go behind de facto preferences generated by given conditions. Therefore expectations are based upon an index of primary goods and the parties make their choice accordingly. The entries in the example are in terms of money and not utility to indicate this aspect of the contract doctrine.

Now, as I have suggested, the original position has been defined so that it is a situation in which the maximin rule applies. In order to see this, let us review briefly the nature of this situation with these three special features in mind. To begin with, the veil of ignorance excludes all but the vaguest knowledge of likelihoods. The parties have no basis for determining the probable nature of their society, or their place in it. Thus they have strong reasons for being wary of probability calculations if any other course is open to them. They must also take into account the fact that their choice of principles should seem reasonable to others, in particular their descendants, whose rights will be deeply affected by it. There are further grounds for discounting that I shall mention as we go along. For the present it suffices to note that these considerations are strengthened by the fact that the parties know very little about the gain-and-loss table. Not only are they unable to conjecture the likelihoods of the various possible circumstances, they cannot say much about what possible circumstances are, much less enumerate them and foresee the outcome of each alternative available. Those deciding are much more in the dark than the illustration by a numerical table suggests. It is for this reason that I have spoken of an analogy with the maximin rule.

Several kinds of arguments for the two principles of justice illustrate the second feature. Thus, if we can maintain that these principles provide a workable theory of social justice, and that they are compatible with reasonable demands of efficiency, then this conception guarantees a satisfactory minimum. There may be, on reflection, little reason for trying to do better. Thus much of the argument ... is to show, by their application to the main questions of social justice, that the two principles are a satisfactory conception. These details have a philosophical purpose. Moreover, this line of thought is practically decisive if we can establish the priority of liberty, the lexical ordering of the two principles. For this priority implies that the persons in the original position have no desire to try for greater gains at the expense of the equal liberties. The minimum assured by the two principles in lexical order is not one that the parties wish to jeopardize for the sake of greater economic and social advantages.

Finally, the third feature holds if we can assume that other conceptions of justice may lead to institutions that the parties would find intolerable. For example, it has sometimes been held that under some conditions the utility principle (in either form) justifies, if not slavery or serfdom, at any rate serious infractions of liberty for the sake of greater social benefits. We need not consider here the truth of this claim, or the likelihood that the requisite conditions obtain. For the moment, this contention is only to illustrate the way in which conceptions of justice may allow for outcomes which the parties may not be able to accept. And having the ready alternative of the two principles of justice which secure a satisfactory minimum, it seems unwise, if not irrational, for them to take a chance that these outcomes are not realized....

Notes

1. As the text suggests, I shall regard Locke's *Second Treatise of Government*, Rousseau's *The Social Contract*, and Kant's ethical works beginning with *The Foundations of the Metaphysics of Morals* as definitive of the contract tradition. For all of its greatness, Hobbes's *Leviathan* raises special problems. A general historical survey is provided by J.W. Gough, *The Social Contract*, 2nd edn (Oxford: Clarendon P, 1957); and Otto Gierke, *Natural Law and the Theory of Society*, trans. with an introduction by Ernest Barker (Cambridge: Cambridge UP, 1934). A presentation of the contract view as primarily an ethical theory is to be found in G.R. Grice, *The Grounds of Moral Judgment* (Cambridge: Cambridge UP, 1967).

2. Kant is clear that the original agreement is hypothetical. See *The Metaphysics of Morals*, pt I *(Rechtslehre)*, especially paragraphs 47, 52; and pt 11 of the essay "Concerning the Common Saying: This May Be True in Theory but It Does Not Apply in Practice," in *Kant's Political Writings*, ed. Hans Reiss and trans. H.B. Nisbet (Cambridge: Cambridge UP, 1970), pp. 73-87. See Georges Vlachos, *La Pensée politique de Kant* (Paris: Presses universitaires de France, 1962), pp. 326-35; and J.G. Murphy, *Kant: The Philosophy of Right* (London: Macmillan, 1970), pp. 109-12, 133-36, for a further discussion.

3. For the formulation of this intuitive idea I am indebted to Allan Gibbard.

4. The process of mutual adjustment of principles and considered judgments is not peculiar to moral philosophy. See Nelson Goodman, *Fact, Fiction, and Forecast* (Cambridge: MA: Harvard UP, 1955), pp. 65-68, for parallel remarks concerning the justification of the principles of deductive and inductive inference.

5. An accessible discussion of this and other rules of choice under uncertainty can be found in W.J. Baumol, *Economic Theory and Operations Analysis*, 2nd edn (Englewood Cliffs, NJ: Prentice-Hall, 1965), chapter 24. Baumol gives a geometric inter-

pretation of these rules, including the diagram used in paragraph 13 to illustrate the difference principle. See pp. 558-62. See also R.D. Luce and Howard Raiffa, *Games and Decisions* (New York: John Wiley and Sons, 1957), chapter XIII, for a fuller account.

6. Here I borrow from William Fellner, *Probability and Profit* (Homewood, IL: R.D. Irwin, 1965), pp. 140-42, where these features are noted.

19.
THE ENTITLEMENT THEORY

✿ ✿ ✿

ROBERT NOZICK

In the following selection from Anarchy, State, and Utopia, *Robert Nozick argues for an entitlement theory of justice. He claims that we are entitled only to those holdings that we have originally acquired in a just manner or that have been transferred to us in a just manner. Principles or practices that distribute wealth, income, or property according to some other schema are morally indefensible because they violate individuals' rights to the holdings they have justly acquired.*

The minimal state is the most extensive state that can be justified. Any state more extensive violates people's rights. Yet many persons have put forth reasons purporting to justify a more extensive state. It is impossible [here] to examine all the reasons that have been put forth. Therefore, I shall focus upon those generally acknowledged to be most weighty and influential, to see precisely wherein they fail. In this chapter we consider the claim that a more extensive state is justified, because necessary (or the best instrument) to achieve distributive justice....

The term "distributive justice" is not a neutral one. Hearing the term "distribution," most people presume that some thing or mechanism uses some principle or criterion to give out a supply of things. Into this process of distributing shares some error may have crept. So it is an open question, at least, whether *re*distribution should take place; whether we should do again what has already been done once, though poorly. However, we are not in the position of children who have been given portions of pie by someone who now makes last minute adjustments to rectify careless cutting. There is no *central* distribution, no person or group entitled to control all the resources, jointly deciding how they are to be doled out. What each person gets, he gets from others who give to him in exchange for something, or as a gift. In a free society, diverse persons control different resources, and new holdings arise out of the voluntary exchanges and actions of persons. There is no more a distributing or distribution of shares than there is a distributing of mates in a society in which persons choose whom they shall marry. The total result is the product of many individual decisions which the different individuals involved are entitled to make. Some uses of the term "distribution," it is true, do not imply a previous distributing appropriately judged by some criterion (for example, "probability distribution"): nevertheless, despite the title of this chapter, it would be best to use a terminology that clearly is neutral. We shall speak of people's holdings; a principle of justice in holdings describes (part of) what justice tells us (requires) about holdings. I shall state first what I take to be the correct view about justice in holdings, and then turn to the discussion of alternate views.

The Entitlement Theory

The subject of justice in holdings consists of three major topics. The first is the *original acquisition of holdings*, the appropriation of unheld things. This includes the issues of how unheld things may come to be held, the process, or processes, by which unheld things may come to be held, the things that may come to be held by these processes, the extent of what comes to be held by a particular process, and so on. We shall refer to the complicated truth about this topic, which we shall not formulate here, as the principle of justice in acquisition.

The second topic concerns the *transfer of holdings* from one person to another. By what processes may a person transfer holdings to another? How may a person acquire a holding from another who holds it? Under this topic come general descriptions of voluntary exchange, and gift and (on the other hand) fraud, as well as reference to particular conventional details fixed upon in a given society. The complicated truth about this subject (with placeholders for conventional details) we shall call the principle of justice in transfer. (And we shall suppose it also includes principles governing how a person may divest himself of a holding, passing it into an unheld state.)

If the world were wholly just, the following inductive definition would exhaustively cover the subject of justice in holdings.

1. A person who acquires a holding in accordance with the principle of justice in acquisition is entitled to that holding.
2. A person who acquires a holding in accordance with the principle of justice in transfer, from someone else entitled to the holding, is entitled to the holding.
3. No one is entitled to a holding except by (repeated) applications of 1 and 2.

The complete principle of distributive justice would say simply that a distribution is just if everyone is entitled to the holdings they possess under the distribution.

A distribution is just if it arises from another just distribution by legitimate means. The legitimate means of moving from one distribution to another are specified by the principle of justice in transfer. The legitimate first "moves" are specified by the principle of justice in acquisition.[1] Whatever arises from a just situation by just steps is itself just. The means of change specified by the principle of justice in transfer preserve justice. As correct rules of inference are truth-preserving, and any conclusion deduced via repeated application of such rules from only true premises is itself true, so the means of transition from one situation to another specified by the principle of justice in transfer are justice-preserving, and any situation actually arising from repeated transitions in accordance with the principle from a just situation is itself just. The parallel between justice-preserving transformations and truth-preserving transformations illuminates where it fails as well as where it holds. That a conclusion could have been deduced by truth-preserving means from premises that are true suffices to show its truth. That from a just situation a situation *could* have arisen via justice-preserving means does *not* suffice to show its justice. The fact that a thief's victims voluntarily *could* have presented him with gifts does not entitle the thief to his ill-gotten gains. Justice in holdings is historical; it depends upon what actually has happened. We shall return to this point later.

Not all actual situations are generated in accordance with the two principles of justice in holdings: the principle of justice in acquisition and the principle of justice in transfer. Some people steal from others, or defraud them, or enslave them, seizing their product and preventing them from living as they choose, or forcibly exclude others from competing in exchanges. None of these are permissible modes of transition from one situation to another. And some persons acquire holdings by means not sanctioned by the principle of justice in acquisition.

The existence of past injustice (previous violations of the first two principles of justice in holdings) raises the third major topic under justice in holdings: the rectification of injustice in holdings. If past injustice has shaped present holdings in various ways, some identifiable and some not, what now, if anything, ought to be done to rectify these injustices? What obligations do the performers of injustice have toward those whose position is worse than it would have been had the injustice not been done? Or, than it would have been had compensation been paid promptly? How, if at all, do things change if the beneficiaries and those made worse off are not the direct parties in the act of injustice, but, for example, their descendants? Is an injustice done to someone whose holding was itself based upon an unrectified injustice? How far back must one go in wiping clean the historical slate of injustices? What may victims of injustice permissibly do in order to rectify the injustices being done to them, including the many injustices done by persons acting through their government? I do not know of a thorough or theoretically sophisticated treatment of such issues. Idealizing greatly, let us suppose theoretical investigation will produce a principle of rectification. This principle uses historical information about previous situations and injustices done in them (as defined by the first two principles of justice and rights against interference), and information about the actual course of events that flowed from these injustices, until the present, and it yields a description (or descriptions) of holdings in the society. The principle of rectification presumably will make use of its best estimate of subjunctive information about what would have occurred (or a probability distribution over what might have occurred, using the expected value) if the injustice had not taken place. If the actual description of holdings turns out not to be one of the descriptions yielded by the principle, then one of the descriptions yielded must be realized.[2]

The general outlines of the theory of justice in holdings are that the holdings of a person are just if he is entitled to them by the principles of justice in acquisition and transfer, or by the principle of rectification of injustice (as specified by the first two principles). If each person's holdings are just, then the total set (distribution) of holdings is just. To turn these general outlines into a specific theory we would have to specify the details of each of the three principles of justice in holdings: the principle of acquisition of holdings, the principle of transfer of holdings, and the principle of rectification of violations of the first two principles. I shall not attempt that task here.

Historical Principles and End-Result Principles

The general outlines of the entitlement theory illuminate the nature and defects of other conceptions of distributive justice. The entitlement theory of justice in distribution is *historical*; whether a distribution is just depends upon how it came about. In contrast, *current time-slice principles* of justice hold that the justice of a distribution is determined by how things are distributed (who has what) as judged by some *structural* principle(s) of just distribution. A utilitarian who judges between any two distributions by seeing which has the greater sum of utility and, if the sums tie, applies some fixed equality criterion to choose the more equal distribution, would hold a current time-slice principle of justice. As would someone who had a fixed schedule of trade-offs between the sum of happiness and equality. According to a current time-slice principle, all that needs to be looked at, in judging the justice of a distribution, is who ends up with what; in comparing any two distributions one need look only at the matrix presenting the distributions. No further information need be fed into a principle of justice. It is a consequence of such principles of justice that any two structurally identical distributions are equally just. (Two distributions are structurally identical if they present the same profile, but perhaps have different persons occupying the particular slots. My having ten and your having five, and my having five and your having ten are structurally identical distributions.) Welfare economics is the theory of current time-slice principles of justice. The subject is conceived as operating on matrices representing only current information about distribution. This, as well as some of the usual conditions (for example, the choice of distribution is invariant under relabeling of columns), guarantees that welfare economics will be a current time-slice theory, with all of its inadequacies.

Most persons do not accept current time-slice principles as constituting the whole story about distributive shares. They think it relevant in assessing the justice of a situation to consider not only the distribution it embodies, but also how that distribution came about. If some persons are in prison for murder or war crimes, we do not say that to assess the justice of the distribution in the society we must look only at what this person has, and that person has, and that person has, ... at the current time. We think it relevant to ask whether someone did something so that he *deserved* to be punished, deserved to have a lower share. Most will agree to the relevance of further information with regard to punishments and penalties. Consider also desired things. One traditional socialist view is that workers are entitled to the product and full fruits of their labor; they have earned it; a distribution is unjust if it does not give the workers what they are entitled to. Such entitlements are based upon some past history. No socialist holding this view would find it comforting to be told that because the actual distribution A happens to coincide structurally with the one he desires D, A therefore is no less just than D; it differs only in that the "parasitic" owners of capital receive under A what the workers are entitled to under D, and the workers receive under A what the owners are entitled to under D, namely very little. This socialist rightly, in my view, holds onto the notions of earning, producing, entitlement, desert, and so forth, and he rejects current time-slice principles that look only to the structure of the resulting set of holdings. (The set of holdings resulting from what? Isn't it implausible that how holdings are produced and come to exist has no effect at all on who should hold what?) His mistake lies in his view of what entitlements arise out of what sorts of productive processes.

We construe the position we discuss too narrowly by speaking of *current* time-slice principles. Nothing is changed if structural principles operate upon a time sequence of current time-slice profiles and, for example, give someone more now to counterbalance the less he has had earlier. A utilitarian or an egalitarian or any mixture of the two over time will inherit the difficulties of his more myopic comrades. He is not helped by the fact that *some* of the information others consider relevant in assessing a distribution is reflected, unrecoverably, in past matrices. Henceforth, we shall refer to such unhistorical principles of distributive justice, including the current time-slice principles, as *end-result principles* or *end-state principles*.

In contrast to end-result principles of justice, *historical principles* of justice hold that past circumstances or actions of people can create differential entitlements or differential deserts to things. An injustice can be worked by moving from one distribution to another structurally identical one, for the second, in profile the same, may violate people's entitlements or deserts; it may not fit the actual history.

Patterning

The entitlement principles of justice in holdings that we have sketched are historical principles of justice. To better understand their precise character, we shall distinguish them from another subclass of the historical principles. Consider, as an example, the principle of distribution according to moral merit. This principle requires that total distributive shares vary directly with moral merit; no person should have a greater share than anyone whose moral merit is greater. (If moral merit could be not merely ordered but measured on an interval or ratio scale, stronger principles could be formulated.) Or consider the principle that results by substituting "usefulness to society" for "moral merit" in the previous principle. Or instead of "distribute according to moral merit," or "distribute according to usefulness to society," we might consider "distribute according to the weighted sum of moral merit, usefulness to society, and need," with the weights of the different dimensions equal. Let us call a principle of distribution *patterned* if it specifies that a distribution is to vary along with some natural dimension, weighted sum of natural dimensions, or lexicographical ordering of natural dimensions. And let us say a distribution is patterned if it accords with some patterned principle. (I speak of natural dimensions, admittedly without a general criterion for them, because for any set of holdings some artificial dimensions can be gimmicked up to vary along with the distribution of the set.) The principle of distribution in accordance with moral merit is a patterned historical principle, which specifies a patterned distribution. "Distribute according to IQ" is a patterned principle that looks to information not contained in distributional matrices. It is not historical, however, in that it does not look to any past actions creating differential entitlements to evaluate a distribution; it requires only distributional matrices whose columns are labeled by IQ scores. The distribution in a society, however, may be composed of such simple patterned distributions, without itself being simply patterned. Different sectors may operate different patterns, or some combination of patterns may operate in different proportions across a society. A distribution composed in this manner, from a small number of patterned distributions, we also shall term "patterned." And we extend the use of "pattern" to include the overall designs put forth by combinations of end-state principles.

Almost every suggested principle of distributive justice is patterned: to each according to his moral merit, or needs, or marginal product, or how hard he tries, or the weighted sum of the foregoing, and so on. The principle of entitlement we have sketched is *not* patterned.[3] There is no one natural dimension or weighted sum or combination of a small number of natural dimensions that yields the distribution, generated in accordance with the principle of entitlement. The set of holdings that results when some persons receive their marginal products, others win at gambling, others receive a share of their mate's income, others receive gifts from foundations, others receive interest on loans, others receive gifts from admirers, others receive returns on investments, others make for themselves much of what they have, others find things, and so on, will not be patterned. Heavy strands of patterns will run through it; significant portions of the variance in holdings will be accounted for by pattern-variables. If most people most of the time choose to transfer some of their entitlements to others only in exchange for something from them, then a large part of what many people hold will vary with what they held that others wanted. More details are provided by the theory of marginal productivity. But gifts to relatives, charitable donations, bequests to children, and the like, are not best conceived, in the first instance, in this manner. Ignoring the strands of pattern, let us suppose for the moment that a distribution actually arrived at by the operation of the principle of entitlement is random with respect to any pattern. Though the resulting set of holdings will be unpatterned, it will not be incomprehensible, for it can be seen as arising from the operation of a small number of principles. These principles specify how an initial distribution may arise (the principle of acquisition of holdings) and how distributions may be transformed into others (the principle of transfer of holdings). The process whereby the set of holdings is generated will be intelligible, though the set of holdings itself that results from this process will be unpatterned.

The writings of F.A. Hayek focus less than is usually done upon what patterning distributive justice requires. Hayek argues that we cannot know enough about each person's situation to distribute to each according to his moral merit (but would justice demand we do so if we did have this knowledge?); and he goes on to say, "our objection is against all attempts to impress upon society a deliberately chosen pattern of distribution, whether it be an order of equality or of inequality." However, Hayek concludes that in a free society there will be distribution in accordance with value rather than with moral merit; that is, in accordance with the perceived value of a person's actions and services to others. Despite his rejection of a patterned conception of distributive justice, Hayek himself suggests a pattern he thinks justifiable: distribution in accordance with the perceived benefits given to others, leaving room for the complaint that a free society does not realize exactly this pattern. Stating this patterned strand of a free capitalist society more precisely, we get "To each according to how much he benefits others who have the resources for benefiting those who benefit them." This will seem arbitrary unless some acceptable initial set of holdings is specified, or unless it is held that the operation of the system over time washes out any significant effects from the initial set of holdings. As an example of the latter, if almost anyone would have bought a car from Henry Ford, the supposition that it was an arbitrary matter who held the money then (and so bought) would not place Henry Ford's earnings under a cloud. In any event, his coming to hold it is not arbitrary. Distribution according to benefits to others is a major patterned strand in a free capitalist society, as Hayek correctly points out, but it is only a strand and does not constitute the whole pattern of a system of entitlements (namely, inheritance, gifts for arbitrary reasons, charity, and so on) or a standard that one should insist a society fit.

Will people tolerate for long a system yielding distributions that they believe are unpatterned? No doubt people will not long accept a distribution they believe is *unjust*. People want their society to be and to look just. But must the look of justice reside in a resulting pattern rather than in the underlying generating principles? We are in no position to conclude that the inhabitants of a society embodying an entitlement conception of justice in holdings will find it unacceptable. Still, it must be granted that were people's reasons for transferring some of their holdings to others always irrational or arbitrary, we would find this disturbing. (Suppose people always determined what holdings they would transfer, and to whom, by using a random device.) We feel more comfortable upholding the justice of an entitlement system if most of the transfers under it are done for reasons. This does not mean necessarily that all deserve what holdings they receive. It means only that there is a purpose or point to someone's transferring a holding to one person rather than to another; that usually we can see what the transferrer thinks he's gaining, what cause he thinks he's serving, what goals he thinks he's helping to achieve, and so forth. Since in a capitalist society people often transfer holdings to others in accordance with how much they perceive these others benefiting them, the fabric constituted by the individual transactions and transfers is largely reasonable and intelligible.[4] (Gifts to loved ones, bequests to children, charity to the needy also are nonarbitrary components of the fabric.) In stressing the large strand of distribution in accordance with benefit to others, Hayek shows the point of many transfers, and so shows that the system of transfer of entitlements is not just spinning its gears aimlessly. The system of entitlement is defensible when constituted by the aims of individual transactions. No overarching aim is needed, no distributional pattern is required.

To think that the task of a theory of distributive justice is to fill in the blank in "to each according to his—" is to be predisposed to search for a pattern; and the separate treatment of "from each according to his—" treats production and distribution as two separate and independent issues. On an entitlement view these are *not* two separate questions. Whoever makes something, having bought or contracted for all other held resources used in the process (transferring some of his holdings for these cooperating factors), is entitled to it. The situation is *not* one of something's getting made, and there being an open question of who is to get it. Things come into the world already attached to people having entitlements over them. From the point of view of the historical entitlement conception of justice in holdings, those who start afresh to complete "to each according to his—" treat objects as if they appeared from nowhere, out of nothing. A complete theory of justice might cover this limit case as well; perhaps here is a use for the usual conceptions of distributive justice.

So entrenched are maxims of the usual form that perhaps we should present the entitlement conception as a competitor. Ignoring acquisition and rectification, we might say:

> From each according to what he chooses to do, to each according to what he makes for himself (perhaps with the contracted aid of others) and what others choose to do for him and choose to give him of what they've been given previously (under this maxim) and haven't yet expended or transferred.

This, the discerning reader will have noticed, has its defects as slogan. So as a summary and great simplification (and not as a maxim with an independent meaning) we have:

> *From each as they choose, to each as they are chosen.*

How Liberty Upsets Patterns

It is not clear how those holding alternative conceptions of distributive justice can reject the entitlement conception of justice in holdings. For suppose a distribution favored by one of these non-entitlement conceptions is realized. Let us suppose it is your favorite one and let us call this distribution D_1; perhaps everyone has an equal share, perhaps shares vary in accordance with some dimension you treasure. Now suppose that Wilt Chamberlain is greatly in demand by basketball teams, being a great gate attraction. (Also suppose contracts run only for a year, with players being free agents.) He signs the following sort of contract with a team: In each home game, twenty-five cents from the price of each ticket of admission goes to him. (We ignore the question of whether he is "gouging" the owners, letting them look out for themselves.) The season starts and people cheerfully attend his team's games; they buy their tickets, each time dropping a separate twenty-five cents of their admission price into a special box with Chamberlain's name on it. They are excited about seeing him play; it is worth the total admission price to them.

Let us suppose that in one season one million persons attend his home games, and Wilt Chamberlain winds up with $250,000, a much larger sum than the average income and larger even than anyone else has. Is he entitled to this income? Is this new distribution D_2, unjust? If so, why? There is *no* question about whether each of the people was entitled to the control over the resources they held in D_1; because that was the distribution (your favorite) that (for the purposes of argument) we assumed was acceptable. Each of these persons *chose* to give twenty-five cents of their money to Chamberlain. They could have spent it on going to the movies, or on candy bars, or on copies of *Dissent* magazine, or of *Monthly Review*. But they all, at least one million of them, converged on giving it to Wilt Chamberlain in exchange for watching him play basketball. If D_1 was a just distribution, and people voluntarily moved from it to D_2 transferring parts of their shares they were given under D_1 (what was it for if not to do something with?), isn't D_2 also just? If the people were entitled to dispose of the resources to which they were entitled (under D_1), didn't this include their being entitled to give it to, or exchange it with, Wilt Chamberlain? Can anyone else complain on grounds of justice? Each other person already has his legitimate share under D_1. Under D_1 there is nothing that anyone has that anyone else has a claim of justice against. After someone transfers something to Wilt Chamberlain, third parties *still* have their legitimate shares; *their* shares are not changed. By what process could such a transfer among two persons give rise to a legitimate claim of distributive justice on a portion of what was transferred, by a third party who had no claim of justice on any holding of the others *before* the transfer?[5] To cut off objections irrelevant here, we might imagine the exchanges occurring in a socialist society, after hours. After playing whatever basketball he does in his daily work, or doing whatever other daily work he does, Wilt Chamberlain decides to put in *overtime* to earn additional money. (First his work quota is set; he works time over that.) Or imagine it is a skilled juggler people like to see, who puts on shows after hours.

Why might someone work overtime in a society in which it is assumed their needs are satisfied? Perhaps because they care about things other than needs. I like to write in books that I read, and to have easy access to books for browsing at odd hours. It would be very pleasant and convenient to have the resources of Widener Library in my back yard. No society, I assume, will provide such resources close to each person who would like them as part of his regular allotment (under D_1). Thus, persons either must do without some extra things that they want, or must be allowed to do something extra to get some of these things. On what basis could the inequalities that would eventuate be forbidden? Notice also that small factories would spring up in a socialist society, unless forbidden. I melt down some of my personal possessions (under D_1) and build a machine out of the material. I offer you, and others, a philosophy lecture once a week in exchange for your cranking the handle on my machine, whose products I exchange for yet other things, and so on. (The raw materials used by the machine are given to me by others who possess them under D_1 in exchange for hearing lectures.) Each person might participate to gain things over and above their allotment under D_1. Some persons even might want to leave their job in socialist industry and work full time in this private sector. I wish merely to note how private property even in means of production would occur in a socialist society that did not forbid people to use as they wished some of the resources they are given under the socialist distribution D_1. The socialist society would have to forbid capitalist acts between consenting adults.

The general point illustrated by the Wilt Chamberlain example and the example of the entrepreneur in a socialist society is that no end-state principle or distributional patterned principle of justice can be continuously realized without continuous interference with people's lives. Any favored pattern would be transformed into one unfavored by the principle, by people choosing to act in various ways; for example, by people exchanging goods and services with other people, or giving things to other people, things the transferrers are entitled to under the favored distributional pattern. To maintain a pattern one must either continually interfere to stop people from transferring resources as they wish to, or continually (or periodically) interfere to take from some persons resources that others for some reason chose to transfer to them. (But if some time limit is to be set on how long people may keep resources others voluntarily transfer to them, why let them keep these resources for any period of time? Why not have immediate confiscation?) It might be objected that all persons voluntarily will choose to refrain from actions which would upset the pattern. This presupposes unrealistically (1) that all will most want to maintain the pattern (are those who don't, to be "re-educated" or forced to undergo "self-criticism"?), (2) that each can gather enough information about his own actions and the ongoing activities of others to discover which of his actions will upset the pattern, and (3) that diverse and far-flung persons can coordinate their actions to dovetail into the pattern. Compare the manner in which the market is neutral among persons' desires, as it reflects and transmits widely scattered information via prices, and coordinates persons' activities.

It puts things perhaps a bit too strongly to say that every patterned (or end-state) principle is liable to be thwarted by the voluntary actions of the individual parties transferring some of their shares they receive under the principle. For perhaps some *very* weak patterns are not so thwarted. Any distributional pattern with any egalitarian component is overturnable by the voluntary actions of individual persons over time; as is every patterned condition with sufficient content so as actually to have been proposed as presenting the central core of distributive justice. Still, given the possibility that some weak conditions or patterns may not be unstable in this way, it would be better to formulate an explicit description of the kind of interesting and contentful patterns under discussion, and to prove a theorem about their instability. Since the weaker the patterning, the more likely it is that the entitlement system itself satisfies it, a plausible conjecture is that any patterning either is unstable or is satisfied by the entitlement system....

Redistribution and Property Rights

Apparently, patterned principles allow people to choose to spend upon themselves, but not upon others, those resources they are entitled to (or rather, receive) under some favored distributional pattern D_1. For if each of several persons chooses to expend some of his D_1 resources upon one other person, then that other person will receive more than his D_1 share, disturbing the favored distributional pattern. Maintaining a distributional pattern is individualism with a vengeance! Patterned distributional principles do not give people what entitlement principles do, only better distributed. For they do not give the right to choose what to do with what one has; they do not give the right to choose to pursue an end involving (intrinsically, or as a means) the enhancement of another's position. To such views, families are disturbing; for within a family occur transfers that upset the favored distributional pattern. Either families themselves become units to which distribution takes place, the column occupiers (on what rationale?), or loving behavior is forbidden. We should note in passing the ambivalent position of radicals toward the family. Its loving relationships are seen as a model to be emulated and extended across the whole society, at the same time that it is denounced as a suffocating institution to be broken and condemned as a focus of parochial concerns that interfere with achieving radical goals. Need we say that it is not appropriate to enforce across the wider society the relationships of love and care appropriate within a family, relationships which are voluntarily undertaken?[6] Incidentally, love is an interesting instance of another relationship that is historical, in that (like justice) it depends upon what actually occurred. An adult may come to love another because of the other's characteristics; but it is the other person, and not the characteristics, that is loved. The love is not transferrable to someone else with the same characteristics, even to one who "scores" higher for these characteristics. And the love endures through changes of the characteristics that gave rise to it. One loves the particular person one actually encountered. Why love is historical, attaching to persons in this way and not to characteristics, is an interesting and puzzling question.

Proponents of patterned principles of distributive justice focus upon criteria for determining who is to receive holdings; they consider the reasons for which someone should have something, and also the total picture of hold-

ings. Whether or not it is better to give than to receive, proponents of patterned principles ignore giving altogether. In considering the distribution of
goods, income, and so forth, their theories are theories of recipient justice;
they completely ignore any right a person might have to give something to
someone. Even in exchanges where each party is simultaneously giver and
recipient, patterned principles of justice focus only upon the recipient role
and its supposed rights. Thus discussions tend to focus on whether people
(should) have a right to inherit, rather than on whether people (should)
have a right to bequeath or on whether persons who have a right to hold also
have a right to choose that others hold in their place. I lack a good explanation of why the usual theories of distributive justice are so recipient oriented;
ignoring givers and transferrers and their rights is of a piece with ignoring
producers and their entitlements. But why is it *all* ignored?

Patterned principles of distributive justice necessitate redistributive activities. The likelihood is small that any actual freely-arrived-at set of holdings fits
a given pattern; and the likelihood is nil that it will continue to fit the pattern
as people exchange and give. From the point of view of an entitlement theory, redistribution is a serious matter indeed, involving, as it does, the violation
of people's rights. (An exception is those takings that fall under the principle
of the rectification of injustices.) From other points of view, also, it is serious.

Taxation of earnings from labor is on a par with forced labor.[7] Some persons find this claim obviously true: taking the earnings of n hours labor is like
taking n hours from the person; it is like forcing the person to work n hours
for another's purpose. Others find the claim absurd. But even these, *if* they
object to forced labor, would oppose forcing unemployed hippies to work for
the benefit of the needy.[8] And they would also object to forcing each person
to work five extra hours each week for the benefit of the needy. But a system
that takes five hours' wages in taxes does not seem to them like one that
forces someone to work five hours, since it offers the person forced a wider
range of choice in activities than does taxation in kind with the particular
labor specified. (But we can imagine a gradation of systems of forced labor,
from one that specifies a particular activity, to one that gives a choice among
two activities, to ...; and so on up.) Furthermore, people envisage a system
with something like a proportional tax on everything above the amount necessary for basic needs. Some think this does not force someone to work extra
hours, since there is no fixed number of extra hours he is forced to work, and
since he can avoid the tax entirely by earning only enough to cover his basic
needs. This is a very uncharacteristic view of forcing for those who *also* think
people are forced to do something *whenever* the alternatives they face are considerably worse. However, *neither* view is correct. The fact that others intentionally intervene, in violation of a side constraint against aggression, to
threaten force to limit the alternatives, in this case to paying taxes or (presumably the worse alternative) bare subsistence, makes the taxation system

one of forced labor and distinguishes it from other cases of limited choices which are not forcings.

The man who chooses to work longer to gain an income more than sufficient for his basic needs prefers some extra goods or services to the leisure and activities he could perform during the possible nonworking hours; whereas the man who chooses not to work the extra time prefers the leisure activities to the extra goods or services he could acquire by working more. Given this, if it would be illegitimate for a tax system to seize some of a man's leisure (forced labor) for the purpose of serving the needy, how can it be legitimate for a tax system to seize some of a man's goods for that purpose? Why should we treat the man whose happiness requires certain material goods or services differently from the man whose preferences and desires make such goods unnecessary for his happiness? Why should the man who prefers seeing a movie (and who has to earn money for a ticket) be open to the required call to aid the needy, while the person who prefers looking at a sunset (and hence need earn no extra money) is not? Indeed, isn't it surprising that redistributionists choose to ignore the man whose pleasures are so easily attainable without extra labor, while adding yet another burden to the poor unfortunate who must work for his pleasures? If anything, one would have expected the reverse. Why is the person with the nonmaterial or non-consumption desire allowed to proceed unimpeded to his most favored feasible alternative, whereas the man whose pleasures or desires involve material things and who must work for extra money (thereby serving whomever considers his activities valuable enough to pay him) is constrained in what he can realize? Perhaps there is no difference in principle. And perhaps some think the answer concerns merely administrative convenience. (These questions and issues will not disturb those who think that forced labor to serve the needy or to realize some favored end-state pattern is acceptable.) In a fuller discussion we would have (and want) to extend our argument to include interest, entrepeneurial profits, and so on. Those who doubt that this extension can be carried through, and who draw the line here at taxation of income from labor, will have to state rather complicated patterned *historical* principles of distributive justice, since end-state principles would not distinguish *sources* of income in any way. It is enough for now to get away from end-state principles and to make clear how various patterned principles are dependent upon particular views about the sources or the illegitimacy or the lesser legitimacy of profits, interest, and so on; which particular views may well be mistaken.

What sort of right over others does a legally institutionalized end-state pattern give one? The central core of the notion of a property right in X, relative to which other parts of the notion are to be explained, is the right to determine what shall be done with X; the right to choose which of the constrained set of options concerning X shall be realized or attempted. The constraints are set by other principles or laws operating in the society; in our theory, by the Lockean rights people possess (under the minimal state). My property rights in my knife allow me to leave it where I will, but not in your chest. I may choose which of the acceptable options involving the knife is to be realized. This notion of property helps us to understand why earlier theorists spoke of people as property in themselves and their labor. They viewed each person as having a right to decide what would become of himself and what he would do, and as having a right to reap the benefits of what he did.

This right of selecting the alternative to be realized from the constrained set of alternatives may be held by an *individual* or by a *group* with some procedure for reaching a joint decision; or the right may be passed back and forth so that one year I decide what is to become of X, and the next year you do (with the alternative of destruction, perhaps, being excluded). Or, during the same time period, some types of decisions about X may be made by me, and others by you. And so on. We lack an adequate, fruitful, analytical apparatus for classifying the *types* of constraints on the set of options among which choices are to be made, and the *types* of ways decision powers can be held, divided, and amalgamated. A *theory* of property would, among other things, contain such a classification of constraints and decision modes, and from a small number of principles would follow a host of interesting statements about the *consequences* and effects of certain combinations of constraints and modes of decision.

When end-result principles of distributive justice are built into the legal structure of a society, they (as do most patterned principles) give each citizen an enforceable claim to some portion of the total social product; that is, to some portion of the sum total of the individually and jointly made products. This total product is produced by individuals laboring, using means of production others have saved to bring into existence, by people organizing production or creating means to produce new things or things in a new way. It is on this batch of individual activities that patterned distributional principles give each individual an enforceable claim. Each person has a claim to the activities and the products of other persons, independently of whether the other persons enter into particular relationships that give rise to these claims, and independently of whether they voluntarily take these claims upon themselves, in charity or in exchange for something.

Whether it is done through taxation on wages or on wages over a certain amount, or through seizure of profits, or through there being a big *social pot* so that it's not clear what's coming from where and what's going where, patterned principles of distributive justice involve appropriating the actions of other persons. Seizing the results of someone's labor is equivalent to seizing hours from him and directing him to carry on various activities. If people force you to do certain work, or unrewarded work, for a certain period of time, they decide what you are to do and what purposes your work is to serve apart from your decisions. This process whereby they take this decision from you makes them a *part-owner* of you; it gives them a property right in you. Just as having such partial control and power of decision, by right, over an animal or inanimate object would be to have a property right in it.

End-state and most patterned principles of distributive justice institute (partial) ownership by others of people and their actions and labor. These principles involve a shift from the classical liberals' notion of self-ownership to a notion of (partial) property rights in *other* people.

Considerations such as these confront end-state and other patterned conceptions of justice with the question of whether the actions necessary to achieve the selected pattern don't themselves violate moral side constraints. Any view holding that there are moral side constraints on actions, that not all moral considerations can be built into end states that are to be achieved, must face the possibility that some of its goals are not achievable by any morally permissible available means. An entitlement theorist will face such conflicts in a society that deviates from the principles of justice for the generation of holdings, if and only if the only actions available to realize the principles themselves violate some moral constraints. Since deviation from the first two principles of justice (in acquisition and transfer) will involve other persons' direct and aggressive intervention to violate rights, and since moral constraints will not exclude defensive or retributive action in such cases, the entitlement theorist's problem rarely will be pressing. And whatever difficulties he has in applying the principle of rectification to persons who did not themselves violate the first two principles are difficulties in balancing the conflicting considerations so as correctly to formulate the complex principle of rectification itself; he will not violate moral side constraints by applying the principle. Proponents of patterned conceptions of justice, however, often will face head-on clashes (and poignant ones if they cherish each party to the clash) between moral side constraints on how individuals may be treated and their patterned conception of justice that presents an end state or other pattern that *must* be realized.

May a person emigrate from a nation that has institutionalized some end-state or patterned distributional principle? For some principles (for example, Hayek's) emigration presents no theoretical problem. But for others it is a tricky matter. Consider a nation having a compulsory scheme of minimal social provision to aid the neediest (or one organized so as to maximize the position of the worst-off group); no one may opt out of participating in it. (None may say, "Don't compel me to contribute to others and don't provide for me via this compulsory mechanism if I am in need.") Everyone above a certain level is forced to contribute to aid the needy. But if emigration from the country were allowed, anyone could choose to move to another country that did not have compulsory social provision but otherwise was (as much as possible) identical. In such a case, the person's *only* motive for leaving would be to avoid participating in the compulsory scheme of social provision. And if he does leave, the needy in his initial country will receive no (compelled) help from him. What rationale yields the result that the person be permitted to emigrate, yet forbidden to stay and opt out of the compulsory scheme of social provision? If providing for the needy is of overriding importance, this does militate against allowing internal opting out; but it also speaks against allowing external emigration. (Would it also support, to some extent, the kidnapping of persons living in a place without compulsory social provision, who could be forced to make a contribution to the needy in your community?) Perhaps the crucial component of the position that allows emigration solely to avoid certain arrangements, while not allowing anyone internally to opt out of them, is a concern for fraternal feelings within the country. "We don't want anyone here who doesn't contribute, who doesn't care enough about the others to contribute." That concern, in this case, would have to be tied to the view that forced aiding tends to produce fraternal feelings between the aided and the aider (or perhaps merely to the view that the knowledge that someone or other voluntarily is not aiding produces unfraternal feelings).

Notes

1. Applications of the principle of justice in acquisition may also occur as part of the move from one distribution to another. You may find an unheld thing now and appropriate it. Acquisitions also are to be understood as included when, to simplify, I speak only of transitions by transfers.

2. If the principle of rectification of violations of the first two principles yields more than one description of holdings, then some choice must be made as to which of these is to be realized. Perhaps the sort of considerations about distributive justice and equality that I argue against play a legitimate role in *this* subsidiary choice. Similarly, there may be room for such considerations in deciding which otherwise arbitrary features a statute will embody, when such features are unavoidable because other considerations do not specify a precise line, yet a line must be drawn.

3. One might try to squeeze a patterned conception of distributive justice into the framework of the entitlement conception, by formulating a gimmicky obligatory "principle of transfer" that would lead to the pattern. For example, the principle that if one has more than the mean income one must transfer everything one holds above the mean to persons below the mean so as to bring them up to (but not over) the mean. We can formulate a criterion for a "principle of transfer" to rule out such obligatory transfers, or we can say that no correct principle of transfer, no principle of transfer in a free society will be like this. The former is probably the better course, though the latter also is true.

Alternatively, one might think to make the entitlement conception instantiate a pattern, by using matrix entries that express the relative strength of a person's entitlements as measured by some real-valued function. But even if the limitation to natural dimensions failed to exclude this function, the resulting edifice would *not* capture our system of entitlements to *particular* things.

4. We certainly benefit because great economic incentives operate to get others to spend much time and energy to figure out how to serve us by providing things we will want to pay for. It is not mere paradox mongering to wonder whether capitalism should be criticized for most rewarding and hence encouraging, not individualists like Thoreau who go about their own lives, but people who are occupied with serving others and winning them as customers. But to defend capitalism one need not think businessmen are the finest human types. (I do not mean to join here the general maligning of businessmen, either.) Those who think the finest should acquire the most can try to convince their fellows to transfer resources in accordance with *that* principle.

5. Might not a transfer have instrumental effects on a third party, changing his feasible options? (But what if the two parties to the transfer independently had used their holdings in this fashion?) I discuss this question below, but note here that this question concedes the point for distributions of ultimate intrinsic noninstrumental goods (pure utility experiences, so to speak) that are transferrable. It also could be objected that the transfer might make a third party more envious because it worsens his position relative to someone else. I find it incomprehensible how this can be thought to involve a claim of justice....

   Here and elsewhere in this chapter, a theory which incorporates elements of pure procedural justice might find what I say acceptable, if kept in its proper place; that is, if background institutions exist to ensure the satisfaction of certain conditions on distributive shares. But if these institutions are not themselves the sum or invisible-hand result of people's voluntary (nonaggressive) actions, the constraints they impose require justification. At no point does our argument assume any background institutions more extensive than those of the minimal night-watchman state, a state limited to protecting persons against murder, assault, theft, fraud, and so forth.

6. One indication of the stringency of Rawls's difference principle, which we attend to in the second part of this chapter, is its inappropriateness as a governing principle even within a family of individuals who love one another. Should a family devote its resources to maximizing the position of its least well off and least talented child, holding back the other children or using resources for their education and development only if they will follow a policy through their lifetimes of maximizing the position of their least fortunate sibling? Surely not. How then can this even be considered as the appropriate policy for enforcement in the wider society? (I discuss below what I think would be Rawls's reply: that some principles apply at the macro-level which do not apply to micro-situations.)

7. I am unsure as to whether the arguments I present below show that such taxation merely *is* forced labor; so that "is on a par with" means "is one kind of." Or alternatively, whether the arguments emphasize the great similarities between such taxation and forced labor, to show it is plausible and illuminating to view such taxation in the light of forced labor. This latter approach would remind one of how John Wisdom conceives of the claims of metaphysicians.

8. Nothing hangs on the fact that here and elsewhere I speak loosely of *needs*, since I go on, each time, to reject the criterion of justice which includes it. If, however, something did depend upon the notion, one would want to examine it more carefully. For a skeptical view, see Kenneth Minogue, *The Liberal Mind* (New York: Random House, 1963), pp. 103-12.

20.
ILLEGAL IMMIGRANTS,
HEALTH CARE, AND SOCIAL RESPONSIBILITY

❋ ❋ ❋

JAMES DWYER

James Dwyer is an associate professor of bioethics and humanities at the State University of New York Upstate Medical University. His research is focused on issues of social justice that arise in connection with health care. In the following article he addresses the question of whether we should provide health care benefits to illegal aliens. Some have argued that those who have no right to be in a country have no claims to health benefits in that country, while others have argued that health care is a basic human right that should be provided for everyone. Dwyer argues that neither view is satisfactory. He offers an alternative position, framed in terms of social justice and social responsibility, which takes account of some of the complexities involved in the situation of illegal immigrants.

Illegal immigrants form a large and disputed group in many countries. Indeed, even the name is in dispute. People in this group are referred as illegal immigrants, illegal aliens, irregular migrants, undocumented workers, or, in French, as *sans papiers*. Whatever they are called, their existence raises an important ethical question: Do societies have an ethical responsibility to provide health care for them and to promote their health?

This question often elicits two different answers. Some people—call them nationalists—say that the answer is obviously no. They argue that people who have no right to be in a country should not have rights to benefits in that country. Other people—call them humanists—say that the answer is obviously yes. They argue that all people should have access to health care. It's a basic human right.

I think both these answers are off the mark. The first focuses too narrowly on what we owe people based on legal rules and formal citizenship. The other answer focuses too broadly, on what we owe people qua human beings. We need a perspective that is in between, that adequately responds to the phenomenon of illegal immigration and adequately reflects the complexity of moral thought. There may be important ethical distinctions, for example, among the following groups: US citizens who lack health insurance, undocumented workers who lack health insurance in spite of working full time, medical visitors who fly to the United States as tourists in order to obtain care at public hospitals, foreign citizens who work abroad for subcontractors of American firms, and foreign citizens who live in impoverished countries. I believe that we—US citizens—have ethical duties in all of these situations, but I see important differences in what these duties demand and how they are to be explained.

In this paper, I want to focus on the situation of illegal immigrants. I will discuss several different answers to the question about what ethical responsibility we have to provide health care to illegal immigrants. (I shall simply assume that societies have an ethical obligation to provide their own citizens with a reasonably comprehensive package of health benefits.) The answers that I shall discuss tend to conceptualize the ethical issues in terms of individual desert, professional ethics, or human rights. I want to discuss the limitations of each of these approaches and to offer an alternative. I shall approach the issues in terms of social responsibility and discuss the moral relevance of work. In doing so, I tend to pull bioethics in the direction of social ethics and political philosophy. That's the direction I think it should be heading. But before I begin the ethical discussion, I need to say more about the phenomenon of illegal immigration.

Human Migration

People have always moved around. They have moved for political, environmental, economic, and familial reasons. They have tried to escape war, persecution, discrimination, famine, environmental degradation, poverty, and a variety of other problems. They have tried to find places to build better lives, earn more money, and provide better support for their families. A strong sense of family responsibility has always been an important factor behind migration.[1]

But while human migration is not new, *illegal* immigration is, since only recently have nation-states tried to control and regulate the flow of immigration. Societies have always tried to exclude people they viewed as undesirable: criminals, people unable to support themselves, people with contagious diseases, and certain ethnic or racial groups. But only in the last hundred years or so have states tried in a systematic way to control the number and kinds of immigrants.

In contrast, what the Athenian polis tried to control was not immigration, but citizenship. Workers, merchants, and scholars came to Athens from all over the Mediterranean world. They were free to work, trade, and study in Athens, although they were excluded from the rich political life that citizens enjoyed. Today, political states try to control both citizenship and residency.

Modern attempts to control residency are not remarkably effective. There are illegal immigrants residing and working all over the globe. When people think about illegal immigrants, they tend to focus on Mexicans in the United States or North-Africans in France. But the phenomenon is really much more diverse and complex. Illegal immigrants come from hundreds of countries and go wherever they can get work. There are undocumented workers from Indonesia in Malaysia, undocumented workers from Haiti in the Dominican Republic, and undocumented workers from Myanmar in Thailand. Thailand is an interesting example because it is both a source of and a destination for undocumented workers: while many people from poorer countries have gone to work in Thailand, many Thais have gone to work in richer countries.

Since illegal activities are difficult to measure, and people are difficult to count, we do not know exactly how many people are illegal immigrants. The following estimates provide a rough idea. The total number of illegal immigrants in the US is probably between five and eight million. About 30-40 per cent of these people entered the country legally, but overstayed their visas. Of all the immigrants in Europe, about one third are probably illegal immigrants. A small country like Israel has about 125,000 foreign workers (not counting Palestinians). About 50,000 of these are in the country illegally.[2]

I believe that a sound ethical response to the question of illegal immigration requires some understanding of the work that illegal immigrants do. Most undocumented workers do the jobs that citizens often eschew. They do difficult and disagreeable work at low wages for small firms in the informal sector of the economy. In general, they have the worst jobs and work in the worst conditions in such sectors of the economy as agriculture, construction, manufacturing, and the food industry. They pick fruit, wash dishes, move dirt, sew clothes, clean toilets.

Japan is a good example of this. In the 1980s many foreign workers came to Japan from the Philippines, Thailand, China, and other countries. Yoshio Sugimoto summarizes the situation:

The unprecedented flow of foreign workers into Japan stemmed from the situations in both the domestic and foreign labor markets.

"Pull" factors within Japan included the ageing of the Japanese workforce and the accompanying shortage of labor in unskilled, manual, and physically demanding areas. In addition, the changing work ethic of Japanese youth has made it difficult for employers to recruit them for this type of work, which is described in terms of the three undesirable Ks (or Ds in English): kitanai (dirty), kitsui (difficult), and kiken (dangerous). Under these circumstances, a number of employers found illegal migrants, in particular from Asia, a remedy for their labor shortage.[3] The pattern is much the same in other countries.

In the global economy, in which a company can shift its manufacturing base with relative ease to a country with cheaper labor, illegal immigrants often perform work that cannot be shifted overseas. Toilets have to be cleaned, dishes have to be washed, and children have to be watched *locally*. This local demand may help to explain a relatively new trend: the feminization of migration. Migrants used to be predominantly young men, seeking work in areas such as agriculture and construction. But that pattern is changing. More and more women migrants are employed in the service sector as, for example, maids, nannies, and health care aides.

Women migrants are also employed as sex workers. The connection between commercial sex and illegal immigration is quite striking. As women in some societies have more money, choices, schooling, and power, they are unwilling to work as prostitutes. These societies seem to be supplying their demands for commercial sex by using undocumented workers from poorer countries. Before brothels were legalized in the Netherlands, about 40 to 75 per cent of the prostitutes who worked in Amsterdam were undocumented workers. About 3,000 of the 7,000 prostitutes in Berlin are from Thailand. Japan has over 150,000 foreign prostitutes, most of them from Thailand, China, and the Philippines. Thailand has about 25,000 prostitutes from Myanmar.[4]

Even when prostitution is voluntary, it is difficult and dangerous. Leah Platt notes that prostitution is

"a job without overtime pay, health insurance, or sick leave—and usually without recourse against the abuses of one's employer, which can include being required to have sex without a condom and being forced to turn tricks in order to work off crushing debts."[5]

And for some illegal immigrants, prostitution is not a voluntary choice. Some are deceived and delivered into prostitution. Others are coerced, their lives controlled by pimps, criminal gangs, and human traffickers.

Some of the worst moral offenses occur in the trafficking of human beings, but even here it is important to see a continuum of activities. Sometimes traffickers simply provide transportation in exchange for payment. Sometimes, they recruit people with deceptive promises and false accounts of jobs, then transport them under horrible and dangerous conditions. If and when the immigrants arrive in the destination country, they are controlled by debt, threat, and force. Some become indentured servants, working without pay for a period of time. Others are controlled by physical threats or threats to expose their illegal status. A few are enslaved and held as property.

Not all illegal immigrants are victims, however, and an accurate account of illegal immigration, even if only sketched, must capture some of its complexity. My task is to consider how well different ethical frameworks deal with that complexity.

A Matter of Desert

The abstract ethical question of whether societies have a responsibility to provide health care for illegal immigrants sometimes becomes a concrete political issue. Rising health care costs, budget reduction programs, and feelings of resentment sometimes transform the ethical question into a political debate. This has happened several times in the United States. In 1996, the Congress debated and passed the "Illegal Immigration Reform and Immigrant Responsibility Act." This law made all immigrants ineligible for Medicaid, although it did allow the federal government to reimburse states for emergency treatment of illegal immigrants.

In 1994, the citizens of California debated Proposition 187, an even more restrictive measure. This ballot initiative proposed to deny publicly funded health care, social services, and education to illegal immigrants. This law would have required publicly funded health care facilities to deny care, except in medical emergencies, to people who could not prove that they were US citizens or legal residents.

This proposition was approved by 59 per cent of the voters. It was never implemented because courts found that parts of it conflicted with other laws, but the deepest arguments for and against it remain very much alive. Because they will probably surface again, at a different time or in different place, it is worthwhile evaluating the ethical frameworks that they assume.

The first argument put forward is that illegal aliens should be denied public benefits because they are in the country illegally. Although it is true that illegal aliens have violated a law by entering or remaining in the country, it is not clear what the moral implication of this point is. Nothing about access to health care follows from the mere fact that illegal aliens have violated a law. Many people break many different laws. Whether a violation of a law should disqualify people from public services probably depends on the nature and purpose of the services, the nature and the gravity of the violation, and many other matters.

Consider one example of a violation of the law. People sometimes break tax laws by working off the books. They do certain jobs for cash in order to avoid paying taxes or losing benefits. Moreover, this practice is probably quite common. I recently asked students in two of my classes if they or anyone in their extended family had earned money that was not reported as taxable income. In one class, all but two students raised their hands. In the other class, every hand went up.

No one has suggested that health care facilities deny care to people suspected of working off the books. But undocumented work is also a violation of the law. Furthermore, it involves an issue of fairness because it shifts burdens onto others and diminishes funding for important purposes. Of course, working off the books and working without a visa are not alike in all respects.

But without further argument, nothing much follows about whether it is right to deny benefits to people who have violated a law.

Proponents of restrictive measures also appeal to an argument that combines a particular conception of desert with the need to make tradeoffs. Proponents of California's Proposition 187 stated that, "while our own citizens and legal residents go wanting, those who chose to enter our country ILLEGALLY get royal treatment at the expense of the California taxpayer."[6] Proponents noted that the legislature maintained programs that included free prenatal care for illegal aliens but increased the amount that senior citizens must pay for prescription drugs. They then asked, "Why should we give more comfort and consideration to illegal aliens than to our own needy American citizens?"

The rhetorical question is part of the argument. I would restate the argument in the following way: Given the limited public budget for health care, US citizens and legal residents are more deserving of benefits than are illegal aliens. This argument frames the issue as a choice between competing goods in a situation of limited resources.

There is something right and something wrong about this way of framing the issue. What is right is the idea that in all of life, individual and political, we have to choose between competing goods. A society cannot have everything: comprehensive and universal health care, good public schools, extensive public parks and beaches, public services, and very low taxes. What is false is the idea that we have to choose between basic health care for illegal aliens and basic health care for citizens. Many other trade-offs are possible, including an increase in public funding.

The narrow framework of the debate pits poor citizens against illegal aliens in a battle for health care resources. Within this framework, the issue is posed as one of desert. Avoiding the idea of desert is impossible. After all, justice is a matter of giving people their due—giving them what they deserve. But a narrow conception of desert seems most at home in allocating particular goods that go beyond basic needs, in situations where the criteria of achievement and effort are very clear. For example, if we are asked to give an award for the best student in chemistry, a narrow notion of desert is appropriate and useful. But publicly funded health care is different and requires a broader view of desert.

The discussion of restrictive measures often focuses on desert, taxation, and benefits. Proponents tend to picture illegal immigrants as free riders who are taking advantage of public services without contributing to public funding. Opponents are quick to note that illegal immigrants do pay taxes. They pay sales tax, gas tax, and value-added tax. They often pay income tax and property tax. But do they pay enough tax to cover the cost of the services they use? Or more generally, are illegal immigrants a net economic gain or a net economic loss for society?

Instead of trying to answer the economic question, I want to point out a problem with the question itself. The question about taxation and benefits tends to portray society as a private business venture. On the business model, investors should benefit in proportion to the funds they put into the venture. This may be an appropriate model for some business ventures, but it is not an adequate model for all social institutions and benefits. The business model is not an adequate model for thinking about voting, legal defense, library services, minimum wages, occupational safety, and many other social benefits.

Consider my favorite social institution: the public library. The important question here is not whether some people use more library services than they pay for through taxation, which is obviously true. Some people pay relatively high taxes but never use the library, while others pay relatively low taxes but use the library quite often. In thinking about the public library, we should consider questions such as the following. What purposes does the library serve? Does it promote education, provide opportunity, and foster public life? Does it tend to ameliorate or exacerbate social injustice? Given the library's purposes, who should count as its constituents or members? And what are the rights and responsibilities of the library users? In the following sections, I shall consider analogous questions about illegal immigrants and the social institutions that promote health.

A Matter of Professional Ethics

Some of the most vigorous responses to restrictive measures have come from those who consider the issue within the framework of professional ethics. Tal Ann Ziv and Bernard Lo, for example, argue that "cooperating with Proposition 187 would undermine professional ethics."[7] In particular, they argue that cooperating with this kind of restrictive measure is inconsistent with physicians' "ethical responsibilities to protect the public health, care for persons in medical need, and respect patient confidentiality."[8]

Restrictive measures may indeed have adverse effects on the public health. For example, measures that deny care to illegal aliens, or make them afraid to seek care, could lead to an increase in tuberculosis. And physicians do have a professional obligation to oppose measures that would significantly harm the public health. But the public health argument has a serious failing, if taken by itself. It avoids the big issue of whether illegal immigrants should be considered part of the public and whether public institutions should serve their health needs. Instead of appealing to an inclusive notion of social justice, the argument suggests how the health of illegal immigrants may influence citizens' health, and then appeals to citizens' sense of prudence. The appeal to prudence is not wrong, but it avoids the larger ethical issues.

The second argument against Proposition 187 is that it restricts confidentiality in ways that are not justified. It requires health care facilities to report people suspected of being in the country illegally and to disclose additional information to authorities. Ziv and Lo argue that "Proposition 187 fails to provide the usual ethical justifications for overriding patient confidentiality."[9] Reporting a patient's "immigration status serves no medical or public health purpose, involves no medical expertise, and is not a routine part of medical care."[10] Thus this restriction on confidentiality is a serious violation of professional ethics.

But if restrictive measures work as designed, issues of confidentiality may not even arise. Illegal aliens will be deterred from seeking medical care or will be screened out before they see a doctor. Thus ·the issue of screening may be more important than the issue of confidentiality. First, if the screening is carried out, it should not be by physicians, because it is not their role to act as agents for the police or the immigration service. Professional ethics requires some separation of social roles, and terrible things have happened when physicians have become agents of political regimes. The bigger issue, though, is not who should do the screening, but whether it should be done at all.

Ziv and Lo note that "clerks will probably screen patients for their immigration status, just as they currently screen them for their insurance status."[11] They object to this arrangement, and they argue that physicians bear some responsibility for arrangements that conflict with professional ethics. In their view, screening out illegal aliens conflicts with physicians' ethical responsibility to "care for persons in medical need."[12]

This claim is important, but ambiguous. It could mean simply that physicians have an obligation to attend to anyone who presents to them in need of emergency care. That seems right. It would be wrong not to stabilize and save someone in a medical emergency. It would be inhumane, even morally absurd, to let someone die because her visa had expired. But a claim that physicians have an enduring obligation to provide emergency care is consistent with measures like Proposition 187 and the 1996 federal law.

The claim might also mean that the selection of patients should be based only on medical need, never on such factors as nationality, residency, immigration status, or ability to pay. This is a very strong claim. It means that all private practice is morally wrong. It means that most national health care systems are too restrictive. It means that transplant lists for organs donated in a particular country should be open to everyone in the world. It might even mean that physicians have an ethical responsibility to relocate to places where the medical need is the greatest. I shall say more about the strong claim in the next section. Here I just want to note one point. This claim goes well beyond professional ethics. It is an ethical claim that seems to be based on a belief about the nature of human needs and human rights.

Finally, Ziv and Lo's claim about physicians' responsibility to care for people in medical need might be stronger than the claim about emergency care but weaker than the universal claim. Perhaps we should interpret it to mean that it is wrong to turn patients away when society has no other provisions and institutions to provide them with basic care. The idea then is that society should provide all members with basic health care and that physicians have some responsibility to work to realize this idea.

There is something appealing and plausible about this interpretation, but it too goes beyond professional ethics. It has more to do with the nature of social justice and social institutions than with the nature of medical practice. It makes an ethical claim based on a belief about social responsibility and an assumption that illegal aliens are to be counted as members of society. I shall try to elaborate this belief and assumption later.

Let me sum up my main points so far. Political measures that restrict medical care for illegal immigrants often involve violations of professional ethics, and health care professionals should oppose such measures. But the framework of professional ethics is not adequate for thinking about the larger ethical issues. It fails to illuminate the obligation to provide medical care. Furthermore, it fails to consider factors such as work and housing that may have a profound impact on health. In the next two sections I shall consider broader frameworks and discourses.

A Matter of Human Rights

To deal with the issue of health care and illegal immigrants, some adopt a humanistic framework and employ a discourse of human rights. They tend to emphasize the right of all human beings to medical treatment, as well as the common humanity of aliens and citizens, pointing to the arbitrary nature of national borders.

National borders can seem arbitrary. Distinctions based on national borders seem even more arbitrary when one studies how borders were established and the disparities in wealth and health that exist between countries. Since it doesn't seem just that some people should be disadvantaged by arbitrary boundaries, it may also seem that people should have the right to emigrate from wherever they are and to immigrate to wherever they wish. But does this follow from the fact that national borders can be seen as arbitrary? John Rawls thinks not. He writes:

> It does not follow from the fact that boundaries are historically arbitrary that their role in the Law of Peoples cannot be justified. On the contrary,
> . to fix on their arbitrariness is to fix on the wrong thing. In the absence of

a world state, there *must* be boundaries of some kind, which when viewed in isolation will seem arbitrary, and depend to some degree on historical circumstances.[13]

Even if boundaries depend on historical circumstances, a defined territory may allow a people to form a government that acts as their agent in a fair and effective way. A defined territory may allow a people to form a government that enables them to take responsibility for the natural environment, promote the well-being of the human population, deal with social problems, and cultivate just political institutions.[14]

From functions like these, governments derive a qualified right to regulate immigration. This right is not an unlimited right of communal self-determination. Societies do not have a right to protect institutions and ways of life that are deeply unjust. Furthermore, even when a society has a right to regulate immigration, there are ethical questions about whether and how the society should exercise that right. And there are ethical questions about how immigrants should be treated in that society.

The committed humanist, who begins with reflections on the arbitrary nature of national boundaries, sometimes reaches the same conclusion as the global capitalist: that all restrictions on labor mobility are unjustified. In their different ways, both the humanist and the capitalist devalue distinctions based on political community. To be sure, there is much to criticize about existing political communities, but we need to be cautious about some of the alternatives. Michael Walzer warns us about two possibilities. He says that to "tear down the walls of the state is not ... to create a world without walls, but rather to create a thousand petty fortresses."[15] Without state regulation of immigration, local communities may become more exclusionary, parochial, and xenophobic. Walzer also notes another possibility: "The fortresses, too, could be torn down: all that is necessary is a global state sufficiently powerful to overwhelm the local communities. Then the result would be ... a world of radically deracinated men and women."[16]

Of course, the humanist need not be committed to an abstract position about open borders. The humanist might accept that states have a qualified right to regulate immigration, but insist that all states must respect the human rights of all immigrants—legal and illegal. That idea makes a lot of sense, although much depends on how we specify the content of human rights.

The idea that all human beings should have equal access to all beneficial health care is often used to critique both national and international arrangements. In an editorial in the *New England Journal of Medicine*, Paul Farmer reflects on the number of people who go untreated for diseases such as tuberculosis and HIV. He writes:

Prevention is, of course, always preferable to treatment. But epidemics of treatable infectious diseases should remind us that although science has revolutionized medicine, we still need a plan for ensuring equal access to care. As study after study shows the power of effective therapies to alter the course of infectious disease, we should be increasingly reluctant to reserve these therapies for the affluent, low-incidence regions of the world where most medical resources are concentrated. Excellence without equity looms as the chief human-rights dilemma of health care in the 21st century.[17]

I too am critical of the gross inequalities in health within countries and between countries, but here I only want to make explicit the framework and discourse of Farmer's critique. His critique appeals to two ideas: that there is a lack of proportion between the medical resources and the burden of disease and that there is a human right to equal access.

What is wrong with the claim that equal access to health care is a human right? First, to claim something as a right is more of a conclusion than an argument. Such claims function more to summarize a position than to further moral discussion. A quick and simple appeal to a comprehensive right avoids all the hard questions about duties and priorities. When faced with grave injustices and huge inequalities, claiming that all human beings have a right to health care is easy. Specifying the kind of care to which people are entitled is harder. Specifying duties is harder yet. And getting those duties institutionalized is hardest of all.

In addition to the general problems with claims about rights, a problem more specific to the issue of illegal immigration exists. Since a claim based on a human right is a claim based on people's common humanity it tends to collapse distinctions between people. Yet for certain purposes, it may be important to make distinctions and emphasize different responsibilities. We may owe different things to, for example, the poor undocumented worker in our country, the middle-class visitor who needs dialysis, the prince who wants a transplant, people enmeshed in the global economy, and the most marginalized people in poor countries.

Rather than claiming an essentially limitless right, it makes more sense to recognize a modest core of human rights and to supplement those rights with a robust account of social responsibility, social justice, and international justice. I do not know if there is a principled way to delineate exactly what should be included in the core of human rights.[18] But even a short list of circumscribed rights would have important consequences if societies took responsibility for trying to protect everyone from violations of these rights. Illegal immigrants are sometimes killed in transport, physically or sexually abused, held as slaves, kept in indentured servitude, forced to work in occupations, and denied personal property. These are clear violations of what should be recognized as human rights. But this core of recognized rights should be supplemented with an account of social justice and responsibility.

A Matter of Social Responsibility

Framing the issue in terms of social responsibility helps to highlight one of the most striking features of illegal immigration: the employment pattern within society. As I noted before, illegal immigrants often perform the worst work for the lowest wages. Illegal immigrants are part of a pattern that is older and deeper than the recent globalization of the economy. Societies have often used the most powerless and marginalized people to do the most disagreeable and difficult work. Societies have used slaves, indentured servants, castes, minorities, orphans, poor children, internal migrants, and foreign migrants. Of course, the pattern is not exactly the same in every society, nor even in every industry within a society, but the similarities are striking.

I see the use of illegal immigrants as the contemporary form of the old pattern. But it is not a natural phenomenon beyond human control. It is the result of laws, norms, institutions, habits, and conditions in society, and of the conditions in the world at large. It is a social construction that we could try to reconstruct.

Some might object that no one forces illegal immigrants to take unsavory jobs and that they can return home if they wish. This objection is too simple. Although most undocumented workers made a voluntary choice to go to another country, they often had inadequate information and dismal alternatives, and voluntary return is not an attractive option when they have substantial debts and poor earning potential at home. More importantly, even a fully informed and voluntary choice does not settle the question of social justice and responsibility. We have gone through this debate before. As the industrial revolution developed, many people agreed to work under horrible conditions in shops, factories, and mines. Yet most societies eventually saw that freedom of contract was a limited part of a larger social ethic. They accepted a responsibility to address conditions of work and to empower workers, at least in basic ways. Decent societies now try to regulate child labor, workplace safety, minimum rates of pay, workers' rights to unionize, background conditions, and much more. But because of their illegal status, undocumented workers are often unable to challenge or report employers who violate even the basic standards of a decent society.

We need to take responsibility for preventing the old pattern from continuing, and the key idea is that of "taking responsibility." It is not the same as legal accountability, which leads one to think about determining causation, proving intention or negligence, examining excuses, apportioning blame, and assigning costs. Taking responsibility is more about seeing patterns and problems, examining background conditions, not passing the buck, and responding in appropriate ways. A society need not bear full causal responsibility in order to assume social responsibility.

Why should society take responsibility for people it tried to keep out of its territory, for people who are not social members? Because in many respects illegal immigrants are social members. Although they are not citizens or legal residents, they may be diligent workers, good neighbors, concerned parents, and active participants in community life. They are workers, involved in complex schemes of social co-operation. Many of the most exploited workers in the industrial revolution—children, women, men without property—were also not full citizens, but they were vulnerable people, doing often undesirable work, for whom society needed to take some responsibility. Undocumented workers' similar role in society is one reason that the social responsibility to care for them is different from the responsibility to care for medical visitors.

If a given society had the ethical conviction and political will, it could develop practical measures to transform the worst aspects of some work, empower the most disadvantaged workers, and shape the background conditions in which the labor market operates. The interests of the worst-off citizens and the interests of illegal immigrants need not be opposed. Practical measures may raise labor costs and increase the price of goods and services, as they should. We should not rely on undocumented workers to keep down prices on everything from strawberries to sex.

I can already hear the objection. "What you propose is a perfect recipe for increasing illegal immigration. All the practical measures that you suggest would encourage more illegal immigration." Whether improving the situation of the worst-off workers will increase illegal immigration is a complex empirical question. The answer probably depends on many factors. But even if transforming the worst work and empowering the worst-off workers leads to an increase in illegal immigration, countries should take those steps. Although we have a right to regulate immigration, considerations of justice constrain the ways we can pursue that aim. A society might also decrease illegal immigration by decriminalizing the killing of illegal immigrants, but no one thinks that would be a reasonable and ethical social policy. Nor do I think that the old pattern of using marginalized people is a reasonable and ethical way to regulate immigration.

I have left out of my account the very point with which I began, namely, health and health care, and I ended up talking about work and social responsibility. Surely work and social responsibility are at the heart of the matter. Where then does health care fit in?

Good health care can, among other things, prevent death and suffering, promote health and well-being, respond to basic needs and vulnerabilities, express care and solidarity, contribute to equality of opportunity, monitor social problems (such as child abuse or pesticide exposure), and accomplish other important aims. But health care is just one means, and not always the most effective means, to these ends. To focus on access to and payment of health care is to focus our ethical concern too narrowly.

I believe that societies that attract illegal immigrants should pursue policies and practices that (1) improve the pay for and conditions of the worst forms of work; (2) structure and organize work so as to give workers more voice, power, and opportunity to develop their capacities; and (3) connect labor to unions, associations, and communities in ways that increase social respect for all workers. I cannot justify these claims in this paper, but I want to note how they are connected to health care. Providing health care for all workers and their families is a very good way to improve the benefit that workers receive for the worst forms of work, to render workers less vulnerable, and to express social and communal respect for them. These are good reasons for providing health care for all workers, documented and undocumented alike. And they express ethical concerns that are not captured by talking about human rights, public health, or the rights of citizens.

The Right Discussion

I have examined the frameworks that are employed in discussions about illegal immigrants and health care. I argued against conceptualizing the issues in terms of desert, professional ethics, or even human rights. Although all of these concepts highlight something important, they tend to be too narrow or too broad. And because they provide the wrong perspective, they fail to focus attention on the crux of the matter.

I have suggested that the issues should be framed in terms of social justice and social responsibility. I realize that I did not fully justify my view, and that other people may give a different account of what social justice requires. But I had a different aim. I did not want to convince everyone of the rectitude of my account, but to shift the discussion into the realm of social justice and responsibility.

Acknowledgements

I would like to thank the following people for their comments and encouragement: Jean Maria Arrigo, Solomon Benarar, Les Chuang, Ruth Macklin, Sara Ruddick, William Ruddick, Mark Wicclair, and Daniel Wikler.

Notes

1. See P. Warshall, "Human Flow," Whole Earth 108 (2002): 39-43.
2. These statistics are taken from the following sources: US Immigration and Naturalization Service, "Illegal Alien Resident Population," available at <http://www.ins.gov/graphics/aboutins/statistics/illegalalien/illegal.pdf>, accessed October 1, 2002; B. Ghosh, *Huddled Masses and Uncertain Shores* (The Hague: Matinus Nijhoff Publishers, 1988); L. Platt, "The Working Caste," *The American Prospect* 13, Part 8 (2001): 32-36.
3. Y. Sumimoto. *An Introduction to Japanese Society* (Cambridge: Cambridge UP, 1997), 187.
4. These statistics are taken from the following sources: L. Platt. "Regulating the Global Brothel," *The American Prospect*, Special Supplement, Summer 2001: 10-14; B. Ghosh. *Huddled Masses and Uncertain Shores*, 27; P. Phongpaichir, "Trafficking in People in Thailand," in *Illegal Immigration and Commercial Sex*, ed. P. Williams (London: Frank Cass, 1999), 89-90.
5. Platt, "Regulating the Global Brothel," 11.
6. This and the following quotations are from the California Ballot Pamphlet, 1994, available at <http://www.holmes.uchastings.edu/cgibin/stardinder/5640/calprop/txt>, accessed September 30. 2002.
7. T.A. Ziv and B. Lo, "Denial of Care to Illegal Immigrants," *NEJM* 332 (1995): 1095-98.
8. Ibid., 1096.
9. Ibid., 1097.
10. Ibid.
11. Ibid., 1096.
12. Ibid.
13. J. Rawls, *The Law of Peoples* (Cambridge, MA: Harvard UP, 1999), 39.
14. Compare Rawls, *The Law of Peoples*, 8.
15. M. Walzer, *Spheres of Justice* (New York: Basic Books, 1983), 39.
16. Ibid.
17. P. Farmer, "The Major Infectious Diseases in the World—To Treat or Not to Treat?" *NEJM* 345 (2001): 208-10.
18. Compare Rawls, *The Law of Peoples*, 79-80.

CHAPTER EIGHT

VIRTUE ETHICS

INTRODUCTION

The central question that concerns modern ethical theorists is "what ought we to do?" The egoist, the divine command theorist, the consequentialist, and the deontologist all propose basic moral principles that are designed to tell us what to do in morally puzzling situations. Imagine that one of these theories, theory X, is much more plausible than the others. Would it then follow that the world's leading expert on theory X is the world's leading moral authority? Would she possess more wisdom than anyone else? Suppose that Dr. Jones is the leading expert on theory X, and that she has published extensively on the structure and implications of this theory. She has a very high IQ and has mastered this theory early in her career. Her success at moral philosophy has gone to her head, and she has become extremely arrogant. Although she always tries to comply with the duties dictated by theory X, she feels bored and impatient with her husband, her children, her friends, and her students. As soon as she has fulfilled her perfect and imperfect duties to them (acting for the sake of duty, of course), she sets them aside and goes back to the project that commands almost all of her attention: achieving even more status and prestige in her profession.

Virtue ethicists believe that something important is missing in modern ethical theories that focus on what we ought to do. They believe that we should be equally concerned, or even centrally concerned, with the question of what character traits we ought to develop in ourselves. Although Dr. Jones may be known as the leading expert on what we ought to *do*, it's obvious that she has devoted very little attention to the question of who she ought to *be* as a person. It seems that something has gone seriously wrong with our approach to ethics if the world's leading moral authority could be a rotten person.

Further, suppose that you are a student of Dr. Jones, you know that she is the world's leading authority on theory X, and you know that theory X is the most plausible theory of obligation that has been developed to date. Suppose also that you are facing a moral dilemma in your personal life. Dr. Jones has offered to work out the solution to any moral dilemma that any of her students may present to her. You could write an abstract description of your dilemma, give it to her, and wait for her to provide the solution in the next class. You could then simply implement the solution she presents. This way, you would not have to struggle with the problem internally, nor would you have to spend much time thinking about it. If the goal is to do the right thing, with the intention of doing the right thing, perhaps this course of action would be your best bet. After all, you are the student and Dr. Jones is the expert. It's more likely that she will find the right solution to the dilemma than you will.

Would you be willing to turn your moral dilemma over to Dr. Jones? Virtue ethicists would argue that you should not. They would hold that it is important for you to forge your own moral character by, among other things, grappling with your own moral dilemmas. If we simply do the right thing according to a "moral expert," or according to the leading theory of obligation, we will miss out on the kind of internal development we need to become wise or virtuous persons. They also hold that there is more to our moral lives than simply following rules. Rules are impersonal. They apply to everyone and set out minimal standards of behaviour. But according to virtue ethicists, a major part of our moral development should consist of establishing our own moral ideals and developing a coherent set of moral commitments that define our own personal characters.

Michael Stocker identifies a paradoxical aspect of modern ethical theories. He argues that these theories necessitate moral schizophrenia. Imagine that you are a proponent of one of these theories and you have decided to give your significant other a beautiful bouquet of flowers for Valentine's Day. She is very touched and says, "Thank you so much. This really means a lot to me." As a good consequentialist, you reply, "Well, I thought this would be the course of action that would maximize preference satisfaction in the community." Or as a good deontologist you answer, "Well this was the maxim that I could will as a universal law of nature." If you want to live a sane and healthy life, if you want to flourish as a human being, you will not seriously make these responses. Nor will you consciously regulate yourself by these moral theories as you develop your personal relationships. Stocker points out that something has gone seriously wrong if we cannot actually allow ourselves to be motivated by the moral theory that supposedly articulates the reasons why we ought to choose one course of action over another.

According to virtue ethicists, these kinds of problems can be avoided if we start not with a set of rules or theories, but by developing worthy character traits in ourselves. This process requires experience, thought, and effort, but it leads to a depth of moral wisdom that cannot be acquired simply by learning a theory or by following a set of abstract rules. With moral wisdom comes the ability to make right decisions in morally puzzling situations and the ability to flourish as a human being—to live a good, sane, healthy life and have meaningful human relationships. If we approach our moral lives in this manner, our character, motivation, emotional responses, and actions will form a coherent package that is informed by the moral wisdom we have acquired.

Virtue ethicists also point out that modern ethical theory is an historical anomaly. Plato and Aristotle were centrally concerned with the development of good character, as were philosophers for several centuries after them. It is only in the past few centuries that we have become preoccupied with constructing abstract moral theories that tell us what we ought to do in any given situation.

Aristotle's *Nichomachean Ethics* is generally considered to be the classic work in virtue ethics, and it provides an example of what a theory of virtue might look like. Structurally, this type of theory is very different from the theories of obligation presented in the previous chapters. Aristotle holds that virtues are those qualities that allow us to achieve a state of *eudaimonia*, or human flourishing. A certain amount of luck and a well-structured political community are also needed to achieve this state. For Aristotle, *eudaimonia* is tied to living rationally, given that rationality sets human beings apart from the other animals. He distinguishes between intellectual virtues and moral virtues. Intellectual virtues enable us to think rationally, whereas moral virtues enable us to handle our desires and emotions rationally. Practical wisdom is an intellectual virtue, but it is needed for the exercise of every moral virtue. To exercise a moral virtue, we must find the mean between the two extremes of defect and excess. For example, courage is the mean between cowardice and rashness, and justice is the mean between suffering injustice and doing injustice. There are no rules or formulas for finding the mean, and we cannot determine where the mean is to be found independent of the circumstances in which it occurs. Judgment is indispensable, and practical wisdom enables us to judge correctly. The other intellectual virtues can be taught, but practical wisdom can only be acquired through experience. We can receive guidance in obtaining the necessary experience from someone who already possesses practical wisdom. The moral virtues are acquired through habitual action and practice. According to Aristotle, the natural outcome of exercising a moral virtue is a right action. If we cultivate the right character traits in ourselves, then we will naturally perform right actions in the situations we encounter. Unlike theories of obligation, then, theories of virtue do not provide us with overarching rules or principles that tell us what we ought to do.

Philosophers have raised some important worries about a virtue-based approach to ethics. We do in fact face many questions about what to do in particular situations, and these questions cannot be avoided. Without a moral theory to fall back on, some of these dilemmas may prove insoluble to us, no matter how well developed are our virtues. For example, suppose that a seventeen-year-old Jehovah's Witness has just been admitted to a hospital and that he will bleed to death without a blood transfusion. He refuses to accept the transfusion because of his religious beliefs. At some point, the hospital personnel must decide whether they will honour his decision or whether they will override his refusal and save his life. It isn't clear that virtue ethics gives us sufficient guidance in these situations. We can say that the hospital personnel involved in the decision should do what a virtuous person (a person of practical wisdom) would do, but what would a virtuous person do in this situation? And how do we identify virtuous persons? It seems that they would be persons who have a consistent disposition to do the right thing, but in this case we would have to know what we ought to do, or what the right thing is to do, before we could identify a virtuous person. Further, it is obviously necessary for us to make broader decisions about public policy. For example, we must decide whether to permit physician-assisted suicide, whether to allow abortion at various stages in a pregnancy, whether to have capital punishment, whether to practice affirmative action in public and private institutions, and so on. The ethical theories presented in the previous chapters provide bases for determining which public policies are morally defensible; it is not clear, however, that we receive sufficient guidance on these matters from virtue ethics. Which public policies are virtuous, or which policies would be endorsed by a person of practical wisdom?

There are two approaches that virtue ethicists can take in responding to these challenges. The first approach is to limit the scope of virtue ethics by saying that the study of character should *supplement* the ethical theories we have previously considered rather than replace them. We need theories of obligation to tell us what to do in particular situations and to help us to determine which public policies are morally defensible. We also need a theory of virtue to guide us in the development of good character. To neglect either of these areas of study is to neglect a centrally important aspect of our moral lives. The second approach is to make the stronger claim that virtue ethics should replace the standard modern approaches to ethical theory, and then to attempt to answer these challenges from within the framework of a theory of virtue. For example, a virtue ethicist could point out that a person of good character might have compassion for the seventeen-year-old Jehovah's Witness, communicate with him honestly, care greatly about his welfare, and at the same time, respect his spirituality. Perhaps an examination of these virtues would ultimately provide clear, practical guidance as to how to handle this situation. Public policy might also be addressed from within the context of a theory of virtue. For example, a virtue ethicist might argue that forgiveness is a virtue, and that a person of good character would attempt to work past her resentment towards criminals to reach a state of genuine forgiveness. At the same time, a person of good character would care deeply about potential victims of crime, and would be moved to try to protect them. Perhaps the public policy that would emerge from considerations of this sort would be to abolish capital punishment and then to mount a serious, systematic program to eradicate the causes of violent crime and prevent violent criminals from regaining unrestrained access to other people.

It remains to be seen if an adequate theory of the virtues can be worked out, and which of these strategies will be more successful. In any case, a careful study of virtue ethics should add an important dimension to our understanding of ethical theory.

21.

SELECTION FROM *NICHOMACHEAN ETHICS*

❧ ❧ ❧

ARISTOTLE

*The Greek philosopher Aristotle (384-322 BC) is considered to be one of the great-
est philosophers of all time. He was a student of Plato's, and the personal tutor
of Alexander the Great. He wrote on a wide range of philosophical and non-
philosophical subjects, including biology, literature, politics, logic, metaphysics,
and ethics. His famous work, the* Nichomachean Ethics, *contains his theory
of the virtues. Aristotle holds that virtues are those qualities that allow us to
achieve a state of eudaimonia, or human flourishing. Since reason is what sets
us apart from the other animals, human flourishing consists in living in accordance with reason. Aristotle distinguishes between intellectual virtues and moral
virtues. Intellectual virtues enable us to think rationally, while moral virtues
enable us to handle our emotions and desires rationally. He then explores the
nature of these virtues and explains how they are acquired.*

Book I

Every art and every inquiry, and similarly every action and pursuit, is thought
to aim at some good; and for this reason the good has rightly been declared
to be that at which all things aim. But a certain difference is found among
ends; some are activities, others are products apart from the activities that
produce them. Where there are ends apart from the actions, it is the nature
of the products to be better than the activities. Now, as there are many
actions, arts, and sciences, their ends also are many; the end of the medical
art is health, that of shipbuilding a vessel, that of strategy victory, that of economics wealth. But where such arts fall under a single capacity—as bridle-
making and the other arts concerned with the equipment of horses fall under
the art of riding, and this and every military action under strategy, in the same
way other arts fall under yet others—in all of these the ends of the master arts
are to be preferred to all the subordinate ends; for it is for the sake of the
former that the latter are pursued. It makes no difference whether the activities themselves are the ends of the actions, or something else apart from the
activities, as in the case of the sciences just mentioned.

If, then, there is some end of the things we do, which we desire for its own
sake (everything else being desired for the sake of this), and if we do not

choose everything for the sake of something else (for at that rate the process would go on to infinity, so that our desire would be empty and vain), clearly this must be the good and the chief good. Will not the knowledge of it, then, have a great influence on life? Shall we not, like archers who have a mark to aim at, be more likely to hit upon what is right? If so, we must try, in outline at least, to determine what it is, and of which of the sciences or capacities it is the object. It would seem to belong to the most authoritative art and that which is most truly the master art. And politics appears to be of this nature; for it is this that ordains which of the sciences should be studied in a state, and which each class of citizens should learn and up to what point they should learn them; and we see even the most highly esteemed of capacities to fall under this, e.g., strategy, economics, rhetoric; now, since politics uses the rest of the sciences, and since, again, it legislates as to what we are to do and what we are to abstain from, the end of this science must include those of the others, so that this end must be the good for man. For even if the end is the same for a single man and for a state, that of the state seems at all events something greater and more complete whether to attain or to preserve; though it is worth while to attain the end merely for one man, it is finer and more godlike to attain it for a nation or for city-states. These, then, are the ends at which our inquiry aims, since it is political science, in one sense of that term.

Our discussion will be adequate if it has as much clearness as the subject-matter admits of, for precision is not to be sought for alike in all discussions, any more than in all the products of the crafts. Now fine and just actions, which political science investigates, admit of much variety and fluctuation of opinion, so that they may be thought to exist only by convention, and not by nature. And goods also give rise to a similar fluctuation because they bring harm to many people; for before now men have been undone by reason of their wealth, and others by reason of their courage. We must be content, then, in speaking of such subjects and with such premises to indicate the truth roughly and in outline, and in speaking about things which are only for the most part true and with premises of the same kind to reach conclusions that are no better. In the same spirit, therefore, should each type of statement be *received*; for it is the mark of an educated man to look for precision in each class of things just so far as the nature of the subject admits; it is evidently equally foolish to accept probable reasoning from a mathematician and to demand from a rhetorician scientific proofs.

Now each man judges well the things he knows, and of these he is a good judge. And so the man who has been educated in a subject is a good judge of that subject, and the man who has received an all-round education is a good judge in general. Hence a young man is not a proper hearer of lectures on political science; for he is inexperienced in the actions that occur in life, but its discussions start from these and are about these; and, further, since he tends to follow his passions, his study will be vain and unprofitable, because the end aimed at is not knowledge but action. And it makes no difference whether he is young in years or youthful in character; the defect does not depend on time, but on his living, and pursuing each successive object, as passion directs. For to such persons, as to the incontinent, knowledge brings no profit; but to those who desire and act in accordance with a rational principle knowledge about such matters will be of great benefit.

These remarks about the student, the sort of treatment to be expected, and the purpose of the inquiry, may be taken as our preface.

Let us resume our inquiry and state, in view of the fact that all knowledge and every pursuit aims at some good, what it is that we say political science aims at and what is the highest of all goods achievable by action. Verbally there is very general agreement; for both the general run of men and people of superior refinement say that it is happiness, and identify living well and doing well with being happy; but with regard to what happiness is they differ, and the many do not give the same account as the wise. For the former think it is some plain and obvious thing, like pleasure, wealth, or honour; they differ, however, from one another—and often even the same man identifies it with different things, with health when he is ill, with wealth when he is poor; but, conscious of their ignorance, they admire those who proclaim some great ideal that is above their comprehension. Now some thought that apart from these many goods there is another which is self-subsistent and causes the goodness of all these as well. To examine all the opinions that have been held were perhaps somewhat fruitless; enough to examine those that are most prevalent or that seem to be arguable....

Let us, however, resume our discussion from the point at which we digressed. To judge from the lives that men lead, most men, and men of the most vulgar type, seem (not without some ground) to identify the good, or happiness, with pleasure; which is the reason why they love the life of enjoyment. For there are, we may say, three prominent types of life—that just mentioned, the political, and thirdly the contemplative life. Now the mass of mankind are evidently quite slavish in their tastes, preferring a life suitable to beasts, but they get some ground for their view from the fact that many of those in high places share the tastes of Sardanapallus. A consideration of the prominent types of life shows that people of superior refinement and of active disposition identify happiness with honour; for this is, roughly speaking, the end of the political life. But it seems too superficial to be what we are looking for, since it is thought to depend on those who bestow honour rather than on him who receives it, but the good we divine to be something proper to a man and not easily taken from him. Further, men seem to pursue honour in order that they may be assured of their goodness; at least it is by men of practical wisdom that they seek to be honoured, and among those who know them, and on the ground of their virtue; clearly, then, according to them, at any rate, virtue is better. And perhaps one might even suppose this to be, rather than honour, the end of the political life. But even this appears somewhat incomplete; for possession of virtue seems actually compatible with being asleep, or with lifelong inactivity, and, further, with the greatest sufferings and misfortunes; but a man who was living so no one would call happy, unless he were maintaining a thesis at all costs. Third comes the contemplative life, which we shall consider later. But enough of this; for the subject has been sufficiently treated even in the current discussions.

The life of money-making is one undertaken under compulsion, and wealth is evidently not the good we are seeking; for it is merely useful and for the sake of something else. And so one might rather take the aforenamed objects to be ends; for they are loved for themselves. But it is evident that not even these are ends; yet many arguments have been thrown away in support of them. Let us leave this subject, then.

Let us again return to the good we are seeking, and ask what it can be. It seems different in different actions and arts; it is different in medicine, in strategy, and in the other arts likewise. What then is the good of each? Surely that for whose sake everything else is done. In medicine this is health, in strategy victory, in architecture a house, in any other sphere something else, and in every action and pursuit the end; for it is for the sake of this that all men do whatever else they do. Therefore, if there is an end for all that we do, this will be the good achievable by action, and if there are more than one, these will be the goods achievable by action. So the argument has by a different course reached the same point; but we must try to state this even more clearly. Since there are evidently more than one end, and we choose some of these (e.g., wealth, flutes, and in general instruments) for the sake of something else, clearly not all ends are final ends; but the chief good is evidently something final. Therefore, if there is only one final end, this will be what we are seeking, and if there are more than one, the most final of these will be what we are seeking. Now we call that which is in itself worthy of pursuit more final than that which is worthy of pursuit for the sake of something else, and that which is never desirable for the sake of something else more final than the things that are desirable both in themselves and for the sake of that other thing, and therefore we call final without qualification that which is always desirable in itself and never for the sake of something else.

Now such a thing happiness, above all else, is held to be; for this we choose always for itself and never for the sake of something else but honour, pleasure, reason, and every virtue we choose indeed for themselves (for if nothing resulted from them we should still choose each of them), but we choose them also for the sake of happiness, judging that by means of them we shall be happy. Happiness, on the other hand, no one chooses for the sake of these, nor, in general, for anything other than itself.

From the point of view of self-sufficiency the same result seems to follow; for the final good is thought to be self-sufficient. Now by self-sufficient we do not mean that which is sufficient for a man by himself, for one who lives a solitary life, but also for parents, children, wife, and in general for his friends and fellow citizens, since man is born for citizenship. But some limit must be set to this; for if we extend our requirement to ancestors and descendants and friends' friends we are in for an infinite series. Let us examine this question, however, on another occasion; the self-sufficient we now define as that which when isolated makes life desirable and lacking in nothing; and such we think happiness to be; and further we think it most desirable of all things, without being counted as one good thing among others—if it were so counted it would clearly be made more desirable by the addition of even the least of goods; for that which is added becomes an excess of goods, and of goods the greater is always more desirable. Happiness, then, is something final and self-sufficient, and is the end of action.

Presumably, however, to say that happiness is the chief good seems a platitude, and a clearer account of what it is is still desired. This might perhaps be given, if we could first ascertain the function of man. For just as for a flute-player, a sculptor, or any artist, and, in general, for all things that have a function or activity, the good and the "well" is thought to reside in the function, so would it seem to be for man, if he has a function. Have the carpenter, then, and the tanner certain functions or activities, and has man none? Is he born without a function? Or as eye, hand, foot, and in general each of the parts evidently has a function, may one lay it down that man similarly has a function apart from all these? What then can this be? Life seems to be common even to plants, but we are seeking what is peculiar to man. Let us exclude, therefore, the life of nutrition and growth. Next there would be a life of perception, but it also seems to be common even to the horse, the ox, and every animal. There remains, then, an active life of the element that has a rational principle; of this, one part has such a principle in the sense of being obedient to one, the other in the sense of possessing one and exercising thought. And, as "life of the rational element" also has two meanings, we must state that life in the sense of activity is what we mean; for this seems to be the more proper sense of the term. Now if the function of man is an activity of soul which follows or implies a rational principle, and if we say "a so-and-so" and "a good so-and-so" have a function which is the same in kind, e.g., a lyre-player and a good lyre-player, and so without qualification in all cases, eminence in respect of goodness being added to the name of the function (for the function of a lyre-player is to play the lyre, and that of a good lyre-player is to do so well): if this is the case, [and we state the function of man to be a certain kind of life, and this to be an activity or actions of the soul implying a rational principle, and the function of a good man to be the good and noble performance of these, and if any action is well performed when it is performed in accordance with the appropriate excellence: if this is the case,] human good turns out to be activity of soul in accordance with virtue, and if there are more than one virtue, in accordance with the best and most complete.

But we must add "in a complete life." For one swallow does not make a summer, nor does one day; and so too one day, or a short time, does not make a man blessed and happy....

We must consider it, however, in the light not only of our conclusion and our premisses, but also of what is commonly said about it; for with a true view all the data harmonize, but with a false one the facts soon clash. Now goods have been divided into three classes, and some are described as external, others as relating to soul or to body; we call those that relate to soul most properly and truly goods, and psychical actions and activities we class as relating to soul. Therefore our account must be sound, at least according to this view, which is an old one and agreed on by philosophers. It is correct also in that we identify the end with certain actions and activities; for thus it falls among goods of the soul and not among external goods. Another belief which harmonizes with our account is that the happy man lives well and does well; for we have practically defined happiness as a sort of good life and good action. The characteristics that are looked for in happiness seem also, all of them, to belong to what we have defined happiness as being. For some identify happiness with virtue, some with practical wisdom, others with a kind of philosophic wisdom, others with these, or one of these, accompanied by pleasure or not without pleasure; while others include also external prosperity. Now some of these views have been held by many men and men of old, others by a few eminent persons; and it is not probable that either of these should be entirely mistaken, but rather that they should be right in at least some one respect or even in most respects.

With those who identify happiness with virtue or some one virtue our account is in harmony; for to virtue belongs virtuous activity. But it makes, perhaps, no small difference whether we place the chief good in possession or in use, in state of mind or in activity. For the state of mind may exist without producing any good result, as in a man who is asleep or in some other way quite inactive, but the activity cannot; for one who has the activity will of necessity be acting, and acting well. And as in the Olympic Games it is not the most beautiful and the strongest that are crowned but those who compete (for it is some of these that are victorious), so those who act win, and rightly win, the noble and good things in life.

Their life is also in itself pleasant. For pleasure is a state of *soul*, and to each man that which he is said to be a lover of is pleasant; e.g., not only is a horse pleasant to the lover of horses, and a spectacle to the lover of sights, but also in the same way just acts are pleasant to the lover of justice and in general virtuous acts to the lover of virtue. Now for most men their pleasures are in conflict with one another because these are not by nature pleasant, but the lovers of what is noble find pleasant the things that are by nature pleasant; and virtuous actions are such, so that these are pleasant for such men as well as in their own nature. Their life, therefore, has no further need of pleasure as a sort of adventitious charm, but has its pleasure in itself. For, besides what we have said, the man who does not rejoice in noble actions is not even good; since no one would call a man just who did not enjoy acting justly, nor any man liberal who did not enjoy liberal actions; and similarly in all other cases. If this is so, virtuous actions must be in themselves pleasant. But they are also *good* and *noble*, and have each of these attributes in the highest degree, since the good man judges well about these attributes; his judgement is such as we have described. Happiness then is the best, noblest, and most pleasant thing in the world, and these attributes are not severed as in the inscription at Delos—

Most noble is that which is justest, and best is health;
But pleasantest is it to win what we love.

For all these properties belong to the best activities; and these, or one—the best—of these, we identify with happiness.

Yet evidently, as we said, it needs the external goods as well; for it is impossible, or not easy, to do noble acts without the proper equipment. In many actions we use friends and riches and political power as instruments; and there are some things the lack of which takes the lustre from happiness, as good birth, goodly children, beauty; for the man who is very ugly in appearance or ill-born or solitary and childless is not very likely to be happy, and perhaps a man would be still less likely if he had thoroughly bad children or friends or had lost good children or friends by death. As we said, then, happiness seems to need this sort of prosperity in addition; for which reason some identify happiness with good fortune, though others identify it with virtue.

Since happiness is an activity of soul in accordance with perfect virtue, we must consider the nature of virtue; for perhaps we shall thus see better the nature of happiness. The true student of politics, too, is thought to have studied virtue above all things; for he wishes to make his fellow citizens good and obedient to the laws. As an example of this we have the lawgivers of the Cretans and the Spartans, and any others of the kind that there may have been. And if this inquiry belongs to political science, clearly the pursuit of it will be in accordance with our original plan. But clearly the virtue we must study is human virtue; for the good we were seeking was human good and the happiness human happiness. By human virtue we mean not that of the body but that of the soul; and happiness also we call an activity of soul. But if this is so, clearly the student of politics must know somehow the facts about soul, as the man who is to heal the eyes or the body as a whole must know about the eyes or the body; and all the more since politics is more prized and better than medicine; but even among doctors the best educated spend much labour on acquiring knowledge of the body. The student of politics, then, must study the soul, and must study it with these objects in view, and do so just to the extent which is sufficient for the questions we are discussing; for further precision is perhaps something more laborious than our purposes require.

Some things are said about it, adequately enough, even in the discussions outside our school, and we must use these; e.g., that one element in the soul is irrational and one has a rational principle. Whether these are separated as the parts of the body or of anything divisible are, or are distinct by definition but by nature inseparable, like convex and concave in the circumference of a circle, does not affect the present question.

Of the irrational element one division seems to be widely distributed, and vegetative in its nature, I mean that which causes nutrition and growth; for it is this kind of power of the soul that one must assign to all nurslings and to embryos, and this same power to full-grown creatures; this is more reasonable than to assign some different power to them. Now the excellence of this seems to be common to all species and not specifically human; for this part or faculty seems to function most in sleep, while goodness and badness are least manifest in sleep (whence comes the saying that the happy are no better off than the wretched for half their lives; and this happens naturally enough, since sleep is an inactivity of the soul in that respect in which it is called good or bad), unless perhaps to a small extent some of the movements actually penetrate to the soul, and in this respect the dreams of good men are better than those of ordinary people. Enough of this subject, however; let us leave the nutritive faculty, alone, since it has by its nature no share in human excellence.

There seems to be also another irrational element in the soul—one which in a sense, however, shares in a rational principle. For we praise the rational principle of the continent man and of the incontinent, and the part of their soul that has such a principle, since it urges them aright and towards the best objects; but there is found in them also another element naturally opposed to the rational principle, which fights against and resists that principle. For exactly as paralysed limbs when we intend to move them to the right turn on the contrary to the left, so is it with the soul; the impulses of incontinent people move in contrary directions. But while in the body we see that which moves astray, in the soul we do not. No doubt, however, we must none the less suppose that in the soul too there is something contrary to the rational principle, resisting and opposing it. In what sense it is distinct from the other elements does not concern us. Now even this seems to have a share in a rational principle, as we said; at any rate in the continent man it obeys the rational principle—and presumably in the temperate and brave man it is still more obedient; for in him it speaks, on all matters, with the same voice as the rational principle.

Therefore the irrational element also appears to be twofold. For the vegetative element in no way shares in a rational principle, but the appetitive and in general the desiring element in a sense shares in it, in so far as it listens to and obeys it; this is the sense in which we speak of "taking account" of one's father or one's friends, not that in which we speak of "accounting" for a mathematical property. That the irrational element is in some sense persuaded by a rational principle is indicated also by the giving of advice and by all reproof and exhortation. And if this element also must be said to have a rational principle, that which has a rational principle (as well as that which has not) will be twofold, one subdivision having it in the strict sense and in itself, and the other having a tendency to obey as one does one's father.

Virtue too is distinguished into kinds in accordance with this difference; for we say that some of the virtues are intellectual and others moral, philosophic wisdom and understanding and practical wisdom being intellectual, liberality and temperance moral. For in speaking about a man's character we do not say that he is wise or has understanding but that he is good-tempered or temperate; yet we praise the wise man also with respect to his state of mind; and of states of mind we call those which merit praise virtues.

Book II

Virtue, then, being of two kinds, intellectual and moral, intellectual virtue in the main owes both its birth and its growth to teaching (for which reason it requires experience and time), while moral virtue comes about as a result of habit.... From this it is also plain that none of the moral virtues arises in us by nature; for nothing that exists by nature can form a habit contrary to its nature. For instance the stone which by nature moves downwards cannot be habituated to move upwards, not even if one tries to train it by throwing it up ten thousand times; nor can fire be habituated to move downwards, nor can anything else that by nature behaves in one way be trained to behave in another. Neither by nature, then, nor contrary to nature do the virtues arise in us; rather we are adapted by nature to receive them, and are made perfect by habit.

Again, of all the things that come to us by nature we first acquire the potentiality and later exhibit the activity (this is plain in the case of the senses; for it was not by often seeing or often hearing that we got these senses, but on the contrary we had them before we used them, and did not come to have them by using them); but the virtues we get by first exercising them, as also happens in the case of the arts as well. For the things we have to learn before we can do them, we learn by doing them, e.g., men become builders by building and lyre-players by playing the lyre; so too we become just by doing just acts, temperate by doing temperate acts, brave by doing brave acts.

This is confirmed by what happens in states; for legislators make the citizens good by forming habits in them, and this is the wish of every legislator, and those who do not effect it miss their mark, and it is in this that a good constitution differs from a bad one.

Again, it is from the same causes and by the same means that every virtue is both produced and destroyed, and similarly every art; for it is from playing the lyre that both good and bad lyre-players are produced. And the corresponding statement is true of builders and of all the rest; men will be good or bad builders as a result of building well or badly. For if this were not so, there would have been no need of a teacher, but all men would have been born good or bad at their craft. This, then, is the case with the virtues also; by doing the acts that we do in our transactions with other men we become just or unjust, and by doing the acts that we do in the presence of danger, and being habituated to feel fear or confidence, we become brave or cowardly. The same is true of appetites and feelings of anger; some men become temperate and good-tempered, others self-indulgent and irascible, by behaving in one way or the other in the appropriate circumstances. Thus, in one word, states of character arise out of like activities. This is why the activities we exhibit must be of a certain kind; it is because the states of character correspond to the differences between these. It makes no small difference, then, whether we form habits of one kind or of another from our very youth; it makes a very great difference, or rather *all* the difference....

Again, the case of the arts and that of the virtues are not similar; for the products of the arts have their goodness in themselves, so that it is enough that they should have a certain character, but if the acts that are in accordance with the virtues have themselves a certain character it does not follow that they are done justly or temperately. The agent also must be in a certain condition when he does them; in the first place he must have knowledge, secondly he must choose the acts, and choose them for their own sakes, and thirdly his action must proceed from a firm and unchangeable character. These are not reckoned in as conditions of the possession of the arts, except the bare knowledge; but as a condition on the possession of the virtues knowledge has little or no weight, while the other conditions count not for a little but for everything, i.e., the very conditions which result from often doing just and temperate acts.

Actions, then, are called just and temperate when they are such as the just or the temperate man would do; but it is not the man who does these that is just and temperate, but the man who also does them as just and temperate men do them. It is well said, then, that it is by doing just acts that the just man is produced, and by doing temperate acts the temperate man; without doing these no one would have even a prospect of becoming good.

But most people do not do these, but take refuge in theory and think they are being philosophers and will become good in this way, behaving somewhat like patients who listen attentively to their doctors, but do none of the things they are ordered to do. As the latter will not be made well in body by such a course of treatment, the former will not be made well in soul by such a course of philosophy....

We must, however, not only describe virtue as a state of character, but also say what sort of state it is. We may remark, then, that every virtue or excellence both brings into good condition the thing of which it is the excellence and makes the work of that thing be done well; e.g., the excellence of the eye makes both the eye and its work good; for it is by the excellence of the eye that we see well. Similarly the excellence of the horse makes a horse both good in itself and good at running and at carrying its rider and at awaiting the attack of the enemy. Therefore, if this is true in every case, the virtue of man also will be the state of character which makes a man good and which makes him do his own work well.

How this is to happen we have stated already, but it will be made plain also by the following consideration of the specific nature of virtue. In everything that is continuous and divisible it is possible to take more, less, or an equal amount, and that either in terms of the thing itself or relatively to us; and the equal is an intermediate between excess and defect. By the intermediate in the object I mean that which is equidistant from each of the extremes, which is one and the same for all men; by the intermediate relatively to us that which is neither too much nor too little—and this is not one, nor the same for all. For instance, if ten is many and two is few, six is the intermediate, taken in terms of the object; for it exceeds and is exceeded by an equal amount; this is intermediate according to arithmetical proportion. But the intermediate relatively to us is not to be taken so; if ten pounds are too much for a particular person to eat and two too little, it does not follow that the trainer will order six pounds; for this also is perhaps too much for the person who is to take it, or too little—too little for Milo, too much for the beginner in athletic exercises. The same is true of running and wrestling. Thus a master of any art avoids excess and defect, but seeks the intermediate and chooses this—the intermediate not in the object but relatively to us.

If it is thus, then, that every art does its work well—by looking to the intermediate and judging its works by this standard (so that we often say of good works of art that it is not possible either to take away or to add anything, implying that excess and defect destroy the goodness of works of art, while the mean preserves it; and good artists, as we say, look to this in their work), and if, further, virtue is more exact and better than any art, as nature also is, then virtue must have the quality of aiming at the intermediate. I mean moral virtue; for it is this that is concerned with passions and actions, and in these there is excess, defect, and the intermediate. For instance, both fear and confidence and appetite and anger and pity and in general pleasure and pain may be felt both too much and too little, and in both cases not well; but to feel them at the right times, with reference to the right objects, towards the right people, with the right motive, and in the right way, is what is both intermediate and best, and this is characteristic of virtue. Similarly with regard to actions also there is excess, defect, and the intermediate. Now virtue is concerned with passions and actions, in which excess is a form of failure, and so is defect, while the intermediate is praised and is a form of success; and being praised and being successful are both characteristic of virtue. Therefore virtue is a kind of mean, since, as we have seen, it aims at what is intermediate.

Again, it is possible to fail in many ways (for evil belongs to the class of the unlimited, as the Pythagoreans conjectured, and good to that of the limited), while to succeed is possible only in one way (for which reason also one is easy and the other difficult—to miss the mark easy, to hit it difficult); for these reasons also, then, excess and defect are characteristic of vice, and the mean of virtue;

For men are good in but one way, but bad in many.

Virtue, then, is a state of character concerned with choice, lying in a mean, i.e., the mean relative to us, this being determined by a rational principle, and by that principle by which the man of practical wisdom would determine it. Now it is a mean between two vices, that which depends on excess and that which depends on defect; and again it is a mean because the vices respectively fall short of or exceed what is right in both passions and actions, while virtue both finds and chooses that which is intermediate. Hence in respect of its substance and the definition which states its essence virtue is a mean, with regard to what is best and right an extreme.

But not every action nor every passion admits of a mean; for some have names that already imply badness, e.g., spite, shamelessness, envy, and in the case of actions adultery, theft, murder; for all of these and suchlike things imply by their names that they are themselves bad, and not the excesses or deficiencies of them. It is not possible, then, ever to be right with regard to them; one must always be wrong. Nor does goodness or badness with regard to such things depend on committing adultery with the right woman, at the right time, and in the right way, but simply to do any of them is to go wrong. It would be equally absurd, then, to expect that in unjust, cowardly, and voluptuous action there should be a mean, an excess, and a deficiency; for at that rate there would be a mean of excess and of deficiency, an excess of excess, and a deficiency of deficiency. But as there is no excess and deficiency of temperance and courage because what is intermediate is in a sense an extreme, so too of the actions we have mentioned there is no mean nor any excess and deficiency, but however they are done they are wrong; for in general there is neither a mean of excess and deficiency, nor excess and deficiency of a mean.

We must, however, not only make this general statement, but also apply it to the individual facts. For among statements about conduct those which are general apply more widely, but those which are particular are more genuine, since conduct has to do with individual cases, and our statements must harmonize with the facts in these cases. We may take these cases from our table. With regard to feelings of fear and confidence courage is the mean; of the people who exceed, he who exceeds in fearlessness has no name (many of the states have no name), while the man who exceeds in confidence is rash, and he who exceeds in fear and falls short in confidence is a coward. With regard to pleasures and pains—not all of them, and not so much with regard to the pains—the mean is temperance, the excess self-indulgence. Persons deficient with regard to the pleasures are not often found; hence such persons also have received no name. But let us call them "insensible."

With regard to giving and taking of money the mean is liberality, the excess and the defect prodigality and meanness. In these actions people exceed and fall short in contrary ways; the prodigal exceeds in spending and falls short in taking, while the mean man exceeds in taking and falls short in spending.... With regard to money there are also other dispositions—a mean, magnificence (for the magnificent man differs from the liberal man; the former deals with large sums, the latter with small ones), an excess, tastelessness and vulgarity, and a deficiency, niggardliness; these differ from the states opposed to liberality....

That moral virtue is a mean, then, and in what sense it is so, and that it is a mean between two vices, the one involving excess, the other deficiency, and that it is such because its character is to aim at what is intermediate in passions and in actions, has been sufficiently stated. Hence also it is no easy task to be good. For in everything it is no easy task to find the middle, e.g., to find the middle of a circle is not for every one but for him who knows; so, too, any one can get angry—that is easy—or to give or spend money; but to do this to the right person, to the right extent, at the right time, with the right motive, and in the right way, *that* is not for every one, nor is it easy; wherefore goodness is both rare and laudable and noble.

Hence he who aims at the intermediate must first depart from what is the more contrary to it, as Calypso advises—

Hold the ship out beyond that surf and spray.

For of the extremes one is more erroneous, one less so; therefore, since to hit the mean is hard in the extreme, we must as a second best, as people say, take the least of the evils; and this will be done best in the way we describe.

But we must consider the things towards which we ourselves also are easi-ly carried away; for some of us tend to one thing, some to another; and this will be recognizable from the pleasure and the pain we feel. We must drag ourselves away to the contrary extreme; for we shall get into the intermediate state by drawing well away from error, as people do in straightening sticks that are bent.

Now in everything the pleasant or pleasure is most to be guarded against; for we do not judge it impartially. We ought, then, to feel towards pleasure as the elders of the people felt towards Helen, and in all circumstances repeat their saying; for if we dismiss pleasure thus we are less likely to go astray. It is by doing this, then, (to sum the matter up) that we shall best be able to hit the mean.

But this is no doubt difficult, and especially in individual cases; for it is not easy to determine both how and with whom and on what provocation and how long one should be angry; for we too sometimes praise those who fall short and call them good-tempered, but sometimes we praise those who get angry and call them manly. The man, however, who deviates little from good-ness is not blamed, whether he do so in the direction of the more or of the less, but only the man who deviates more widely; for *he* does not fail to be noticed. But up to what point and to what extent a man must deviate before he becomes blameworthy it is not easy to determine by reasoning, any more than anything else that is perceived by the senses; such things depend on par-ticular facts, and the decision rests with perception. So much, then, is plain, that the intermediate state is in all things to be praised, but that we must incline sometimes towards the excess, sometimes towards the deficiency; for so shall we most easily hit the mean and what is right.

Book X

If happiness is activity in accordance with virtue, it is reasonable that it should be in accordance with the highest virtue; and this will be that of the best thing in us. Whether it be reason or something else that is this element which is thought to be our natural ruler and guide and to take thought of things noble and divine, whether it be itself also divine or only the most divine ele-ment in us, the activity of this in accordance with its proper virtue will be per-fect happiness. That this activity is contemplative we have already said.

Now this would seem to be in agreement both with what we said before and with the truth. For, firstly, this activity is the best (since not only is reason the best thing in us, but the objects of reason are the best of knowable objects); and, secondly, it is the most continuous, since we can contemplate truth more continuously than we can *do* anything. And we think happiness has pleasure mingled with it, but the activity of philosophic wisdom is admittedly the pleasantest of virtuous activities; at all events the pursuit of it is thought to offer pleasures marvelous for their purity and their enduringness, and it is to be expected that those who know will pass their time more pleasantly than those who inquire. And the self-sufficiency that is spoken of must belong most to the contemplative activity. For while a philosopher, as well as a just man or one possessing any other virtue, needs the necessaries of life, when they are sufficiently equipped with things of that sort the just man needs people towards whom and with whom he shall act justly, and the temperate man, the brave man, and each of the others is in the same case, but the philosopher, even when by himself, can contemplate truth, and the better the wiser he is; he can perhaps do so better if he has fellow-workers, but still he is the most self-sufficient. And this activity alone would seem to be loved for its own sake; for nothing arises from it apart from the contemplating, while from practical activities we gain more or less apart from the action. And happiness is thought to depend on leisure; for we are busy that we may have leisure, and make war that we may live in peace. Now the activity of the practical virtues is exhibited in political or military affairs, but the actions concerned with these seem to be unleisurely. Warlike actions are completely so (for no one chooses to be at war, or provokes war, for the sake of being at war; any one would seem absolutely murderous if he were to make enemies of his friends in order to bring about battle and slaughter); but the action of the statesman is also unleisurely, and—apart from the political action itself—aims at despotic power and honours, or at all events happiness, for him and his fellow citizens—a happiness different from political action, and evidently sought as being different. So if among virtuous actions political and military actions are distinguished by nobility and greatness, and these are unleisurely and aim at an end and are not desirable for their own sake, but the activity of reason, which is contemplative, seems both to be superior in serious worth and to aim at no end beyond itself, and to have its pleasure proper to itself (and this augments the activity), and the self-sufficiency, leisureliness, unweariedness (so far as this is possible for man), and all the other attributes ascribed to the supremely happy man are evidently those connected with this activity, it follows that this will be the complete happiness of man, if it be allowed a complete term of life (for none of the attributes of happiness is *in*complete).

But such a life would be too high for man; for it is not in so far as he is man that he will live so, but in so far as something divine is present in him; and by so much as this is superior to our composite nature is its activity superior to that which is the exercise of the other kind of virtue. If reason is divine, then, in comparison with man, the life according to it is divine in comparison with human life. But we must not follow those who advise us, being men, to think of human things, and, being mortal, of mortal things, but must, so far as we can, make ourselves immortal, and strain every nerve to live in accordance with the best thing in us; for even if it be small in bulk, much more does it in power and worth surpass everything. This would seem, too, to be each man himself, since it is the authoritative and better part of him. It would be strange, then, if he were to choose not the life of his self but that of something else.... [T]hat which is proper to each thing is by nature best and most pleasant for each thing; for man, therefore, the life according to reason is best and pleasantest, since reason more than anything else *is* man. This life therefore is also the happiest.

But in a secondary degree the life in accordance with the other kind of virtue is happy; for the activities in accordance with this befit our human estate. Just and brave acts, and other virtuous acts, we do in relation to each other, observing our respective duties with regard to contracts and services and all manner of actions and with regard to passions; and all of these seem to be typically human. Some of them seem even to arise from the body, and virtue of character to be in many ways bound up with the passions. Practical wisdom, too, is linked to virtue of character, and this to practical wisdom, since the principles of practical wisdom are in accordance with the moral virtues and rightness in morals is in accordance with practical wisdom. Being connected with the passions also, the moral virtues must belong to our composite nature; and the virtues of our composite nature are human; so, therefore, are the life and the happiness which correspond to these. The excellence of the reason is a thing apart; we must be content to say this much about it, for to describe it precisely is a task greater than our purpose requires. It would seem, however, also to need external equipment but little, or less than moral virtue does. Grant that both need the necessaries, and do so equally, even if the statesman's work is the more concerned with the body and things of that sort; for there will be little difference there; but in what they need for the exercise of their activities there will be much difference. The liberal man will need money for the doing of his liberal deeds, and the just man too will need it for the returning of services (for wishes are hard to discern, and even people who are not just pretend to wish to act justly); and the brave man will need power if he is to accomplish any of the acts that correspond to his virtue, and the temperate man will need opportunity; for how else is either he or any of the others to be recognized? It is debated, too, whether the will or the deed is more essential to virtue, which is assumed to involve both; it is surely clear that its perfection involves both; but for deeds many things are needed, and more, the greater and nobler the deeds are. But the man who is contemplating the truth needs no such thing, at least with a view to the exercise of his activity; indeed they are, one may say, even hindrances, at all events to his contemplation; but in so far as he is a man and lives with a number of people, he chooses to do virtuous acts; he will therefore need such aids to living a human life.

But that perfect happiness is a contemplative activity will appear from the following consideration as well. We assume the gods to be above all other beings blessed and happy; but what sort of actions must we assign to them? Acts of justice? Will not the gods seem absurd if they make contracts and return deposits, and so on? Acts of a brave man, then, confronting dangers and running risks because it is noble to do so? Or liberal acts? To whom will they give? It will be strange if they are really to have money or anything of the kind. And what would their temperate acts be? Is not such praise tasteless, since they have no bad appetites? If we were to run through them all, the circumstances of action would be found trivial and unworthy of gods. Still, every one supposes that they live and therefore that they are active; we cannot suppose them to sleep like Endymion. Now if you take away from a living being action, and still more production, what is left but contemplation? Therefore the activity of God, which surpasses all others in blessedness, must be contemplative; and of human activities, therefore, that which is most akin to this must be most of the nature of happiness.

This is indicated, too, by the fact that the other animals have no share in happiness, being completely deprived of such activity. For while the whole life of the gods is blessed, and that of men too in so far as some likeness of such activity belongs to them, none of the other animals is happy, since they in no way share in contemplation. Happiness extends, then, just so far as contemplation does, and those to whom contemplation more fully belongs are more truly happy, not as a mere concomitant but in virtue of the contemplation; for this is in itself precious. Happiness, therefore, must be some form of contemplation.

But, being a man, one will also need external prosperity; for our nature is not self-sufficient for the purpose of contemplation, but our body also must be healthy and must have food and other attention. Still, we must not think that the man who is to be happy will need many things or great things, merely because he cannot be supremely happy without external goods; for self-sufficiency and action do not involve excess, and we can do noble acts without ruling earth and sea; for even with moderate advantages one can act virtuously (this is manifest enough; for private persons are thought to do worthy acts no less than despots—indeed even more); and it is enough that we should have so much as that; for the life of the man who is active in accordance with virtue will be happy. Solon, too, was perhaps sketching well the happy man when he described him as moderately furnished with externals but as having done (as Solon thought) the noblest acts, and lived temperately; for one can with but moderate possessions do what one ought. Anaxagoras also seems to have supposed the happy man not to be rich nor a despot, when he said that he would not be surprised if the happy man were to seem to most people a strange person; for they judge by externals, since these are all they perceive. The opinions of the wise seem, then, to harmonize with our arguments. But while even such things carry some conviction, the truth in practical matters is discerned from the facts of life; for these are the decisive factor. We must therefore survey what we have already said, bringing it to the test of the facts of life, and if it harmonizes with the facts we must accept it, but if it clashes with them we must suppose it to be mere theory. Now he who exercises his reason and cultivates it seems to be both in the best state of mind and most dear to the gods. For if the gods have any care for human affairs, as they are thought to have, it would be reasonable both that they should delight in that which was best and most akin to them (i.e., reason) and that they should reward those who love and honour this most, as caring for the things that are dear to them and acting both rightly and nobly. And that all these attributes belong most of all to the philosopher is manifest. He, therefore, is the dearest to the gods. And he who is that will presumably be also the happiest; so that in this way too the philosopher will more than any other be happy.

22

ON SOME VICES OF VIRTUE ETHICS

⁂ ⁂ ⁂

ROBERT B. LOUDEN

Robert Louden is a professor of philosophy at the University of Southern Maine who specializes in ethics and the history of philosophy. In the following article he examines some of the differences between virtue ethics and consequentialist and deontological ethical theories. Virtue ethics shifts the focus from rules and actions to character traits, and Louden points out that some problems will arise for virtue ethicists as a result of this shift. According to Louden, virtue ethics alone cannot give a full account of morality, but neither can an ethical theory that is focused exclusively on rules and actions. A full account of our moral reasoning requires an analysis of both character and obligation.

It is common knowledge by now that recent philosophical and theological writing about ethics reveals a marked revival of interest in the virtues. But what exactly are the distinctive features of a so-called virtue ethics? Does it have a special contribution to make to our understanding of moral experience? Is there a price to be paid for its different perspective, and if so, is the price worth paying?

Contemporary textbook typologies of ethics still tend to divide the terrain of normative ethical theory into the teleological and deontological. Both types of theory, despite their well-defined differences, have a common focus on acts as opposed to qualities of agents. The fundamental question that both types of theory are designed to answer is: What ought I to do? What is the correct analysis and resolution of morally problematic situations? A second feature shared by teleological and deontological theories is conceptual reductionism. Both types of theory start with a primary irreducible element and then proceed to introduce secondary derivative concepts which are defined in terms of their relations to the beginning element. Modern teleologists (the majority of whom are utilitarians) begin with a concept of the good—here defined with reference to states of affairs rather than persons. After this criterion of the good is established, the remaining ethical categories are defined in terms of this starting-point. Thus, according to the classic maxim, one ought always to promote the greatest good for the greatest number. Duty, in other words, is defined in terms of the element of ends—one ought always to maximize utility. The concepts of virtue and rights are also treated as derivative categories of secondary importance, definable in terms of utility. For the classic utilitarian, a right is upheld "so long as it is upon the whole advantageous to the society that it should be maintained," while virtue is construed as a "tendency to give a net increase to the aggregate quantity of happiness in all its shapes taken together."[1]

For the deontologist, on the other hand, the concept of duty is the irreducible starting-point, and any attempt to define this root notion of being morally bound to do something in terms of the good to be achieved is rejected from the start. The deontologist is committed to the notion that certain acts are simply inherently right. Here the notion of the good is only a derivative category, definable in terms of the right. The good that we are to promote is right action for its own sake—duty for duty's sake. Similarly, the virtues tend to be defined in terms of pro-attitudes towards one's duties. Virtue is important, but only because it helps us do our duty.

But what about virtue ethics? What are the hallmarks of this approach to normative ethics? One problem confronting anyone who sets out to analyze the new virtue ethics in any detail is that we presently lack fully developed examples of it in the contemporary literature. Most of the work done in this genre has a negative rather than positive thrust—its primary aim is more to criticize the traditions and research programs to which it is opposed rather than to state positively and precisely what its own alternative is. A second hindrance is that the literature often has a somewhat misty antiquarian air. It is frequently said, for instance, that the Greeks advocated a virtue ethics, though what precisely it is that they were advocating is not always spelled out. In describing contemporary virtue ethics, it is therefore necessary, in my opinion, to do some detective work concerning its conceptual shape, making inferences based on the unfortunately small number of remarks that are available.

For purposes of illustration, I propose briefly to examine and expand on some key remarks made by two contemporary philosophers—Elizabeth Anscombe and Philippa Foot—whose names have often been associated with the revival of virtue movement. Anscombe, in her frequently cited article "Modern Moral Philosophy," writes: "you can do ethics without it [viz., the notion of 'obligation' or 'morally ought'], as is shown by the example of Aristotle. It would be a great improvement if, instead of 'morally wrong,' one always named a genus such as 'untruthful,' 'unchaste,' 'unjust.'"[2] Here we find an early rallying cry for an ethics of virtue program, to be based on contemporary efforts in philosophical psychology and action theory. On the Anscombe model, strong, irreducible duty and obligation notions drop out of the picture, and are to be replaced by vices such as unchasteness and untruthfulness. But are we to take the assertion literally, and actually attempt to do moral theory without any concept of duty whatsoever? On my reading, Anscombe is not really proposing that we entirely dispose of moral oughts.

Suppose one follows her advice, and replaces "morally wrong" with "untruthful," "unchaste," etc. Isn't this merely shorthand for saying that agents *ought* to be truthful and chaste, and that untruthful and unchaste acts are *morally wrong* because good agents don't perform such acts? The concept of the moral ought, in other words, seems now to be explicated in terms of what the good person would do.[3]

A similar strategy is at work in some of Foot's articles. In the Introduction to her recent collection of essays, *Virtues and Vices and Other Essays in Moral Philosophy*, she announces that one of the two major themes running throughout her work is "the thought that a sound moral philosophy should start from a theory of virtues and vices."[4] When this thought is considered in conjunction with the central argument in her article "Morality as a System of Hypothetical Imperatives," the indication is that another virtue-based moral theory is in the making. For in this essay Foot envisions a moral community composed of an "army of volunteers," composed, that is, of agents who voluntarily commit themselves to such moral ideals as truth, justice, generosity, and kindness.[5] In a moral community of this sort, all moral imperatives become hypothetical rather than categorical: there are things an agent morally ought to do if he or she wants truth, justice, generosity, or kindness, but no things an agent morally ought to do if he or she isn't first committed to these (or other) moral ideals. On the Foot model (as presented in "Morality as a System"), what distinguishes an ethics of virtue from its competitors is that it construes the ideal moral agent as acting from a direct desire, without first believing that he or she morally ought to perform that action or have that desire. However, in a more recent paper, Foot has expressed doubts about her earlier attempts to articulate the relationship between oughts and desires. In "William Frankena's Carus Lectures" (1981), she states that *"thoughts* [emphasis added] about what is despicable or contemptible, or low, or again admirable, glorious or honorable may give us the key to the problem of rational moral action."[6] But regardless of whether she begins with desires or with thoughts, it seems clear her strategy too is not to dispense with oughts entirely, but rather to employ softer, derivative oughts.

In other words, conceptual reductionism is at work in virtue ethics too. Just as its utilitarian and deontological competitors begin with primitive concepts of the good state of affairs and the intrinsically right action respectively and then drive secondary concepts out of their starting-points, so virtue ethics, beginning with a root conception of the morally good person, proceeds to introduce a different set of secondary concepts which are defined in terms of their relationship to the primitive element. Though the ordering of primitive and derivatives differs in each case, the overall strategy remains the same. Viewed from this perspective, virtue ethics is not unique at all. It has adopted the traditional mononomic strategy of normative ethics. What sets it apart from other approaches, again, is its strong agent orientation.

So for virtue ethics, the primary object of moral evaluation is not the act or its consequences, but rather the agent. And the respective conceptual starting-points of agent—and act—centered ethics result in other basic differences as well, which may be briefly summarized as follows. First of all, the two camps are likely to employ different models of practical reasoning. Act theorists, because they focus on discrete acts and moral quandaries, are naturally very interested in formulating decision procedures for making practical choices. The agent, in their conceptual scheme, needs a guide—hopefully a determinate decision procedure—for finding a way out of the quandary. Agent-centered ethics, on the other hand, focuses on long-term characteristic patterns of action, intentionally down-playing atomic acts and particular choice situations in the process. They are not as concerned with portraying practical reason as a rule-governed enterprise which can be applied on a case-by-case basis.

Secondly, their views on moral motivation differ. For the deontological act theorist, the preferred motive for moral action is the concept of duty itself; for the utilitarian act theorist, it is the disposition to seek the happiness of all sentient creatures. But for the virtue theorist, the preferred motivation factor is the virtues themselves (here understood non-reductionistically). The agent who correctly acts from the disposition of charity does so (according to the virtue theorist) not because it maximizes utility or because it is one's duty to do so, but rather out of a commitment to the value of charity for its own sake.

While I am sympathetic to recent efforts to recover virtue from its long-standing neglect, my purpose in this essay is not to contribute further to the campaign for virtue. Instead, I wish to take a more critical look at the phenomenon, and to ask whether there are certain important features of morality which a virtue-based ethics either handles poorly or ignores entirely. In the remainder of this essay, I shall sketch some objections which (I believe) point to genuine shortcomings of the virtue approach to ethics. My object here is not to offer an exhaustive or even thoroughly systematic critique of virtue ethics, but rather to look at certain mundane regions of the moral field and to ask first what an ethics of virtue might say about them, and second whether what it says about them seems satisfactory.

Agents vs. Acts

As noted earlier, it is a commonplace that virtue theorists focus on good and bad agents rather than on right and wrong acts. In focusing on good and bad agents, virtue theorists are thus forced to de-emphasize discrete acts in favor of long-term, characteristic patterns of behavior. Several related problems arise for virtue ethics as a result of this particular conceptual commitment.

a. Casuistry and Applied Ethics. It has often been said that for virtue ethics the central question is not "What ought I to *do*" but rather "What sort of person ought I to *be*?"[7] However, people have always expected ethical theory to tell them something about what they ought to do, and it seems to me that virtue ethics is structurally unable to say much of anything about this issue. If I'm right, one consequence of this is that a virtue-based ethics will be particularly weak in the areas of casuistry and applied ethics. A recent reviewer of Foot's *Virtues and Vices,* for instance, notes that "one must do some shifting to gather her view on the virtues." "Surprisingly," he adds, "the studies of abortion and euthanasia are not of much use."[8] And this is odd, when one considers Foot's demonstrated interest in applied ethics in conjunction with her earlier cited prefatory remark that a "sound moral theory should start from a theory of virtues and vices." But what can a virtues and vices approach say about specific moral dilemmas? As virtue theorists from Aristotle onward have rightly emphasized, virtues are not simply dispositions to behave in specified ways, for which rules and principles can always be cited. In addition, they involve skills of perception and articulation, situation-specific "know-how," all of which are developed only through recognizing and acting on what is relevant in concrete moral contexts as they arise. These skills of moral perception and practical reason are not completely routinizable, and so cannot be transferred from agent to agent as any sort of decision procedure "package deal." Owing to the very nature of the moral virtues, there is thus a very limited amount of advice on moral quandaries that one can reasonably expect from the virtue-oriented approach. We ought, of course, to do what the virtuous person would do, but it is not always easy to fathom what the hypothetical moral exemplar would do were he in our shoes, and sometimes even he will act out of character. Furthermore, if one asks him why he did what he did, or how he knew what to do, the answer—if one is offered—might not be very enlightening. One would not necessarily expect him to appeal to any rules or principles which might be of use to others.

We can say, à la Aristotle, that the virtuous agent acts for the sake of the noble (*tou kalou heneka*), that he will not do what is base or depraved, etc. But it seems to me that we cannot intelligently say things like: "The virtuous person (who acts for the sake of the noble) is also one who recognizes that all mentally deficient eight-month-old fetuses should (or should not) be aborted, that the doctor/patient principle of confidentiality must always (or not always) be respected, etc." The latter simply sound too strange, and their strangeness stems from the fact that motives of virtue and honor cannot be fully routinized.

Virtue theory is not a problem-oriented or quandary approach to ethics: it speaks of rules and principles of action only in a derivative manner. And its derivative oughts are frequently too vague and unhelpful for persons who have not yet acquired the requisite moral insight and sensitivity. Consequently, we cannot expect it to be of great use in applied ethics and casuistry. The increasing importance of these two subfields of ethics in contemporary society is thus a strike against the move to revive virtue ethics.

b. Tragic Humans. Another reason for making sure that our ethical theory allows us to talk about features of acts and their results in abstraction from the agent and his conception of what he is doing is that sometimes even the best person can make the wrong choices. There are cases in which a man's choice is grounded in the best possible information, his motives honorable and his action not at all out of character. And yet his best-laid plans may go sour. Aristotle, in his *Poetics*, suggests that here lies the source of tragedy: we are confronted with an eminent and respected man, "whose misfortune, however, is brought upon him not by vice (*kakia*) and depravity (*moktheira*) but by some error of judgement (*amartia*)" (1453a8-9). But every human being is morally fallible, for there is a little Oedipus in each of us. So Aristotle's point is that, *regardless of character*, anyone can fall into the sort of mistake of which tragedies are made. Virtue ethics, however, since its conceptual scheme is rooted in the notion of the good person, is unable to assess correctly the occasional (inevitable) tragic outcomes of human action.

Lawrence Becker, in his article "The Neglect of Virtue," seems at first to draw an opposite conclusion from similar reflections about virtue theory and tragedy, for it is his view that virtue ethics makes an indispensable contribution to our understanding of tragedy. According to him, "there are times when the issue is not how much harm has been done, or the value to excusing the wrongdoer, or the voluntary nature of the offending behavior, but rather whether the sort of character indicated by the behavior is 'acceptable' or not—perhaps even ideal—so that the 'wrongful' conduct must be seen simply as an unavoidable defect of it."[9] As Becker sees it, Oedipus merely comes off as a fool who asked too many questions when viewed from the perspective of act theories. Only a virtue ethics, with its agent perspective, allows us to differentiate tragic heroes from fools, and to view the acts that flow from each character type in their proper light. And the proper light in the case of tragic heroes is that there are unavoidable defects in this character type, even though it represents a human ideal. Becker's point is well taken, but its truth does not cancel out my criticism. My point is that virtue ethics is in danger of blinding itself to the wrongful conduct in Oedipal acts, simply because it views the Oedipuses of the world as honorable persons *and* because its focus is on long-term character manifestations rather than discrete acts. To recognize the wrong in Oedipal behavior, a theory with the conceptual tools enabling one to focus on discrete acts is needed. (Notice, incidentally, that Becker's own description does just this.)

c. Intolerable Actions. A third reason for insisting that our moral theory enable us to assess acts in abstraction from agents is that we need to be able to identify certain types of action which produce harms of such magnitude that they destroy the bonds of community and render (at least temporarily) the achievement of moral goods impossible. In every traditional moral community one encounters prohibitions or "barriers to action" which mark off clear boundaries in such areas as the taking of innocent life, sexual relations, and the administration of justice according to local laws and customs.[10] Such rules are needed to teach citizens what kinds of actions are to be regarded not simply as bad (a table of vices can handle this) but as intolerable.[11] Theorists must resort to specific lists of offences to emphasize the fact that there are some acts which are absolutely prohibited. We cannot articulate this sense of absolute prohibition by referring merely to characteristic patterns of behavior.

In rebuttal here, the virtue theorist may reply by saying: "Virtue ethics does not need to articulate these prohibitions—let the law do it, with its list of do's and don'ts." But the sense of requirement and prohibition referred to above seems to me to be at bottom inescapably moral rather than legal. Morality can (and frequently does) invoke the aid of law in such cases, but when we ask *why* there is a law against, e.g., rape or murder, the proper answer is that it is morally intolerable. To point merely to a legal convention when asked why an act is prohibited or intolerable raises more questions than it answers.

d. Character Change. A fourth reason for insisting that a moral theory be able to assess acts in abstraction from agents and their conception of what they're doing is that peoples' moral characters may sometimes change. Xenophon, towards the beginning of his *Memorabilia* (1.11.21), cites an unknown poet who says: "Ah, but a good man is at one time noble (*esthlos*), at another wicked (*kakos*)." Xenophon himself agrees with the poet: "... many alleged (*phaskonton*) philosophers may say: A just (*dikaios*) man can never become unjust; a self-controlled (*sophron*) man can never become wanton (*hubristes*); in fact no one having learned any kind of knowledge (*mathesis*) can become ignorant of it. I do not hold this view ... For I see that, just as poetry is forgotten unless it is often repeated, so instruction, when no longer heeded, fades from the mind."[12]

Xenophon was a practical man who was not often given to speculation, but he arrived at his position on character change in the course of his defense of Socrates. One of the reasons Socrates got into trouble, Xenophon believed, was because of his contact with Critias and Alcibiades during their youth. For of all Athenians, "none wrought so many evils to the *polis*." However, Xenophon reached the conclusion that Socrates should not be blamed for the disappearance of his good influence once these two had ceased their close contact with him.

If skills can become rusty, it seems to me that virtues can too. Unless we stay in practice we run the risk of losing relative proficiency. We probably can't forget them completely (in part because the opportunities for exercising virtues are so pervasive in everyday life), but we can lose a certain sensitivity.

People do become morally insensitive, relatively speaking—missing opportunities they once would have noticed, although perhaps when confronted with a failure they might recognize that they had failed, showing at least that they hadn't literally "forgotten the difference between right and wrong." If the moral virtues are acquired habits rather than innate gifts, it is always possible that one can lose relative proficiency in these habits. Also, just as one's interests and skills sometimes change over the course of a life as new perceptions and influences take hold, it seems too that aspects of our moral characters can likewise alter. (Consider religious conversion experiences.) Once we grant the possibility of such changes in moral character, the need for a more "character-free" way of assessing action becomes evident. Character is not a permanent fixture, but rather plastic. *A more reliable yardstick is sometimes needed.*[13]

e. Moral Backsliding. Finally, the focus on good and bad agents rather than on right and wrong actions may lead to a peculiar sort of moral backsliding. Because the emphasis in agent ethics is on long-term, characteristic patterns of behavior, its advocates run the risk of overlooking occasional lies or acts of selfishness on the ground that such performances are mere temporary aberrations—acts out of character. Even the just man may on occasion act unjustly, so why haggle over specifics? It is unbecoming to a virtue theorist to engage in such pharisaic calculations. But once he commits himself to the view that assessments of moral worth are not simply a matter of whether we have done the right thing, backsliding may result: "No matter how many successes some people have, they still feel they 'are' fundamentally honest."[14] At some point, such backsliding is bound to lead to self-deception.

I have argued that there is a common source behind each of these vices. The virtue theorist is committed to the claim that the primary object of moral evaluation is not the act or its consequences but rather the agent—specifically, those character traits of the agent which are judged morally relevant. This is not to say that virtue ethics does not ever address the issue of right and wrong actions, but rather that it can only do so in a derivative manner. Sometimes, however, it is clearly acts rather than agents which ought to be the primary focus of moral evaluation.

Who Is Virtuous?

There is also an epistemological issue which becomes troublesome when one focuses on qualities of persons rather than on qualities of acts. Baldly put, the difficulty is that we do not seem to be able to know with any degree of certainty who really is virtuous and who vicious. For how is one to go about establishing an agent's true moral character? The standard strategy is what might be called the "externalist" one: we try to infer character by observing conduct.

While not denying the existence of some connection between character and conduct, I believe that the connection between the two is not nearly as tight as externalists have assumed. The relationship is not a necessary one, but merely contingent. Virtue theorists themselves are committed to this claim, though they have not always realized it. For one central issue behind the "Being vs. Doing" debate is the virtue theorist's contention that the moral value of Being is not reducible to or dependent on Doing; that the measure of an agent's character is not exhausted by or even dependent on the values of the actions which he may perform. On this view, the most important moral traits are what may be called "spiritual" rather than "actional."[15]

Perhaps the most famous example of a spiritual virtue would be Plato's definition of justice (*dikaiosune*). Plato, it will be remembered, argued that attempts to characterize *dikaiosune* in terms of an agent's conduct are misguided and place the emphasis in the wrong place. *Dikaiosune* for Plato is rather a matter of the correct harmonious relationship between the three parts of the soul: "It does not lie in a man's external actions, but in the way he acts within himself (*ten entos*), really concerned with himself and his inner parts (*peri eauton kai ta eautou*)" (*Republic* 443d). Other spiritual virtues would include such attitudes as self-respect and integrity. These are traits which do have a significant impact on what we do, but whose moral value is not wholly derivable from the actions to which they may give rise.

If there are such spiritual virtues, and if they rank among the most important of moral virtues, then the externalist strategy is in trouble. For those who accept spiritual virtues, the Inner is not reducible to or dependent on the Outer. We cannot always know the moral value of a person's character by assessing his or her actions.

But suppose we reject the externalist approach and take instead the allegedly direct internalist route. Suppose, that is, that we could literally "see inside" agents and somehow observe their character traits first hand. (The easiest way to envision this is to assume that some sort of identity thesis with respect to moral psychology and neurophysiology is in principle correct. Lest the reader object that this is only a modern materialist's silly pipe dream, I might add that at least one commentator has argued that Aristotle's considered view was that the presence of the virtues and vices depends on modifications of the brain and nervous system; and that the relevant mental processes in ethics have accompanying bodily states.[16]) Here the goal will be to match specific virtues with specific chemicals, much in the manner that identity theorists have sought to match other types of mental events with other specific neurophysiological events. However, even on this materialistic reading of the internalist strategy, nothing could be settled about virtues by analyzing chemicals without first deciding who has what virtue. For we would first need to know who possessed and exhibited which virtue, and then look for specific physical traces in him that were missing in other agents. But as indicated earlier in my discussion of the externalist strategy, this is precisely what we don't know. An analogy might be the attempt to determine which objects have which colors. Regardless of how much we know about the physical make-up of the objects in question, we must first make color judgements. However, at this point the analogy breaks down, for the epistemological problems involved in making color judgements are not nearly as troublesome as are those involved in making virtue judgements.[17]

To raise doubts about our ability to know who is virtuous is to bring skepticism into the center of virtue ethics, for it is to call into question our ability to identify the very object of our inquiry. This is not the same skepticism which has concerned recent writers such as Bernard Williams and Thomas Nagel, when they reflect on the fact that "the natural objects of moral assessment are disturbingly subject to luck."[18] Theirs is more a skepticism *about* morality, while mine is a skepticism *within* morality. The sort of skepticism to which I am drawing attention occurs after one has convinced oneself that there are genuine moral agents who really do things rather than have things happen to them. As such, my skepticism is narrower but also more morality-specific: it concerns not so much queries about causality and free will as doubts about our ability to know the motives of our own behavior. As Kant wrote, "the real morality of actions, their merit or guilt, even that of our own conduct ... remains entirely hidden from us."[19] Aquinas too subscribed to a similar skepticism: "Man is not competent to judge of interior movements, that are hidden, but only of exterior acts which are observable; and yet for the perfection of virtue it is necessary for man to conduct himself rightly in both kinds of acts."[20]

Now it may be objected here that I am making too much of this epistemological error, that no one actually "lives it" or contests the fact that it is an error. But I think not. To advocate an ethics of virtue is, among other things, to presuppose that we can clearly differentiate the virtuous from the vicious. Otherwise, the project lacks applicability.

Consider for a moment the Aristotelian notion of the *spoudaios* (good man) or *phronimos* (man of practical wisdom)—two essentially synonymous terms which together have often been called the touchstone of Aristotle's ethics. Again and again in the *Nicomachean Ethics* the *spoudaios/phronimos* is pointed to as the solution to a number of unanswered problems in Aristotle's ethical theory. For instance, we are told to turn to the *spoudaios* in order to learn what really is pleasurable (1113ª 26-8). And we must turn to an actual *phronimos* in order to find out what the abstract and mysterious *orthos logos* really is (right reason or rational principle—a notion which plays a key role in the definition of virtue) (1107ª 2, 1144ᵇ 24). Even in discussing the intellectual virtue of *phronesis* or practical wisdom, Aristotle begins by announcing that "we shall get at the truth by considering who are the persons we credit with it" (1140ª 24). But who are the *phronimoi*, and how do we know one when we see one? Aristotle does say that Pericles "and men like him" are *phronimoi*, "because they can see what is good for themselves and what is good for men in general" (1140^b 8-10). However, beyond this rather casual remark he does not give the reader any hints on how to track down a *phronimos*. Indeed, he does not even see it as a problem worth discussing.

The reasons for this strange lacuna, I suggest, are two. First, Aristotle is dealing with a small face-to-face community, where the pool of potential *phronimoi* generally come from certain well established families who are well known throughout the *polis*. Within a small face-to-face community of this sort, one would naturally expect to find wide agreement about judgements of character. Second, Aristotle's own methodology is itself designed to fit this sort of moral community. He is not advocating a Platonic ethics of universal categories.

Within the context of a polis and an ethical theory intended to accompany it, the strategy of pointing to a *phronimos* makes a certain sense. However, to divorce this strategy from its social and economic roots and then to apply it to a very different sort of community—one where people really do not know each other all that well, and where there is wide disagreement on values—does not. And this, I fear, is what contemporary virtue ethicists have tried to do.[21]

Style Over Substance

In emphasizing Being over Doing, the Inner over the Outer, virtue theorists also lay themselves open to the charge that they are more concerned with style than with substance. For as I argued earlier, virtue theorists are committed to the view that the moral value of certain key character traits is not exhausted by or even dependent on the value of the actions to which they may give rise. When this gulf between character and conduct is asserted, and joined with the claim that it is agents rather than actions which count morally, the conclusion is that it is not the substance of an agent's actions which is the focus of moral appraisal. The implication here seems to be that if you have style, i.e., the style of the virtuous person, as defined in the context of a concrete moral tradition, it doesn't so much matter what the results are. ("It's not whether you win or lose, but how you play the game that counts.") As Frankena remarks, in a passage which underscores an alleged basic difference between ancient and contemporary virtue ethics:

> The Greeks held ... that being virtuous entails not just having good motives or intentions but also doing the right thing. Modern views typically differ from Greek views here; perhaps because of the changed ways of thinking introduced by the Judeo-Christian tradition, we tend to believe that being

morally good does not entail doing what is actually right ... even if we believe (as I do) that doing what is actually right involves more than only having a good motive or intention. Today many people go so far as to think that in morality it does not matter much *what* you do; all that matters, they say, *is how* you do it. To parody a late cigarette advertisement; for them it's not how wrong you make it, it's how you make it wrong.[22]

But it is sophistry to claim that the consequences of the lies of gentlemen or Aristotelian *kaloikagathoi* aren't very important, or that the implications of their rudeness are somehow tempered by the fact that they are who they are. This line of thought flies in the face of our basic conviction that moral assessment must strive towards impartiality and the bracketing of morally irrelevant social and economic data.

It seems to me that this particular vice of virtue ethics is analogous to the Hegelian "duty for duty's sake" critique of formalist deontologies. Virtue-based and duty-based theories are both subject to the "style over substance" charge because their notion of ends is too weak. Both types of theory speak of ends only in a derivative sense. For the duty-based theorist, the good is an inherent feature of dutiful action, so that the only proclaimed end is right action itself. For the virtue-based theorist, the good is defined in terms of the virtuous agent. ("Virtue is its own reward.") Aristotle, as noted earlier, in distinguishing the true from the apparent good, remarks that "that which is in truth an object of wish is an object of wish to the good man (*spoudaios*), while any chance thing may be so to the bad man" (*En* 1113ª 26-28).

While no one (except the most obstinate utilitarian) would deny these two respective ends their place in a list of moral goods, it appears that there is another important type of end which is left completely unaccounted for. This second type of end is what may be called a *product-end*, a result or outcome of action which is distinct from the activity that produces it. (An example would be a catastrophe or its opposite.) Virtue-based and duty-based theories, on the other hand, can account only for *activity-ends*, ends which are inherent features of (virtuous or dutiful) action. Virtue-based theories then, like their duty-based competitors, reveal a structural defect in their lack of attention to product-ends.[23]

Now it might be said that the "style-over-substance" charge is more appropriately directed at those who emphasize Doing over Being, since one can do the right things just to conform or for praise. One can cultivate the externalities, but be inwardly wretched or shallow. I grant that this is a problem for act theorists, but it is a slightly different criticism from mine, using different senses of the words "style" and "substance." "Style," as used in my criticism, means roughly: "morally irrelevant mannerisms and behavior," while "substance," as I used it, means something like: "morally relevant results of action." The "substance" in this new criticism refers to good moral character and the acts which flow from it, while "style" here means more "doing the right thing, but without the proper fixed trait behind it." However, granted that both "style over substance" criticisms have some validity, I would also argue that mine points to a greater vice. It is one thing to do what is right without the best disposition, it is another not to do what is right at all.

Utopianism

The last vice I shall mention has a more socio-historical character. It seems to me that there is a bit of utopianism behind the virtue theorist's complaints about the ethics of rules. Surely, one reason there is more emphasis on rules and regulations in modern society is that things have become more complex. Our moral community (in so far as it makes sense to speak of "community" in these narcissistic times) contains more ethnic, religious, and class groups than did the moral community which Aristotle theorized about. Unfortunately, each segment of society has not only its own interests but its own set of virtues as well. There is no general agreed upon and significant expression of desirable moral character in such a world. Indeed, our pluralist culture prides itself on and defines itself in terms of its alleged value neutrality and its lack of allegiance to any one moral tradition. This absence of agreement regarding human purposes and moral ideals seems to drive us (partly out of lack of alternatives) to a more legalistic form of morality. To suppose that academic theorists can alter the situation simply by re-emphasizing certain concepts is illusory. Our world lacks the sort of moral cohesiveness and value unity which traditional virtue theorists saw as prerequisites of a viable moral community.[24]

The table of vices sketched above is not intended to be exhaustive, but even in its incomplete state I believe it spells trouble for virtue-based moral theories. For the shortcomings described are not esoteric—they concern mundane features of moral experience which any minimally adequate moral theory should be expected to account for. While I do think that contemporary virtue theorists are correct in asserting that any adequate moral theory must account for the fact of character, and that no ethics of rules, pure and unsupplemented, is up to this job, the above analysis also suggests that no ethics of virtue, pure and unsupplemented, can be satisfactory.

My own view (which can only be stated summarily here) is that we need to begin efforts to coordinate irreducible or strong notions of virtue along with irreducible or strong conceptions of the various act notions into our conceptual scheme of morality. This appeal for coordination will not satisfy those theorists who continue to think in the single-element or mononomic tradition (a tradition which contemporary virtue-based theorists have inherited from their duty-based and goal-based ancestors), but I do believe that it will result in a more realistic account of our moral experience. The moral field is not unitary, and the values we employ in making moral judgements sometimes have fundamentally different sources. No single reductive method can offer a realistic means of prioritizing these different values. There exists no single scale by means of which disparate moral considerations can always be measured, added, and balanced.[25] The theoretician's quest for conceptual economy and elegance has been won at too great a price, for the resulting reductionist definitions of the moral concepts are not true to the facts of moral experience. It is important now to see the ethics of virtue and the ethics of rules as adding up, rather than as canceling each other out.

Notes

1. The rights definition is from Bentham, "Anarchical Fallacies," repr. in A.I. Melden (ed.), *Human Rights* (Belmont, CA, 1970), 32. The virtue definition is from Bentham, "The Nature of Virtue," repr. in Bhiku Parekh (ed.), *Bentham's Political Thought* (New York, 1973), 89.

2. G.E.M. Anscombe, "Modern Moral Philosophy," *Philosophy*, vol. 33 (1958), pp. 1-19.

3. Anscombe appears to believe also that moral oughts and obligations only make sense in a divine law context, which would mean that only divine command theories of ethics employ valid concepts of obligation. I see no reason to accept such a narrow definition of duty. See ibid. pp. 30-31, 38-40. For one argument against her restrictive divine law approach to moral obligation, see Alan Donagan, *The Theory of Morality* (Chicago, 1977), 3.

4. Philippa Foot, *Virtues and Vices and Other Essays in Moral Philosophy* (Oxford, 1978), p. xi.

5. Philippa Foot, "Morality as a System of Hypothetical Imperatives," *Philosophical Review*, 81 (1972), 305-16; repr. in *Virtues and Vices*, 157-73. See especially the long concluding footnote, added in 1977.

6. Philippa Foot, "William Frankena's Carus Lectures," *The Monist*, 64 (1981), 311.

7. For background on this "Being vs. Doing" debate, see Bernard Mayo, *Ethics and the Moral Life* (London, 1958), 211-14, and William K. Frankena, *Ethics*, (2nd edn., Englewood Cliffs, NJ, 1973), 65-66.

8. Arthur Flaming, "Reviving the Virtues," review of Foot's *Virtues and Vices* and James Wallace's "Virtues and Vices," *Ethics*, 90 (1980), 588.

9. Lawrence Becker, "The Neglect of Virtue," *Ethics*, 85 (1975), 111.

10. Stuart Hampshire (ed.), *Private and Public Morality* (Cambridge, 1978), 7.

11. Alasdair MacIntyre, *After Virtue* (London, 1895), 142.

12. It is curious to note that contemporary philosophers as different as Gilbert Ryle and H.G. Gadamer have argued, against Xenophon and myself, that character cannot change. See H.G. Gadamer, "The Problem of Historical Consciousness,"

in P. Rabinow and W.M. Sullivan (eds.), *Interpretive Social Science* (Berkeley and Los Angeles, 1979), 140, and Gilbert Ryle, "On Forgetting the Difference Between Right and Wrong," in A.I. Melden (ed.), *Essays in Moral Philosophy* (Seattle, 1958).

13. One possibility here might be to isolate specific traits and then add that the virtuous agent ought to retain such traits throughout any character changes. (E.g., "The good man will not do what is base, regardless of whether he be Christian, Jew, or atheist.") However, it is my view that very few if any moral traits have such a "transcharacter" status. The very notion of what counts as a virtue or vice itself changes radically when one looks at different traditions. (Compare Aristotle's praise for *megalopsuchia* or pride as the "crown of the virtues" with the New Testament emphasis on humility.) Also, one would expect basic notions about what is base or noble to themselves undergo shifts of meaning as they move across traditions.

14. Becker, "The Neglect of Virtue," 112.

15. I have borrowed this terminology from G.W. Trianosky-Stillwell, "Should We Be Good? The Place of Virtue in Our Morality" (doctoral dissertation, University of Michigan, 1980).

16. W.F.R. Hardie, *Aristotle's Ethical Theory* (2nd edn., Oxford, 1980), ch. VI, esp. pp. 111-13.

17. I am indebted to Bill Robinson for help on this criticism of the internalist strategy.

18. Thomas Nagel, "Moral Luck," in *Mortal Questions* (Cambridge, 1979), 28. See also Bernard Williams, "Moral Luck," in *Moral Luck* (Cambridge, 1981).

19. Kant, *Critique of Pure Reason*, A552 = B580, n. 1.

20. Thomas Aquinas, Saint. *Summa Theologica*, I-II Q. 91, a. 4.

21. I would like to thank Arthur Adkins for discussion on these points.

22. William K. Frankena, *Thinking About Morality* (Ann Arbor, 1980), 52-3.

23. My own position on this topic is contra that of utilitarianism. I believe that activity-ends are clearly the more important of the two, and that most product-ends ultimately derive their moral value from more fundamental activity-ends. (The importance of saving lives, for instance, borrows its value from the quality of life it makes possible. "Life at any price" is nonsense.) But I also believe, contra deontology and virtue ethics, that any adequate moral theory must find room for both types of ends.

24. For similar criticism, see Mayo, *Ethics and the Moral Life*, 217; and MacIntyre, *After Virtue*.

25. See Thomas Nagel, "The Fragmentation of Value," in *Mortal Questions*, 131-2, 135. A similar position is defended by Charles Taylor in his recent essay, "The Diversity of Goods," in A. Sen and B. Williams (eds.), *Utilitarianism and Beyond* (Cambridge, 1982).

Earlier versions of this essay were read at the 1982 American Philosophical Association Pacific Division Meetings, and at the 1981 Iowa Philosophical

Society Meeting at Grinnell College. I am very grateful for useful criticisms and suggestions offered on these occasions. I would also like to thank Marcia Baron, Lawrence Becker, James Gustafson, W.D. Hamlyn, Bob Hollinger, Joe Kupfer, and Warner Wick for criticisms of earlier drafts. Portions of the present version are taken from my doctoral dissertation, "The Elements of Ethics: Toward a Topography of the Moral Field" (University of Chicago, 1981).

23

Virtue Theory and Abortion

※ ※ ※

Rosalind Hursthouse

Rosalind Hursthouse is a professor of philosophy at the University of Auckland, and has published several books and articles on virtue ethics. In "Virtue Theory and Abortion" she examines several of the objections that have been raised against virtue ethics and argues that they are misplaced. She rejects in particular what she takes to be the major criticism of virtue ethics: that it does not help us to know what we ought to do. She addresses this criticism with a detailed discussion of how a virtue ethicist might deal with the concrete moral issue of abortion.

The sort of ethical theory derived from Aristotle, variously described as virtue ethics, virtue-based ethics, or neo-Aristotelianism, is becoming better known, and is now quite widely recognized as at least a possible rival to deontological and utilitarian theories. With recognition has come criticism, of varying quality. In this article I shall discuss nine separate criticisms that I have frequently encountered, most of which seem to me to betray an inadequate grasp either of the structure of virtue theory or of what would be involved in thinking about a real moral issue in its terms. In the first half I aim particularly to secure an understanding which will reveal that many of these criticisms are simply misplaced, and to articulate what I take to be the major criticism of virtue theory. I reject this criticism, but do not claim that it is necessarily misplaced. In the second half I aim to deepen that understanding and highlight the issues raised by the criticisms by illustrating what the theory looks like when it is applied to a particular issue, in this case, abortion.

Virtue Theory

Virtue theory can be laid out in a framework that reveals clearly some of the essential similarities and differences between it and some versions of deontological and utilitarian theories. I begin with a rough sketch of familiar versions of the latter two sorts of theory, not, of course, with the intention of suggesting that they exhaust the field, but on the assumption that their very familiarity will provide a helpful contrast with virtue theory. Suppose a deontological theory has basically the following framework. We begin with a premiss providing a specification of right action:

P.1. An action is right iff it is in accordance with a moral rule or principle.

This is a purely formal specification, forging a link between the concepts of *right action* and *moral rule*, and gives one no guidance until one knows what a moral rule is. So the next thing the theory needs is a premiss about that:

P.2. A moral rule is one that ...

Historically, an acceptable completion of P.2 would have been

(i) is laid on us by God
or
(ii) is required by natural law.

In secular versions (not, of course, unconnected to God's being pure reason, and the universality of natural law) we get such completions as

(iii) is laid on us by reason
or
(iv) is required by rationality
or
(v) would command universal rational acceptance
or
(vi) would be the object of choice of all rational beings

and so on. Such a specification forges a second conceptual link, between the concepts of *moral rule* and *rationality*.

We have here the skeleton of a familiar version of a deontological theory, a skeleton which reveals that what is essential to any such version is the links between *right action*, *moral rule*, and *rationality*. That these form the basic structure can be seen particularly vividly if we lay out the familiar act-utilitarianism in such a way as to bring out the contrasts.

Act-utilitarianism begins with a premiss that provides a specification of right action:

P.1. An action is right iff it promotes the best consequences.

It thereby forges the link between the concepts of *right action* and *consequences*. It goes on to specify what the best consequences are in its second premiss:

P.2. The best consequences are those in which happiness is maximized.

It thereby forges the link between *consequences* and *happiness.*

Now let us consider what a skeletal virtue theory looks like. It begins with a specification of right action:

P.1. An action is right iff it is what a virtuous agent would do in the circumstances.[1]

This, like the first premisses of the other two sorts of theory, is a purely formal principle, giving one no guidance as to what to do, which forges the conceptual link between *right action* and *virtuous agent.* Like the other theories, it must, of course, go on to specify what the latter is. The first step towards this may appear quite trivial, but is needed to correct a prevailing tendency among many critics to define the virtuous agent as one who is disposed to act in accordance with a deontologist's moral rules.

P.1a. A virtuous agent is one who acts virtuously, that is, one who has and exercises the virtues.

This subsidiary premiss lays bare the fact that virtue theory aims to provide a non-trivial specification of the virtuous agent *via* a non-trivial specification of the virtues, which is given in its second premiss:

P.2. A virtue is a character trait a human being needs to flourish or live well.

This premiss forges a conceptual link between *virtue* and *flourishing* (or *living well* or *eudaimonia*). And, just as deontology, in theory, then goes on to argue that each favoured rule meets its specification, so virtue ethics, in theory, goes on to argue that each favoured character trait meets its.

There are the bare bones of virtue theory: here follow five brief comments directed to some misconceived criticisms which should be cleared out of the way.

First, the theory does not have a peculiar weakness or problem in virtue of the fact that it involves the concept of *eudaimonia* (a standard criticism being that this concept is hopelessly obscure). Now no virtue theorist will pretend that the concept of human flourishing is an easy one to grasp. I will not even claim here (though I would elsewhere) that it is no more obscure than the concepts of *rationality* and *happiness*, since, if our vocabulary were more limited, we might, *faute de mieux*, call it (human) *rational happiness*, and thereby reveal that it has at least some of the difficulties of both. But virtue theory has never, so far as I know, been dismissed on the grounds of the *comparative* obscurity of this central concept; rather, the popular view is that it has a problem with this which deontology and utilitarianism in no way share. This, I think, is clearly false. Both *rationality* and *happiness*, as they figure in their respective theories, are rich and difficult concepts—hence all the disputes about the various tests for a rule's being an object of rational choice, and the disputes, dating back to Mill's introduction of the higher and lower pleasures, about what constitutes happiness.

Secondly, the theory is not trivially circular; it does not specify right action in terms of the virtuous agent and then immediately specify the virtuous agent in terms of right action. Rather, it specifies her in terms of the virtues, and then specifies these, not merely as dispositions to right action, but as the character traits (which are dispositions to feel and react as well as act in certain ways) required for *eudaimonia.*[2]

Thirdly, it does answer the question "What should I do?" as well as the question "What sort of person should I be?" (That is, it is not, as one of the catchphrases has it, concerned only with Being and not with Doing.)

Fourthly, the theory does, to a certain extent, answer this question by coming up with rules or principles (contrary to the common claim that it does not come up with any rules or principles). Every virtue generates a positive instruction (act justly, kindly, courageously, honestly, etc.) and every vice a prohibition (do not act unjustly, cruelly, like a coward, dishonestly, etc.). So trying to decide what to do within the framework of virtue theory is not, as some people seem to imagine, necessarily a matter of taking one's favoured candidate for a virtuous person and asking oneself, "What would they do in these circumstances?" (as if the raped 15-year-old girl might be supposed to say to herself, "Now would Socrates have an abortion if he were in my circumstances?" and as if someone who had never known or heard of anyone very virtuous were going to be left, according to the theory, with no way to decide what to do at all). The agent may instead ask herself, "If I were to do such and such now, would I be acting justly or unjustly (or neither), kindly or unkindly [and so on]?" I shall consider below the problem created by cases in which such a question apparently does not yield an answer to "What should I do?" (because, say, the alternatives are being unkind or being unjust); here my claim is only that it sometimes does—the agent may employ her concepts of the virtues and vices directly, rather than imagining what some hypothetical exemplar would do.

Fifthly, (a point that is implicit but should be made explicit), virtue theory is not committed to any sort of reductionism which involves defining all our moral concepts in terms of the virtuous agent. On the contrary, it relies on a lot of very significant moral concepts. Charity or benevolence, for instance, is the virtue whose concern is the *good* of others; that concept of *good* is related to the concept of *evil* or *harm*, and they are both related to the concepts of the *worthwhile*, the *advantageous*, and the *pleasant*. If I have the wrong conception of what is worthwhile and advantageous and pleasant, then I shall have the wrong conception of what is good for, and harmful to, myself and others, and, even with the best will in the world, will lack the virtue of charity, which involves getting all this right. (This point will be illustrated at some length in the second half of this article; I mention it here only in support of the fact that no virtue theorist who takes her inspiration from Aristotle would even contemplate aiming at reductionism.[3])

Let me now, with equal brevity, run through two more standard criticisms of virtue theory (the sixth and seventh of my nine) to show that, though not entirely misplaced, they do not highlight problems peculiar to that theory but, rather, problems that are shared by familiar versions of deontology.

One common criticism is that we do not know which character traits are the virtues, or that this is open to much dispute, or particularly subject to the threat of moral scepticism or "pluralism"[4] or cultural relativism. But the parallel roles played by the second premisses of both deontological and virtue theories reveal the way in which both sorts of theory share this problem. It is at the stage at which one tries to get the right conclusions to drop out of the bottom of one's theory that, *theoretically*, all the work has to be done. Rule deontologists know that they want to get "don't kill," "keep promises," "cherish your children," and so on as the rules that meet their specification, whatever it may be. They also know that any of these can be disputed, that some philosopher may claim, of any one of them, that it is reasonable to reject it, and that at least people claim that there has been, for each rule, some culture which rejected it. Similarly, the virtue theorists know that they want to get justice, charity, fidelity, courage, and so on as the character traits needed for *eudaimonia*; and they also know that any of these can be disputed, that some philosopher will say of any one of them that it is reasonable to reject it as a virtue, and that there is said to be, for each character trait, some culture that has thus rejected it.

This is a problem for both theories, and the virtue theorist certainly does not find it any harder to argue against moral scepticism, "pluralism," or cultural relativism than the deontologist. Each theory has to stick out its neck and say, in some cases, "This person/these people/other cultures are (or would be) in error," and find some grounds for saying this.

Another criticism (the seventh) often made is that virtue ethics has unresolvable conflict built into it. "It is common knowledge," it is said, "that the requirements of the virtues can conflict; charity may prompt me to end the frightful suffering of the person in my care by killing him, but justice bids me to stay my hand. To tell my brother that his wife is being unfaithful to him would be honest and loyal, but it would be kinder to keep quiet about it. So which should I do? In such cases, virtue ethics has nothing helpful to say." (This is one version of the problem, mentioned above, that considering whether a proposed action falls under a virtue or vice term does not always yield an answer to "What should I do?")

The obvious reply to this criticism is that rule deontology notoriously suffers from the same problem, arising not only from the fact that its rules can apparently conflict, but also from the fact that, at first blush, it appears that one and the same rule (e.g., preserve life) can yield contrary instructions in a particular case.[5] As before, I agree that this is a problem for virtue theory, but deny that it is a problem peculiar to it.

Finally, I want to articulate, and reject, what I take to be the major criticism of virtue theory. Perhaps because it is *the* major criticism, the reflection of a very general sort of disquiet about the theory, it is hard to state clearly—especially for someone who does not accept it— but it goes something like this.[6] My interlocutor says:

> Virtue theory can't *get* us anywhere in real moral issues because it's bound to be all assertion and no argument. You admit that the best it can come up with in the way of action-guiding rules are the ones that rely on the virtue and vice concepts, such as, "act charitably," "don't act cruelly," and so on; and, as if that weren't bad enough, you admit that these virtue concepts, such as charity, presuppose concepts such as the *good*, and the *worthwhile*, and so on. But that means that any virtue theorist who writes about real moral issues must rely on her audience's agreeing with her application of all these concepts, and hence accepting all the premises in which those applications are enshrined. But some other virtue theorist might take different premises about these matters, and come up with very different conclusions, and, within the terms of the theory, there is no way to distinguish between the two. While there is agreement, virtue theory can repeat conventional wisdom, preserve the status quo, but it can't get us anywhere in the way that a normative ethical theory is supposed to, namely, by providing rational grounds for acceptance of its practical conclusions.

My strategy will be to split this criticism into two: one (the eighth) addressed to the virtue theorist's employment of the virtue and vice concepts enshrined in her rules—act charitably, honestly, and so on—and the other (the ninth) addressed to her employment of concepts such as that of the *worthwhile*. Each objection, I shall maintain, implicitly appeals to a certain *condition of adequacy* on a normative moral theory, and in each case, I shall claim, the condition of adequacy, once made explicit, is utterly implausible.

Yes, it is true that when she discusses real moral issues, the virtue theorist has to assert that certain actions are honest, dishonest, or neither; charitable, uncharitable, or neither. And it is true that this is often a very difficult matter to decide; her rules are not always easy to apply. But this counts as a criticism of the theory only if we assume, as a condition of adequacy, that any adequate action-guiding theory must make the difficult business of knowing what to do if one is to act well easy, that it must provide clear guidance about what ought not to be done which any reasonably clever adolescent could follow if she chose. But such a condition of adequacy is implausible. Acting rightly is difficult, and *does* call for much moral wisdom, and the relevant condition of adequacy, which virtue theory meets, is that it should have built into it an explanation of a truth expressed by Aristotle,[7] namely, that moral knowledge— unlike mathematical knowledge—cannot be acquired merely by attending lectures and is not characteristically to be found in people too young to have had much experience of life. There are youthful mathematical geniuses, but rarely, if ever, youthful moral geniuses, and this shows us something significant about the sort of knowledge that moral knowledge is. Virtue ethics builds this in straight off precisely by couching its rules in terms whose application may indeed call for the most delicate and sensitive judgement.

Here we may discern a slightly different version of the problem that there are cases in which applying the virtue and vice terms does not yield an answer to "What should I do?" Suppose someone "youthful in character," as Aristotle puts it, having applied the relevant terms, finds herself landed with what is, unbeknownst to her, a case not of real but of apparent conflict, arising from a misapplication of those terms. Then she will not be able to decide what to do unless she knows of a virtuous agent to look to for guidance. But her quandary is (*ex hypothesi*) the result of her lack of wisdom, and just what virtue theory expects. Someone hesitating over whether to reveal a hurtful truth, for example, thinking it would be kind but dishonest or unjust to lie, may need to realize, with respect to these particular circumstances, not that kindness is more (or less) important than honesty or justice, and not that honesty or justice sometimes requires one to act unkindly or cruelly, but that one does people no kindness by concealing this sort of truth from them, hurtful as it may be. This is the *type* of thing (I use it only as an example) that people with moral wisdom know about, involving the correct application of *kind*, and that people without such wisdom find difficult.

What about the virtue theorist's reliance on concepts such as that of the *worthwhile*? If such reliance is to count as a fault in the theory, what condition of adequacy is implicitly in play? It must be that any good normative theory should provide answers to questions about real moral issues whose truth is in no way determined by truths about what is worthwhile, or what really matters in human life. Now although people are initially inclined to reject out of hand the claim that the practical conclusions of a normative moral theory have to be based on premises about what is truly worthwhile, the alternative, once it is made explicit, may look even more unacceptable. Consider what the condition of adequacy entails. If truths about what is worthwhile (or truly good, or serious, or about what matters in human life) do *not* have to be appealed to in order to answer questions about real moral issues, then I might sensibly seek guidance about what I ought to do from someone who had declared in advance that she knew nothing about such matters, or from someone who said that, although she had opinions about them, these were quite likely to be wrong but that this did not matter, because they would play no determining role in the advice she gave me.

I should emphasize that we are talking about real moral issues and real guidance; I want to know whether I should have an abortion, take my mother off the life-support machine, leave academic life and become a doctor in the Third World, give up my job with the firm that is using animals in its experiments, tell my father he has cancer. Would I go to someone who says she has *no* views about what is worthwhile in life? Or to someone who says that, as a matter of fact, she tends to think that the only thing that matters is having a good time, but has a normative theory that is consistent both with this view and with my own rather more puritanical one, which will yield the guidance I need?

I take it as a premiss that this is absurd. The relevant condition of adequacy should be that the practical conclusions of a good normative theory *must* be in part determined by premisses about what is worthwhile, important, and so on. Thus I reject this "major criticism" of virtue theory, that it cannot get us anywhere in the way that a normative moral theory is supposed to. According to my response, a normative theory which any clever adolescent can apply, or which reaches practical conclusions that are in no way determined by premisses about what is truly worthwhile, serious, and so on, is guaranteed to be an inadequate theory.

Although I reject this criticism, I have not argued that it is misplaced and that it necessarily manifests a failure to understand what virtue theory is. My rejection is based on premisses about what an adequate normative theory must be like—what sorts of concepts it must contain, and what sort of account it must give of moral knowledge—and thereby claims, implicitly, that the "major criticism" manifests a failure to understand what an *adequate normative theory* is. But, as a matter of fact, I think the criticism is often made by people who have no idea of what virtue theory looks like when applied to a real moral issue; they drastically underestimate the variety of ways in which the virtue and vice concepts, and the others, such as that of the *worthwhile*, figure in such discussion.

As promised, I now turn to an illustration of such discussion, applying virtue theory to abortion. Before I embark on this tendentious business, I should remind the reader of the aim of this discussion. I am not, in this article, trying to solve the problem of abortion; I am illustrating how virtue theory directs one to think about it. It might indeed be said that thinking about the problem in this way "solves" it by *dis*solving it, in so far as it leads one to the conclusion that there is no single right answer, but a variety of particular answers, and in what follows I am certainly trying to make that conclusion seem plausible. But, that granted, it should still be said that I am not trying to "solve the problem*s*" in the practical sense of telling people that they should, or should not, do this or that if they are pregnant and contemplating abortion in these or those particular circumstances.

I do not assume, or expect, that all of my readers will agree with everything I am about to say. On the contrary, given the plausible assumption that some are morally wiser than I am, and some less so, the theory has built into it that we are bound to disagree on some points. For instance, we may well disagree about the particular application of some of the virtue and vice terms; and we may disagree about what is worthwhile or serious, worthless or trivial. But my aim is to make clear how these concepts figure in a discussion conducted in terms of virtue theory. What is at issue is whether these concepts are indeed the ones that should come in, that is, whether virtue theory should be criticized for employing them. The problem of abortion highlights this issue dramatically, since virtue theory quite transforms the discussion of it.

Abortion

As everyone knows, the morality of abortion is commonly discussed in relation to just two considerations: first, and predominantly, the status of the foetus and whether or not it is the sort of thing that may or may not be innocuously or justifiably killed; secondly, and less predominantly (when, that is, the discussion concerns the *morality* of abortion rather than the question of permissible legislation in a just society), women's rights. If one thinks within this familiar framework, one may well be puzzled about what virtue theory, as such, could contribute. Some people assume the discussion will be conducted solely in terms of what the virtuous agent would or would not do (cf. the third, fourth, and fifth criticisms above). Others assume that only justice, or at most justice and charity,[8] will be applied to the issue, generating a discussion very similar to Judith Jarvis Thomson's.[9]

Now if this is the way the virtue theorist's discussion of abortion is imagined to be, no wonder people think little of it. It seems obvious in advance that in any such discussion there must be either a great deal of extremely tendentious application of the virtue terms *just*, *charitable*, and so on or a lot of rhetorical appeal to "this is what only the virtuous agent knows." But these are caricatures; they fail to appreciate the way in which virtue theory quite transforms the discussion of abortion by dismissing the two familiar dominating considerations as, in a way, fundamentally irrelevant. In what way or ways, I hope to make both clear and plausible.

Let us first consider women's rights. Let me emphasize again that we are discussing the *morality* of abortion, not the rights and wrongs of laws prohibiting or permitting it. If we suppose that women do have a moral right to do as they choose with their own bodies, or, more particularly, to terminate their pregnancies, then it may well follow that a *law* forbidding abortion would be unjust. Indeed, even if they have no such right, such a law might be, as things stand at the moment, unjust, or impractical, or inhumane: on this issue I have nothing to say in this article. But, putting all questions about the justice or injustice of laws to one side, and supposing only that women have such a moral right, *nothing* follows from this supposition about the morality of abortion, according to virtue theory, once it is noted (quite generally, not with particular reference to abortion) that in exercising a moral right I can do something cruel, or callous, or selfish, light-minded, self-righteous, stupid, inconsiderate, disloyal, dishonest—that is, act viciously.[10] Love and friendship do not survive their parties' constantly insisting on their rights, nor do people live well when they think that getting what they have a right to is of pre-eminent importance; they harm others, and they harm themselves. So whether women have a moral right to terminate their pregnancies is irrelevant within virtue theory, for it is irrelevant to the question "In having an abortion in these circumstances, would the agent be acting virtuously or viciously or neither?"

What about the consideration of the status of the foetus—what can virtue theory say about that? One might say that this issue is not in the province of any moral theory; it is a metaphysical question, and an extremely difficult one at that. Must virtue theory then wait upon metaphysics to come up with the answer?

At first sight it might seem so. For virtue is said to involve knowledge, and part of this knowledge consists in having the *right* attitude to things. "Right" here does not just mean "morally right" or "proper" or "nice" in the modern sense; it means "accurate, true." One cannot have the right or correct attitude to something if the attitude is based on or involves false beliefs. And this suggests that if the status of the foetus is relevant to the rightness or wrongness of abortion, its status must be known, as a truth, to the fully wise and virtuous person.

But the sort of wisdom that the fully virtuous person has is not supposed to be recondite; it does not call for fancy philosophical sophistication, and it does not depend upon, let alone wait upon, the discoveries of academic philosophers.[11] And this entails the following, rather startling, conclusion: that the status of the foetus—that issue over which so much ink has been spilt—is, according to virtue theory, simply not relevant to the rightness or wrongness of abortion (within, that is, a secular morality).

Or rather, since that is clearly too radical a conclusion, it is in a sense relevant, but only in the sense that the familiar biological facts are relevant. By "the familiar biological facts" I mean the facts that most human societies are and have been familiar with—that, standardly (but not invariably), pregnancy occurs as the result of sexual intercourse, that it lasts about nine months, during which time the foetus grows and develops, that standardly it terminates in the birth of a living baby, and that this is how we all come to be.

It might be thought that this distinction—between the familiar biological facts and the status of the foetus—is a distinction without a difference. But this is not so. To attach relevance to the status of the foetus, in the sense in which virtue theory claims it is not relevant, is to be gripped by the conviction that we must go beyond the familiar biological facts, deriving some sort of conclusion from them, such as that the foetus has rights, or is not a person, or something similar. It is also to believe that this exhausts the relevance of the familiar biological facts, that all they are relevant to is the status of the foetus and whether or not it is the sort of thing that may or may not be killed.

These convictions, I suspect, are rooted in the desire to solve the problem of abortion by getting it to fall under some general rule such as "You ought not to kill anything with the right to life but may kill anything else." But they have resulted in what should surely strike any non-philosopher as a most bizarre aspect of nearly all the current philosophical literature on abortion, namely, that, far from treating abortion as a unique moral problem, markedly unlike any other, nearly everything written on the status of the foetus and its bearing on the abortion issue would be consistent with the facts of human reproduction (to say nothing of family life) being totally different from what they are. Imagine that you are an alien extraterrestrial anthropologist who does not know that the human race is roughly 50 per cent female and 50 per cent male, or that our only (natural) form of reproduction involves heterosexual intercourse, viviparous birth, and the female's (and only the female's) being pregnant for nine months, or that females are capable of childbearing from late childhood to late middle age, or that childbearing is painful, dangerous, and emotionally involving—do you think you would pick up these facts from the hundreds of articles written on the status of the foetus? I am quite sure you would not. And that, I think, shows that the current philosophical literature on abortion has got badly out of touch with reality.

Now if we are using virtue theory, our first question is not "What do the familiar biological facts show—what can be derived from them about the status of the foetus?" but "How do these facts figure in the practical reasoning, actions and passions, thoughts and reactions, of the virtuous and the non-virtuous? What is the mark of having the right attitude to these facts and what manifests having the wrong attitude to them?" This immediately makes essentially relevant not only all the facts about human reproduction I mentioned above, but a whole range of facts about our emotions in relation to them as well. I mean such facts as that human parents, both male and female, tend to care passionately about their offspring, and that family relationships are among the deepest and strongest in our lives—and, significantly, among the longest-lasting.

These facts make it obvious that pregnancy is not just one among many other physical conditions; and hence that anyone who genuinely believes that an abortion is comparable to a haircut or an appendectomy is mistaken.[12] The fact that the premature termination of a pregnancy is, in some sense, the cutting-off of a new human life, and thereby, like the procreation of a new human life, connects with all our thoughts about human life and death, parenthood, and family relationships, must make it a serious matter. To disregard this fact about it, to think of abortion as nothing but the killing of something that does not matter, or as nothing but the exercise of some right or rights one has, or as the incidental means to some desirable state of affairs, is to do something callous and light-minded, the sort of thing that no virtuous and wise person would do. It is to have the wrong attitude not only to foetuses, but more generally to human life and death, parenthood, and family relationships.

Although I say that the facts make this obvious, I know that this is one of my tendentious points. In partial support of it I note that even the most dedicated proponents of the view that deliberate abortion is just like an appendectomy or haircut rarely hold the same view of spontaneous abortion, that is, miscarriage. It is not so tendentious of me to claim that to react to people's grief over miscarriage by saying, or even thinking, "What a fuss about nothing!" would be callous and light-minded, whereas to try to laugh someone out of grief over an appendectomy scar or a botched haircut would not be. It is hard to give this point due prominence within act-centred theories, for the inconsistency is an inconsistency in attitude about the seriousness of loss of life, not in beliefs about which acts are right or wrong. Moreover, an act-centred theorist may say, "Well, there is nothing wrong with *thinking* 'What a fuss about nothing!' as long as you do not say it and hurt the person who is grieving. And besides, we cannot be held responsible for our thoughts, only for the intentional actions they give rise to." But the character traits that virtue theory emphasizes are not simply dispositions to intentional actions, but a seamless disposition to certain actions and passions, thoughts and reactions.

To say that the cutting-off of a human life is always a matter of some seriousness, at any stage, is not to deny the relevance of gradual foetal development. Notwithstanding the well-worn point that clear boundary lines cannot be drawn, our emotions and attitudes regarding the foetus do change as it develops, and again when it is born, and indeed further as the baby grows. Abortion for shallow reasons in the later stages is much more shocking than abortion for the same reasons in the early stages in a way that matches the fact that deep grief over miscarriage in the later stages is more appropriate than it is over miscarriage in the earlier stages (when, that is, the grief is solely about the loss of *this* child, not about as might be the case, the loss of one's only hope of having a child or of having one's husband's child). Imagine (or recall) a woman who already has children; she has not intended to have more, but finds herself unexpectedly pregnant. Though contrary to her plans, the pregnancy, once established as a fact, is welcomed—and then she loses the embryo almost immediately. If this were bemoaned as a tragedy, it would, I think, be a misapplication of the concept of what is tragic. But it may still properly be mourned as a loss. The grief is expressed in such terms as "I shall always wonder how she or he would have turned out" or "When I look at the others, I shall think, 'How different their lives would have been if this other one had been part of them.'" It would, I take it, be callous and light-minded to say, or think, "Well, she has already *got* four children; what's the problem?"; it would be neither, nor arrogantly intrusive in the case of a close friend, to try to correct prolonged mourning by saying, "I know it's sad, but it's not a tragedy; rejoice in the ones you have." The application of tragic becomes more appropriate as the foetus grows, for the mere fact that one has lived with it for longer, conscious of its existence, makes a difference. To shrug off an early abortion is understandable just because it is very hard to be fully conscious of the foetus's existence in the early stages and hence hard to appreciate that an early abortion is the destruction of life. It is particularly hard for the young and inexperienced to appreciate this, because appreciation of it usually comes only with experience.

I do not mean "with the experience of having an abortion" (though that may be part of it) but, quite generally, "with the experience of life." Many women who have borne children contrast their later pregnancies with their first successful one, saying that in the later ones they were conscious of a new life growing in them from very early on. And, more generally, as one reaches the age at which the next generation is coming up close behind one, the counterfactuals "If I, or she, had had an abortion, Alice, or Bob, would not have been born" acquire a significant application, which casts a new light on the conditionals "If I or Alice have an abortion then some Caroline or Bill will not be born."

The fact that pregnancy is not just one among many physical conditions does not mean that one can never regard it in that light without manifesting a vice. When women are in very poor physical health, or worn out from childbearing, or forced to do very physically demanding jobs, then they cannot be described as self-indulgent, callous, irresponsible, or light-minded if they seek abortions mainly with a view to avoiding pregnancy as the physical condition that it is. To go through with a pregnancy when one is utterly exhausted, or when one's job consists of crawling along tunnels hauling coal, as many women in the nineteenth century were obliged to do, is perhaps heroic, but people who do not achieve heroism are not necessarily vicious. That they can view the pregnancy only as eight months of misery, followed by hours if not days of agony and exhaustion, and abortion only as the blessed escape from this prospect, is entirely understandable and does not manifest any lack of serious respect for human life or a shallow attitude to motherhood. What it does show is that something is terribly amiss in the conditions of their lives, which makes it so hard to recognize pregnancy and childbearing as the good that they can be.

In relation to this last point I should draw attention to the way in which virtue theory has a sort of built-in indexicality. Philosophers arguing against anything remotely resembling a belief in the sanctity of life (which the above claims clearly embody) frequently appeal to the existence of other communities in which abortion and infanticide are practised. We should not automatically assume that it is impossible that some other communities could be morally inferior to our own; maybe some are, or have been, precisely in so far as their members are, typically, callous or light-minded or unjust. But in communities in which life is a great deal tougher for everyone than it is in ours, having the right attitude to human life and death, parenthood, and family relationships might well manifest itself in ways that are unlike ours. When it is essential to survival that most members of the community fend for themselves at a very young age or work during most of their waking hours, selective abortion or infanticide might be practised either as a form of genuine euthanasia or for the sake of the community and not, I think, be thought callous or light-minded. But this does not make everything all right; as before, it shows that there is something amiss with the conditions of their lives, which are making it impossible for them to live really well.[13]

The foregoing discussion, in so far as it emphasizes the right attitude to human life and death, parallels to a certain extent those standard discussions of abortion that concentrate on it solely as an issue of killing. But it does not, as those discussions do, gloss over the fact, emphasized by those who discuss the morality of abortion in terms of women's rights, that abortion, wildly unlike any other form of killing, is the termination of a pregnancy, which is a condition of a woman's body and results in *her* having a child if it is not aborted. This fact is given due recognition not by appeal to women's rights but by emphasizing the relevance of the familiar biological and psychological facts and their connection with having the right attitude to parenthood and family relationships. But it may well be thought that failing to bring in women's rights still leaves some important aspects of the problem of abortion untouched.

Speaking in terms of women's rights, people sometimes say things like, "Well, it's her life you're talking about too, you know; she's got a right to her own life, her own happiness." And the discussion stops there. But in the context of virtue theory, given that we are particularly concerned with what constitutes a good human life, with what true happiness or *eudaimonia* is, this is no place to stop. We go on to ask, "And is this life of hers a good one? Is she living well?"

If we are to go on to talk about good human lives, in the context of abortion, we have to bring in our thoughts about the value of love and family life, and our proper emotional development through a natural life cycle. The familiar facts support the view that parenthood in general, and motherhood and childbearing in particular, are intrinsically worthwhile, are among the things that can be correctly thought to be partially constitutive of a flourishing human life.[14] If this is right, then a woman who opts for not being a mother (at all, or again, or now) by opting for abortion may thereby be manifesting a flawed grasp of what her life should be, and be about—a grasp that is childish, or grossly materialistic, or shortsighted, or shallow.

I said "may thereby": this *need* not be so. Consider, for instance, a woman who has already had several children and fears that to have another will seriously affect her capacity to be a good mother to the ones she has—she does not show a lack of appreciation of the intrinsic value of being a parent by opting for abortion. Nor does a woman who has been a good mother and is approaching the age at which she may be looking forward to being a good grandmother. Nor does a woman who discovers that her pregnancy may well kill her, and opts for abortion and adoption. Nor, necessarily, does a woman who has decided to lead a life centred around some other worthwhile activity or activities with which motherhood would compete.

People who are childless by choice are sometimes described as "irresponsible," or "selfish," or "refusing to grow up," or "not knowing what life is about." But one can hold that having children is intrinsically worthwhile without endorsing this, for we are, after all, in the happy position of there being more worthwhile things to do than can be fitted into one lifetime. Parenthood, and motherhood in particular, even if granted to be intrinsically worthwhile, undoubtedly take up a lot of one's adult life, leaving no room for some other worthwhile pursuits. But some women who choose abortion rather than having their first child, and some men who encourage their partners to choose abortion, are not avoiding parenthood for the sake of other worthwhile pursuits, but for the worthless one of "having a good time," or for the pursuit of some false vision of the ideals of freedom or self-realization. And some others who say "I am not ready for parenthood yet" are making a mistake about the extent to which one can manipulate the circumstances of one's life so as to make it fulfil some dream that one has. Perhaps one's dream is of having two perfect children, a girl and a boy, within a perfect marriage, in financially secure circumstances, with an interesting job of one's own. But to care too much about that dream, to demand of life that it give it to one and to act accordingly, may be both greedy and foolish, and is to run the risk of missing out on happiness entirely. Not only may fate make the dream impossible, or destroy it, but one's own attachment to it may make it impossible. Good marriages, and the most promising children, can be destroyed by just one adult's excessive demand for perfection.

Once again, this is not to deny that girls may quite properly say "I am not ready for motherhood yet," especially in our society, and, far from manifesting irresponsibility or light-mindedness, show an appropriate modesty or humility, or a fearfulness that does not amount to cowardice. However, even when the decision to have an abortion is the right decision—one that does not itself fall under a vice-related term and thereby one that the perfectly virtuous could recommend—it does not follow that there is no sense in which having the abortion is wrong, or guilt appropriate. For, by virtue of the fact that a human life has been cut short, some evil has probably been brought about,[15] and that circumstances make the decision to bring about some evil the right decision will be a ground for guilt if getting into those circumstances in the first place itself manifested a flaw in character.

What "gets one into those circumstances" in the case of abortion is, except in the case of rape, one's sexual activity and one's choices, or the lack of them, about one's sexual partner and about contraception. The virtuous woman (which here of course does not mean simply "chaste woman" but "woman with the virtues") has such character traits as strength, independence, resoluteness, decisiveness, self-confidence, responsibility, serious-mindedness, and self-determination—and no one, I think, could deny that many women become pregnant in circumstances in which they cannot welcome or cannot face the thought of having this child precisely because they lack one or some of these character traits. So even in the cases where the decision to have an abortion is the right one, it can still be the reflection of a moral failing—not because the decision itself is weak or cowardly or irresolute or irresponsible or light-minded, but because lack of the requisite opposite of these failings landed one in the circumstances in the first place. Hence the common universalized claim that guilt and remorse are never appropriate emotions about an abortion is denied. They may be appropriate, and appropriately inculcated, even when the decision was the right one.

Another motivation for bringing women's rights into the discussion may be to attempt to correct the implication, carried by the killing-centred approach, that in so far as abortion is wrong, it is a wrong that only women do, or at least (given the preponderance of male doctors) that only women instigate. I do not myself believe that we can thus escape the fact that nature bears harder on women than it does on men,[16] but virtue theory can certainly correct many of the injustices that the emphasis on women's rights is rightly concerned about. With very little amendment, everything that has been said above applies to boys and men too. Although the abortion decision is, in a natural sense, the woman's decision, proper to her, boys and men are often party to it, for well or ill, and even when they are not, they are bound to have been party to the circumstances that brought it up. No less than girls and women, boys and men can, in their actions, manifest self-cen-tredness, callousness, and light-mindedness about life and parenthood in relation to abortion. They can be self-centred or courageous about the pos-sibility of disability in their offspring; they need to reflect on their sexual activity and their choices, or the lack of them, about their sexual partner and contraception; they need to grow up and take responsibility for their own actions and life in relation to fatherhood. If it is true, as I maintain, that in so far as motherhood is intrinsically worthwhile, being a mother is an impor-tant purpose in women's lives, being a father (rather than a mere generator) is an important purpose in men's lives too, and it is adolescent of men to turn a blind eye to this and pretend that they have many more important things to do.

Conclusion

Much more might be said, but I shall end the actual discussion of the prob-lem of abortion here, and conclude by highlighting what I take to be its sig-nificant features. These hark back to many of the criticisms of virtue theory discussed earlier.

The discussion does not proceed simply by our trying to answer the ques-tion "Would a perfectly virtuous agent ever have an abortion and, if so, when?"; virtue theory is not limited to considering "Would Socrates have had an abortion if he were a raped, pregnant 15-year-old?" nor automatically stumped when we are considering circumstances into which no virtuous agent would have got herself. Instead, much of the discussion proceeds in the virtue- and vice-related terms whose application, in several cases, yields practical conclusions (cf. the third and fourth criticisms above). These terms are difficult to apply correctly, and anyone might challenge my application of any one of them. So, for example, I have claimed that some abortions, done for certain reasons, would be callous or light-minded; that others might indicate an appropriate modesty or humility; that others would reflect a greedy and foolish attitude to what one could expect out of life. Any of these examples may be disputed, but what is at issue is, should these difficult terms be there, or should the discussion be couched in terms that all clever adolescents can apply correctly? (Cf. the first half of the "major objection" above.)

Proceeding as it does in the virtue- and vice-related terms, the discussion thereby, inevitably, also contains claims about what is worthwhile, serious and important, good and evil, in our lives. So, for example, I claimed that par-enthood is intrinsically worthwhile, and that having a good time was a worth-less end (in life, not on individual occasions); that losing a foetus is always a serious matter (albeit not a tragedy in itself in the first trimester) whereas acquiring an appendectomy scar is a trivial one; that (human) death is an evil. Once again, these are difficult matters, and anyone might challenge any one of my claims. But what is at issue is, as before, should those difficult claims be there or can one reach practical conclusions about real moral issues that are in no way determined by premises about such matters? (Cf. the fifth criticism, and the second half of the "major criticism.")

The discussion also thereby, inevitably, contains claims about what life is like (e.g., my claim that love and friendship do not survive their parties' constantly insisting on their rights; or the claim that to demand perfection of life is to run the risk of missing out on happiness entirely). What is at issue is, should those disputable claims be there, or is our knowledge (or are our false opinions) about what life is like irrelevant to our understanding of real moral issues? (Cf. both halves of the "major criticism.")

Naturally, my own view is that all these concepts should be there in any discussion of real moral issues, and that virtue theory, which uses all of them, is the right theory to apply to them. I do not pretend to have shown this. I realize that proponents of rival theories may say that, now that they have understood how virtue theory uses the range of concepts it draws on, they are more convinced than ever that such concepts should not figure in an adequate normative theory, because they are sectarian, or vague, or too particular, or improperly anthropocentric, and reinstate what I called the "major criticism." Or, finding many of the details of the discussion appropriate, they may agree that many, perhaps even all, of the concepts should figure, but argue that virtue theory gives an inaccurate account of the way the concepts fit together (and indeed of the concepts themselves) and that another theory provides a better account; that would be interesting to see. Moreover, I admitted that there were at least two problems for virtue theory: that it has to argue against moral scepticism, "pluralism," and cultural relativism, and that it has to find something to say about conflicting requirements of different virtues. Proponents of rival theories might argue that their favoured theory provides better solutions to these problems than virtue theory can. Indeed, they might criticize virtue theory for finding problems here at all. Anyone who argued for at least one of moral scepticism, "pluralism," or cultural relativism could presumably do so (provided their favoured theory does not find a similar problem); and a utilitarian might say that benevolence is the only virtue and hence that virtue theory errs when it discusses even apparent conflicts between the requirements of benevolence and some other character trait such as honesty.

Defending virtue theory against all possible, or even likely, criticisms of it would be a lifelong task. As I said at the outset, in this article I aimed to defend the theory against some criticisms which I thought arose from an inadequate understanding of it, and to improve that understanding. If I have succeeded, we may hope for more comprehending criticisms of virtue theory than have appeared hitherto.[17]

Notes

1. It should be noted that this premiss intentionally allows for the possibility that two virtuous agents, faced with the same choice in the same circumstances, may act differently. For example, one might opt for taking her father off the life-support machine and the other for leaving her father on it. The theory requires that neither agent thinks that what the other does is wrong (see n. 4 below), but it explicitly allows that no action is uniquely right in such a case—both are right. It also intentionally allows for the possibility that in some circumstances—those into which no virtuous agent could have got herself—no action is right. I explore this premiss at greater length in "Applying Virtue Ethics," in *Virtues and Reasons*, ed. Rosalind Hursthouse, Gavin Lawrence, and Warren Quinn (Oxford, 1995).

2. There is, of course, the further question of whether the theory eventually describes a larger circle and winds up relying on the concept of right action in its interpretation of *eudaimonia*. In denying that the theory is trivially circular, I do not pretend to answer this intricate question. It is certainly true that virtue theory does not claim that the correct conception of *eudaimonia* can be got from "an independent 'value-free' investigation of human nature" (John McDowell, "The Role of *Eudaimonia* in Aristotle's Ethics," Amelie O. Rorty (ed.), *Essays on Aristotle's Ethics* (Berkeley and Los Angeles, 1980)). The sort of training that is required for acquiring the correct conception no doubt involves being taught from early on such things as "Decent people do this sort of thing, not that" and "To do such and such is the mark of a depraved character" (cf. *Nicomachean Ethics* 1110[a]22). But whether this counts as relying on the concept of right (or wrong) action seems to me very unclear and requiring much discussion.

3. Cf. Bernard Williams's point in *Ethics and the Limits of Philosophy* (London, 1985) that we need an enriched ethical vocabulary, not a cut-down one.

4. I put *pluralism* in scare quotes to serve as a warning that virtue theory is not incompatible with all forms of it. It allows for "competing conceptions" of *eudaimonia* and the worthwhile, for instance, in the sense that it allows for a plurality of flourishing lives—the theory need not follow Aristotle in specifying the life of contemplation as the only one that truly constitutes *eudaimonia* (if he does). But the conceptions "compete" only in the sense that, within a single flourishing life, not everything worthwhile can be fitted in; the theory does not allow that two people with a correct conception of *eudaimonia* can disagree over whether the way the other is living constitutes flourishing. Moreover, the theory is committed to the strong thesis that the same set of character traits is needed for any flourishing life; it will not allow that, for instance, soldiers need courage but wives and mothers do not, or that judges need justice but can live well despite lacking kindness.

(This obviously is related to the point made in n. 1 above.) For an interesting discussion of pluralism (different interpretations thereof) and virtue theory, see Douglas B. Rasmussen, "Liberalism and Natural End Ethics," *American Philosophical Quarterly*, 27 (1990). 153-61.

5. e.g., in Williams's Jim and Pedro case in J.J.C. Smart and Bernard Williams, *Utilitarianism: For and Against* (London, 1973).

6. Intimations of this criticism constantly come up in discussion; the clearest statement of it I have found is by Onora O'Neill, in her review of Stephen Clark's *The Moral Status of Animals*, in *Journal of Philosophy*, 77 (1980),440-46. For a response I am much in sympathy with, see Cora Diamond, "Anything But Argument?," *Philosophical Investigations*, 5 (1982), 23-41.

7. Aristotle, *Nicomachean Ethics* 1142ᵃ 12-16.

8. It seems likely that some people have been misled by Foot's discussion of euthanasia (through no fault of hers) into thinking that a virtue theorist's discussion of terminating human life will be conducted exclusively in terms of justice and charity (and the corresponding vice terms) (Philippa Foot, "Euthanasia," *Philosophy and Public Affairs*, 6/2 (Winter 1977), 85-112). But the act-category *euthanasia* is a very special one, at least as defined in her article, since such an act must be done "for the sake of the one who is to die." Building a virtuous motivation into the specification of the act in this way immediately rules out the application of many other vice terms.

9. Judith Jarvis Thomson, "A Defense of Abortion," *Philosophy and Public Affairs*, 1/1 (Fall 1971), 47-66. One could indeed regard this article as proto-virtue theory (no doubt to the surprise of the author) if the concepts of callousness and kindness were allowed more weight.

10. One possible qualification: if one ties the concept of justice very closely to rights, then if women do have a moral right to terminate their pregnancies it *may* follow that in doing so they do not act unjustly. (Cf. Thomson, "A Defense of Abortion.") But it is debatable whether even that much follows.

11. This is an assumption of virtue theory, and I do not attempt to defend it here. An adequate discussion of it would require a separate article, since, although most moral philosophers would be chary of claiming that intellectual sophistication is a necessary condition of moral wisdom or virtue, most of us, from Plato onwards, tend to write as if this were so. Sorting out which claims about moral knowledge are committed to this kind of elitism and which can, albeit with difficulty, be reconciled with the idea that moral knowledge can be acquired by anyone who really wants it would be a major task.

12. Mary Anne Warren, in "On the Moral and Legal Status of Abortion," *Monist*, 57 (1973), sect. 1, says of the opponents of restrictive laws governing abortion that "their conviction (for the most part) is that abortion is not a *morally* serious and extremely unfortunate, even though sometimes justified, act, comparable to killing in self-defense or to letting the violinist die, but rather is closer to being a morally *neutral* act, like cutting one's hair" (emphasis added). I would like to

think that no one *genuinely* believes this. But certainly in discussion, particularly when arguing against restrictive laws or the suggestion that remorse over abortion might be appropriate, I have found that some people *say* they believe it (and often cite Warren's article, albeit inaccurately, despite its age). Those who allow that it is morally serious, and far from morally neutral, have to argue against restrictive laws, or the appropriateness of remorse, on a very different ground from that laid down by the premiss "The foetus is just part of the woman's body (and she has a right to determine what happens to her body and should not feel guilt about anything she does to it)."

13. For another example of the way in which "tough conditions" can make a difference to what is involved in having the right attitude to human life and death and family relationships, see the concluding sentences of Foot, "Euthanasia."

14. I take this as a premiss here, but argue for it in some detail in my *Beginning Lives* (Oxford, 1987). In this connection I also discuss adoption and the sense in which it may be regarded as "second best," and the difficult question of whether the good of parenthood may properly be sought, or indeed bought, by surrogacy.

15. I say "some evil has probably been brought about" on the ground that (human) life is (usually) a good and hence (human) death usually an evil. The exceptions would be (a) where death is actually a good or a benefit, because the baby that would come to be if the life were not cut short would be better off dead than alive, and (b) where death, though not a good, is not an evil either, because the life that would be led (e.g., in a state of permanent coma) would not be a good. (See Foot, "Euthanasia.")

16. I discuss this point at greater length in *Beginning Lives*.

17. Versions of this article have been read to philosophy societies at University College, London, Rutgers University, and the Universities of Dundee, Edinburgh, Oxford, Swansea, and California-San Diego; at a conference of the Polish and British Academies in Cracow in 1988 on "Life, Death and the Law," and as a symposium paper at the Pacific Division of the American Philosophical Association in 1989. I am grateful to the many people who contributed to the discussions of it on these occasions, and particularly to Philippa Foot and Anne Jaap Jacobson for private discussion.

CHAPTER NINE

FEMINIST ETHICS

INTRODUCTION

One of the most dramatic challenges to traditional ethical theory comes from feminist ethics. The challenge focuses on three aspects of the traditional approach to ethical theory: the assumed universality of moral theories, moral autonomy, and moral principles. Our focus will primarily be on an influential and important feminist alternative to the traditional approaches, namely the ethics of care.

One of the most important feminist challenges came not from a philosopher but from a psychologist, Carol Gilligan, who was working on moral development. Her conclusions about moral development were in stark contrast with those of Lawrence Kohlberg, another leading scholar in the area of moral development. After conducting a long term study of about seventy males from the United States, Kohlberg had concluded that moral development progressed through three levels—the preconventional level, the conventional level, and the postconventional level—each of which consisted of two stages.

The preconventional level is the level of most children under the age of nine, some adolescents, and adult criminals. Persons at the first stage of this level try to obey laws and rules, but in the second stage they do so only if this course of action is in their immediate best interest. The conventional level is the level of most adolescents and adults. At this level people conform to and uphold the rules of society simply because they are the rules of society. At the first stage in the conventional level people try to live up to the expectations of those who are close to them. Mutual relationships, trust, respect, and loyalty become important. At the second stage people start to focus more on their social system and the importance of maintaining it.

It is only at the postconventional level that people start to understand the basic principles that underlie their society's rules of conduct. If people at this level accept the rules of society, it is because they accept the reasoning that supports these rules. It is therefore at the postconventional level that people start to judge by moral principles rather than by moral conventions. The postconventional level, according to Kohlberg, is reached by a minority of adults, and then only after the age of twenty. During the first stage of the postconventional level people are aware of the multitude of values and rules that might be important to a particular social group. People at this stage often have a feeling of contractual obligations and tend to believe that rules and laws should be based on utilitarian calculations. During the second stage people move away from utilitarianism and social contracts towards universal principles of justice and human rights and towards respect for all persons. The moral attitude at this stage takes on a Kantian flavour.

Kohlberg's conclusions were surprising, especially in the light of further studies. It turned out that those who reached the highest level of moral maturity according to Kohlberg's theory tended to be males. Females tended to reach only the second stage of the second level, where the main focus is on social systems and the importance of maintaining them. This conclusion seemed appropriate to some males. It fit the traditional stereotype of gender roles, in which the male takes care of business and the female stays at home to keep the family going. The father's role is to maintain discipline while the mother's role is to smooth things over and to help everyone get along. Men in particular were inclined to find Kohlberg's views persuasive. Being labelled as generally morally inferior was something that many women, however, found disturbing. An antidote was on the way with the results of the studies of another renowned psychologist, Carol Gilligan.

Gilligan's results were based on three long-term studies, two of which used females as subjects, and one of which used both males and females as subjects. Her studies showed that male and female moral development did not conform to Kohlberg's outline. Males and females exhibit different patterns of moral development. They have different moral outlooks and different approaches to moral issues and problems. There are, in short, two moralities: male morality and female morality. The account that Kohlberg had given had emphasized the idea that those who reach the greatest moral maturity act according to moral rules, and ultimately deontological rules rather than utilitarian ones. The account that Gilligan gave emphasized the fact that women tend to solve moral problems not by acting on rules, but rather by establishing a context that eschews abstract moral rules and deductive reasoning. Gilligan discovered that it was common for women to favour an approach to moral conflicts that maintains ties between people without sacrificing anyone's integrity.

It is actually possible to interpret Gilligan's results as corroboration of Kohlberg's conclusions, but we can do so only if we make the implausible assumption that women (as well as people of some other cultures that don't fit neatly into Kohlberg's schema) do not reach full moral maturity. Once we assume that members of both genders can reach full moral maturity, we are led to Gilligan's conclusion that males and females mature in different ways and end up with significantly different moral outlooks.

How does all of this relate to moral theory? In one significant respect, these studies have no real bearing on our ethical theories. Kohlberg and Gilligan studied how people do act, and this is a question of psychology that must be answered empirically. Ethicists study how people should act, and this is a question of philosophy. Ethicists generally agree that how people do act does not define how we ought to act. Even though people used to enslave each other, we ought not to practice slavery. And even if men oppress (or used to oppress) women, that is not what they should do. So in a significant respect

Kohlberg's and Gilligan's studies have nothing to do with ethical theory, and their results should not be taken as guidelines for how people ought to behave. But with this point established, we might still wonder whether these psychological studies have any lessons to teach us about our approach to ethical theory.

Nel Noddings thinks so. Noddings supports Gilligan in her criticism of Kohlberg. Noddings points out that ethics of care represents an alternative to Kohlberg's last stage of moral development. Women, she claims, do not abstract away from the concrete situations they find themselves in. Instead they embrace relationships and caring, thus finding themselves at a lower stage in Kohlberg's hierarchy. Nevertheless, Nodding points out, we should not view those who embrace caring as being less developed morally than those who are at the most advanced stage of Kohlberg's scale. Instead, they simply have a different sort of world view that represents a powerful ethic.

At the very least the psychological studies serve to call attention to the fact that there are different moral perspectives. They raise the question of whether moral rules should always be viewed as the ultimate outcome of moral theorizing, as has been the presumption in Western normative ethics.

Western normative theories can be divided into two camps: rule-based ethics and virtue ethics. As the name indicates, rule-based ethics uses moral rules to guide actions. If someone who uses a rule-based ethic finds herself in a situation that requires a moral decision, she consults the relevant moral rule, whether it is the Principle of Utility, the Categorical Imperative, or perhaps a rule of a divine command theory. She uses the appropriate principle to help her assess the various options open to her, and then chooses the best option. Ethics of care has no such rules to fall back on. Instead, the emphasis is on the interdependance of all individuals as well as on the importance of being sensitive to the context of each situation in order to safeguard the interests of those involved. This talk of relationships and responsibilities to others is not captured in the rule-oriented moral theories.

It might be argued that ethics of care is not comprehensive enough to stand on its own. Critics point out, for example, that when care and justice conflict then impartiality might be called for rather than empathy with particular individuals. Other have pointed out that while care is important, justice is more important. In light of these and other criticism one might think that ethics of care should be viewed as a part of a more comprehensive moral theory, namely virtue ethics. Like ethics of care, virtue ethics has no such rules to fall back on. The virtues are character traits that have been appropriately developed over time, and they are not based on moral rules. Rule-based ethics has dominated moral theorizing in the Western world, and teleological and deontological moral theories are firmly established within this tradition. Although virtue ethics was developed by Aristotle in Ancient Greece, it fell out of favor for several centuries and has only recently started to receive significant attention once again.

We might wonder why anyone would think of virtue ethics as "female" ethics. After all, Aristotle, who initially developed virtue ethics, was a male and a notoriously male-centric thinker. He modelled his theory on the Greek society of his day which was indisputably highly male-oriented. During the eighth and ninth centuries, the Vikings terrorized the seasides of northern Europe. Judging from Nordic poems and stories, their moral outlook is best described as that of virtue ethics. Still, no one would be likely to claim that the Vikings adopted "female" ethics. And when virtue ethics was resurrected to some extent during the late nineteenth century, it was by Friedrich Nietzsche, another male who (like Aristotle) did not think very highly of women.

In response to this line of reasoning, we should note that psychological research after Gilligan has revealed that the division between "male" and "female" moral outlooks is not empirically rigid. It is not the case that there are distinct male ethics and female ethics. Instead there are different moral outlooks that people of either gender might accept when they are morally mature. It may be more common for females to accept the ethics of care that Gilligan attributes to females and it may be more common for males to accept the rule-based model that she attributes to males. However, there are no sharp divisions on these models on the basis of gender that can be used to define these models. This later research helps to explain the seemingly contradictory fact that the main advocates of virtue ethics have been males, as well as the fact that the moral outlook of some male-dominated cultures is still best described in terms of virtue ethics.

Even if there is not a sharp division between male and female ethics, feminist ethics has questioned the universality of ethical theories and the validity of moral principles. Gender aside, different genuinely "mature" people can have different moral outlooks and different approaches to resolving moral issues. Most feminists argue that no single rule-based moral theory can claim to be the "right" theory, and that no single moral theory can claim to be universal.

Further, feminist ethics has changed how we look at moral autonomy. Ethical theories that emphasize moral rules and abstract reasoning have typically assumed that a moral agent is separate from others and that making moral decisions requires a certain degree of impartiality. According to these theories, one cannot get too caught up in special relationships, for this might taint the reasoning process. Against this position, feminist ethics has argued that a morally responsible person is one who recognizes that she is entangled in a network of relations with other people and who orients her moral deliberations with a view to maintaining these relations.

24.
STANDARD MORAL THEORIES
FROM A FEMINIST PERSPECTIVE

❧ ❧ ❧

HILDE LINDEMANN

Hilde Lindemann is a professor of philosophy at Michigan State University. Her books include An Invitation to Feminist Ethics, *from which the following selection is taken. In this selection, Lindemann examines some prominent moral theories: utilitarianism, Kantian ethics, and social contract theory. While she acknowledges that these theories have real value and warrant careful study, she suggests that they are also seriously deficient. In particular, they fail to address the concerns and circumstances that make up the greater part of the lives of many women, men of colour, and others who are socially disadvantaged. They are written from the perspective of persons who are privileged (generally at the expense of others) and who assume that their own situations should inform all of our moral theorizing.*

What's Wrong with This Picture?

These thumbnail sketches of the most prominent moral theories are meant to give you an idea of the differences among them, which are surely considerable. Less visible, perhaps, is how much the theories have in common. But it's their commonalities that trouble many feminists, so rather than offer criticisms of each theory in turn, I'll show you three pictures that underlie all of them and explain what it is that feminists think the pictures get wrong. These pictures are simplifications, of course. And what they portray emerges only if you stand back and notice the things the theories emphasize, the things they take for granted, and the things they don't mention. When you do that you start to see, first, the picture of the person who is supposed to act on the theories; second, the picture of the society in which this person lives; and third, the picture of human reason that the person exercises when making moral judgments. Let's examine these pictures with an awareness of how power operates in the guise of gender, so that we can see more clearly what they distort, paint over, or leave out altogether. (This is an instance of Lindemann's ad hoc rule Number 37: When the Wizard of Oz says, "Pay no attention to the man behind the screen," be sure to take a closer look.)

The Picture of the Person

The first thing to notice about the people who are meant to lead their lives in accordance with the theories is that they are detached from other people. They act on their own, unconstrained by their relationships to family or friends. They might *have* such relationships, but the theories aren't much interested in them. Hobbes populates the State of Nature with individuals who spring up out of the ground full grown, like mushrooms. The citizens of the Kingdom of Ends don't seem to have had parents either, not to mention lovers or children. And if utilitarian moral agents have special responsibilities to housemates, siblings, or grandparents, you won't find that out by reading Mill. None of the theories does much to ensure that people will have any connections to one another aside from the minimal ones needed to keep the society from collapsing, and all of them picture the agent as what the philosopher Charles Taylor calls a "punctual self"—a dot on a page, unconnected to other dots.

The second thing to notice is that these people are self-sufficient. You can tell this because they all want to be let alone. Hobbes isn't worried about what would happen if he became ill—he's worried that his neighbors will attack him. The Categorical Imperative operates primarily to tell you what you *mustn't do to* other people, not what you *should do for* them. Mill is worried more about state interference in people's lives than about the ways the state might be able to give aid to the needy. For the most part, the theories take it for granted that the people they are talking about can look after themselves without any help from anybody.

The third thing to notice is that each of these people has just as much social power as everyone else. None of them is socially disadvantaged and none has to report to a higher-up. The parties to the social contract are presumed to negotiate from positions of equality, and indeed in the Rawlsian version of the theory, this presumption is explicitly built in. Kantian persons are lawgivers and judges, powerful enough so they don't have to notice that the laws they'd be willing to accept might not be equally acceptable to socially disadvantaged people for whom the laws could be harmful or beside the point. And utilitarian persons don't have to report to any higher-up because they *are* the higher-ups. As Sidgwick so revealingly put it, utilitarianism is for "a class of persons defined by exceptional qualities of intellect, temperament, or character," who by virtue of these qualities are fitted to make policies for the public good. Williams calls these people "government house" utilitarians, because it's easy to imagine them as bureaucrats, government officials, or corporate managers.

The fourth thing to notice is that the people are calculators and planners. The individuals who are hammering .out the social contract are trying in a self-interested fashion to get the best bargain they can for themselves, which requires a certain amount of gamesmanship—knowledge of the maximin strategy, for example—as each determines his own advantage by figuring out what other people are likely to do. Rawlsian social contractors all have rational life plans: They know where they're going in the long run, and they exercise the watchful self-control that's required to get them there. Bentham's and Mill's moral agents are rational planners too, though as managers and policy makers, they typically direct their planning toward others rather than themselves. And Kantian moral agents are the quintessential calculators: What's morally valuable about them—and the *only* source of their value—is their ability to reason.

The trouble with the picture of the persons who populate these theories— the judge, the policy maker, the manager, the contractor, the gamesman—is that it represents, in ideal form, the responsibilities, privileges, and concerns of only *some* actual people in a certain kind of society and, even then, only at a particular time in their lives. The kind of person who is supposed to act on these theories is both unattached and self-sufficient; he's the powerful equal of the other people to whom the theory applies; he promotes his own interests or the interests of those he's responsible for and assumes his peers will do the same; he enters freely into contracts with other free contractors; he uses his reason to plan out the course of his own life or to manage and coordinate the efforts of others; and he commands the resources needed to do these things.

What a number of you will find missing from these accounts is large chunks of your own experience of life. Indeed, what many of you won't find there is *yourselves*. Though the theories don't acknowledge it, the picture of the ideal or representative person they offer is, as Margaret Urban Walker (1998) aptly puts it, "none of us at all times, and many of us at no times" (21-22). In particular, the idealized picture of independent, powerful agents seeking to promote their own interests, plan for themselves and others, or enhance their autonomy through voluntary and impersonal interactions misrepresents many *women's* lives. Which people get to live the kind of life these theories depict depends on their gender, race, age, class, and the other factors on which the uneven distribution of social privilege is based. And this is a problem for three different reasons.

First of all, it's a problem because, as a representation of what real people are really like, it's false. None of us stands on our own; we all live firmly embedded within a thick web of social relationships. We couldn't even *be* the persons we are if it weren't for all the other persons who respond to us, care for us, teach us, include us in their activities, and find room for us in their society. This is what Annette Baier means when she says we are all "second persons," persons produced by other persons rather than punctual selves. Moreover, all of us have needed help at various points in our lives and will doubtless need it again. Then too, many people aren't in a position to pursue their own interests by bargaining on equal terms with other contractors—to quote Baier (1994) again, "Contract is a device for traders, entrepreneurs, and capitalists, not for children, servants, indentured wives, and slaves" (113). Many people have to follow policies made by others, rather than make policy themselves. And the circumstances of many people's lives don't permit them to make long-range plans, while other people don't think it's very important to live their lives according to a long-range plan.

Second, if the picture of persons underlying these theories isn't supposed to represent real people but instead is meant to be an ideal toward which all real people ought to strive, then it's still false, because it's impossible. If you're going to get anywhere near the ideal yourself, you need vast amounts of support from other people who, because they're supporting you, can't have the kind of life you live. Who is supposed to nurture, protect, and socialize children so that they can grow up to be self-sufficient utilitarians? Who is supposed to take care of autonomous individuals when they fall ill or are badly injured? Who is supposed to do the social contractors' laundry, clean their bathrooms, or cook their meals so that they are free to pursue their life plans? To realize the ideal you need people—mostly, they've been women— to look after you, but because they're looking after you, they aren't free to realize the ideal for themselves.

Third, the idealized representation of persons on which these theories are based isn't just false, it's harmful. Though all of us are supposed to aim at it, the ideal isn't necessarily the best or only one. Some people—those suffering from Alzheimer's dementia or mentally retarded people, for example— couldn't possibly hope to be autonomous in the sense that Kant means, but they might have very good lives if they (and the rest of us) aimed at something else. Other people have excellent reasons to reject various aspects of the ideal on moral, political, religious, or personal grounds. But because the standard theories are dominant in our culture, the actual people who can't or don't conform to their picture of the ideal person appear substandard or morally defective, not what "we" are or should be. When people appear to be morally defective, they are often treated as morally defective, and this restricts their ability to live responsibly and well.

The Picture of Society

The second picture on which these prominent moral theories are based is that of a society consisting of two spheres: the public and the private. The public sphere is the one in which people's freedom is secured by rights. These rights are couched negatively, in terms of things the state or other individuals may not do to you, and can fairly be summed up as the right not to be interfered with. Because freedom is the central value of this sphere, it is governed by a "thin" conception of the good life—that is, the view of what it means to live well is left deliberately sketchy so that each person can decide for himself what's important in life and how best to achieve it. The public sphere is therefore the sphere in which people make choices. The public sphere is also the place for impartiality: No one's interests or rights are to count for more than anyone else's. And finally, in the public sphere the laws or principles for conduct are universal and impersonal. The supposedly impersonal and universal nature of truth itself gives these laws their authority.

If the public sphere is the sphere of rights, the private sphere is the sphere of the good. It's here that people pursue their various "thick" visions of the best way to live, whether as a practicing Catholic, a housewife, a fraternity brother, or whatever. The private sphere is the one in which relationships and the responsibilities that arise from them are frequently unchosen. It's the place for favoritism, because it's the sphere of friendship, love, and families— relationships in which another person is singled out for special consideration rather than treated like everybody else. The private sphere is particularistic rather than universal; it's quirky, unsystematic, and personal.

Any theory that is primarily concerned with the basic structure of society, or says each person is to count for one and none for more than one, or tells you that if you do something for one person you have to be willing to do it for all, is focusing on relationships in the public sphere, not the private. For that reason it's sometimes said that the dominant theories treat the private sphere as if it isn't the business of morality. This isn't strictly true, of course. None of the theories permits you to kill your girlfriend as long as you do it in the privacy of your own home, for example. But all three theories fail utterly to acknowledge the morally crucial labor that must be done in families and other private places if society is to function at all. It's in the places marked "private" that vast amounts of unpaid and socially unrecognized work goes on—the work of forming and maintaining selves, caring for children and others who need it, and transmitting morality from one generation to the next. And because this work is *gendered,* in that it's primarily women who are expected to do it, the theories in effect withhold moral recognition from many of the activities that make up most women's lives.

Because the dominant moral theories offer a picture of the public sphere as one in which each person is just as free as every other, they represent women as having choices about whether to engage in the reproductive labor of the private sphere. The theories show women choosing to provide loving maternal care, or persuading their husbands to provide loving paternal care, or deciding to have an abortion. But here again the picture is false. Many women don't have these choices: The fathers of their children walk out on them; they have no access to abortion or their moral beliefs forbid it; the child is a niece or granddaughter with nobody else to look after her. Even if reproductive choices really *were* optional, though, it could still be objected that no decent moral theory leaves the care of new or future children solely up to those who choose to provide it.

Although social contract theory, utilitarianism, and Kantian ethics offer a picture of society whose public sphere is supposed to be governed by impartiality and universality, this too is false. As the picture of the persons who inhabit this society has already shown us, the theories are not impartial. Instead, they favor persons whose social standing, concerns, and occupations look suspiciously like those of well-to-do white men. The ideal of impartiality is intended to emphasize the ways in which we're all alike, which is why the theories assume that in the public sphere, people's basic interests are the same. They assume, for example, that while we all might have different plans for how to get ahead in our jobs, we all basically care about living according to plan. But even in the workplace or marketplace, not all people basically care about living according to plan, or about not being interfered with, or about bargaining on equal terms with others. The assumption that they do tends to steamroll over the differences in people's needs, their cultural traditions, and how they're expected to act when they're in public.

Nor are the theories in fact universal, because they center on relations among independent strangers in the male-dominated public world of work and politics. Those relations are important only to certain sorts of people, and they're out of the question or a matter of indifference to many others. If the theories were truly concerned with including as many people as possible, wouldn't they focus instead on the lack of control, the dependency, and the relations of love and friendship that make up the fabric of most people's everyday lives?

Attention to these matters would quickly reveal the importance of the particular and the personal in all of morality, not just the part that's supposed to govern the public sphere. A great many of the choices we make in our everyday lives can't and shouldn't be universalized. I may not be aiming at the same things you are striving for; I might not want or need to go where you do. The notion of universality effectively excludes people who look (suspiciously) like women and men of color from the society the liberal theories depict. By carving that society into two spheres and populating the private sphere with anybody who doesn't fit the "universal" norm, the theories keep such people from participating fully in the social contract, pure Kantian rationality, or the promotion of the public good.

All of which is to say that the division of society into two spheres is a fiction. It serves the social contract, Kantian, and utilitarian theories well, because it creates a boundary that can be policed so that the preoccupations of powerful people in a certain kind of society are seen as the important ones—the ones that are governed by morality. The reality, however, is that morality can't be boxed off in this way. It permeates all of society, including the parts where the misfits live.

The Picture of Rationality

What gives morality its hold over us? Why, that is, should we do the right thing if it's inconvenient or embarrassing or even costs us our life? One possible answer is "Because God commands it," but that answer doesn't satisfy people who (a) don't believe in God or (b) believe in God but aren't sure we know precisely what he wants us to do ("Thou shalt not kill." Not even in self-defense? In war? How about animals?). The dominant theories, rejecting religious faith as the basis for morality, tell us we have to do the right thing because *reason* commands it. Now, reason is a fine thing. Feminist moral theorists are delighted when people offer reasons for what they do and tackle their moral disagreements with other people in a rational manner. But they aren't altogether happy with the picture of rationality that underlies social contract, Kantian, and utilitarian theories.

For one thing, the picture leaves a lot out. It excludes the emotions, rather than acknowledging that feelings such as empathy, resentment, or anger play a useful role in our moral thinking. It excludes what we care about, rather than acknowledging that what we care about often *is* the reason we ought to do something. It excludes trust, rather than acknowledging that trust is what keeps our moral judgments from being paranoid. And it excludes narrative or other representational modes of reasoning, rather than acknowledging that stories and images are powerful tools for making moral sense of the world and our place in it.

Furthermore, the picture exaggerates the role of reason in morality. The method of reasoning recommended by Rawls, for example, is that you put your considered moral judgments into reflective equilibrium with your moral principles so that none of your beliefs contradict any other. But suppose you were raised to believe that the white race is superior to all other races, and when you grew up, having never interacted with people who weren't white, you thought it over carefully and concluded that whites really *are* superior, with the result that you now hold the belief very firmly. And suppose all of your moral principles are consistent with this belief. In that case, your system of beliefs is in reflective equilibrium, so it's rational. The trouble is, it's also *evil.* Even if you follow the method very carefully, you can't count on it to rid you of bigotry and prejudice.

And finally, the picture shows reason operating at high levels of abstract idealization, which tends to produce bad arguments. Consider this one, from the philosopher Christine Korsgaard's *Sources of Normativity* (1996, 143). Korsgaard imagines that you are tormenting a stranger and he calls on you to stop, asking how you would like it if someone did the same to you. Unless you take the stranger's words as mere noise, she says, you are acknowledging that this is a human being speaking. Then, like the good Kantian philosopher she is, she argues that since you see *yourself* as worthy of moral consideration "in so far as you are just human, just *someone*," your rationality compels you to see that the stranger's humanity deserves moral consideration as well. If you don't, she concludes, you're being inconsistent. But as Walker points out in *Moral Contexts* (143-45), this argument assumes that you think the stranger is just like you in being human, and you're just like him in being human. In many cases, though, people *don't* think that others are just human beings exactly like themselves. They think there are different *kinds* of human beings and that some kinds may be enslaved, others may be slaughtered, still others may be outlawed, and others yet again are fit only to satisfy the sexual and domestic wants of men. If you think there are different kinds of human beings, then you *aren't* being inconsistent in doing to a stranger what you wouldn't want done to you. We can deplore the fact that many people do think certain kinds of people are fair game for abusive treatment, but the problem isn't that they're irrational. They only look that way if rationality is idealized and abstracted from the social and moral contexts in which actual people live.

The PowerPoint Problem

Taken together, then, the three pictures underlying social contract theory, utilitarianism, and Kantian ethics suggest that the theories really aren't up to the job of illuminating the moral experience of all people, everywhere. In particular, they are silent about a number of the activities, concerns, and circumstances that make up the greater part of the lives of many women and many men of color, especially if they are poor, disabled, gay, old, or otherwise disadvantaged by their social situation.

Well, *could* the theories speak to the moral situation of the people they have neglected? Do these silences imply in a strictly logical way that the theories can't handle the moral realities of socially disadvantaged people? No. I suspect that in fact they can't, but my talk of pictures is deliberate, because pictures don't logically imply anything—they represent a state of affairs. It's the actual state of affairs that's important here, not what might in principle be possible. The question isn't whether the theories *couldn't* accommodate the experience of women and relatively powerless men; the point is that they don't. Their repeated, intensive focus on certain topics in moral theorizing and their consistent exclusion of others has created what Cheshire Calhoun calls an "ideology of the moral life." It's an ideology because it's politically loaded in favor of privileged white men and because it represents as natural and normal what is actually the effect of social power. As a direct result of what it emphasizes and what it leaves out, certain kinds of moral capacities and knowledge, important differences among people, and the moral demands that make up the bulk of many people's day-to-day lives don't get registered as the proper concerns of a moral theory at all. The ideology keeps forcing our attention back on the topics and problems that matter to the ideal man who is supposed to, but doesn't, symbolize all of us.

You could think of this as the PowerPoint problem. If you've ever put together a PowerPoint presentation, you know that while the software offers you a number of content layouts, text-and-content layouts, and text-and-graph layouts, it offers only two standardized text layouts: a page-width layout with a title and bullet-points, and a two-column layout with a title and bullet-points. The page-width layout lets you display a string of facts with supporting points under each, and the two-column layout lets you compare or contrast two items. That's it. If you want to compare three items, you're out of luck, and if you want to circle around an idea instead of laying it out in a linear fashion, you can't do that either. Nor can you present a conversation or a story. If you're very clever you might be able to customize the layout, but there's no easy way to do it, so the chances are you won't. As a result, you are repeatedly forced into a very limited kind of thinking—the kind that's used by the corporate executives for which the software program seems to have been designed. And because PowerPoint is the dominant technology for making presentations, the more you use it, the more likely it is that you'll consider that kind of thinking normal and right.

I believe that the three most widely known moral theories are plagued by a feminist version of the PowerPoint problem. As Baier (1994) puts it, "The great moral theorists in our tradition not only are all men, [but] with a few significant exceptions ... they are a collection of clerics, misogynists, and puritan bachelors" (3). The theories reflect their authors' social circumstances, focusing on the sorts of preoccupations and concerns that mark a certain kind of prosperous and respectable masculine life. And because they are *dominant* theories, they offer no incentive to take account of other kinds of lives: If you study them long enough, you'll consider that way of doing ethics normal and right.

Is there any point, then, in studying Kant and Mill and Rawls? Of course there is. In the first place, the dominant theorists should be studied just because they *are* dominant. They've provided a vocabulary and a set of ideas that help us to make moral sense of each other. The second reason to study them is that many of the concepts, arguments, distinctions, and methodologies they have developed are well worth having: They help us sort out what we ought to do and why we ought to do it. These theorists are powerful voices in a long-standing conversation in Western culture about crucially important questions concerning human existence: How might we best live together? Who should I strive to be? What should I care about? What must I take responsibility for? All morally developed persons must find their own answers to questions of this kind, but they don't have to do it all by themselves. There are rich resources at their disposal in the standing theories.

While the theories can't be dismissed, then, their neglect of gender and other factors that determine who has power over whom means that those of us who want to think clearly and carefully about ethics have got our work cut out for us. We have to get a better understanding of the consequences for ethics of taking seriously the moral claims and perspectives of people who don't occupy positions of social privilege. What happens when moral theory becomes skeptical of ideal relationships of equality as the basis for morality and shifts its focus to relationships of dependency and vulnerability? What happens when moral selves are represented as having bodies and emotions as well as minds? What happens when ethical attention moves from an idealized, supposedly universal human nature to particular persons and social groups? ...

References

Baier, Annette C. 1994. *Moral Prejudices: Essays on Ethics.* Cambridge, MA: Harvard UP.

Korsgaard, Christine M. 1996. *The Sources of Normativity.* Cambridge: Cambridge UP.

Walker, Margaret Urban. 1998. *Moral Contexts.* Lanham, MD: Rowman & Littlefield.

25.
WOMEN AND CARING

✽ ✽ ✽

NEL NODDINGS

Nel Noddings is a professor of education, emerita, at Stanford University. She specializes in ethics, feminist philosophy, and philosophy of education, and is the author of Caring: A Feminist Approach to Ethics and Moral Education, *from which this selection is taken. Noddings gives some examples of the typical differences between masculine and feminine approaches to ethics, and explicates the feminine approach which is based on caring in specific interpersonal relationships. She suggests that instead of regarding women as typically occupying an inferior stage of moral development, we can develop a powerful and coherent approach to ethics based on the type of caring that is so familiar to women.*

Women often define themselves as both persons and moral agents in terms of their capacity to care. When we move from natural caring to an ethic of caring, we shall consider the deep psychological structures that may be responsible for this mode of definition. Here I wish to concentrate on the caring itself—on particular examples of feminine courage in relating and remaining related and on the typical differences between men and women in their search for the ethical in human relationships.

We may find the sorts of examples and contrasts we seek in legend, Biblical accounts, biography, and fiction. I shall do no more than sample the possibilities here. The legend of Ceres, for example, can be interpreted beautifully to illustrate the attitude and conflicts of one-caring.[1] Recall that Ceres was the goddess who cared for the earth. It was she who made the fields fertile and watched over the maturation and harvest of crops. She had a daughter, Proserpine, whom she dearly loved. One day, Pluto, god of the underworld, crazed by love from Cupid's arrow, snatched Proserpine from her play and abducted her to his underground kingdom. Ceres searched the world for her daughter without success and was grief-stricken. Next something happens in the legend that is especially instructive for the one-caring: Ceres, in all her misery, is approached by an old man, Celeus, and his little girl. They respond to her grief and invite her to visit their cottage; indeed, they respond by weeping with her. Ceres is moved by this show of compassion and accompanies them. Here is a concrete illustration of the power of the cared-for in contributing to the caring relation. Ceres knows that she is the one-caring, that

373

she has the power to confer good or ill on these passersby. But, in her misery, she needs the active response of the cared-for to maintain herself as one-caring. Typical of one-caring who would be one-caring, she answers Celeus by saying: "Lead on, ... I cannot resist that appeal."[2]

Arriving at the cottage, Ceres finds a little boy very ill, probably dying. She is received, however, by the child's mother, Metanira, and moved to pity, Ceres cures the child with a kiss. Later, when Ceres tries to make the child immortal by tempering his body in flaming ashes, Metanira snatches the child fearfully from her. Ceres chides the mother for depriving her son of immortality but, still, she assures Metanira that he will nevertheless be "great and useful." The boy, Triptolemus, will someday teach humankind the secrets of agriculture as revealed to him by Ceres. Here, then, is a second facet of the ideal for one-caring. The cared-for shall be blessed not with riches, luck, and power but with the great gift of *usefulness*. The conversation between Ceres intending immortality for Triptolemus and Metanira afraid to risk her son in the flames is illustrative, again, of the feminine striving for an attainable ideal. It stands in bold contrast to the story we shall consider next—that of Abraham's willingness to sacrifice his son to divine command.

Eventually, Ceres finds the place where Proserpine was swallowed up by the earth, but she mistakenly supposes that the earth itself did this terrible thing. She is stricken by a double grief. Not only has she lost her beloved Proserpine but another cared-for, her fruitful earth, has turned against her. Now Ceres does not fly into a destructive rage and visit the earth with lightning, fire and flood. She merely ceases to care; she withdraws as one-caring, and the earth dries up in mud and weeds and brambles. Ceres, the one-caring, has nothing to sustain her in caring. Here, we see foreshadowed the power of the cared-for in maintaining the caring relationship.

Finally, Ceres learns the truth and entreats Jove to intercede on her behalf with Pluto. As you may recall, Pluto, in fear of losing his kingdom entirely, agrees to return Proserpine but induces her to eat some pomegranate seeds so that she will be unable to spend more than half of each year with her mother. When Proserpine returns each spring, Ceres bestows great fruitfulness on the earth and, when she leaves each fall, Ceres is overcome by grief and allows winter to settle on the earth.

This story is widely understood as an allegory of the seasons, of sleeping grain and awakening fruitfulness, but it may be interpreted also as a fable of caring and being cared-for.[3] It illustrates the vulnerability of the one-caring, her reception of the proximate stranger, her generosity upon being herself received, and the munificent displacement of motivation that occurs when she is sustained as one-caring.

Now, someone is sure to point out that, in contrast to the legend of one-caring as the pinnacle of feminine sensibility, feminine skull-duggery lies at the root of the problem described in the legend.[4] It was, after all, Venus who prompted her son, Cupid, to shoot Pluto with the arrow of love. I am not denying the reality of this dark side of feminine character,[5] but I am rejecting it in my quest for the ethical. I am not, after all, suggesting a will to power but rather a commitment to care as the guide to an ethical ideal.

This commitment to care and to define oneself in terms of the capacity to care represent a feminine alternative to Kohlberg's "stage six" morality.[6] At stage six, the moral thinker transcends particular moral principles by appealing to a highest principle—one that allows a rearrangement of the hierarchy in order to give proper place-value to human love, loyalty, and the relief of suffering. But women, as ones-caring, are not so much concerned with the rearrangement of priorities among principles; they are concerned, rather, with maintaining and enhancing caring. They do not abstract away from the concrete situation those elements that allow a formulation of deductive argument; rather, they remain in the situation as sensitive, receptive, and responsible agents. As a result of this caring orientation, they are perceived by Kohlberg as "being stuck" at stage three—that stage in which the moral agent wants to be a "good boy or girl." The desire to be good, however, to be one-caring in response to these cared-for here and now, provides a sound and lovely alternative foundation for ethical behavior. Like Ceres, the one-caring will not turn from the real human beings who address her. Her caring is the foundation of—and not a mere manifestation of—her morality.

In contrast to the story of Ceres, who could not abandon her child even for the sake of her beloved Earth, we may consider Abraham. In obedience to God, Abraham traveled with his son, Isaac, to Moriah, there to offer him as a sacrifice: "And they came to the place which God had told him of, and Abraham built an altar there, and laid the wood in order, and bound Isaac his son, and laid him on the altar upon the wood. And Abraham stretched forth his hand, and took the knife to slay his son."[7]

Kierkegaard interprets Abraham's action as supra-ethical, that is, as the action of an individual who is justified by his connection to God, the absolute. For him, as for us, the individual is higher than the universal, but for him that "higher" status is derived from "absolute duty toward God." Hence a paradox is produced. Out of duty to God, we may be required to do to our neighbor what is ethically forbidden. The ethical is, for Kierkegaard, the universal, and the individual directly obedient to God is superior to the universal. He says: "In the story of Abraham we find such a paradox. His relation to Isaac, ethically expressed, is this, that the father should love the son. This ethical relation is reduced to a relative position in contrast with the absolute relation to God."[8]

But for the mother, for us, this is horrendous. Our relation to our children is not governed first by the ethical but by natural caring. We love not because we are required to love but because our natural relatedness gives natural birth to love. It is this love, this natural caring, that makes the ethical possible. For us, then, Abraham's decision is not only ethically unjustified but it is in basest violation of the supraethical—of caring. The one-caring can only describe his act—"You would kill your own son!"—and refuse him forgiveness. Abraham's obedience fled for protection under the skirts of an unseeable God. Under the gaze of an abstract and untouchable God, he would destroy this touchable child whose real eyes were turned upon him in trust, and love, and fear. I suspect no woman could have written either *Genesis* or *Fear and Trembling*, but perhaps I should speak only for myself on that. The one-caring, male or female, does not seek security in abstractions cast either as principles or entities. She remains responsible here and now for this cared-for and this situation and for the forseeable futures projected by herself and the cared-for.

Now, of course, the scholar may argue that I have interpreted the story too literally, and even that Kierkegaard did so in an agony of faith against ethical reason. He will point out that, on another interpretation, God used Abraham and Isaac to teach His people that human sacrifice was unacceptable to Him and, henceforth, forbidden. This interpretation will not satisfy the mother. The mother in Abraham's position would respond to the fear and trust of her child—not to the voice of abstraction. The Mother-as-God would not use a parent and child so fearfully and painfully to teach a welcome lesson to her other children. The Mother-God must respond caringly to Abraham as cared-for and to Isaac as cared-for, and she must preserve Abraham as one-caring in relation to Isaac.

Everything that is built on this sacrificial impulse is anathema to woman. Here, says woman, is my child. I will not sacrifice him for God, or for the greatest good, or for these ten others. Let us find some other way. The devotion to "something beyond" that is revealed in traditional, masculine ethics is often devotion to deity, but sometimes it is devotion to principle. Recall the story of Manlius, a Roman commander who laid down harsh laws for the conduct of his legions. One of the first to disobey a rule about leaving camp to engage in individual combat was his own son. In compliance with the rules, Manlius ordered the execution of his son. A principle had been violated; for this violation, X must be executed. That "X" was replaced by "my son" gave Manlius no release from obedience to the principle. Why, then, did he not think concretely before establishing the rule? Why do men so often lay out their own clear paths to tragedy? The one-caring would want to think carefully about the establishment of rules and even more carefully about the prescription of penalties. Indeed, she would prefer to establish a climate of cooperative "we-ness" so that rules and penalties might be kept to a minimum. For her, the hypothetical is filled with real persons, and, thus, her rules are tempered a priori with thoughts of those in her inner circle. A stranger might, then, be spared death because she would not visit death upon her own child.

She does not, in whatever personal agony, inflict death upon her child in devotion to either principle or abstract entity.

History, legend, and biography might profitably be reinterpreted in light of feminine experience. Both men and women may participate in the "feminine" as I am developing it, but women have suffered acutely from its lack of explication. They have felt and suffered and held fast, but they have—as a result—been accused of deficiency in abstract reasoning, of capricious behavior, of emotional reaction. Even in parenting, perhaps especially in parenting, the typical differences between concrete and abstract, between here-and-now and here-and-after, between flesh-and-blood and spirit, stand out in life and literature. In Robert Frost's "Home Burial," the conflict between man and woman in the loss of their child is dramatic. He tries to relieve his grief by speaking of ordinary things; she is convinced because of this that he feels no grief. He makes matters worse by saying:

> What was it brought you up to think it the thing
> To take your mother-loss of a first child
> So inconsolably—in the face of love.
> You'd think his memory might be satisfied—[9]

What is the man doing here? He is not callous, and he has not escaped suffering, but he has not met his wife on the level of feeling. He accuses her of thinking "it the thing" to grieve deeply; he speaks of "mother-loss" and "first child," but he avoids the child's name and any concrete reference to him. He speaks of "his memory" but not of the small, warm body his wife nurtured. It is this difference in language and direction of reference that forms the difference between an ethic of caring and an ethic of principle.

Examples appear in real life as well as in poetry and fiction. Pearl Buck describes the difference in her own parents.

> The fascinating thing about Andrew and Carie was that from the two of them we always got entirely different stories about the same incident. They never saw the same things or felt the same way about anything, and it was as though they had not gone to the same place or seen the same people.[10]

Andrew was spirit—all heaven and abstraction; Carie was completely human. He was a preacher, a missionary in China, and cared for the souls of his parishioners. Carie cared for them as persons, ministering to their bodies and earthly minds. She had no preconceived notion of what her children should be; she did not cast them in the image of a catechism-produced God. Rather, she loved their warm bodies, cherished their laughter and childish pranks, nurtured their earthly courage and compassion for each other. The greatest joy in her life came through her children, and her greatest suffering was incurred by their loss. When Andrew was seventy years old, some time after Carie had died, he wrote the story of his life. The record fit into twenty-five pages. His daughter remarks:

> It was the story of his soul, his unchanging soul. Once he mentioned the fact of his marriage to Carie, his wife. Once he listed the children he had had with her, but in the listing he forgot entirely a little son who lived to be five years old and was Carie's favorite child, and he made no comment on any of them.[11]

Yet all of her life Carie was made to feet spiritually inferior to her husband and, as she lay near death, he expressed concern about her soul!

Today we are asked to believe that women's "lack of experience in the world" keeps them at an inferior stage in moral development. I am suggesting, to the contrary, that a powerful and coherent ethic and, indeed, a different sort of world may be built on the natural caring so familiar to women.

Circles and Chains

We find ourselves at the center of concentric circles of caring. In the inner, intimate circle, we care because we love. In particularly trying situations we may act out of ethical sense even here. After all, sometimes we are tired, the other has behaved abominably, and our love is frayed. Then we remind ourselves of the other's location in our system of circles: He is (was) my friend; she is my child; he is my father. The engrossment remains, although its color changes, and we may vacillate between the once natural caring-for other to growing concern for ourselves.

As we move outward in the circles, we encounter those for whom we have personal regard. Here, as in the more intimate circles, we are guided in what we do by at least three considerations: how we feel, what the other expects of us, and what the situational relationship requires of us. Persons in these circles do not, in the usual course of events, require from us what our families naturally demand, and the situations in which we find ourselves have, usually, their own rules of conduct. We are comfortable in these circles if we are in compliance with the rules of the game. Again, these rules do not compel us, but they have an instrumental force that is easily recognized. I listen with a certain ready appreciation to colleagues, and I respond in a polite, acceptable fashion. But I must not forget that the rules are only aids to smooth passage through unproblematic events. They protect and insulate me. They are a reflection of someone's sense of relatedness institutionalized in our culture. But they do not put me in touch; they do not guarantee the relation itself. Thus rules will not be decisive for us in critical situations, but they will be acknowledged as economies of a sort. As such they will be even less important than the "illuminative maxims" described by Joseph Fletcher.[12] For us, the destructive role of rules and principles must be clarified and acknowledged.

Beyond the circles of proximate others are those I have not yet encountered. Some of these are linked to the inner circle by personal or formal relations. Out there is a young man who will be my daughter's husband; I am prepared to acknowledge the transitivity of my love. He enters my life with potential love. Out there, also, are future students; they are linked formally to those I already care for and they, too, enter my life potentially cared-for. Chains of caring are established, some linking unknown individuals to those already anchored in the inner circles and some forming whole new circles of potential caring. I am "prepared to care" through recognition of these chains.

But what of the stranger, one who comes to me without the bonds established in my chains of caring? Is there any sense in which I can be prepared to care for him? I can remain receptive. As in the beginning, I may recognize the internal "I must," that natural imperative that arises as I receive the other, but this becomes more and more difficult as my world grows more complex. I may be bombarded with stimuli that arouse the "I must," and I learn to reduce the load. As we have seen, a standard fashion of controlling what comes in is to rely on situational rules. These protect me. What, under normal circumstances, I must do for a colleague is different from what I must do for my child. I may come to rely almost completely on external rules and, if I do, I become detached from the very heart of morality: the sensibility that calls forth caring. In an important sense, the stranger has an enormous claim on me, because I do not know where he fits, what requests he has a formal right to make, or what personal needs he will pass on to me. I can meet him only in a state of wary anticipation and rusty grace, for my original innocent grace is gone and, aware of my finiteness, I fear a request I cannot meet without hardship. Indeed, the caring person, one who in this way is prepared to care, dreads the proximate stranger, for she cannot easily reject the claim he has on her. She would prefer that the stray cat not appear at the back door—or the stray teenager at the front. But if either presents himself, he must be received not by formula but as individual.

The strain on one who would care can be great. Literature is filled with descriptions of encounters of this sort: the legitimate dread of the one-caring and the ultimate acceptance or rejection of the internal "I must." One thinks of John Steinbeck's Carl Tiflin and Mr. Gitano in *The Red Pony*.[13] In defiance of a loud and insistent "I must," Tiflin diminishes his ethical ideal and turns the old man away. In contrast, Robert Frost has the farm wife, Mary, express the one-caring as she accepts the "hired man" into her home:

Yes, what else but home? It all depends on what you mean by home.
Of course he's nothing to us, any more
Than was the hound that came a stranger to us
Out of the woods, worn out upon the trail.
Home is the place where, when you have to go there,
They have to take you in.[14]

Both imperatives expressed here, the "have to's" of the one-caring and the cared-for, are internal imperatives. An observer can see alternatives clearly, but the "I must" suggests itself as binding upon the one in whom it occurs. We are both free and bound in our circles and chains.

Notes

1. Carol Gilligan cites D. McClelland as interpreting the myth as a description of the feminine attitude toward power. See Gilligan, "Woman's Place in Man's Life Cycle," *Harvard Educational Review* 49 (1979), 445.

2. Thomas Bulfinch, *Mythology: The Age of Fable* (New York: The New American Library, Inc., 1962), p. 86.

3. The legend of Ceres has been variously interpreted. The ancient myth clearly referred to the conferral of special gifts on young males by creative and powerful female figures. In this sense, we find a long-standing tradition for the interpretation of Ceres as one-caring, bestowing the gifts of competence and usefulness on her protégés. See Erich Neumann, *The Great Mother* (Princeton: Princeton UP, 1955). On p. 321, Neumann states: "This investiture is not an 'agricultural' rite, although in the earliest primordial age it was probably bound up with such a rite. In the mysteries at least, it has a far more profound significance. It is the investiture of the male with his chthonic and spiritual fecundating function, which is transmitted to him by woman."

4. See the account in Bulfinch, *Mythology: The Age of Fable.*

5. For a fascinating account of the dark and light in feminine thinking and legend, see M. Esther Harding, *Woman's Mysteries* (New York: Harper and Row, 1971).

6. See Lawrence Kohlberg and R. Kramer, "Continuities and Discontinuities in Childhood and Moral Development," *Human Development* (1969), 93-120.

7. Genesis 22: 9,10.

8. Søren Kierkegaard, *Fear and Trembling*, transl. Walter Lowrie (Princeton UP, 1941), p. 71.

9. Robert Frost, "Home Burial," in *The Complete Poems of Robert Frost* (New York: Henry Holt and Company, 1949), p. 71.

10. Pearl S. Buck, *Fighting Angel* (New York: Pocket Books, 1964), p. 38.

11. Ibid., p. 2.

12. Joseph Fletcher, *Situational Ethics* (Philadelphia: Westminster P, 1966).

13. John Steinbeck, *The Red Pony* (New York: Viking, 1945).

14. Robert Frost, "The Death of the Hired Man," *The Complete Poems of Robert Frost*, p. 53.

26.
PROSTITUTION
AND THE CASE FOR DECRIMINALIZATION

❧ ❧ ❧

LAURIE SHRAGE

Laurie Shrage is Director of the Women's Studies Center and Professor of both Philosophy and Women's Studies at Florida International University. Her areas of research include feminist political theory, reproductive rights, and feminist debates about sex work and women's health issues. In this article she argues that we should eliminate legal and social institutions that criminalize prostitution, appealing to both worker's rights and the dignity of low-status work. She suggests that the exploitation of prostitutes is similar to the exploitation of other workers, and should therefore be addressed through social policies that improve the conditions of workers generally.

Responses to prostitution from the left have been radically contradictory. Marxist thinkers, for example, are committed to study social phenomena in terms of systems of production and their related labor forms. But they rarely treat prostitution as a kind of work; instead they treat it as a side effect of the moral decay, corruption, or cultural collapse that occurs under particular social conditions. Why? Leftists generally respect working-class people and their political and economic struggles. Yet they rarely exhibit respect toward prostitute organizations or their political activists and intellectuals. For the most part, such groups and individuals are ignored.[1] Again, why?

Many on the left want to believe that prostitution would not exist or would not be common or tolerated in a world free of economic, gender, and sexual exploitation. The problem of prostitution would solve itself once other problems are solved. Yet speculative judgments like this one are abstract and academic. Prostitution isn't any single thing—a unitary social phenomenon with a particular origin—and so it doesn't make sense to argue about whether it would or wouldn't be present in this or that type of society. Working from crosscultural and historical studies, I have examined institutionalized and commodified exchanges of sexual services between women providers and their male customers in many different social contexts.[2] I conclude that there are (or have been) places and times where exchanges of sexual services between women and men are (or were) relatively free of gender and class domination. How then should leftists respond to the varieties of prostitution in the contemporary United States, where the labor practices involved are shaped by pernicious class and gender asymmetries?

I want to argue that we should include in our political agendas the dismantling of the legal and social structures that criminalize prostitution and stigmatize prostitutes. In conjunction with this project, we will need to invent regulatory alternatives to the current punitive systems of control. These are the primary aims of numerous prostitute civil rights and labor groups, and I think both feminists and socialists should support them, though not for the libertarian reasons many representatives of these groups give. Arguments for decriminalizing prostitution can be made by appealing to notions of workers' rights and the dignity of low-status work; they need not appeal to the libertarian ideal of total freedom from governmental intrusion into the lives of presumably independent individuals. These arguments can also be strengthened by accepting a robust pluralism with regard to sexual customs and practices. I don't mean that we cannot criticize sexual practices, only that the criticism must take into account different cultural conceptions of human sexuality and not dismiss out of hand those that are unfamiliar. Again, this desire to understand alien customs should not be confused with a libertarian laissez-faire morality. The libertarian sees sexual desires as a natural force that society should respect; the pluralist understands that desire, including the desire for noncommodified sex, is shaped by cultural and social forces.

Feminist theorists have argued that prostitution involves the sexual and economic subordination, degradation, and exploitation of women and girls. Many forms of prostitution are indeed brutal and oppressive: the near slave conditions that have been reported recently in brothels in Thailand, the use of "comfort women" by the Japanese during the Second World War, the prostitution that exists around US military bases and in many contemporary urban spaces ("streetwalking," "massage parlors," "escort services," and so on). Women and girls have been tricked, or physically and economically coerced, into the prostitution business and then kept in it against their will. Women have contracted fatal diseases; they have been beaten and raped. These are common aspects of contemporary prostitution that anyone concerned with social justice must address. But we must also ask whether the legal structures that have been set up to control and discourage prostitution—including voluntary prostitution where it exists—also oppress women. Both women who work as prostitutes and women who are suspected of doing so (usually poor women of color) are frequently harassed, manipulated, and exploited by police officers and others who have power over them. Criminalization contributes to the stigma that prostitutes bear, making them more vulnerable to hate crimes, housing and employment discrimination, and other violations of their basic rights.

Because both the operation of prostitution businesses and their legal suppression typically sacrifice women's interests, feminists generally oppose both prostitution and its criminalization. Many feminists aim to devise nonpunitive, extralegal responses, such as providing other work opportunities. Yet there has been no concerted feminist attempt to undo the laws that define acts of prostitution as criminal offenses and impose penalties on participants—more often the female vendors than the male customers. Certainly feminist groups have not given the decriminalization of prostitution the same priority they have given to other issues, such as ensuring the legality of abortion, reforming rape and sexual harassment laws, and desegregating corporate management and the professions. Moreover, feminists have been more vocal in opposing sex businesses than the laws that criminalize the activities of commercial providers, and thus have contributed to creating a climate conducive to the continued degradation of prostitutes.

Feminists have not mobilized around the decriminalization of prostitution because of our lingering ambivalence about the subject. Some question whether commodified exchanges of sexual services are ever voluntary and regard prostitutes always as manipulated victims rather than autonomous agents—a view that requires us to second guess the motives, desires, and values of all prostitutes. Other feminists argue for decriminalizing only the prostitute's work while maintaining the criminal status of pimping, pandering, and so on. But this requires the state to determine which of the prostitute's partners are exploiting her and which are not unless we wish to punish all the prostitute's possible business partners, including her spouse, boyfriend or girlfriend, parents and siblings, and other comrades.

Although feminists are fully aware of the varieties of abuse prostitutes suffer, many of them fear that decriminalization will lead to more prostitution and thus more exploitation of women and children. So they are willing to tolerate the often brutal enforcement of laws against it. Yet realistically, we are more likely to discourage the exploitation of women and children by regulating the labor practices followed by sex businesses. If businesses that provide customers with personal sexual services could operate legally, then they would be subject to the same labor regulations that apply to other businesses (given the nature of the work, additional regulations might be necessary).[3] Such businesses would not be allowed to treat workers like slaves, hire underage workers, deprive them of compensation for which they contracted, or expose them to unnecessary risks. The businesses could be required to enforce health and safety codes, provide workers with a minimum income and health insurance, and allow them to form collectives to negotiate for improved working conditions, compensation, and benefits.

Many feminists find it frightening to imagine a society where sex can be purchased as easily as soap, where selling sex is an occupational option like selling shoes, and where businesses that profit from commercial sex are as legitimate as Ben and Jerry's. Such imaginings usually lead to the question, "What next?" This is the slippery-slope argument, which is elaborated as follows: "Are we now going to allow the sale of *x*?" where *x* is your favorite tabooed object (babies, vital organs, bombs, and so on). The answer to this question is "No—not unless by tolerating the commercial distribution of *x* we can better protect the rights of particular people or better realize some moral ideal." By tolerating the commercial distribution of sexual services within certain limits, we can better protect the rights and interests of those who seek these services and, importantly, those who choose to earn income by providing them.

Though it is useful to ask what social forces lead some people to seek the relatively *impersonal* provision of *personal* sexual services, we should be equally critical of the cultural assumptions embedded in this question and in our various answers. At best, such excursions may help us understand how prostitution is shaped by large and small capital interests, as well as dominant gender, racial, and sexual ideologies, and thus how to devise regulatory instruments that discourage the recognizable forms of abuse, exploitation, and humiliation.

The argument I am making is simply this: that the forms of exploitation and abuse suffered by prostitutes are similar to those suffered by other workers (though they are often more intense because of the illegal status of this work). Therefore these abuses should be addressed by mechanisms that improve the condition of workers generally. Sweatshop conditions should not be tolerated, violations of workers' constitutionally protected rights should not be tolerated, customers should not be permitted to engage in behaviors that endanger the workers' health or well being, care should be taken to avoid harm to noninvolved third parties, contracts for compensation and services should be voluntary and take into account the interests of all affected, and when these conditions are met such contracts should be respected (though not necessarily enforced by outside authorities). If the sex trade were regulated like other businesses, we would not have a perfect world— labor would still be underpaid and exploited and needs would still go unmet—but the world would be modestly improved.

The prostitute has often served as a symbol for the degraded status of the worker in capitalist societies, and prostitution itself has been evoked as a metaphor for the general relationship between workers and owners under capitalism. It is also used to represent other often exploitative social relationships, between husbands and wives, for example. But the metaphor works only if we assume that prostitution is universally exploitative and degrading, so that activities likened to it are cast as illegitimate. Rather than make the Marxist point that exchanges of sex or labor for money in a capitalist market are necessarily exploitative, the point of the metaphor is that the exchange of labor for money under capitalism is like the exchange of sex for money in *any* circumstances. But the assumption that all sex commerce is inherently exploitative fails to take into account the diversity of actual and possible practices. The degradation of the worker under capitalism is more like the degradation of someone who is forced to sell his/her labor—sexual or nonsexual—but it seems redundant to point this out. By insisting on the inherent and unqualified degradation of sex commerce, those who use the metaphor only add to the degradation they presumably oppose.

Prostitutes—like gays, lesbians, and other sexual dissidents—are commonly viewed as threatening to families. But those who see them in this light often have a very narrow notion of what constitutes a family. In her book *The Comforts of Home: Prostitution in Colonial Nairobi*, Luise White describes relationships between prostitutes and their customers that might be compared to informal polyandrous unions, where a variety of physical and social needs are met—needs that more conventional families also serve.[4] In the United States and elsewhere, many prostitutes have children, partners, and parents that they support through their work. Prostitutes and those with whom they are socially intimate and interdependent, and with whom they share households, are in fact families, and they deserve the same social supports as other families. Laws that criminalize prostitution tear families apart, separate parents and children, and render sex workers and their intimate partners criminals.

All this said, some may feel that there is still something immoral or objectionable about the prostitute's work, and that we would be better off suppressing the practice and finding other livelihoods for the people involved. At least three articles appearing in academic journals and books in recent years bear the title "What's Wrong with Prostitution?" Each attempts to locate just what it is that distinguishes prostitution from other human activities, although one concludes contrary to the others that nothing is deeply wrong with waged sex work.[5] Perhaps one way to approach the intuition that there is something inherently wrong is to compare commercial sex to other work that is very similar to it. For example, many prostitutes like to compare themselves to sex therapists, educators, and entertainers. Annie Sprinkle likens her work to both bodily and spiritual forms of guidance and help. Either we must show that there is something wrong with these activities or we must show that the analogy between prostitution and sex therapy/education/entertainment doesn't hold. Frankly, I can't see how to show either.

One fear that many feminists have about legalizing prostitution is that this would create just one more female job ghetto where women are coerced into stereotypical and subordinate roles, and low-paying, low-status, dead-end work. Furthermore, the industry's "products" would very likely reproduce status hierarchies among people based on age, race, class, gender, physical ability, and so on. Subordinate service roles would be filled—as they already are in the illegally run sex industry—by age, class, race, and gender subordinates, and their commercial sexual availability would perpetuate myths about the inferiority of persons from the subordinated groups. These are legitimate fears, and supporters of decriminalization have to consider how such outcomes might be avoided.

One of the first things to be said is that although the overwhelming majority of customers for prostitution are male, not all prostitutes are women. It's important to notice that some prostitutes serve customers of the same gender as themselves, the same economic class, and the same socially defined racial category. Though a great deal of contemporary prostitution involves heterosexual white, bourgeois males exploiting working-class or underclass women (especially women of color), keeping prostitution illegal will not affect this situation. Instead, by developing programs and policies that address poverty, racism, and sexism, and by regulating a legal sex industry, we can hope to make those who are socially oppressed less vulnerable to exploitation from those who aren't.

Anyone who advocates the legalization of prostitution needs to address the "But would you want your daughter ...?" argument. I suppose the only way to answer this question/objection is to take it personally—I happen to have a daughter who is now eight. This argument is meant to expose the hypocrisy of anyone who has made the assertions I've made. For, not surprisingly, my answer is "No, I wouldn't want my daughter to be a prostitute." So how can I accept this occupation for others? Well, first of all, this isn't all of my answer. The more nuanced answer is that, although I would prefer my daughter to be a mathematician, pianist, or labor organizer, were she to seek employment in the sex trade, I would still want the best for her. Her choice would be less heartbreaking to me if the work were legal, safe, reasonably well paid, and moderately respectable. In arguing for the decriminalization of prostitution, we need not go from the extreme of deploring it to the other extreme of romanticizing it. This objection works only if these are our only alternatives.

If prostitution remains criminalized, what can we expect? In Hollywood, some prostitutes will continue to profit from the instant celebrity status that being arrested at the right time and with the right customer can bring. But the average prostitute will continue to be abused by her (or his) clients and co-workers, exposed unnecessarily to disease, socially marginalized and demonized, harassed by public officials, and separated from her children and other family members; her children will suffer from neglect and poverty. And underage workers will continue to be used, with or without their or their family's consent. Perhaps, a large and coordinated effort to decriminalize prostitution for the sake of workers and their families is one more battle we need to wage with the radical religious right.

Notes

1. One recent notable exception to this is Shannon Bell's *Reading, Writing, and Rewriting the Prostitute Body* (Bloomington: Indiana UP, 1994).
2. *Moral Dilemmas of Feminism: Prostitution, Adultery, and Abortion* (New York: Routledge, 1994).
3. Roger Matthews proposes some general guidelines for regulating prostitution informed by radical rather than liberal principles in "Beyond Wolfenden?: Prostitution, Politics and the Law," in R. Matthews and J. Young, eds., *Confronting Crime* (London: Sage, 1986). See also my discussion of his proposals in *Moral Dilemmas of Feminism*, pp. 83-87 and 158-61.
4. Luise White, *The Comforts of Home: Prostitution in Colonial Nairobi* (Chicago: U of Chicago P, 1990).
5. See Christine Overall, "What's Wrong with Prostitution?: Evaluating Sex Work" in *Signs* 17 (Summer 1992), pp. 705-24; Carole Pateman, "What's Wrong with Prostitution?" in *The Sexual Contract* (Stanford: Stanford UP, 1988), pp. 189-218; and Igor Primoratz, "What's Wrong with Prostitution?" in *Philosophy* 68 (1993), pp. 159-82.

Sources

Aristotle, from "Nicomachean Ethics," translated by W.D. Ross from Aristotle's *Ethics* from *The Oxford Translation of Aristotle*, edited by W.D. Ross, vol. 9. Oxford University Press, 1925. Reprinted by permission of Oxford University Press.

Dwyer, James. "Illegal Immigrants, Health Care, and Social Responsibility," *The Hastings Center Report*, vol. 34, no. 1 (Jan.-Feb., 2004): 34-41.

Fins, Joseph J. "Encountering Diversity: Medical Ethics and Pluralism," Journal *of Religion and Health*, Vol. 33, No. 1, Spring 1994.

Gilligan, Carol. Selection from *In A Different Voice*, Reprinted by permission of the publisher from *In A Different Voice* by Carol Gilligan, Cambridge, MA: Harvard University Press, Copyright © 1982, 1993 by Carol Gilligan.

Hill, Thomas E., Jr. "The Message of Affirmative Action." *Social Philosophy and Policy* 8:2 (1991): 108-29. Reprinted with permission of Cambridge University Press.

Hood, Robert. "Global Warming" in *A Companion to Applied Ethics: Blackwell Companions to Philosophy*, edited by R.G. Frey (Malden, MA: Blackwell, 2003) 674-84.

Hursthouse, Rosalind. "Virtue Theory and Abortion," *Philosophy and Public Affairs* 20 (1991): 223-46. Copyright © 1991. Reprinted by permission of Princeton University Press.

Kekes, John. "Pluralism and the Value of Life" in *Cultural Pluralism and Moral Knowledge*, edited by Ellen Frankel Paul, Fred D. Miller, Jr., and Jeffrey Paul (Cambridge, UK: Cambridge UP, 1994) 44-60.

Kitcher, Philip. *The Lives to Come: The Genetic Revolution and Human Possibilities* (New York: Simon and Schuster, 1997). Selection.

Lindemann, Hilde. *An Invitation to Feminist Ethics* (McGraw Hill, 2005) 72-83.

Louden, Robert B. "On Some Vices of Virtue Ethics," *American Philosophical Quarterly* 21 (1984): 227-36. Reprinted by permission of the publisher.

Marquis, Donald. "Why Abortion Is Immoral." *Journal of Philosophy* 86:4 (1989): 183-202. Reprinted with permission of the author and the publisher.

Noddings, Nel. "Women and Caring" from *Caring: A Feminine Approach to Ethics*. Berkeley, CA: University of California Press. Copyright © 1984 The Regents of the University of California. Reprinted with permission of the press and the author.

Nozick, Robert. "The Experience Machine" and "The Entitlement Theory of Justice." From *Anarchy, State and Utopia* by Robert Nozick. Copyright © 1974 by Basic Books, Inc. Reprinted by permission of Basic Books, a member of Perseus Books, L.L.C.

O'Neill, Onora. "Perplexities of Famine and World Hunger," from *Matters of Life and Death: New Introductory Essays in Moral Philosophy*, 2nd ed., edited by Tom Regan. Random House, 1986: 319-29. Reprinted with permission of the McGraw-Hill Companies.

Plato, "Euthyphro," and "The Myth of Gyges," from *Defence of Socrates; Euthyphro; Crito*, translated with an introduction by David Gallop. Oxford University Press, World's Classics, 1997. Reprinted with permission of Oxford University Press.

Rachels, James. "Egoism and Moral Scepticism," from *A New Introduction to Philosophy*, ed. Steven M. Cahn. Harper & Row, 1971. Reprinted by permission of Steven M. Cahn.

Rawls, John. Selection from *A Theory of Justice*. Reprinted by permission of the publisher from *A Theory of Justice* by John Rawls. Cambridge, MA: The Belknap Press of Harvard University Press, Copyright © 1971 by the President and Fellows of Harvard College.

Rawls, John. "Two Concepts of Rules," *The Philosophical Review* 64 (1955): 3-32.

Ross, W.D. Selection from *The Right and The Good* by W.D. Ross. Oxford University Press, 1930. Reprinted with permission of Oxford University Press.

Shaw, William H. "Relativism and Objectivity in Ethics," from *Morality and Moral Controversies*, edited by John Arthur. Prentice Hall, 1981. Reprinted with permission of the author.

Shrage, Laurie. "Prostitution and the Case for Decriminalization," *Dissent* (Spring 1996): 41-45.

Singer, Peter. "Rich and Poor," *Practical Ethics*, 2nd ed. Cambridge University Press, pp. 218-46. Reprinted with permission of Cambridge University Press.

Smart, J.J.C. "An Outline of a System of Utilitarian Ethics," from *Utilitarianism: For and Against*, by J.J.C. Smart and Bernard Williams. Cambridge University Press, 1973. Reprinted with permission of Cambridge University Press and the author.

Sumner, William Graham. Selection from *Folkways*. © Ginn & Co., 1907. Reprinted with permission of the publisher.

Van Wyk, Robert N. "Perspectives on World Hunger and the Extent Of Our Positive Duties." *Public Affairs Quarterly* 2 (1988): 75-90. Reprinted with permission of the publisher.